THE WEB OF
PREACHING

The Web of Preaching

New Options in
Homiletic Method

Richard L. Eslinger

To Richard, Dear Friend and colleague, and servant of the Word.

Abingdon Press
Nashville

THE WEB OF PREACHING
NEW OPTIONS IN HOMILETIC METHOD

Library of Congress Cataloging-in-Publication Data

Eslinger, Richard L. (Richard Laurence), 1940-
    The web of preaching : new options in homiletic method / Richard L. Eslinger
        p. cm.
Includes bibliographical references.
    ISBN 0-687-01297-X (pbk. : alk. paper)
1. Preaching.   I. Title.
BV4211.3 .E85 2002
251—dc21

                                                                                                2002009191

02 03 04 05 06 07 08 09 10 11—10 9 8 7 6 5 4 3 2 1

MANUFACTURED IN THE UNITED STATES OF AMERICA

To my cherished sisters and brothers
of faith and family—
Suellen Eslinger
Mark and Emily Matheny
Cindy and Phil Brooks
Jim and Kristen Matheny

Contents

Acknowledgments

As a fifteen-year-later sequel to *A New Hearing: Living Options in Homiletic Method, The Web of Preaching* remains indebted to the five homileticians whose methods I originally surveyed. Charles Rice spoke for the (then) new movement of preaching as storytelling, Henry Mitchell labored to interpret the preaching tradition of the African American church to a wider audience, Eugene Lowry had just presented his narrative homiletical plot to preachers, Fred Craddock was already one of the mature spokespersons for the new homiletics, and David Buttrick would publish his *Homiletic* the same year as *A New Hearing* (in 1987). In the intervening years, each of these movements has continued, although the state of North American homiletics has become a much more diverse and expansive enterprise. This sequel, then, is indebted not only to those "pioneers" and their continuing influence, but also to the analytic and creative work of my colleagues in the Academy of Homiletics. I am grateful to be a part of such a remarkable "college of preachers." My gratitude extends to all of the preachers who both bring these methods to their ministry of proclamation and continually refine and reshape the homiletical terrain. The preachers who have contributed their sermons to this new survey of method model this lively interplay beween homiletical theory and practice. I am grateful for their contributions.

I deeply appreciate other colleagues who have assisted me in the preparation of *The Web of Preaching*. Research librarians Sarah D. Brooks Blair and Janet McDermott at United Theological Seminary in Dayton, Ohio, and Elizabeth Hamilton at Mount St. Mary's Seminary of the West in Cincinnati, Ohio, provided invaluable assistance. Also, I have reaped wonderful bibliographic harvests from my friend and fine homiletician, Robert Howard, whose sermon also appears in this work. Nicole Duran watched over my Koine Greek transliterations. My faculty colleagues, homiletician and Dean Kendall McCabe, and President Edwin Zeiders have become a family of encouragement at United Theological Seminary.

Finally, I continue to grow in gratitude for my wife, Elise, for her constant love, her continual encouragement, and her evocative partnership in mind and spirit. I give thanks to God for our covenant.

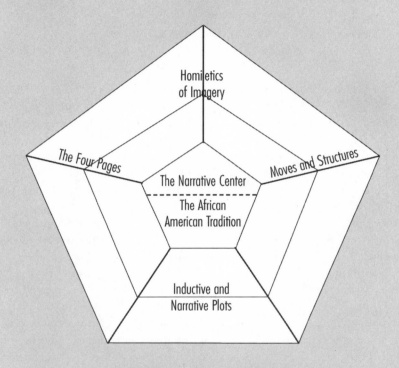

The Web of Preaching

Introduction

Preaching is in the midst of a remarkable renewal in the churches. The number of books on preaching has exploded in volume and in quality and diversity. Theological schools that just a few decades ago had severely reduced their offerings in preaching and eliminated faculty positions entirely in many cases are now expanding both course offerings and faculty positions. Most important, the insistent voices from local congregations regarding the priority of competence in preaching is increasingly heard and acknowledged in judicatory settings ecumenically. Even *Time* magazine featured a cover story on preachers in America several years ago![1] The scene in contemporary homiletics is one of ferment and even argument, yet it is remarkably productive with regard to the church's ministry of proclamation. The strong emergence of women's voices in pulpits and positions of homiletics has richly contributed to the renewal of preaching. Moreover, the field of homiletics now is wonderfully multicultural, with ethnic minority preaching valued as a gift for the entire community of faith. Studies in African American preaching, for example, have multiplied at an astounding rate over the past two decades. This harvest of resources related to the African American preaching tradition is, likewise, serving to propel the renewal of preaching across the churches. Preaching is in renewal.

Of course, it is important to place some qualifications on such a judgment—we are not yet where we need to be as those called to preach. First, we might locate ourselves with regard to the old orthodoxy of discursive preaching, the model built upon argument and organized by points and propositions. The "new homiletics"[2] began to emerge in the late 1960s and early 1970s, with early pioneers including Charles Rice, Fred Craddock, Edmund Steimle, and others. "A Copernican revolution in preaching" is the way I described the situation by the middle of the 1980s. It was time for an initial survey of the homiletical terrain, method-wise, with my book, *A New Hearing: Living Options in Homiletic Method*. The publication of this survey of methods in preaching, then, might be viewed as a "second generation" mapping of the emerging homiletic field. From this vantage point, we have come two generations beyond the old rationalistic homiletic. Ironically, the old model persists and dies hard.

A second way to interpret the contemporary homiletical scene is to track the enduring elements of that revolution and to call our attention to newer voices in the field. By way of introducing *A New Hearing*, I quoted Wellford Hobbie who had just offered an observation of deep insight. He noted in 1982 that there seemed to be three major movements in homiletics that were moving churches beyond the topical preaching orthodoxy: an inductive approach, a narrative or story form, and a method based on the movement and structure of the biblical text.[3]

Based on Hobbie's analysis, I shaped *A New Hearing* around five homileticians who represented in some way these movements—Charles Rice (storytelling); Henry Mitchell (narrative preaching in the black tradition); Eugene Lowry (the narrative sermonic plot); Fred Craddock (his inductive model); and David Buttrick (a phenomenological approach). Hobbie's analysis remains remarkably apt, though a survey of homiletic method fifteen years later involves some adaptations to his model. The three approaches he listed remain vital movements within the field of homiletics.

A fourth method, best seen in the work of David Buttrick, looks to assemble plotted language within the consciousness of the listeners. Since *A New Hearing's* publication, Buttrick has expanded his system by way of proposing three modes of hermeneutic consciousness: the mode of immediacy, of reflectivity, and of praxis. The methodological implications of these three modes—not available in *A New Hearing*—are interpreted in this volume's chapter on Buttrick's moves and structures. Also, since Hobbie's article was written, Paul Scott Wilson has produced a fully developed methodology for preaching dealing with the four pages of the sermon. One chapter is devoted to this proposal. Finally (a word to be used with caution in this quite fluid homiletic situation), enough time and sufficient preaching, in which biblical and contemporary images organize the sermonic plot, has taken place that we can begin to sketch out the methodological implications here. We are indebted in large part to faithful women preachers for this evocative approach to shaping the movement and logic of the sermon.

The question that confronted this author once these positions were identified for this new review and assessment related to the organization of the project. In *A New Hearing*, I simply dealt with the approaches of the five colleagues in no particular order. In each chapter, there is a development of that person's method, followed by an evaluation and a sermon written on that respective subject. For this sequel on homiletic method, a model for organizing the volume was suggested by Abingdon Press editor, Paul Franklyn. "How about titling your new work *The Web of Preaching*"? Paul wrote me. Yes! This metaphor of the web is richly evocative and provides a model by which we can locate each position and envision the relationship of the various methods to one another. The web in nature (as in those of the spider) implies a system that is tensive, yet remaining connective. Moreover, there is the implication of dynamic interaction across the web. Touch a web at the bottom and the situation is reshaped at all other points as well. This is a nice metaphor for the mutually interactive quality of contemporary homiletics. A new insight or retrieval of some virtue in homiletic tradition at one location on the web of preaching will soon influence (or even disrupt) other locations also.

A second layer of meaning related to the web of preaching is suggested by today's Internet and the worldwide web. Here, we are offered the notion of an ongoing conversation that enriches the meanings already derived from nature's webs. I have sought in this new survey of method to enhance this element of conversation around preaching's web. What would David Buttrick and Paul Scott Wilson, for example, say to each other regarding the homiletics of imagery? I have sought to imagine just such a conversation. Finally, we hear various specialists speaking of the neural web of the human brain. Here is added the notion of embodiment. Preaching in most all of its manifestations is embodied within the body of Christ, within particular liturgical contexts, and for the most part within specific congregations. Therefore, I have attempted, where possible, to assess the relationship between each homiletic approach and its liturgical and sacramental context. Some delightful findings emerged from this quest: for example, the central emphasis within African American narrative preaching on the sermon's organic relationship to the entire event of worship. So we will speak of the web of preaching.

The model of preaching's web has also liberated this survey from focusing only on one homiletician in each chapter. To be sure, David Buttrick and Paul Scott Wilson demanded separate chapters dealing solely with their systems. (They did not personally demand this treatment, but their distinctive approaches did insist on such individual analysis.) However, now we can begin to speak, even with Buttrick and Wilson, about "locations on the web and the interaction of those locations." Most every location, moreover, finds a number of colleagues producing good fruit for proclamation. For this writer, at the center of the web of preaching lies a complex of theology and practice that has narrativity as its shared foundation. Two chapters, then, are designed to explore this narrative center of the web of preaching, one representing a rather postliberal stance including my own and the second reflecting the narrative preaching tradition within the African American church. (See the sketch of the web of preaching that precedes this introduction for a visualization of this model.)

Extending out from the center on each side of the narrative center of the web are the approaches of our two "distinctive" contributors, David Buttrick and Paul Scott Wilson. Notice that their methodologies connect in each case with the narrative center. But, imagining the outer rim of the web as the more conceptual and discursive location, each also connects in distinctive ways to that discursive rim of the web. I locate the approaches of Fred Craddock with his inductive method and the model of Eugene Lowry's "loop" on an intermediate strand between the web's center and edge. (Lowry is also a significant contributor to the material at the narrative center.) Finally, I imagine the narrative center connected vertically by the emerging homiletics of imagery. It is important both that these schools connect methodologically and that preachers live out those connections in their sermons. Also by way of this model of the web of preaching, I was freed to invite a wonderfully gifted and diverse group of preachers to provide sermons illustrating and modeling the various positions surveyed. I am awed by their approaches that at once are so distinctive and yet so joined together within the one Body.

Once again, as one who continues to be privileged to teach in Roman Catholic and Protestant seminary contexts, I will give a word about terminology. For most Protestants, we find it easy to speak of biblical preaching within the Sunday worship of God's people as "the sermon." For most of us, a "homily" connotes a lesser thing—some sort of meditation or edifying remarks. However, in the Catholic context (along with many Episcopalians), the terminology is almost exactly reversed. A "sermon" is some topical address—perhaps on the bishop's latest appeal—but having little or no connection to the texts of the day and to the liturgical and sacramental context. A "homily," on the other hand, is shaped in and through the Scriptures and is intentionally designed to lead the worshipers (the assembly) to a deeper sharing in the liturgy that then responds to the Word. I therefore request a bit of "translation" by both my Catholic and Protestant colleagues. We speak here of biblical preaching in the Sunday assembly, most fully realized when that worship is fulfilled in the breaking of bread and the sharing of the cup.

Also, a word of gratitude to my colleagues who have contributed the sermon/homilies that model the various locations on preaching's web. This ecumenical college of preachers provides outstanding examples of the methods surveyed in this project. These preachers, moreover, are nifty friends in Christ. I am grateful for their faith and their word.

CHAPTER 1

Inductive and Narrative Homiletic Plots: Fred Craddock and Eugene Lowry

A frequent critique of narrative preachers and homileticians is that of the inherent limitations built into their methods by the Scriptures themselves. After all, the critics point out, biblical texts come in all sorts of literary forms—poetry, apocalyptic, discourses, Wisdom sayings, as well as the rhetoric of the Epistles and, of course, narrative. Can it not be the case that narrative approaches to preaching work well with narrative texts, but fail the preacher and people when the text at hand derives from a source other than narrative? The issues raised by this evaluation of narrative preaching's adequacy, of course, need to be aligned with the critique narrative homileticians have raised regarding the adequacy of the old discursive preaching to deal with most any biblical texts. The latter approach—preaching's modern expression in points and themes and main ideas—is perhaps best conceived as a spatial kind of activity in which the preacher constructed sermons from static themes and propositions. Recall, as Eugene Lowry observes, that most of us "were trained to think space and not time, unconsciously of course, when we sit down to begin sermon preparation."[1] Lowry continues, "The result is that without conscious consent we immediately set about to order ideas."[2] The alternative, doing "time" in the pulpit, is to take up a narrative model of preaching with its mobility and emphasis on plot rather than outline. So the question may be sharpened somewhat

15

regarding preaching methods and diverse literary forms of the Scripture: How can the dynamics of narrative biblical texts inform our preaching whatever the literary form we preach? More simply put, we ask about methods in preaching that can "do time" no matter what the lesson or occasion.

The Inductive Homiletics of Fred Craddock

The Old Deductive Preaching

Colleague Eugene Lowry put it this way: "When Fred Craddock's work *As One Without Authority* was published in 1971, a new era in North American homiletics was born."[3] And as is the case with the other pioneers in preaching's new era, Fred Craddock begins his revolution by critiquing the old homiletic orthodoxy. The prior era in preaching was beholden to a deductive methodology that has held sway for centuries, having its origins in Aristotle. The method derives its name from an internal movement and logic; beginning with a general truth, its goal is to lead to specific applications for a particular situation. Within homiletical tradition, this deductive method has long been established as normative for preaching regarding both the structure of the sermon and its exegetical underpinnings. Structurally, a recognizable form is consistently detected: The thesis of the sermon is stated and broken down into its constitutive "points"; these subtheses are then expanded, illustrated, and applied to some particular life situation. This approach is immediately familiar, expressing "the main stream of traditional preaching."[4]

If the formal characteristics of this mainstream approach to preaching are familiar, so, too, are its uses of Scripture. Deductive preaching has exemplified a minimalist and often arbitrary relationship to biblical material throughout its history. The thesis or topic may or may not be drawn from the Bible, biblical warrant being by no means essential to the deductive method. Rather, Scripture can be found within the range of illustrative material, or may contribute "a governing image or basic vocabulary."[5] Deductive preaching's use of Scripture, however, most often constitutes genuine misuse. Passages evaluated for employment within the deductive preaching model are first boiled down, revealing a thematic residue. Otherwise, serving as illustrations, biblical texts are viewed as merely ornamental to the argument already presented. Such use, according to Craddock, only offers "the illusion rather than the reality of listening to the text."[6]

Beyond deductive preaching's exegetical deficiencies, two other serious problems have flawed this mainstream tradition. Craddock notes that the thesis of the sermon first is expounded and only later is related to particular situations. He then adds that such an approach is "a most unnatural mode of communication, unless, of course, one presupposes passive listeners who accept the right or authority of the speaker to state conclusions which he then applies to their faith and life."[7] There is, therefore, an inherent bias in the whole project of deductive preaching, which assumes authoritarian address of God's Word and passive reception. What is lacking in such a downward movement of truth is any possibility of dialogue or democracy. There is "no listening by the speaker, no contributing by the hearer. If the congregation is on the team, it is as javelin catcher."[8] Such an attitude is seriously out of touch with contemporary American congregations, Craddock believes. Some other, less autocratic method of preaching should replace the deductive sermon's condescending manner.

A second major flaw in deductive preaching relates to issues of structure and movement. As the main thesis is broken down into subsidiary points, a structure emerges that presents almost insurmountable problems regarding homiletic movement. The hearers of a traditional three-point sermon frequently experience three sermonettes instead, since the transition from the end of one point to the beginning of the next is usually unsuccessful. "There may have been movement within each point," Craddock observes, "and there may have been some general kinship among the points, but there was not one movement from beginning to end."[9] Points that are conceptually equal in force cannot evoke a sense of sermonic movement and unity. Attempts at communication through such a static system are experienced by people in the church today as unnatural and as a violation of a sense of community.[10]

Bridges to the New Era in Preaching

As is the case with the other pioneers in the new homiletics, a series of cultural and intellectual movements have been identified that served to bridge the chasm between the old era in homiletics and the new. For Fred Craddock, three of these are especially noteworthy—the rapidly shifting nature of public language, the new biblical studies, and contemporary hermeneutics. Each involves a look back at what has gone before and an assessment of what is new. Of course, Craddock would argue, if communal language, biblical studies, and hermeneutics have all experienced a Copernican revolution, so, too, will the practice of preaching.

1. Language in transition

There is a crisis in language, a diminution in the ability of words to express potency: "to create or to destroy, to bind or to loose, to bless or to curse."[11] Affecting both the culture in general and the church's language as well, the crisis is experienced as a loss in the power of words. Several factors contribute to the phenomenon. First, Craddock invites his readers to assess the impact of the media on social language; they are bombarded by words day in and day out. "The eyes and ears have no relief, and all the old silent haunts are now scarred with billboards and invaded by public-address systems."[12] Without a necessary silence, the power of words decays, again, within both a social and ecclesial context. Biblically speaking, the Word of God is born in silence, and when silence is lost, words and the Word seem to lose their potency: "How one understands a word as an event in the world of sound depends to a great extent upon whether that word is experienced against a backdrop of silence or in a room of many words."[13] Most of the time, we live in rooms of many words.

A second factor relates to the lost efficacy in the traditional language of the church. Although a crisis of culture-wide proportions, the language of the church seems most susceptible to this infection. On one level, this may relate to the inability of the church to slough old and worn-out words that functioned effectively at one time but that no longer communicate the faith. These words "fought well at Nicea, Chalcedon and Augsburg," but "they are kept in the line of march even if the whole mission is slowed to a snail's pace and observers on the side are bent double in laughter."[14] This loss in efficacy related to the church's traditional language may also stem from the radical shift in the way persons access information and express thoughts and feelings.

In spite of these losses with regard to the linguistic support for the task of preaching, there are signs of hope. In particular, Craddock notes the contributions of Martin Heidegger who insists on the centrality of language. Language precedes human existence and gives rise to it. Viewed from this perspective, language is constitutive of human existence and is essential to it. A person, Craddock notes, "is a conversation."[15] And since preaching is by its very nature born out of an oral tradition and becomes an event by returning the Word to its oral/aural immediacy, the performative power of its language is now being reaffirmed. Recalling the insights of Carl Michalson, Craddock concludes that "preaching is by its nature an acoustical event, having its home in orality not textuality."[16]

2. Cultural factors influencing the state of preaching

Fred Craddock joins with the other first-generation shapers of the new homiletics in pointing to the profound changes that have undercut the foundations of preaching. He singles out a philosophical shift from an interest in metaphysics to a focus on ontology and historicity. Resulting from this transition is a setting aside of a perspective that saw reality as substance within a static modality in favor of positions emphasizing being (ontology) and time (historicity). The ordered and changeless qualities of a previous era are gone, replaced by art and literature that expresses rapid change and even fragmentation. Architecturally, Craddock adds, even churches "do not look like churches any more."[17] Within such a worship space, where the cultural winds have swept through even the church's liturgy, the static and timeless verities contained within a three-point sermon seem oddly out of place and out of touch. The hearers of such preaching receive it as the imposition of a false symmetry on contemporary life, caught up in rapid and discordant change.

But on the other hand, Fred Craddock suggests that it is precisely this erosion of the old cultural stasis that ironically creates a new environment in which the spoken word may well be heard anew. Resonating with the new cultural situation is the fact that "sound is always present, always an existential experience."[18] Moreover, the spoken word in a nonrehearsed context such as preaching conveys the qualities of openness, polyvalence, and spontaneity, qualities held in high favor within the contemporary culture. The polyvalence in preaching means that more may be received in such an oral/aural event than was initially intended. This "more than was intended" opens up a new future; the spoken word is capable of leading "toward a goal as yet undetermined."[19]

3. The role of media

If human perception "is no longer polarized around sound and person but rather around sight and object, the difficulties for the preaching task are all too obvious."[20] These difficulties for preaching, as noted earlier, derive from a prior shift in language's center of gravity. With the advent of a print-oriented culture, oral communication was viewed as subsidiary to the written word, radically altering the previous experience of Scripture: "Words fixed in space by print tended to create the idea that the meanings of these words were fixed also. As a result, the written word was more authoritative than the spoken."[21] Now, this more recent shift from a literary to a visually oriented culture in fact represents the second profound shift in social consciousness away from the primacy of oral communication. The situation, however, is not this neat in its cultural and linguistic manifestations, and this is a sign of hope for

Craddock. With this caveat in mind, it is now appropriate to assess those factors that are borne within the new cultural situation and that are making for the renewal of the ministry of preaching.

4. Biblical studies

Once again, Fred Craddock identifies a sequence in which a prior situation that was detrimental to the task of preaching has moved to a new, much more supportive location. In this case, the situation is that of modern biblical interpretation. The dominant tenor of the relationship between biblical studies and preaching had been somewhat negative and abrasive during the ascendancy of historical-critical interpretation. Ironically, while one of this discipline's objectives had been the understandability of the Bible by the church, the reverse became the norm. What was conveyed to the church, and especially to the preacher, by the probings of historical criticism was an increasing awareness of the differences between the contemporary world and the biblical world. As it was dissected by historical research, the text seemed to recede further and further, as if viewed through the wrong end of a telescope. An experience of distance was the outcome: The preacher felt a disturbing distance from the biblical world and a confusing distance from the scholarly one. Faced with this quandary, some preachers reverted to preseminary methods of dealing with a text and simply ignored the critical apparatus a seminary education sought to impart. More to the point was the insight that "biblical studies always moved [the preacher] backward, behind the texts to sources and antecedent, while [the preacher] at the same time sensed that in actuality, the story of the Gospel had always moved forward."[22] What was needed was "a new angle of vision" within biblical interpretation that would allow the preacher to transverse this distance between himself or herself and the world of the biblical text.[23]

It is in the emergence of the new methods of biblical criticism within the last twenty-five years, Fred Craddock celebrates, that "the distance between the modern pulpit and the ancient text, a distance of which historical-critical methods made us so aware, no longer seems so frightening and non-negotiable."[24] Particularly in the rhetorical and literary criticism of Amos Wilder, Robert Funk, and Ernst Fuchs, the "inseparable relation of the Gospel and the forms of its communication" has been established.[25] Faced with such a multiplicity of literary forms in Scripture—narrative, sayings, epistolary discourse, and so on—the preacher may finally be convinced to let go of the constraints of the old topical outline with its points and poems. Whatever sermonic method is chosen, its "modes of discourse" will be appropriate to the form of the pericope itself.[26] Just as there is no one normative form of biblical discourse, a biblical sermon will not impose any particular sermonic form, especially one derived from Hellenistic rhetorical, upon every text. Although not supplanting the historical-critical approach, an invaluable contribution of literary criticism is its capability of helping the preacher understand what a biblical text does and learning what it says.[27]

Aligned with this new angle of vision on the text for Craddock are some central theological emphases that may have become obscured in preaching's modern era. They are now reemerging within the church's theology of interpretation and disclose a continuum between the two ends of the hermeneutical arch that is essential for preaching. Biblical texts not only are discovered to have a past (form and redaction criticism) but a future also. Theologically, this futurity of the text that is fulfilled in preaching is based for Craddock on several fundamental assumptions. The Scriptures:

> [1] . . . are normative in the life of the church. To sever preaching from that norm either by neglect or intent would be to cut the church off from its primary source of nourishment and discipline. Sermons not informed and inspired by Scripture are objects dislodged, orphans in the world, without mother or father.
>
> [2] . . . by keeping sentinel watch over the life and faith of the church, blow the whistle on lengthy exercises in self-analysis and self-serving. . . . Sermons that are self-serving are called into question by the very texts that had been selected to authenticate the message.
>
> [3] . . . continually remind pulpit and pew not only what but how to preach. . . . A stirring text well read creates an expectation in listeners, which the sermon should not disappoint.[28]

If that expectation is to be fulfilled in the hearing of the congregation, it will not be through the imposition of a condescending, deductive method. Now, Fred Craddock invites, it is time to consider more deeply the implications of the new biblical studies for a method of biblical preaching.

From Biblical Studies to Hermeneutics

There is tension in the distance between preacher and text that of necessity will persist throughout the process of interpretation. Attempts at overcoming the distance through, for instance, existentialism (which dissolves it) or positivism (which simply remains in the past and thus avoids interpretation), are for Craddock unacceptable alternatives. The distance remains and needs to remain, though the task of interpretation changes the quality of that distance, a shift that will be decisive for preaching. At the beginning of interpretation, however, the preacher will need to approach the ancient text "*anticipating* meaning"; that is, come to it with interest and expectation.[29] The preacher, then, "can come with *interest* knowing that interest is an accepted hermeneutical principle."[30] Moreover, this interest should not be narrowly circumscribed by specifically homiletical concerns: "What is this text's message?" To shut down the interpretive process in such a fashion is to deny Scripture its polyvalent quality. A text contains a "surplus of meaning," even beyond that which was intended by the writer.[31] No single interpretation will exhaust the meaning latent in a text for interpretation or for preaching. Anticipating the text's surplus of meaning, then, is a principle that stands at the outset of the preacher's challenge of negotiating the distance between Scripture and the contemporary situation.

The interpretation of Scripture begins with the selection of a text, although Craddock notes that sermons themselves may be prompted by occasions as well as texts and still remain biblical preaching. The text may be chosen by the preacher (Craddock encourages using some sort of preaching plan) or commended by way of the lectionary. In any case, the initial question becomes, "How is the preacher to approach the text?"[32] How is the "conversation" between the text and the listener to be initiated? Craddock indicates a three-staged process of interaction.

The first and perhaps most important aspect of interpretation is a sensitive, but unassisted, listening to the text. This is not the time for consulting secondary sources concerning the Scripture lesson—those investigations will come later. First, the text should be read, several times in fact, and the preacher should respond immediately with "ideas, questions, feelings, and triggered recollections."[33] These preliminary readings should have a quality of naïveté about them, and the thoughts and feelings that constitute the interpreter's first response should be as spontaneous as possible. However, because of the spontaneity of this interaction, the responses are fragile and so it is best to write down everything that comes to mind.[34] Through such a discipline of naive reading and listening, the preacher is more closely identified with the congregation "who will also come to the text unaided except for their own thoughts, feelings, and needs."[35] For this first reading, the preacher should find herself or himself among the parishioners rather than among the scholars. Questions raised and recorded here will be most likely derived from the concerns of the text itself. One important reason for recording these reactions and responses, for Craddock, is that "these early notes will provide more than half [of] one's introductions to sermons."[36] For this purpose and several others as well, this naive first reading and rereading of the text is essential, "foundational for all other study."[37]

The second stage in the interpretive process involves the contributions of commentaries and other resources. The timing of this stage is crucial, though, since to consult a commentary too early may result in a weakening of the centrality of the text. Consulted too late, a commentary's influence is diminished and simply becomes another potential source for sermonic material. Craddock underlines this assertion: "A commentary consulted too soon tends to be a master over the interpreter and consulted too late tends to be an agreeable subordinate. At the right time, a commentary can be the interpreter's colleague."[38] Among the significant purposes of this second stage, an early activity involves "establishing the text." Variants in the text are checked along with its parameters, even if they are already indicated by the lectionary. "Taking the text seriously," Craddock notes, "begins by asking, What words did the writer write?"[39] Later in the second stage, the interpreter will seek the assistance of the commentaries in answering questions related to the meaning of the text in its original context. As clearly as possible, the preacher will want to discover how original listeners understood the text when they heard it. Finally, the more specific issues raised as early as the first reading are investigated and given some resolution, if possible. The movement within this stage, then, is from the more general concerns to the more specific and concrete.

The third and final stage of this particular process involves a movement away from the secondary sources and toward the text once more. Now, it is carefully reread and the notes made during the first reading are reviewed. What has happened, the preacher may observe, is that "the intervening exegetical work has clarified some early questions, confirmed some impressions, and destroyed others."[40] By this latter reading much of the initial distance in the text has disappeared and a deep engagement is taking place. "If this is indeed the case," Craddock states, "then the process of withdrawing from the text and recovering one's distance from it should begin."[41] This new step of withdrawal is characterized by a more analytic relationship to the text that involves the following considerations:

1. "Position" in the text

The preacher is now called to become self-conscious about the "point of identification" or "position" in relation to the text. Redactional questions concerning the levels of the text are raised now and will soon become important for the development of the sermon. (For example, will the sermon focus on the parable alone or the evangelist's redactional context as well?) But to raise the question of position in the text is also to insist that the interpreter become aware of the place in the text he or she has already assumed. Where has the preacher stood within the biblical narrative? With what character or characters? Is it not time for other perspectives to be taken? An intentionality about these considerations is important for two reasons, Craddock believes. In the first place, such identification will bear "not only upon the interpretation of the text but also upon the sermon soon to be designed."[42] In the second place, a lack of self-consciousness at this point will almost certainly assure that in both interpretation and preaching, the preacher will take the most favored places in the text. Given this temptation, it is certainly healthy "to stand elsewhere now and then."[43]

2. Discerning the theme

A major achievement in interpretation is the ability to state in one affirmative sentence the theme or message of the text. The affirmative mode of this theme sentence serves to avoid "the hortatory terms that too often characterize entire sermons: we must, we ought, we should, let us, let us not."[44] Craddock does not mean to say that such exhortation is out of place in preaching; rather, this step is intended to relate such imperatives functionally to the theme. The ability to capture the meaning of the text in one sentence, he affirms, "marks a genuine achievement, rewarded not only by a sense of satisfaction but by a new appetite for the next task: the sermon itself."[45]

3. Discerning the action

A text not only says something (its theme), but also does something. Actions along with words constitute the fullness of human communication. With reference to Scripture, this activity of the text is best discerned by attention to its historical and literary contexts and to its form.[46] For Fred Craddock, what a text does reveals its intentionality—that is, does a passage of scripture reprove, encourage, mistrust, or correct? An awareness of the scripture's context, of course, is vital to the discernment of the action of the text.

Discovering what a text does, moreover, is intimately related to sermon preparation, especially if the sermon intends to do what the text does. The preacher, then, "will want to hold on to the form, since form captures and conveys function, not only during the interpretation of the text but during the designing of the sermon as well."[47] The difficulty with a theme-deductive approach to the sermon would be that this principle is consistently violated. The form of the text is abandoned for a deductive model presumed to be normative apart from the form and function of the text. It is little wonder,

Craddock notes, that such literary forms as the parables of Jesus suffered homiletical violence through such a thematic approach.

These canons for biblical interpretation, Fred Craddock believes, will provide the preacher/interpreter with a broad understanding of the text, its message, its context, and its literary form. However, while quite a bit may now be known about the scripture, little may be known about the sermon itself. This awareness is critical for preaching: "the process of arriving at something to say is to be distinguished from the process of determining how to say it."[48] For Craddock, a distinction of interpretive method from homiletical method, strictly speaking, is based on several key assumptions. First, it is assumed that work on the sermon itself is systematically subsequent to the exegetical and interpretive tasks that will provide the sermon's message. Until that message has been determined, "getting up a sermon" is a fruitless and potentially chaotic activity. On the other hand, the achievement of a text's theme and form does not necessarily provide the preacher with the shape and context of the sermon. Each process, interpretation, and sermon design is distinct, having its own goals, skills, and climax.[49] Moreover, each process has its own critical focus or position, with a distance between them that gives rise to the hermeneutical task. While "factors of time, space, language, worldview, and immediate circumstances" separate the two, the distance may be negotiated. However, as Craddock insists, the two enterprises are simply not susceptible to one encompassing methodology.

The shift from arriving at a message to determining how that message will be preached occurs as the preacher turns to the task of interpreting the listeners. Not only does the preacher interpret the Scriptures with understanding, she or he must interpret the congregation as well. Otherwise, the sermon will remain in the past or, perhaps worse, the message will be presented in an overly objective manner, removed from the concerns of the hearers. When undertaking this second project of interpretation, the same question of distance that was so crucial to biblical interpretation also stands with regard to the hearers. For Craddock, it is best to begin the process of interpreting the listeners at a considerable distance; the congregation should first be viewed by the preacher as an audience. This at least removes the temptation to gear the sermon from the start according to the likes and dislikes of specific members of the congregation. Viewed positively, the goal here is "to get enough distance to understand and accept the listeners in and of themselves, apart from their relationship to the minister."[50] The purpose of this act of imagination is to remind the preacher of the needs and values held in common by a congregation, apart from those brought to the foreground by pastoral involvements.

Here, the challenge is to see the congregation as a guest minister would see them—as those created in the image of God, yet an image distorted by sin and rebellion. There is, still, "the faint recollection of Eden" within any group of listeners that will evoke a sense of recognition when the preacher speaks of the Christian faith and the human condition.[51] Other qualities of listeners seen as audience will also begin to gain definition. "They are all seeking a place to stand, a place that feels like home"; they want "room to say no to the sermon but a genuine invitation to say yes."[52] Finally, the listeners understood as audience have a longing to be brought into God's presence. Any sermon that addresses these needs will have significantly overcome the distance between pulpit and pew. Even those hearers who are not church members will feel that the minister has understood them well.[53]

Although the listeners as audience are viewed as strangers, this sense of distance is diminished when the listeners are seen as a congregation. The specific characteristics of the persons and groups within the church are taken into account. What is also considered is the powerful relationship that exists between pastor and congregation. Put together, the knowledge accumulated through this process will enable the pastor "to preach with a power and effectiveness unavailable to the guest speaker, whatever may be the skills, credentials, and reputation of that speaker."[54] Whether by way of formal means (initial pastoral contact with community officials), informal means (the daily pastoral contacts), or by way of "empathic imagination" (putting oneself in the place of the parishioners), such an understanding of listeners as congregation is indispensable to effective preaching. Yet Craddock notes that this more intimate and specific awareness does not displace the understanding gained by viewing the hearers as audience. On the contrary, the concrete details gained through pastoral ministry and empathic imagination build on the foundation gained from viewing the listeners from a greater distance. By employing both approaches, "ministers will likely be surprised to discover how much understanding of the human condition they already have but which has not been adequately reflected in either the words or music of their preaching."[55] Put simply, there is a need for both critical distance from and close identification with a preacher's congregation.

It is this close identification with the congregation that allows the preacher to speak for the people as well as to them. That is, the congregation would be allowed to recover what was experienced in the past and sense it as being familiar. "It is part of the power of preaching," Craddock affirms, "that the people are familiar with what we are saying."[56] Effective preaching evokes these past experiences and a corresponding sense of familiarity, creating what Craddock terms a "nod of recognition." In other words, the power of preaching is not located in its constant novelty, but in its ability to bring to recognition what people already know, allowing them to say, "amen." With regard to sermon preparation, Craddock underscores two values that need to be inherent if a nod of recognition is to occur: "First, it means that the preacher will share, not omit, details."[57] People need to be entrusted with the biblical story, but recognition will occur only if enough detail is present for that story to be recalled. Second, the nod of recognition is evoked when the preacher recounts the familiar passage of scripture with interest and enthusiasm. Craddock notes that some preachers deal ponderously with biblical material because the people have heard it before. What these preachers are failing to grasp is the excitement created when people recognize their stories, and thereby recognize themselves in the messages. "The principle of recognition liberates the preacher to move through familiar territory with more, not less, conviction and enthusiasm."[58]

Preaching is not exhausted by Craddock's homiletics of recognition, for buried within the *nod* of recognition is the *shock* of recognition. Consistently effective preaching, he believes, will convey within it the shock of recognition. But that shock is always latent within the nod, and without the latter, there will be no shock at all, but only anger. Such a negative reaction is almost inevitable, and results from an association of the shock with "the messenger and not with the message."[59] Once more, Craddock insists that for this shock to occur with effectiveness, considerable attention must be given to details. His refrainlike admonition is for preachers to stay with the story longer: "The power is in the details."[60] For the hearer to be addressed, convicted, or motivated, calls for a prior awareness of the familiarity of the story, an assent to it, and a nod of recognition. Then, the shock can occur when that person realizes that he or she is "the one called, the one addressed, the one guilty, the one responsible, the one commissioned."[61] But without the antecedent "amen," such a shock will not be experienced, for the story will not be recognized as our story.

This dynamic involving the interpretation of listeners is as fundamental to the process of sermon preparation as is the interpretation of scripture. In fact, any movement from exegesis directly to preaching is inappropriate to the extent that it circumvents an evaluation of the congregational context for that preaching. Two distinct foci, therefore, are seen by Craddock as essential to effective preaching: one related to the listeners and their personal and social contexts and the other related to the biblical text and its historical, literary, and theological contexts.[62] Hence, he concludes:

> The practical question, long discussed by homileticians, has to do with whether one begins with the text or with the people in sermon preparation.

. . . [But] in the movement here recommended, the experience is not of a trip from text to people or from people to text. . . . Both are actively involved.[63]

The listeners and the text must both be interpreted, with canons of interpretation appropriate to each respective context. What results is a message that has successfully negotiated the distance between the biblical past and the contemporary pastoral situation. What has not resulted yet, Craddock insists, is a sermon, for the methodology for designing a sermon is distinct from those processes that have been utilized to interpret text and listeners.[64]

From Interpretation to Sermonic Method

An overriding concern for homiletic method for Fred Craddock is that of sermonic movement. Although sermons take a myriad of shapes, they tend to move generally in one of two basic directions—along either deductive or inductive patterns of thought. While the liabilities of the former seem to rule out a continuation of those deductive patterns, an inductive approach em-bodies a number of values that commend it as a living option in homiletic method. The inductive method of preaching is founded on a central conviction held by Craddock: that the congregation on Sunday morning should be permitted to take the same inductive trip that brought the preacher to the pulpit and be granted the freedom to arrive at its own conclusion.[65] Such a trip is sermonically possible and, in fact, may make the explicit statement of its conclusion unnecessary. Moreover, if the people have made the inductive trip with the preacher, then "it is *their* conclusion, and the implications for their own situations is not only clear but personally inescapable."[66]

Exactly what constitutes an inductive sermon is not answerable in as immediate a fashion as the identifying characteristics of the old deductive approach. There is for Fred Craddock no one normative structure that will predictably mark an effective sermon. In fact, he cautions, "a sermon is defined more by content and purpose than by form."[67] Nevertheless, there are a number of formal considerations that need to be taken into account if one is to preach inductively. Inductive method in preaching will be effective to the extent that a number of qualities are present within the sermon. Given their presence, the preacher is then released to focus more specifically on formal and organizational considerations. Craddock lists these as follows:

1. Movement

Inductive method in preaching subordinates structure to movement to the extent that the former may not even be noticeable by the congregation. Furthermore, inductive preaching demands that the form or outline used move consistently "from the present experience of the hearers to the point at which the sermon will leave [the congregation] to their own decisions and conclusion."[68] The beginning point in sermon preparation, consequently, is not with the introduction, but the conclusion. And the completed sermon will be a journey from the jumping off place that deals seriously with the thoughts and feelings of the hearers, to a conclusion in which that human situation is seen in the light of the presence of Christ. The message itself is the end of the sermon, arrived at by both preacher and people.

For this inductive movement to occur, however, the persistent challenge to the preacher is first to create a sense of anticipation and then to sustain it. In fact, Craddock states, evoking such anticipation becomes "a primary burden of movement in the sermon."[69] The hearer's attention in an inductive sermon is much more critical than in the old deductive approach, since the message is the terminus of the sermon and not its point of origin. Not only will interest need to be maintained in order for both preacher and congregation to arrive at the sermon conclusion, but the quality of anticipation also serves "to prepare the hearer's mood or mind set to grasp and participate in the central idea when it comes."[70]

While there are numerous ways in which the quality of anticipation is sustained throughout a sermon, Craddock highlights the following three factors: First, the oral character of preaching is a vital element in the maintenance of sermonic interest and movement. Preaching is not a literary medium, and the rhetoric of preaching must be that of oral address. Second, Craddock suggests that in preparation, the preacher sequentially list in tersely worded phrases the ideas of the sermon and then ask of this series of thoughts: "Does the material move along, evoking ideas and sustaining anticipation until the end?"[71] Third, a similar scrutiny should search out transitional movements in the sermon denoted by such words as "and," "therefore," and "beyond this."[72] These transitional markers should be well identified by the preacher since they serve "as pegs on which to hang series of ideas, preserving the hard-won flow of material."[73]

2. Unity

Not only must a sermon have movement as a primary characteristic, it must also manifest a unity within which that movement is located. "The contribution to the movement and power of a sermon made by the restraint of a single idea can hardly be overstated."[74] Inductive sermons will not have points, but will have a point, the message toward which all material will tend. Therefore, it is essential that the preacher be able to clearly articulate the main idea of the sermon in a single sentence. Such a statement, for Craddock, is the appropriate and necessary outcome of the twin processes of scriptural and congregational interpretation. It is also to be maintained throughout the process of sermon preparation as the ground of the sermon's unity.

The governing theme serves on one hand as a magnet to attract appropriate material to the sermon in an ordered sequence. On the other hand, the statement will constantly serve as guardian against the introduction of extraneous or potentially distracting material. Nothing can be more disastrous for a sermon than an illustration that arrogantly masters rather than serves. The sermonic theme will filter out such arrogant material.[75] The main idea will also serve to enhance the delivery of the sermon itself. Confident of the unity of the material, the preacher can enter the pulpit knowing that the sermon has a destination and that its various ideas and illustrations will build to a conclusion. Finally, the seminal idea of the sermon is needed because only such a grasp of the sermon's purpose and destination can release the imagination of the preacher, sustaining interest and even excitement. The imaginative faculties of the preacher will not remain focused and fruitful unless this crucial unity is maintained.

3. Imagination

Images are distinct from illustrations, according to Fred Craddock, the latter serving an ornamental function while the former are "essential to the form and inseparable from the content of the entire sermon."[76] They are not to be confined to the introduction or inserted into the body of the sermon to pick up interest, nor are they susceptible to replacement by concepts. Within a person's imaginative consciousness, images "are replaced not by concepts but by other images, and that quite slowly."[77] Since images function to recreate the way life is experienced, their function in both preparing and hearing a sermon is decisive. The minister will need an empathetic imagination, both to interpret the congregation and to form the sermon so that it reflects the realities of the listeners' life experiences.

The question now becomes for Craddock how the preacher's images are "formed in the imagination of [the] hearers with clarity and force sufficient to effect changes in attitudes, values, and life directions."[78] Several principles, he notes, are operative in this process of imaginative communication. First, it is important that the images be taken from real life, "cast in forms recognizable as real and possible."[79] Then, the language used in the pulpit needs to be as concrete as possible, evoking immediate and familiar sensory experience. Generalized language—e.g., speaking of "holy matrimony" rather than imaging a specific wedding—serves to distance listeners from life and thereby severely reduces the sermon's effectiveness. Further, the effectiveness and power of language employed in preaching are eroded when adjectives and adverbs are overused. Parenthetically, such use robs the hearers of their own judgments regarding the ideas and images. Craddock also admonishes the preacher to "avoid all self-conscious interruptions in narration and description."[80] These interruptions not only jar the vital sense of sermonic movement, but also serve to quash the congregation's imaginative faculties in favor of a focus on the preacher. Finally, in order for images to be effectively shared, the language used in preaching must be that of the preacher and not of someone else or of an assumed "pulpit personality." This is a call, Craddock states, "for the vernacular in the pulpit."[81] Employment of these three principles is essential to the task of conveying the concrete realities of life within an inductive sermon. These principles also serve to heighten the emphatic imagination of the preacher so that impression precedes expression.

To have dealt effectively with the issues of unity, movement, and concrete imagining still does not provide a sermon with a specific form. Actually, Craddock observes, there is no one pattern to which preaching should invariably conform. Yet the shape a sermon takes is not an inconsequential issue; rather, "the form itself is active, contributing to what the speaker wishes to say and do, sometimes no less persuasive than the content itself."[82] Form and content, then, are interrelated and interdependent. With an inductive approach to preaching, though, Craddock sets considerable stake on sermonic forms that will evoke and sustain congregational interest. The structure of a sermon will determine "the degree of participation demanded of the hearers," and deductive preaching's inability to invite congregational participation is one of its primary deficiencies.[83] He reminds us that if the message is given first, with supportive material following the conclusions, the congregation is assumed to be passive throughout the process. Among the variety of forms available to the preacher, the goal is to choose those "that are both adequate and congenial to the message and the experience to be generated by the sermon."[84]

An increasingly popular approach among ministers, Craddock notes, is to derive the form of the sermon from the biblical text that provided the sermon's message. Not only does this approach provide the preacher with variety in sermonic forms, but it also helps ensure a fundamental integrity to preaching by deriving both the message and design of the sermon from the same biblical source. Especially in situations where the sermon is based upon a biblical narrative, Craddock encourages the preacher to achieve this congruence of form and message. "Why should I take something that comes to me as a parable," he asks, "and preach it as an outline?"[85] There are limitations to this strategy, perhaps related to the non-narrative character of a good deal of biblical material. However, the unity and movement of a sermon are optimized when sermonic form is grounded in the literary form of a biblical text.

Finally, some forms have endured through long periods of the church's preaching, and it behooves the contemporary preacher to renew acquaintance with these homiletical traditions. The validity of forms that have persisted in the tradition is based, for Craddock, upon their persistently demonstrated ability to carry "the burden of truth with clarity, thoroughness, and interest."[86] This storehouse of readily available forms from the past includes such standards as:

"Explore, explain, apply
The problem, the solution
....
Either/or
Both/ and
....
Ambiguity, clarity
Major premise, minor premise, conclusion
....
From the lesser, to the greater."[87]

While these examples include deductive as well as inductive models, their value is shown in their persistence throughout church tradition and in their ability to offer the preacher a variety of sermon structures. Moreover, a varied diet of sermon patterns is critical if congregational interest is to be maintained: "No form is so good that it does not eventually become wearisome to both listener and speaker."[88] The preacher's alternatives regarding sermonic form, then, involve either the selection of a form—from the biblical text or homiletical tradition—or the creation of a form more immediately in accord with inductive principles.

In spite of the normative character of the inductive approach to biblical interpretation and congregational interpretation, the question of sermonic form remains open for the preacher. Both deductive and inductive approaches remain available and effective for preaching. The enduring question for Fred Craddock, however, is the adequacy and congeniality of the sermonic form to the message at the heart of the sermon. Biblical preaching, then, will not so much focus on form as on the appropriateness of any sermonic form with regard to that sermon's message and its expression of the gospel.

Eugene Lowry and the Homiletical Plot

At the narrative center of preaching, we delight in the abundance of biblical stories whose plots offer a way for the sermon. Narrative preaching on narrative texts gains its movement and sequencing from the story itself; preachers need not look much further for resources on the form of the sermon. However, Lowry notes with others that there can be a narrative movement of the sermonic form without a dependence on any specific narrative text. In the former—preaching on the narrative text—the form of the sermon is quite fully informed by the biblical story's plot. In the latter—preaching as narrative oral discourse—there is a "narrative sequencing of the presentation" while not dependent upon a specific story text.[89] Lowry summarizes the held-in-common identity of narrative sermons as follows:

> What identifies the usual narrative sermon most readily is its plot form, which always—one way or another—begins with a felt *discrepancy* or conflict, and then makes its way through *complication* (things get worse), makes a decisively sharp turn or *reversal*, and then moves finally toward *resolution* or closure.[90]

At the same time, Lowry calls attention to the distinctions within the scope of narrative sermons. On one hand, the sermon may be largely a story, with its story derived from Scripture; on the other hand, it may embody a narrative form in which the movement and structure follow the inherent sequences of a narrative plot.

Eugene Lowry offers preachers and homileticians a remarkable study in the development of a location within the new homiletics. In 1980, he wrote *The Homiletical Plot: The Sermon as Narrative Art Form*.[91] This work introduced preachers to "the Lowry Loop," the stages within a narrative sermonic plot. Then, after much fruitful work at the narrative center of preaching's web (reflected in his *Doing Time in the Pulpit*[92] and *How to Preach a Parable: Designs for Narrative Preaching*[93]), he returned to a reconsideration and refinement of his narrative sermonic form. It is profitable to scrutinize both Lowry's original analysis of the narrative sermonic form as depicted in the 1980 publication and then to assess the most recent alterations and continuities within his approach. We will then attempt an application of his revised narrative method with regard to a specific biblical text and liturgical occasion. We may think of Lowry's work in exploring narrative sermonic forms as being comprised of two levels—level one depicted in *The Homiletical Plot* (1980) and level two in *The Sermon* (1997).

Level 1: A Problem-solutional Approach

What generates the plot form of a sermon is the interaction of some human problem and a theme, yielding a sermon idea. In the beginning, there is a felt need that is experienced as discrepancy and that will need to be sustained throughout the sermon as suspense. At the same time, the need, the discrepancy, longs for some kind of solution, a "scratch" that will specifically address the "itch." The primary clue to the formation of a sermon idea, then, is this tension between problem and theme that offers up the needed suspense that will both sustain and propel the sermonic plot. The resulting sermons are of necessity "always problem-solutional."[94] This movement from itch to scratch involves two particular challenges for the preacher, according to Lowry. First, the preacher will need to establish a relationship of trust with his or her listeners. Second, the preacher will also possess the skills necessary to maintain suspense throughout the movement of the sermon's narrative plot. The two tasks—establishing trust and maintaining suspense—are interrelated: "The listeners knowing we are about to lead them down a risky road—hopefully to some resolution born of the gospel—must have the confidence that we are capable of doing the job credibly, convincingly, theologically, and hopefully."[95]

Suspense in the homiletical plot derives in its effectiveness through a sweep of movement from ambiguity to resolution. Inherent within every sermonic plot is a sense of issues and actions not yet disclosed. There is necessarily "the suspension of revelation and decision."[96] Yet this essential ambiguity does not mean preaching that is ambiguous as to focus or relevance. Such preaching is vague rather than suspenseful and far removed from the particularities of both the congregation's needs and the gospel's response. If the message is clearly conveyed that nothing significant is at stake, congregational trust and attentiveness will be lost.

In order to avoid such a loss of trust, preaching must express genuine problems of human existence thrown against the particularity of the gospel. Moreover, in its essential form, the sermon is "a premeditated plot which has as its key ingredient a sensed discrepancy, a homiletical bind."[97] There are two general types of plots that offer themselves for homiletical usage, Lowry observes. A movie plot will typically begin with a felt discrepancy and move to an unknown resolution. Complications thicken the plot as it moves toward its unknown conclusion. On the other hand, a television series plot will begin in a similar manner, but move toward a known conclusion (the crew of the Enterprise will all be on the next episode of "Star Trek" along with their intrepid captain and starship). Sermons, Lowry observes, fall most accurately into the latter plot form, since the community of faith already knows that the resolution of the issues of human existence is provided through the Incarnation of Jesus Christ. How the gospel will respond to the particular binds and discrepancies of our lives, however, is the issue open to ambiguity. And for Lowry, "this unknown middle ground provides the context for sermonic tension."[98] In order for this movement from ambiguity and homiletical bind to resolution through the gospel to occur, it is essential to identify and appropriate the specific stages of the sermon plot. Initially, Lowry defined these stages as "(1) upsetting the equilibrium, (2) analyzing the discrepancy, (3) disclosing the clue to resolution, (4) experiencing the gospel, and (5) anticipating the consequences."[99]

Lowry's students, he remarks, came up with a helpful shorthand version of these stages: (1) Oops; (2) Ugh; (3) Aha; (4) Whee; (5) Yeah.[100]

Stage 1: Upsetting the equilibrium

At the sermon's opening, interest must be created before it can be maintained, and this is best done by upsetting the equilibrium of the listeners. Within only a few minutes (two or three) the preacher's itch will need to become that of the congregation, through the introduction of an attendant ambiguity or "bind." Lowry likens this stage to "the opening scene of a play or movie in which some kind of conflict or tension is introduced."[101] The preacher is granted an important opportunity within this first stage since the opening tension may or may not relate to the main theme of the sermon. Just as a good story may have several subplots and could begin by introducing any one of them, a sermon can similarly begin by focusing on an ambiguity that is subsidiary to the central issue. It is crucial, however, that the preacher not leave the minor ambiguity unresolved when the point for the introduction of the sermon's central bind has been reached. Closure must be given to any subsidiary ambiguities quite early in the sermon's development. Lowry's advice to preachers regarding this decision is as follows:

> As a general rule, when a context of a sermon is the contemporary human situation, whether at a personal or social level, it is likely that the opening ambiguity will be the central or fundamental discrepancy. In the case of

expository or doctrinal preaching, it is more likely that the opening ambiguity will serve to engage the congregation in a preliminary bind, which in turn opens into the central problem.[102]

Lowry offers one other suggestion related to this first stage of the homiletical plot. While the resolution of the plot should never be disclosed here, some direction to the ambiguity should be provided. "Undifferentiated ambiguity," he notes, "soon becomes no ambiguity at all."[103] Given adequate clarity and direction, however, ambiguity is the sense of the beginning of any narrative and consequently of the homiletical plot as well.

Stage 2: Analyzing the discrepancy

Once the opening bind of the sermon has been disclosed, it can easily be lost through either premature resolution on one hand or persistent vagueness on the other. The challenge for the preacher in this second stage of the homiletical plot is to retain and even enhance the ambiguity introduced within stage one. Such retention and interest is sustained here by virtue of the sermon's analysis or diagnosis of the discrepancy, a process usually resulting in greater length than any of the other stages. The suspense is maintained during this diagnosis since the listeners' knowledge of the outcome is not yet possible or methodologically desirable. Stage two is a time for "diagnostic wrestling—of theologizings"; the congregation's attention is held "because the bind is not yet solved and there is therefore no option but to stay involved in the sermonic process."[104] Once a discrepancy has been introduced, it is the preacher's duty to perform sufficiently extensive analysis so that some particular aspect of the gospel responds to something now made equally concrete and explicit. Moreover, this process of diagnosis is crucial since it will determine the consequent form of the sermon, "including the form of the good news proclaimed."[105]

The difficulty for preaching, Lowry observes, is that while such diagnosis is crucial for the effectiveness of the plot, in practice, it is usually the weakest aspect of the sermon. Rather than engaging in the serious and challenging work of this diagnostic wrestling, many preachers simply make do with simple description or illustration. Neither will do, however. In the case of the former, the preacher will trade in generalizations concerning the human condition, with the assumption made that to so label something is really to explain it. In the latter approach, illustration is even more frequently invoked as a substitute for analysis. Illustrations, after all, are much more specific than generalized descriptions, and seen therefore as more helpful. Nevertheless, illustrations tend to deal with human life at a behavioral level alone, and rarely disclose, let alone analyze, motives. Treated only from the empirical evidence offered in an illustration, situations and decisions may be conveyed as relatively uncomplicated and unambiguous. Yet the factors underlying the behavioral outcome of a situation may be incredibly complex. The purpose of this analysis, then, is "to uncover the areas of inner motivation where the problem is generated, and hence expose the motivational setting toward which any cure need be directed."[106]

The need for in-depth diagnosis is critical as well for Lowry's inductive approach since it assumes a principle of correlation between the human bind and the gospel's response. Superficial or nonexistent analysis will result in a gospel response sounding both stereotyped and incredible. The good news will come out sounding like a collection of "poetic answers" to life's little changes. Furthermore, the preacher's role as a theologian demands that the diagnostic task be carried out with seriousness and precision. Homiletically, this process of analysis provides the most appropriate context for testing and refining the theological positions held by the preacher.

Stage 3: Disclosing the clue to resolution

The goal of diagnosis is to provide some sort of explanation and with it some sense of outcome. In our cause-and-effect world, a scientific, medical, or homiletical investigator assumes there is a missing link, which, when found, will lead from problem to solution, from itch to scratch. The process, however, is not usually one of ever-increasing insight and awareness. Rather, a number of possible solutions are scrutinized during stage two and rejected, thereby sustaining suspense—the sense of "bind." And when a clue to resolution is finally uncovered, it is frequently experienced as a surprise, as revelatory. "In gestalt terms, it is the 'aha,' the one piece which allows the whole puzzle to come into sharp focus."[107] Such clues, Lowry reports, are more "experienced" than "known" by the listeners.

When the clue to resolution is given through the distinctive movement of the homiletical plot, there is typically a reversal of prior expectation. A radical change in direction significantly alters the congregation's sense of outcome, based on the prior analysis. Attendant on such a revelatory experience is often the need to rethink the "common sense" used in some of the diagnosis provided during stage two. Consequently, the new and revelatory clue is received as an intuitive leap, turning normal expectations, and the sermon, upside down. As a paradigm of biblical narratives, Jesus' parables consistently embody this principle of reversal and surprise. A hated Samaritan becomes the one who extends mercy and grace. The prodigal son is welcomed home, and it is revealed that the older son rejects the father's grace and hospitality.

However, this principle should not be evident only in sermons based upon such biblical reversals. The gospel will invariably come as reversal of human expectations and overturn the consequences that were disclosed through our analysis of the homiletical bind. In contrast to this principle of reversal, Lowry notes that "the fundamental mistake of the liberal Protestant pulpit of the last forty years is that it presumes that the gospel is continuous with human experience."[108] Such is the case, he adds, only after that experience has been overturned by the power of the gospel.

Stage 4: Experiencing the gospel

The ability to experience the gospel through the homiletical plot depends to a large degree upon the success of the analysis provided in the two prior stages of the sermon. By the time the preacher and congregation have arrived at the fourth stage, the bind that provided for ambiguity needs to be explored through insightful diagnosis. Only when such in-depth analysis has occurred are listeners ready to hear the good news of the gospel. Unfortunately, a "homiletical short circuit" frequently interrupts this process; there is often "a giant, and ill-fated leap from the beginning of stage two (analysis) to stage five—which is the stage of anticipating what can or ought to be done in light of the intersection of the problem and proclamation of the gospel."[109] Such short-circuiting not only fails to take life seriously and thereby the gospel as well, but also serves to prematurely release the sermon's necessary tension and ambiguity. The time-oriented sermonic plot loses control of movement essential to its character.

When the first three stages convey a sense of discrepancy, which is then insightfully analyzed, the gospel is heard effectively—that is, the Word does what it proclaims. This intersection of the specific form of the proclamation of the gospel with in-depth diagnosis of some specific human bind is at the heart of the homiletical plot. All previous diagnosis of the discrepancy has led now to the declaration of God's response in Jesus Christ. Identifying the latter is relatively simple if the prior diagnostic work has been done well. "When I have done my diagnostic homework and the decisive clue has emerged," Lowry states, "the good news has fallen into place sermonically as though pulled by a magnet."[110]

Stage 5: Anticipating the consequences

The sense of the ending within Lowry's homiletical plot differs considerably from that usually encountered in conceptual preaching. What marks the

conclusion of a conceptual sermon is its character as climax and call—a sermonic "asking." Within a sermon plot based upon narrative movement, however, the climax comes earlier, in stage three when the reversal occurs, and
again when the gospel is experienced in the next stage. The similarity of the
two approaches—that an anticipation of the gospel is located in the same relative position as a conceptual sermon's "call"—is really only superficial.
Methodologically, the climax in the narrative plot has *already* occurred by the
time stage five has begun, and closure now occurs. This ending is critical to
the plot, however, since it explicates the future "now made new by the
gospel."[111] The preacher now asks, "What—in light of this intersection of
human condition with the gospel—can be expected, should be done, or is
now possible"?[112] Congregations and preachers now jointly consider the consequences of the surprising reversals introduced by the gospel.

There is a second, more theological consideration raised by this comparison of topical and narrative plot ending. Lowry attacks the tendency of the
former to make the sermonic climax synonymous with the sermonic call as a
form of works righteousness. That theological problem, he claims, is inherent within conceptual preaching's method. To the contrary, the focus of our
preaching "is upon the decisive activity of God, not upon us, and hence the
climax of any sermon must be stage four—the experiencing of the gospel of
grace."[113] Our response to that proclamation is important, but is not the center of gravity for the sermon. What *is* at the center is the good news of Jesus
Christ. Methodologically, the preacher can call for a response at stage five
only because a new freedom to choose has been effected through hearing the
gospel. "Freedom," Lowry asserts, "is a consequence of the grace of God."[114]
The ability to respond to the good news is not a natural human endowment;
it is given through the experienced grace of the gospel. And while the specific expressions of the consequences explored in stage five may be quite varied, they are all based on the grace of "a new situation being created by the
gospel—a new freedom to make choices we could never before make."[115]

The homiletic plot, according to Eugene Lowry, moves in sequence
through the stages of upsetting the equilibrium, analyzing the discrepancy,
disclosing the clue to resolution, experiencing the gospel, and anticipating
the consequences. It is an "event-in-time" or, more accurately, an ordering of
time that derives its shape and movement from the formal organization of
narrative art. This sequential movement, moreover, is essential for the effective proclamation of the gospel. As has been seen, dire homiletical consequences will predictably follow from a disregard of the plot; that is, if the
bind is not specifically portrayed and diagnosed, or if the clue to resolution

leading to reversal is not appropriately disclosed. Some modifications of the stages in the plot can and should be made, however, as dictated by pastoral circumstances. A funeral sermon, for example, needs little if any attention to the first stage, for congregational equilibrium is already quite upset. And festive occasions may call for less time spent in diagnosis of the discrepancy. Moreover, "there come those extraordinary moments in the life of a church when a pastor faithful to the gospel and to conscience must bring a prophetic, healing, troubled, or celebrative witness to the congregation which by its very nature violates any and all sermonic rules."[116]

Apart from such special and infrequent occasions, the major exemption of the homiletical plot occurs when preaching from biblical narrative itself. The reasoning here is that such narrative material already has a plot of its own and therefore contains its own ambiguity to be resolved. "It does not need another plot line superimposed on top of it."[117] Such biblical narrative "should be allowed to run its own narrative course."[118] And Lowry joins with others in attending to that preaching at the narrative center of the web of preaching, especially in his work, *How to Preach a Parable: Designs for Narrative Preaching*. But when the sermonic focus is elsewhere—life situational, doctrinal, or expository—the homiletical plot enables this preaching to become a "narrative event" as well. And when the biblical text is other than narrative, the five stages of the homiletic plot advocated by Eugene Lowry likewise render a narrative event of preaching. For Lowry, the purpose is, after all, that all preaching becomes an ordering of time into narrative time, the time of *our* story and *the* story.

Level 2: Revising the Homiletical Plot: A Play in Four Acts

In a recent book, *The Sermon: Dancing the Edge of Mystery*, Eugene Lowry proposes a modest revision of his five-stage homiletical plot. What persists, though, are the dual assumptions that underlie his construal of the essential qualities of a narrative sermon. First, Lowry continues to maintain that along with other living options in homiletic method, narrative preaching involves "a *sequencing strategy*" in which the arrangement of ideas takes the form of a plot involving a strategic delay of the preacher's meaning."[119] Second, Lowry specifies the quality of that strategic delay in the unfolding of the sermonic plot as one of "an ever-increasingly difficult bind, which moves toward the apparently impossible—until the surprise of the unanticipated turn happens."[120] A narrative sermon, then, will embody a sequential logic, inviting the hearers to move toward some intensifying quandary, then surprising them with a sudden shift that resolves the bind in unanticipated directions. In Lowry's *The Homiletical Plot,* the "loop" of any narrative sermon plot was composed of five stages—analyzed in some depth in the above section. Now, in *The Sermon,* the names of the stages are changed and the number of stages is reduced to four. What remains consistent are the two foundational assumptions: the sequential quality of any narrative sermon's plot and a sequential movement from problem through intensifying bind to sudden, unexpected resolution. Now, in *The Sermon,* the four stages Lowry proposes are:

Conflict ↷ Complication ↷ Sudden Shift ↷ Unfolding

The five stages of Lowry's earlier work, we recall, are as follows:

Oops   ↷   Ugh   ↷   Aha   ↷   Whee   ↷   Yeah

| Upsetting the Equilibrium | Analyzing the Discrepancy | Disclosing the Clue to Resolution | Experiencing the Gospel | Anticipating the Consequences |

Instead of surveying the new four-stage plot, which would involve considerable reiteration of the earlier survey, we will employ its format as a means of sketching out a narrative sermon based on a non-narrative biblical text. The question here is as follows: How is a sermon shaped according to the four-stage model, retaining the essential sequencing and complicating logic of the homiletical plot?

Joel 2:23-32: A Narrative Sermon Plot

The pericope, Joel 2:23-32, is the first lesson for the twenty-first Sunday after Pentecost in the Revised Common Lectionary, Year B. It was preached early in a new pastorate that followed a period of significant dislocation within the congregational family system. This sermon may be sketched as follows employing Lowry's four stages:

1. Conflict

If the preacher must have "a kind of thirst for chaos," then this passage from Joel is a perfect text.[121] The reader confronts chaos in abundance. Here, the conflict is blatantly clear, an opposition between life as God's covenant people and the locust plague that has engulfed them. The destroyers have eaten everything (1:4), and there are images by the prophet of invaders, as like lion's teeth (1:6), a raging fire (2:3), and as an all-conquering army (2:2, 4-5). The response of the people to this overwhelming catastrophe is dismay and a joyless lament; God's people and even their livestock wail and wander aimlessly. It is "a day of darkness and gloom" (2:2) that portends the end time itself. Certainly the congregation can sense the chaos brought by the invading locusts. What the preacher must now accomplish is to locate the hearers within some contemporary expressions of analogous chaos and conflict. The profound sense of being overwhelmed and of a despair as to a "happy ending" will need to be experienced by the congregation with regard both to Israel's plight and their own religious situation. Given the pastoral context in the new church setting, a series of examples was developed, each linked to the other by means of a tag line, *"and it's locust time, and we are overcome."* The pastoral situation invited a number of analogous experiences to Joel's plague of locusts. Some members of the congregation had just overdone traumatic illnesses and surgery. Their family members were present and were themselves signs of this distinctive form of being overwhelmed. Another example came readily in the new pastoral setting—the devouring fire of corporate downsizing had affected some families in the church. Suddenly, lifelong breadwinners were without jobs. Finally, the communal experience of the congregation over the past eighteen months had left them feeling hopeless and in despair much like Joel. The sermon did not pause overly to elaborate the details of this congregational time of chaos; it was simply mentioned, again with the tag line about it being locust time.

2. Complication

Recall that for Eugene Lowry, a narrative plot does not proceed from a statement of the problem to an immediate announcement of the resolution; in the words of *The Homiletical Plot,* the listeners are not given a shortcut that moves directly from "Oops" to "Whee." After an opening statement of the problem, the conflict, the task now presents itself to the preacher as regards a strategy for complication. Certainly diagnosis, as advocated by Lowry in *The Homiletical Plot*, remains a viable means of complicating the initial conflict or bind. However, other narrative strategies offer themselves for consideration as well.[122] Which approach is finally selected has much to do both with the listeners and the pastoral situation on one hand and the specific type of sermon involved on the other hand. A story sermon will find its complication typically in the actions of its characters, for example, whereas in an inductive sermon, "complication may be achieved by the accumulation of conflictual data, which repeatedly short circuit obvious conclusion after obvious conclusion. . . ."[123] Lowry concludes regarding these strategic considerations:

> Whatever the forms of complication in whatever sermonic types, the critical key is the move to fluidity where matters are not indefinite, but yet clearly are indeterminate. The movement at this stage of the plot must be movement toward the actually irresolute, the truly dilemmic, the really bound.[124]

The challenge for the preacher is to now select an appropriate strategy for complication.

In the Joel text, the complication is handed to us by the prophet. What has begun as an external crisis—the locusts "out there"—has become a profound, "in here" spiritual crisis. The devastation created by the locust plague has reached deep within the cultic system as well, rendering it null and void. So Joel laments:

> The grain offering and the drink offering are cut off from the house of the Lord. The priests mourn, the ministers of the LORD. The fields are devastated, the ground mourns; for the grain is destroyed, the wine dries up, the oil fails. (1:9-10)

With the failure of the oil, the wine, and the grain, the material conditions necessary for coming before God in supplication are now absent. Put simply, no hope remains; the people cannot even come before their God by way of a sacrifice of intercession. There is nothing to sacrifice. The locusts have consumed the offering, too. This is, indeed, a profound crisis—a "complication."

Now as the sermon moves into this second, complicating stage of its plot, it is the task of the preacher to invite the congregation to experience the bind for themselves. *"How is it when the answer of God's people to the gospel hymn's question, 'What Shall I Render?' is a flat 'Nothing'? There is nothing I can render back to God."* In the sermon preached early in that pastoral transition, my strategy was both to complicate the opening bind, yet to be careful to demark the boundaries of such complication. One issue, especially, is raised as we track Joel's prophetic poetics—the question of theodicy. Notice that while Joel will call the people to lamentation and fasting, he directs no indictment that the locust disaster is an expression of divine wrath and judgment. This is an important point to make when preaching on Joel. A locust plague may sweep across our personal and communal lives, however, the issue may or not be one of personal or communal culpability. In the case of those locusts, Joel does not point to the evil of those who are suffering as the cause of their plight. On the other hand, the locusts have left the people seemingly bereft of any means of affecting their condition. Oil, wine, and grain are gone, and along with their disappearance, the possibility of any sacrifice to the Lord.

In the sermon, then, the gospel song's question "What shall I render?" is employed within a rhetorical system in which our answer comes despairingly, "Nothing. There is nothing I can render back to God." Since we have used a threefold example system during the elaboration of stage one, selecting another illustrative approach will be useful here.[125] The approach that was selected—after declining a number of alternatives—was to image the personal experience of having the imposition of ashes for the first time. (This was a United Methodist congregation that did not have such a prior tradition.) Several advantages seemed to accrue to this imaging of the complication. First, the illustration focused attention on an occasion when it is absolutely clear what we bring to God, what we can render. The answer is that we bring only ourselves, claiming no merit or privilege. Another asset of this particular illustration is that it locates this particular coming before God within a liturgical context, within the community. The experience is both personal and deeply communal. Then, too, the liturgical location begins a season that looks forward to the Paschal mystery of Christ's death and resurrection. Lowry proposes that some clue to resolution of our bind be provided during the first two stages of the homiletical plot. By introducing the Lent-Easter cycle, liturgically, the hearers may well begin to locate themselves within the baptismal Body that dies and rises with Christ. With the above in mind, the illustration was given from a personal, yet corporate, perspective.

3. Sudden shift

There is always the question, for Lowry, as to when the good news occurs within the sermonic plot. Clearly, the good news is the sudden shift from the news complicating conflict developed in stages one and two. And likewise, the preacher would not want to subvert the narrative movement of the plot by introducing the good news prematurely.[126] According to the style of the sermon, Lowry sees most possibilities for experiencing the gospel as relating to the third stage, the "sudden shift." Whether at its beginning, middle, or ending, it is the imperative claim of the gospel that makes possible any unfolding of grace. "There can be no *imperative claim,*" Lowry insists, "*without the indicative* based on the Good News of Christ."[127] This good news is disclosed within the Joel text as an expression of the prophetic imagination. The prophet announces, "Sanctify a fast, call a solemn assembly. Gather the elders and all the inhabitants of the land to the house of the LORD your God, and cry out to the LORD" (2:14). The surprising shift is made by way of an imaginative renaming of the condition of the people. Previously, the images were those pertaining to victimhood, along with an attendant helplessness and despair. But when the prophet renames the disaster as a fast, a remarkable and sudden shift occurs. The people are invited to experience their deprivation as a spiritual sacrifice to the Lord. They are no longer passive victims, but engaged once more in a covenantal relationship with their God, a relationship based upon divine mercy and grace. Within stage three of the sermon, this surprising shift in point of view was explored, first in relation to the text and its religious situation. The invitation was extended to the congregation to rename their bitter months and years as a "fast" to their God!

The illustrative system expressing this sudden shift of renaming is the most important of the entire sermon. Recalling David Buttrick, it is much easier for preachers to image the darkness, sin, law (and locust plagues) than it is to image the sudden shift of good news and grace. If the sermon's conflict has been successfully portrayed along with the stage of complication, we cannot simply gesture toward good news. A powerful illustration is needed here, yet with a cautionary note. To introduce another liturgical experience—say the movement from darkness to light at the Easter Vigil—would risk a collapsing of this stage with the prior one. Ash Wednesday and Easter could merge into one single meaning rather than remain distinct. The image that was employed in stage three of the sermon focused the congregation on the signboard under the church's name out by the facing roadway. What was imaged was an imagined message that had hung there for months—"Church of the Locust Plagues." The point of view was that of passersby driving along the road. Then, while the point of view remained the same, the hearers were invited to watch as those letters were taken down and a new message was put in their place—"A Fasting Church!" The congregation was renamed, just as Joel renamed God's people during another time of disaster.

4. Unfolding

In *The Sermon,* Eugene Lowry renamed this last stage of the homiletical plot from "anticipating the consequences" to "unfolding." He reflects that "the term consequences does carry some unnecessary freight."[128] This last stage of unfolding will need to have a rhetorical discipline about it; the last stage "is a crucial time for powerful economy with words."[129] And while matters developed during the first two stages will, of necessity, be resolved following the sudden shift toward the good news, Lowry cautions against a construal of this unfolding as an arrival at a place of final homiletical rest. This unfolding is a location of "dynamic equilibrium," a stasis born when opposing forces are made equal."[130] Lowry's description of the concluding stage of the homiletical plot concludes,

> It could be called "settling in to tomorrow." The focus here is anticipated genesis, imagined effect, gracious inducement, expected responding, consequential flowering, surprising releasing, unexpected blossoming—indeed, unfolding.[131]

The sense of unexpected blossoming is signaled in Joel by the phrase, "Who knows . . . ?"; "Who knows whether he will not turn and relent, and leave a blessing behind him, a grain offering and a drink offering for the LORD, your God?" (2:14). The striking sudden shift has at its core a grace-filled gift of God that restores covenant, making intercession possible at all. The indicative good news of Christ will appear at this point in the sermon, as the question is raised, "Who knows . . . ?" with its implied answer that God will provide all things necessary for restoration and new life.

It is now the opportunity to image these intriguing possibilities of new life suggested by the prophetic "Who knows . . . ?" What was selected as the illustration within stage four was a rhetorical system that imagined a series of new children's ministries, each introduced with the phrase, "Who knows . . . ?" (There had been no children's ministry within the parish for more than a year!) The listing included a children's choir, a return to Sunday school activity, and a vision of the children and youth off at church camp next summer. Each of the possibilities was introduced by Joel's "Who knows . . . ?" phrase. Then the sequence was intentionally disrupted. "Who knows," the last stage concluded, "maybe we will now need to change the sign once more. 'Welcome to ———,' it might read. 'A People Rejoicing in God!' "

Evaluation

Fred Craddock and Eugene Lowry (when Lowry is using his loop model) share a common interest that binds them together with regard to homiletic method. Both are reacting against the assumptions of the old, discursive approach to the sermon in which propositions and subthemes organize the material. Craddock labels this discursive approach deductive preaching, while Lowry added that it attempts a spatial rather than a temporal sense of sermonic organization. Both agree that the deductive method is seriously flawed in its assumptions about biblical interpretation (the Scriptures are not simply a collection of themes disguised as parables, sayings, signs, apocalyptic), in its rhetoric (entirely too dependent on third person, conceptual language), and in its pastoral sensibilities (the congregation remains largely passive, an "audience" rather than a partner in a dialogue). However, enough distinctions exist between the two homiletic methods that warrant independent evaluations.

Fred Craddock

Fred Craddock remains a pioneer in the emergence of "the new homiletics." His seminal work, *As One Without Authority,* first published in 1971, remains both valid in its assessment of the old homiletic and prophetic in its outline of the issues for reform. Both that volume and *Preaching* (a summation of his homiletic program) continue to serve well as texts in seminary introduction to preaching classes and as guides for practicing preachers. As many are aware, Fred Craddock not only teaches the art and craft of preaching, he is a consummate preacher as well. Through his publications, lectures, and preaching, Craddock has a central place in the renewal of preaching in our day.

Among the many strengths evidenced in Craddock's writings, several have clear implications for an inquiry into homiletic method. First, he has not wavered in his insistence that preaching be *biblical* preaching. Responsible exegesis of the text is not an option, Craddock believes, and he employs his own expertise as a New Testament scholar to model the pastor's necessary work of interpretation.[132] This insistence on an attentive listening to the text exposes one of deductive preaching's most serious flaws: its regular misuse of the text. On the other hand, a careful listening to the text is, for Craddock, a necessary and felicitous aspect of the inductive approach to preaching.

Sensitive and insightful attention to the function of language also marks his research. Among Fred Craddock's many laurels is his early warnings to the American pulpit that its traditional language of preaching was in serious trouble. While he could have remained content with that "watcher at the gates" role regarding language and preaching, Craddock also drew on the linguistic analysis of Martin Heidegger by way of his early reconstruction of the rhetoric of the sermon. Among his many positive contributions to this reformed rhetoric, he is widely known for his emphasis on a certain economy and discipline to the language of preaching, an admonition that many preachers still need to hear and heed. Interestingly, this attention to the language of preaching also focuses on deductive preaching's tendency to moralize the gospel. The "ought," "must," and "should" hortatory that still afflicts the American pulpit is inherently in conflict with biblical preaching expressed in a language congenial to the gospel.

One of the most valuable contributions for homiletic method is Craddock's pastoral emphasis on the role of the assembly. The preacher is called to listen to the congregation and the biblical text. Lacking the former, a sermon becomes a positivistic restatement of scriptural "truth," while remaining other than biblical preaching. For an inductive approach, the real, lived experience of those within the community of faith is essential to the formation of the sermon and, in conjunction with the text, provides the sermon's message. Deductive preaching's use of life situations to illustrate themes and topics violates the integrity of the congregation's participation in the shaping of the sermon. Its experience is essential to preaching, not an ornament to it.

As an approach to preaching deeply attuned to the pastoral context of the listeners, Fred Craddock's inductive method commends itself particularly in those cases when the message or text may be perceived as dull or disagreeable. Ron Allen helpfully notes that "inductive tension creates interest that helps the congregation want to be involved in the sermon," adding that this method "can particularly help the listening environment when the congregation disagrees with the viewpoint of the sermon, or when the sermon needs to help the congregation alter its interpretation of a text or topic."[133]

Finally, Craddock has consistently maintained that preaching must have a persistent sense of movement within its sermonic form. For him as much as for Eugene Lowry, preaching without movement is a homiletical sin. While there can be any number of forms through which the inductive method can come to fruition, the resulting sermon will always move in a way that sustains congregational interest and allows the hearers to arrive at a common destination. Craddock is accurate in his analysis that the deductive method precludes authentic movement within the sermon. There may be some movement within each point, but the overall effect is as static as moths pinned to a corkboard.

The liabilities of the inductive method as espoused by Fred Craddock center on issues related to hermeneutics and sermonic form. A cluster of questions surrounds that crucial shift in methodology when the preacher turns from interpreting the text and begins the work of shaping or selecting a form for the sermon. The first of these issues relates to the distance experienced between the text and the interpreter. To be sure, a sense of distance from the text is experienced as a preacher deals responsibly with a text—Craddock sees this awareness as a necessary stage in the process of interpretation. His assumption, however, that an exegetical living with the text serves to overcome the distance encountered earlier is, however, problematic. In fact, certain types of biblical forms seem highly resistant to such an outcome (apocalyptic literature, miracles and signs, and the resurrection/ascension accounts, for example). Even the parable form, of which Craddock is particularly fond, has proved resistant to conventional historical-critical interpretation, especially when it partners with a main idea hermeneutic. Although reference is made to the contributions of literary criticism, it is difficult to identify how this latter approach to the text figures into Craddock's hermeneutics or affects his homiletic method.

A second issue that relates to both biblical interpretation and sermonic form is that of thematic unity. Fred Craddock is quite explicit in his latest work that the end product of the interpretation of the text and the congregation is a message that will then become the *telos* for the movement and form of the sermon. What happens, one must ask, when an interpreter encounters a pericope that simply refuses such ideational redaction (this being the case precisely with the parables and probably with other narrative material such as the Johannine signs)? Either the preacher must impose a thematic on the text from outside, or be threatened with a collapse of sermonic unity. The literary critics of biblical narrative and their narrative theology fellow travelers have demonstrated that plot serves more effectively as a principle of homiletical control than the notion of a text's message, at least as regarding narrative literature in Scripture. The implications of this insight are undeveloped by Craddock, however, and the weak link in his approach remains the assumption that the interpretive payoff of every text is a proposition, which in turn becomes the homiletical payoff of every sermonic form. Viewed from this perspective, the distance between a homiletics of induction and that of deduction closes considerably. Both seem bound to a rationalistic hermeneutic, notwithstanding the inductive method's clear advantages in sustaining congregational interest and involvement in the sermon.

A final issue relates specifically to homiletic form. The inductive method yields a sermon whose form and movement are readily detectable to the hearer. Hence, an inductive sermon is a relatively easy species for the listener to spot. We are invited to begin a journey in the sermon on the common ground of our common experience. Yet by the conclusion of his discussion of form, Craddock has also offered as viable options a series of forms from homiletic tradition, most of which are variations on the deductive model. What is confusing to the reader/preacher here is that after so much attention to biblical interpretation and the contemporary situation, the message of the sermon may still gain form through multiple choices: by way of the shape of the text, through some kind of inductive movement, or from deductive models provided by the tradition. Perhaps the problem here is the rather sharp delineation between exegesis and homiletical method. What if hermeneutics informed more immediately both the interpretation of the text and the emergence of homiletic form and movement? The African American narrative sermon typically shows a much more intimate relationship between the analysis of the text and the shape and movement of the sermon. Similar intimacy abounds within related methods at the narrative center of the web of preaching. It may well be, then, that Fred Craddock is most vulnerable with regard to a hermeneutic that inadequately provides for the alignment of scriptural interpretation and sermonic formation.

Eugene Lowry

Any assessment of the homiletics of Eugene Lowry must begin with a celebration of his role in articulating a narrative-based approach to preaching. This contribution is actually twofold. First, Lowry among a small band of prophets, including Fred Craddock, David Buttrick, and Henry Mitchell among others, provided a compelling critique of the old discursive homiletic with its points and argumentation model of rhetoric. Lowry labeled this approach "doing space," involving the ordering of ideas and resulting in a construction model of creating a sermon. Then, Lowry picked up the constructive side of his project. He offered a literal barrage of images for this alternative approach: "ordering experience," "doing time," and "shaping the process of the sermon." The underlying shift in homiletic paradigms was from that of ordering ideas to ordering experience. Plot, rather than a theme-based outline, was now the organizing principle for the preacher. This achievement by Eugene Lowry was by way of both his telling criticism of a spatial-oriented rationalistic homiletic and his proposal of a time-based narrative model. Also, it should be noted, and celebrated, that Lowry's writing both clearly and carefully interpreted the two competing paradigms and invited the reader on a journey from the place of doing space to the process of doing time. In this regard, Lowry is to be commended by a congruence between his pedagogy and his homiletic method.

Lowry's contribution to constructive homiletic method remains centered in the loop model of movement—from itch to scratch, from conflict through resolution. Whether expressed by way of his original five-stage loop in *The Homiletical Plot* or in his revised four sequences proposed in *The Sermon*, the qualities of this narrative sermonic form remain central. These qualities include the mobility of the sermonic plot, its sequential ordering, and the notion of "torque." Lowry has trained many of us well with regard to the first two qualities—mobility and episodic ordering. Interestingly, many preachers these days take these two aspects of the homiletic plot and then turn to David

Buttrick and speak of the episodes as "moves," all the while borrowing any number of rhetorical insights from African American preaching. (This messy eclecticism in the pulpit today should come as a caution to those of us in the homiletic guild not to overdo our drawing of distinctions between the alternatives available in this postmodern context.) It is in the notion of the homily's torque, however, that Lowry makes a distinctive contribution. Whether embodied in the five- or four-stage loop, there comes that occasion rather late in the sermon when the plot shifts from a downward to an upward trajectory. A sermon, Lowry insists, "needs some kind of internal expansive force."[134] This force of turning is not like an option tacked on to escalate the price of a new car. It is at the heart of the matter, this turning force. Of course, Lowry would also add that this internal expansive force is really the gospel of Jesus Christ. A sermon lacking such torque thereby gives away an opportunity to experience this turning force of the gospel in preaching.

It is precisely at the point of Eugene Lowry's strongest methodological contention that there is the most homiletical contentiousness. For David Buttrick, the shift from a set of negative moves to positive ones is either determined by the text—as in the mode of immediacy—or by the logic of reflective consciousness. Typically, the torque in a Buttrick-style homiletical plot will come certainly in the latter portion of the sermon. However, there is no compelling reason in Buttrick's method to locate such a plot shift so consistently late in the sermon as Lowry seems to advocate. Just at this point is where Paul Scott Wilson has chosen to contrast his Four Page model with Lowry's narrative approach (see pp. 237-38). For Wilson, the sermon's torque lies precisely at midpoint, between Page Two (trouble in the world) and Page Three (grace in the text). For his part, Lowry has seen the need to make some adjustments in his own earlier position. It is "readily apparent," he states, "that not all plotted sermons involve a polar reversal of one-hundred-eighty-degree turn."[135] Referring to "this decisive moment in the sermon process," Lowry notes the rich variety of reversals in secular literature as well as biblical texts and speaks of a necessary "fluidity" to the homiletic plot.[136] However, the fundamental shape of the Lowry loop persists, even as the torque comes in different flavors (a full 180-degree turn or perhaps only 93.7 degrees). "What is important," Lowry concludes, "is that the turn be so decisive that there is no way to go back to the previous view."[137] However, the trend for Lowry is, in spite of the emphasis on fluidity of form, to position the sudden shift later in the homiletic plot. He now prefers the turn at perhaps five-sixths rather than three-fourths of the sermon, and adds that, "On rare occasions it may happen on the last line."[138]

This new note regarding the fluidity of the sermon's reversal or shift, then, serves to diminish several criticisms of Lowry's methodology. First, the comments by Paul Scott Wilson condemning sermons in which grace appears only in a last tag line needs further qualification. The more recent emphasis on the fluidity of the sermon's plot and the tensiveness of the essential shift certainly calls for a reconsideration by Wilson regarding the interplay of the dynamics of grace and the shifts in the plot. (Wilson would, to be sure, continue to argue against those "rare occasions" when the tag line of a sermon is to carry the full freight of the shift to the gospel!) Another comment, being of a less negative sort, comes from Ronald Allen. The latter observes that Lowry's model "even with its permeating tension can become familiar if the preacher follows it every week."[139] What the congregation may need from time to time, Allen cautions, may be "less the new discovery of an 'Aha' than the patient reassurance that what they believe and do is adequate to the gospel and their situation."[140] Here, the response by Lowry would perhaps emphasize two nuances of his more recent statement of the method. On one hand, Lowry may respond, the elements of mobility and sequencing would need to obtain even in a sermon designed to reassure and confirm the congregation. Addressing such pastoral needs is not sufficient warrant to abandon a doing of time, relapsing into a doing of space. On the other hand, Lowry might respond that even a situation in which reassurance is the pastoral felt need, some sense of conflict probably lurks beneath the somewhat placid homiletical waters. In fact, where the need for reassurance is at its most intense—at a liturgical situation at the time of death—the complications and conflicts are all too obvious. In such cases, Lowry advises, there is little need to add to the "itch" in the sermon, but rather move on to a resolution fitting to the gospel.[141]

Nick at Night

Eugene L. Lowry

John 3:1-17

It happened in the middle of the night. Perhaps one might say that it happened in the middle of *his* night. Maybe as late as two in the morning, the streets were dark and deserted. Not a soul could be seen—at least he hoped so. There *was* someone out there in the dark, jumping from shadow to shadow. But he didn't want to be seen. His name was Nicodemus. He was indeed Nick at night. Apparently no sunrise evident yet, as he jumps from shadow to shadow. And you wonder: What's he doing out there? Why is he coming across town in the shadows and back alleys to see Jesus who is staying with friends?

You understand, Nick is a big shot. Nick is a ruler of his religious community. He is the sort of person who can walk anywhere he pleases, day or night. If he crosses the street into a group of people on the corner, they part automatically to allow him through. He seldom has his hand on a doorknob, because before he can reach for it, someone else has already opened the door. Nicodemus is "Mister Big."

So what's he doing coming in the middle of the night to see this itinerant preacher? Do you sense that there must be some yearning, some ache in his soul—this stranger in the night?

Well, as I imagine it, they wake up Jesus, he goes to greet this visitor in the night, and they open a conversation—the strangest opening lines to a conversation I think I have ever heard. Catch the opening exchange. Nicodemus says, "Rabbi, you must come from God because nobody could do what you do unless God were with them." That is Nicodemus's opening line. So what is Jesus' response? Well, he says: "Unless you have been born anew (or again, or on high) you cannot even see the kingdom of God." Do you sense that those first two statements seem not to compute? The sentences miss each other. Apparently, they are both strangers, all right, and *they* are missing in the night. "Nobody could do what you do unless God were with them." "Truly I say, unless you have been born anew, you cannot even see the kingdom of God." I'm kind of shocked at Jesus. At least he could thank him for the compliment.

I should hope that any minister greeting people after the Sunday service and hearing the words, "Preacher, you must have been inspired from God, for no one could preach the way you preached today unless God were with them"—would at least say, "Well, thank you very much." Or at least, "How long did it take you to figure this out?" I hope the preacher wouldn't just say: "Well it's about twelve hundred miles from Kansas City to New York." That is true, but what has that got to do with this? Well, actually, Jesus and Nicodemus are not missing in the night as much as it may first appear.

What Nicodemus was doing was to cite an old tradition—about the several criteria used to determine the authenticity of someone being a prophet—such factors as having an ecstatic experience and making a prophetic announcement. He was saying to Jesus: "I have counted up the score and declare that you pass the test as a true prophet of the Lord." And I think

Jesus' response about being born anew in order to even see the Kingdom was to say to Nicodemus: "You can't get here from there."

One does not first count up the score and wind up with faith; only those within the circle of faith who have the eyes to see count the score. This is not unique in our human experience. What does it mean to be a student? Only a student can reply. What is it like to be a plumber? Ask one. What is the quality of the marriage covenant? Only those who are married need respond. If you want to know something about faith, you have to get inside the circle of its community to really know. That's what Jesus was saying: "You can't get here from there." You must be born anew to know. That's what he said.

But, poor Nick. He wasn't big on metaphor. Not much of a poet. Jesus is trying to use an image, a phrase to talk about spiritual things. Poor Nicodemus. He thinks Jesus is talking gynecology. So when Jesus says, "You must be born again," he asks: "How do I reenter my mother's womb?" The question is a little crude, but it's in the Book. Well, Jesus says the truth. He says, "The wind blows where it will." The *ruach*, the breath of God, blows where it will. You don't know where it comes from and you don't know where it's going, but you hear the sound—or as I would put it, you can feel it as it comes across your face. It *is* mysterious. Well, they talk some more, but Nicodemus just doesn't get it. Finally, in desperation he exclaims: "How can this be?" And I must say, there is a part of me that understands this exactly.

I remember as a child looking out the backseat car window on long Kansas roads—looking for anything to see—and we would pass an ugly-painted billboard announcing: "Ye must be born again." I never liked it; it seemed pushy, rude. I wanted to say: "Why don't you mind your own business?" Well, I don't see so many of those roadside signs anymore. We get our instructions from high-tech media experts—advertisers who also seem pushy, even rude sometimes. There is one ad I have great trouble with. It's shown on television by a company that sells shoes. And the ad says, "Just do it!" Perhaps Nicodemus had a bumper sticker on his car, and it said, "Just do it." But he was uncertain as to just what it was that he was to do. I think that's why he came in the middle of the night to see Jesus.

Now, as a slogan for a church budget, the phrase "Just do it" isn't bad, but as a principle for living it carries an incredible burden. It is a weight that bears down on everyone who listens to it. Generally, on television the phrase comes just after some super athlete does something almost impossible. Then, we're told to follow suit: "Just do it." Underneath that advice is an assumption—namely that we *can* all do it, if we have a mind to. But of course, the truth is, *we cannot all do it*, period. And underneath all of this is a more basic theological claim—not only *do* it, you *can* do it, but now you *must* do it. Your soul is at stake. Just do it.

Every March we see one form of this tragic assumption. It's called "March Madness"—you know, the NCAA collegiate basketball tournament. It's not just March madness—it is *lunacy for a lifetime*.

Notice the system. The sixty-four best college teams in the nation are invited to play one another until a national champion is finally determined. If you are among the other several hundred teams starting with number sixty-five and beyond, you need not apply. Just the best of the best. Can you hear the coach before the game instructing the squad, "Now team, you can do it; you've got what it takes. Now just get out there on the floor, focus, and get it done." Only trouble is, the opposing team's coach is saying the very same thing. Only one team wins the game. Then the locker-room interviews begin.

Listen to the answers to such innocuous questions as: "Well, what about that game?" Says one on the winning team: "Well, we saw what we had to do, and we did it." In the losing team's locker room, heads are bowed. One looks up long enough to say: "Well, I guess they wanted it more than we did." Nonsense. It's quite possible that one team was just plain better than the other one. Worse yet, when all is said and done, and the national champion crowned, only one of the best sixty-four teams ends their season on a note of victory. Sixty-three of the best end their season with a monumental defeat. Do you hear the tragedy? "Just do it?"

Could it be that one day somebody might have whispered in Nicodemus's ear: "Just do it"? So, in spite of his achievements, he came to Jesus that night to ask: "What *yet* must I do?" So when Jesus said "You must be born anew," Nicodemus took it to mean that *that* was what he now *must* do. But, actually what Jesus said was the exact reverse of all that. Because you see, no matter how talented, bright, clever, industrious and all the rest, *the one thing no one can ever do is to birth oneself*. Birth is always a gift of another. So, when Jesus told Nicodemus that he must be born anew, he wasn't talking about another task for Nick to accomplish. Instead, he was speaking about a gift that he was to receive. The wind blows where it will, Jesus said, and you may feel the breeze across your face. But not Nick—he's too busy running, even at night to find out what to do next. Oh, Nick, give it up. Stop trying so hard. This "just do it" business is killing you. Well, actually, it's killing a lot of us.

But, the wind blows; the breeze of the spirit is blowing across this universe. If we could just stop trying so hard to earn our way, running the race of merit, we might just feel the gift.

Heather, give it up; Gene, give it up; LaNita, give it up.

Nick, for heaven's sake, give it up. Feel the breeze, for God so loved the world . . .

CHAPTER 2

The Narrative Center

The Eclipse of Biblical Narrative

As long as the lively play of biblical narrative remained in eclipse in the churches, narrative preaching also remained dormant.[1] With the one great exception of narrative preaching in the African American churches, the same Enlightenment assumptions that propelled interpretation also drove homiletics. That is to say, the interpreter came to narrative texts in Scripture with an interest in the moral or spiritual truths that were extracted from those stories. Once the thematic was isolated, it was framed in a propositional format and the narrative itself became disposable. The rationalist model of interpretation viewed biblical narratives as containing a message, existing for illustrations of the timeless truths of the Bible. Of course, once these truths were spotted by the interpreter, the narrative, with its storied world, could be left behind. Biblical narrative remained in eclipse. Since the Enlightenment, Western preaching—with the exception noted—came equipped with a "hermeneutic of distillation"[2] in which the text was raided for some discursive theme. The narrative elements of plot, character, setting, tone, and narrative time were considered as decorative of that theme, and therefore were essentially disposable. Narrative preaching was in eclipse by virtue of the loss of a narrative model of scriptural interpretation.

To speak of the "narrative center" of biblical preaching, then, is to bear testimony, first, to the surprising ways in which story has become recovered as a preferred mode for interpreting self and world. The preaching-as-storytelling movement of the 1970s and 1980s comes most immediately to mind for many of us who are called to preach. In fact, the pioneering explorers of the world of narrative interpretation included several schools of theological ethicists, the literary critics, and those engaged in "the poetics of imagination, i.e., modern hermeneutics."[3] A singular contribution remains that of phenomenologist Stephen Crites. In his "The Narrative Quality of Human Experience," he provides a striking distinction between what he labels as "mundane stories" and "sacred stories."[4] Contemporary narrative homiletics, then, is a postmodern discipline that has its roots within all of these pioneering movements. To our initial list of narrative pioneers—ethicists, literary critics, and hermeneuts—we must also add the contributions of those working in the fields of biblical studies, liturgics, psychology, and feminist and liberation studies. All of these citations are intended to direct the reader's attention to two important realities: Contemporary narrative homiletics is derivative, emerging by virtue of the seminal work of those narrative pioneers, and narrative homiletics continues to be an energetic, multidisciplinary endeavor.

After a long season of dormancy, finally the eclipse of biblical narrative is now coming to an end. It is this recovery of biblical narrative that stands at the heart of narrative preaching's project. As long as interpretation sought after the rationalistic residue of biblical texts, narrative would remain in eclipse. What is clear by now is that biblical narrative continues its recovery and that narrative preaching is becoming the most favored strategy for preaching narrative texts. However, it is necessary to pause and reflect on the various aspects that constitute this project of narrative homiletics. For John McClure, narrative preaching finds expression in narrative hermeneutics, narrative semantics, narrative enculturation, and in a narrative worldview.[5] Eugene Lowry translates these categories, identifying the first narrative hermeneutics, as "the focus on biblical literary forms and their impact on the sermon."[6] Lowry redescribes narrative semantics as "narrative homiletical form," that is, the shape of a narrative semon.[7] McClure's "narrative enculturation" speaks to the connection between meaning in sermon and culture while "narrative worldview" relates to larger issues of sermonic context. And while Lowry considers the latter two categories "a bit more confusing," they are essential to the performance of narrative preaching.[8] Just as essential, however, is a prior element within narrative homiletics, and that component relates to a necessary competence by the preacher who is reading narrative biblical texts. The skills involved in reading biblical narrative are a necessary precondition to competencies achieved within the subsequent arenas of narrative homiletic method and cultural and social analysis. We now turn to an overview of these essential skills in reading biblical narrative.

Elements of Biblical Narrative

Causality and Plot

A narrative's plot holds the story together and provides for a sense of movement, purpose, climax, and outcome. All of these dynamics are consti-tutive of the genre of biblical narrative—lacking any, we no longer have a story. For example, the sense of movement within a narrative is conveyed by a "this," which leads us on toward a "that." In John 9, it is the blind man's awkward blurtings about Jesus that led to growing opposition from the reli-gious authorities. Each of these interactions then sets up the occasion for a deeper insight by the blind man as to the identity of Jesus. Clearly, the nar-rative's plot is driven by an interplay of cause and effect. Lacking this dynamic of causation and response, it is questionable whether we have a story in the first place. So, E. M. Forester's famous statement to the effect that "The king died and then the queen died"[9] does not meet this funda-mental criterion of causality. Ergo, the statement is not really a story. For Forester, we would need to add "of grief" to complete the statement and inject a note of causality. But notice how we strain to see a cause-and-effect pattern within the two royal demises. We assume that there is some rela-tionship, and invent reasons ourselves. Clearly, we surmise, there is some underlying reason that Her Royal Highness died so soon following His Royal Highness' death. A story is born in such connections dealing with causality, and lacking explicit clues ("The king died and then the queen died"), we assume them to be there and search for the causal connection. Stories, then, are coterminous with their plots. And their plots have to do with cause and effect.[10]

Episodic movement

The achievement of plot's causality is dependent upon its episodic quality. Look at any narrative within the Hebrew Scripture or the New Testament. What we find is a succession of episodes or scenes that propel the story's plot along. These episodes may be only very brief depictions of action and dia-logue or they may become quite extended episodes within the range of the particular narrative. Turning to the parables, for example, we have become accustomed to their clearly delineated, but rather terse little scenes. On the other hand, in some biblical narratives, a scene or episode may extend through a considerable number of verses. The latter gain their more extended quality mainly by way of descriptions, either of character or of setting. (The parables are examples of narratives in which description is noticeably sketchy, contributing to a sense of ambiguity, of suspense, and surprise.)[11] Whether stated most briefly or drawn out more, the function of these episodes or scenes concern the progress of the plot's causality.

Narrative Time

Narrative time, Alan Culpepper remarks, "is determined by the order, duration, and frequency of events in the narrative."[12] Each of these factors serves a distinctive role in creating the overall sense of time within a narrative.

1. Order

The "normal" order of events involves a series of events that have some causal relationship with each other and are arranged chronologically. That is, we expect some event B to follow event A, and it does. In Luke's account of the disciples on the Emmaus Road (24:13-35), the sequence of events is ordered temporally, and we follow Luke's order as one event leads to the next. At the conclusion of the story, however, Luke introduces an *analepses,* namely, "any evocation after the fact of an event that took place earlier than the point in the story where we are at a given moment."[13] Upon returning to Jerusalem "that very hour," the two disciples were greeted by the community's report, "The Lord has risen indeed, and he has appeared to Simon!" (24:34). The order of the story both moves ahead, but is now given impetus by reference to an event that had occurred prior to the present story time. Analepses in biblical narrative can refer to events happening just prior to the present story time—as with the community's confession in Luke 24—or the prior event can span over centuries—as when Luke cites the prophet Isaiah as speaking of the appearance and vocation of John the Baptist (3:4-6). When the order of the narrative is qualified by reference to a future event, a *prolepses,* that reference may either occur later in the narrative or be projected beyond the narrative time of the story itself. Both internal and external prolepses are devices employed frequently by the biblical writers. The former can be seen in Luke's story of the Transfiguration (9:28-38). As Jesus is transfigured, Moses and Elijah appear and were "speaking of his departure which he was about to accomplish at Jerusalem" (9:31). This internal prolepses subtly contains an analepses as well. The evangelist employs the word "exodus" *(exodon)* for "departure," hence evoking God's saving act for Israel at the Passover. An obvious example of an external prolepses occurs at the end of Luke's Gospel.

The risen and about to ascend Christ commands his followers to "stay here in the city until you have been clothed with power from on high." That promised event lies outside the narrative of the Gospel, but is the subject of the second chapter of the book of Acts.

2. Duration

We must begin this analysis with a distinction between narrative time and story time. The latter is the entire sweep of time referred to within the narrative. In Mark's Gospel, for example, story time spans from the advent of the Baptist in 1:4 to the flight of the women from the tomb in 16:8. (The promised appearance of Jesus in Galilee is an external prolepses. It occurs outside the duration of the Gospel's story.) Narrative time, however, varies considerably within the scope of the story. In Mark, the sense of narrative time is rapid and insistent as Jesus begins his ministry with a succession of healings, journeys, and teachings. Mark intensifies narrative time by linking episodes or scenes with an introductory "and," as well as by denoting that events followed "immediately" upon each other. Narrative time may skip over a period of story time either by simply having a gap in the action or by providing a summary of a sequence of events otherwise not depicted. The closest that the reader comes to an alignment of narrative and story time is when a dialogue is reported in detail as in Mark 10:17-22. As the story of Mark's Gospel reaches toward its climax, narrative time slows down to an almost unbearable pace. The story time of the Crucifixion may be from 9:00 A.M. to 3:00 P.M., but the silences and darkness within the narrative add up to an eternity.

3. Frequency

By this term, Gérard Gennette means to describe the variety of ways events can be reported within a story. They can be told once as an episode within a sequence, or, in more complex narrative forms, they may be repetitively depicted.[14] For the most part, biblical narrative proceeds by way of events happening singularly, even though a past event may be evoked later through an explicit reference—"this was said to fulfill the prophecy"—or by way of a more implicit reference. One implicit device that conveys a sense of repetition is *typology*. In a biblical type scene, certain structures of plot, character, or symbol evoke in the hearer other prior scenes sharing a similar pattern. The Gospel of John employs both internal and external references of this sort. Internally, each of the three Passovers in the narrative sets up a symbolic structure that harks back (and ahead) to the others. Motifs of Jesus' "hour," of a sign of his glory, and of his being "lifted up," cluster at all of the Passover accounts. A powerful reference to external type scenes occurs in the fourth chapter of the Gospel as Jesus meets with the woman at the well.[15] In another episode within the Gospel, the entire sixth chapter evokes a repetition of the Exodus through the typological images of wilderness, crowd/leader-sent-from-God, and bread from heaven.

Opposition

Conflicts of some sort or other are persistent indicators that we have entered into a storied world. "It is difficult to imagine," Mark Allan Powell observes, "a story that does not contain some elements of conflict."[16] We have already spotted the conflict within the story of the Man Born Blind in John 9. Here, the oppositions are most evident in the encounters of the characters—the blind man and the religious authorities and, briefly, the parents of the man and the authorities. Conflicts within narratives most obviously occur between various characters. Yet there are deeper levels at which narrative oppositions are also taking place. Take the parable of the good Samaritan. The most obvious—or perhaps we should say "the most obvious in recent parable criticism"—conflict is between the social and religious world of the Jews and the Samaritans. (A "good Samaritan," for a "good Jew," would be either a humorous oxymoron or a world-threatening new piece of information.) The oppositions that underlie the characters and their own particular conflict, then, may be ideological in nature where characters represent different national, ethnic, or theological interests. Or the oppositions may be signaled in a biblical story through conflicts regarding specific actions that are expressive of ideological worlds that are in conflict. For example, at the beginning of Jesus' ministry in Mark's Gospel, the demon possessing the man in the synagogue at Capernaum speaks not just for itself, but for the realm of evil that this Holy One of God has come to overturn.[17]

To interrogate a text with regard to its oppositions, according to Daniel Patte, is to be about the discernment of the author's "system of convictions." Such a convictional system operates at a different level than issues related to the ideas present in a narrative. The latter (ideas), Patte suggests, are controlled by the author or reader in that they are produced and can be studied, thought through, or rejected. Narratives do contain embodied ideas, but can never be reduced to their ideational contents. Convictions, on the other hand, control us, "they impose themselves upon us."[18] Patte continues:

> [Convictions] are truths that we take to be self-evident, obvious, and thus, that we do not view as needing any demonstration. . . . Furthermore, convictions as self-evident truths (i.e., as truths that we do not question) con-

trol us in the sense that they have the power to impose certain kinds of behavior upon us.[19]

Since convictions are held so deeply and are manifest in our values and behavior, we will typically state them both with respect to a positive affirmation (for example, "I am a pacifist"). In order to state our convictions unambiguously, as Patte observes, we will "more or less spontaneously set an *opposition* between what we actually want to say and what we do not want to say."[20] We may then add regarding our pacifism, "I will not take up arms." Biblical narrative is replete with oppositions, which thereby serve to disclose the convictional system of the author. From the point of view of our interest in preaching these narrative texts, oppositions within the discourse also provide clues to the way in which the plot of the sermon may eventually be formed.

Character and Narrative

Among the many attempts at a definition of narrative, a kind of shorthand summary might be as follows: "narrative is the representation of action in words."[21] So, it follows that some kind of action—others would specify a cause-and-effect action—is the essential threshold to the category of narrative. Hence, to say "I am queasy" is not yet a narrative. Notice that we almost unconsciously begin to explore the why of this queasiness—what causes could result in the condition. Propose a cause, for example, "I must have caught that new bug that's going around." We are now entering into the incipient world of story. No action, no cause and effect. The result may be sheer description of internal (queasy) states or external ones. What we do not have, however, is a narrative. To follow this line of reasoning one step further, in answer to the question, "What or who acts, enacts the causes and effects of a narrative?" the role of a story's characters is raised. In fact, a character is shaped by actions even though as we enter into the story it appears that the characters are the ones doing the acting. So, Beaumont asserts:

> In narrative, character is derived from action. Though in real life we might wish to give priority to the agent, because, as it seems to us for there to be an act there must be an agent, in narrative discourse the situation is different. There, I would contend, the act must be conceded a certain priority over the agent.[22]

For narrative to emerge, there must be action, and the detectability of cause and effect as well.[23]

There is another perspective on the nature of characterization within narratives, and it is one that gains particular force within biblical narrative. While it may be said that the essence of character is action, within the stories of Scripture there are other means of revealing a character, and in many instances these other approaches reveal more about a character than does a report of actions. Among these other means for revealing information about a character, Robert Alter lists appearance, gesture, posture, comments by one character about another, a character's direct speech, or comments concerning the character provided by the narrator.[24] Ironically, although actions may be claimed to have a precedence over character in narrative discourse in general, within the biblical narratives, a character's actions are often less revealing than most all of these other modes of disclosure.

Turning to the Fourth Gospel, the actions of certain characters are sufficiently ambiguous that the narrator interjects directly as to the true motivation of a character's actions. Therefore, in John 9:20-21, when the parents of the man born blind answer the religious authorities in a rather equivocating manner ("Ask him, he is of age"), the narrator enters the discourse to inform the readers that the parents were afraid of being expelled from the synagogue. Even Jesus' actions occasionally need their true meaning revealed by direct narration. So when the temple cleansing was completed, Jesus leaves the crowd with a cryptic saying about his raising the temple in three days (2:19). And while the crowd, typically, seizes onto the literal meaning of Jesus' words, the narrator tells us the truth: "But he was speaking of the temple of his body" (2:21).[25]

Once again, the art of biblical narrative qualifies more general and conventional notions of character and story. In this instance, we notice that much of the material designated "narrative" in the Bible is composed almost entirely of dialogue. A modern novel, on the other hand, may focus our attention on, first, the outer action of a character ("She walked down to the beach, tracing the old path through the dunes"), and, second, the inner state of the character ("She felt such a peace here, this place of her childhood adventures among the dunes"). In biblical narrative, characters are depicted by attention to such outer and inner descriptions. The story of David and Goliath (1 Sam. 17) revels in depicting the outer appearance of the two protagonists in striking and humorous detail—David's appearance dressed in Saul's armor.[26] Here, the outer description is a reliable clue about the inner state of the two champions. Biblical narratives do attend to outer description—of a character, a group of persons, animals, and, of course, of natural and social setting. Still, in comparison to modern narrative, we will conclude that the stories of Scripture are sparser in their attention to outer appearance.

The relative sparsity of outer description of a character is even more obvious when the issue of inner description is raised. In the Gospels, the issue of a character's inner motivations, feelings, or intent is infrequently disclosed directly. Looking to the parables for strategies of character depiction, two aspects dominate—the actions of the character and the character's speech. Only infrequently does the parable refer to an inner state directly. However, this scarcity of inner reference only serves to emphasize the importance of that state when it is provided. So, our attention is riveted on the outcome when the owner of the house becomes angry (Luke 14:21) or when the Samaritan is "moved with pity" (Luke 10:33). Rather than either direct outer or inner depiction, character in biblical narratives is often rendered through dialogue, by means of what two characters say to each other. In the striking case of the parable of the rich fool (Luke 12:16-20), that man's character is disclosed through the device of an inner dialogue between himself and his *psyche*.[27] Whether in the parables of Jesus or elsewhere in biblical narrative, there is a persistent dependence on dialogue as the means of disclosing keys to the identity of the character and of propelling the plot.

The voice of the story

The reader is guided through a story by the narrator, a voice whose presence is persistent yet, in Scripture, rarely intrusive. There is a strange but usually unnoticed process at work in biblical narrative, an implicit contract between the reader or hearer and the narrator such that trust and reliability are extended by the former to the latter. This contract obtains even when, as Wayne Booth notes, one biblical narrator begins, "There was a man in the land of Uz, whose name was Job; and that man was perfect and upright, one that feared God, and eschewed evil."[28] This opening statement, when scrutinized apart from the story, "is incredible, yet the reader accepts it without question."[29] We are formed to accept the canons of this implicit contract between ourselves and the narrator of most every biblical story. At the heart of those canons is the concurrence with the narrator's stance of trustworthiness and reliability. Therefore, when the narrator of the Fourth Gospel intrudes into the story to directly inform us of significant information, we accept this interruption, receive the newly disclosed point of view, and then continue with the story. We encounter this more direct example of trustworthy intervention as the narrator directly informs us that the pious comments of Judas concerning the poor are hypocrisy: "He said this not because he cared about the poor, but because he was a thief; he kept the common purse and used to steal what was put into it" (John 12:6). We accept this information, allow it to shape our point of view toward Judas, and therefore, continue to regard Mary's act of anointing Jesus' feet as one of selfless devotion. The contract between reader and narrator endures and is even deepened in its canons of trust and reliability.

Underneath these direct and obvious interventions by the narrator are the ongoing descriptions that provide clues about external conditions and events along with information about the internal conditions of one or more of the characters. With Meir Sternberg, we may speak of such information as "exposition," expressing "the basic norm of straightforward communication."[30] Many of these pass almost unnoticed, assimilated into the story as they enrich its telling. So, in the course of the Fourth Gospel's story of Jesus, the narrator sprinkles information here and there to help us locate time and place or to set the circumstances of the story. We are told: "Lazarus was ill," that "it was a sabbath day" when Jesus healed the blind man, and that "it was winter, and Jesus was walking in the temple, in the portico of Solomon." Likewise, we easily receive information that propels the story of Saul and David in 1 Samuel: Saul and the men of Israel "were in the valley of Elah, fighting with the Philistines," a necessary bit of stage setting prior to the introduction of Goliath (1 Sam. 17:19). This imparting of information necessary to the story's movement and direction comes naturally and reliably. Yet in the same voice, the narrator provides us with material that is rich in symbolism or laden with irony. The story of David and Bathsheba begins with the famous line, "In the spring of the year, the time when kings go out to battle." The narrator then tells us, "David remained at Jerusalem" (2 Sam. 11:1). Mark tells the readers that after the second feeding miracle, during the sea crossing, "the disciples had forgotten to bring any bread; and they had only one loaf with them in the boat" (Mark 8:14).

The narrator we name "John" frequently conveys rich symbolism by way of description. Hence, Nicodemus comes to Jesus at night. There is a further escalation of the dimensions of biblical narration as the reader is told what the God of Israel's position is regarding persons or events in the story: "The Lord took note of Hannah" (1 Sam. 2:21; and "the thing that David had done displeased the Lord" (2 Sam. 12:1). God intervenes in the story and "an evil spirit from God rushed upon Saul" (1 Sam. 18:10). Whether it is the relating of the "mere facts" (exposition) that assist us with the story or the narrator's information about the actions and attitude of the Lord God, we come to rely on the trustworthiness of the biblical narrator.[31] The implicit contract between reader and narrator remains intact.

Based on this analysis, we may identify two core qualities that mark the narrators of biblical stories. Each builds on the other to provide a dominant point of view on the whole story at hand. And these qualities of narration are mutually interdependent; if one is to crumble into disbelief, all will be in jeopardy.

Biblical narrators are knowledgeable

In modern fiction, this quality may or may not be the case, especially if the narration is in the first person. In a good detective thriller, for example, the suspense may be driven precisely by a perplexing lack of knowledge held by the first-person narrator. However, biblical narrators, as we have seen, have a great deal of knowledge about the events depicted, the actions and motivations of the characters, and sometimes even the thoughts and acts of God.

Narrators are able to report not only public events, but also private ones in which a character is supposed alone (e.g., Mark 14:32-42). They are able to tell us what happened in two different places at the same time (e.g., John 18:12-27). They even know the inner thoughts and motivations of the characters they describe (e.g., Matt. 2:3).[32]

Nevertheless, there are limits to the knowledge of the biblical narrator. Or to rephrase this assertion, there are limits on information the narrator chooses to impart to the reader. Therefore, in certain cases, we are *not* privileged by the narrator to have insight into the inner motives of a character. (Witness the extraordinary lengths preachers have gone to interpret Jesus' motive for seemingly referring to the Syrophonecian woman as one of the dogs in Mark 7:24-30. The narrator remains silent on this disturbing comment.) Among the company of narrators of Scripture, it is the Fourth Gospel, however, that most thoroughly expands a sense of knowledgeability. This story is told by a voice whose knowledge includes the very act of creation itself (John 1:1-18) and who knows much more about Jesus than is even contained in the Gospel (John 21:25). Additionally, many commentators on the Gospel of John have noted that a common point of view is shared by the narrator and Jesus—they speak with the same voice theologically and both share intimate knowledge of the Father. However, one thread is shared by the entire company of biblical narrators: They speak in a way that claims "free access to the minds ("hearts") of his dramatis personae, not excluding God himself."[33]

Biblical narrators are reliable

We have noted that the reader's reliance on the narrator for essential facts of the account lends support to a sense of trustworthiness of the former for the latter. We take these items of exposition at face value and proceed, thus informed, whether about the time of day, the season of the year, or the appearance of a character in the story.

However, the quality of reader-narrator relationship dealing with this trustworthiness is as much posited by the reader as it is earned by the narrator. Otherwise, how reliable could Mark's opening assertion be for a reader that this is "The beginning of the good news of Jesus Christ, the Son of God" (Mark 1:1)? The reliability of the narrator, then, is derived from the entirety of the account, its narrative integrity, along with the location of the reader within the community of faith. So, Ronald Thiemann notes that the biblical stories in general (and narrations in particular, we would add) "call forth a remarkable act from the reader: Christians call it faith."[34] He continues by adding that faith "presupposes that the meaning of the narrative is latent within their rich and nuanced depictions."[35]

The silent voices of biblical narrative

Throughout the drama of the biblical narrative, the author engages in a deeper level of communication with the reader, whether through the exposition of the narrator or the depiction of the characters. There is a "silent" communication at play in a biblical narrative wherein the author "smiles, winks, and raises his eyebrows as the story is told."[36] These strategies of silent communication include the use of symbolism, misunderstanding (particularly in John's Gospel), and, most centrally, irony. Symbolic images and actions abound in Scripture, making a flat, literal reading a daunting task. So in the Fourth Gospel, the narrator reports—and emphasizes the reliability of the account—that upon Jesus' death, a guard pierced his side with a spear, "and at once blood and water came out" (John 19:34). The layers of symbolism here seem unending. The blood and water resonate back to the discourse with Nicodemus, the conversation with the woman at the well, the Dominical sign at Cana, and the bread of life discourse in John 6. Yet the symbolic depth remains. By way of this piercing rather than the breaking of Jesus' legs, the story connects with the date of Jesus' death to undergird the reliability of the Baptist's conviction that this is the lamb of God (John 1:36). And the narrator comments that this act of this piercing Jesus' side "occurred so that the scripture might be fulfilled" (John 19:36-37).

Misunderstanding is both a literary employed by the Fourth Evangelist and a reflection of the Gospel's ideology of light and darkness/the earthly and heavenly/flesh and spirit. Nicodemus seizes on the earthly meaning, asking how it could be that a person reenter his or her mother's womb to be born again. This misunderstanding provides the occasion for Jesus to teach about heavenly things: "You must be born from above" (John 3:7). In John's Gospel, the misunderstanding is frequently generated by double-meaning words, such as the Greek word *anōthen,* or by statements that are ambiguous. An example of misunderstanding born of ambiguity occurs at the outset of the story of the raising of Lazarus as Jesus declares that "Our friend Lazarus has fallen asleep" (John 11:11). The disciples once again grab onto the earthly meaning, believing that Lazarus has fallen asleep and will recover from his illness. Jesus must clarify the misunderstanding plainly: "Lazarus is dead" (11:14). Of course, this reality then sets the stage for the full glory of Christ to be revealed to those with the eyes to see as he calls Lazarus out of the tomb. Misunderstanding, then, results in John from either double-meaning words, from ambiguous language or events, or from deliberate metaphors (such as "bread of heaven" in chapter 6). Culpepper notes that these misunderstandings "provide an opportunity to explain the meaning of Jesus' words and develop significant themes further." He adds, "They are more, however, and their effect on the reader is greater than if the meaning had merely been stated plainly from the beginning."[37]

Among all of the "silent voices" of biblical narrative, irony speaks the loudest. The stories of Scripture are replete with irony; it seems that you cannot tell these stories without recourse to this mode of indirection. And the irony extends to the way in which this silent voice speaks—it speaks through the audible voices of the characters in the text. We hear the sons of Zebedee ask Jesus to reign at his right and left hand (Mark 10:35-40), but discover that those places will be occupied by two thieves. We listen to Caiaphas argue that "it is better for you to have one man die for the people than to have the whole nation destroyed" (John 11:50); not knowing the truth of his words—that one man will die for the people, yet the nation will, in fact, be destroyed. It is not only the characters of biblical narrative who speak this silent language through their discourse. Some of the most powerful irony is spoken by the narrator, who pretends to be telling a simple and forthright tale.[38] Clearly, several qualities are at play in the ironically "silent voice" of biblical irony. Preeminently, with Wayne Booth, the ironies of narrative are intended.[39] They deftly employ the active voices of the text to speak in ways profoundly at odds with the ostensible meanings at hand. In this sense, irony is a matter of intentionally saying one thing and meaning another. But a second issue is also of critical importance. Since we have come to trust the reliability of the voice of the narrator within a biblical story, how does the reader identify that a particular statement, action, or episode is not to be taken at face value? Even among the characters of the story, how is it that we are able to sense when a situation has become ironic? Several competencies, it would seem, are needed by faithful readers and hearers of the narratives of Scripture. They are all essential to achieving an ironic reading of the text.

1. The reader must be able to discern a certain incongruity in the narrative. Interestingly, this awareness is not shared with the characters within the story, otherwise the irony evaporates. This creates, according to Robert Fowler, "a two-layered structure to (the story), a built-in dialectical relationship between what is not understood within the story and what is understood in the audience's encounter with the story."[40] Fowler then concludes, "Dramatic irony is inherently revelatory."[41] We now risk an early observation: *Biblical narrative has as one intention, the formation of a community of faith capable of detecting these surface-level incongruities by spotting the author's wink over the text.* If the audience is incapable of an ironic vision, the incongruities remain undetected. This situation itself—becoming more prevalent in a postmodern culture and an ideologically driven church—becomes ironic.

2. The reader, having assessed the surface meaning of the text as not to be trusted, is now faced with the challenge of discerning various covert meanings and choosing among them. So during the bread of life discourse of John 6, the crowds follow Jesus after he fed them on the mountain and ask "What sign are you going to give us then, so that we may see it and believe you?" (John 6:30). We cannot trust the surface meaning of this request of the crowd, primarily because it is the same group of people who on the previous day were fed the loaves and fishes. What, then, are we to conclude? Do they have collective amnesia, that they were a different group of people than were fed? John says they were the same crowd. Or can they not recognize a sign from Jesus and believe because their very question belies their seeing and believing? Here is a "two-story phenomenon" at work; having rejected the first story, the reader is forced down to the second.[42] However, within biblical narrative, this deep level is one containing many rooms. We are now forced to make a decision among the latent meanings of the text about which one was sig-

naled in the author's wink. It is a critical decision down here; to enter one of the rooms involves a risk of faith.

3. The reader now has before him or her the challenge of community. Once the surface reading is rejected and the choice made among the latent meanings of the story, that interpreter now discovers others within the same room, all sharing in the once-hidden revelation. A community is born, although, to be sure, one that excludes others who remain with the victims at the surface level of the text. Biblical narrative thus embodies an exclusionary strategy on behalf of gathering a more faithful community of covenantal faith. Commenting on this exclusionary strategy, Fowler adds that "all persons reading the Gospel, to the extent that they see through the irony, become a community—a community not bound by race, culture, or politics but by the common experience of reading and coming to terms with Mark's irony."[43]

Equipped with these competencies, readers are invited more and more into the biblical story. It becomes their world.

A Narrative Hermeneutic

If the world of the biblical narrative is to become the world of the contemporary community of faith, several successive theses must be argued on behalf of a narrative hermeneutics. Each builds on its predecessor and each is essential to the entire model of interpretation.

1. The narrative mode of interpretation is primary to reading and proclaiming Scripture

Certainly we mean here that the Bible is filled with stories—an insight the preaching-as-storytelling movement recovered for the churches several decades ago.[44] However, to claim a narrative mode of interpretation as central to reading and proclaiming Scripture, we must mean more than the fact that we have stories to tell from the Bible. The next step in the argument is to celebrate the abundance of stories in Scripture and add the judgment "that narrative is central to the Bible's own interests in communicating its message."[45] If the Bible's self-interest in disclosing the story of God's people and the character of God is primarily through narrative, then our preaching on these narrative texts may well need to embody a narrative form. Put the other way around, to preach biblical narrative persistently through non-narrative homiletic methods would seem at some level to work against the intent of Scripture's self-interest! A further claim is involved here whereby all of Scripture is located with reference to the narrative center of the Bible. The status of non-narrative biblical material immediately emerges as the claim is made that the narrative mode of interpretation encompasses all of Scripture. Certainly the relationship of certain non-narrative material to narrative texts is rather clear. These former texts seem "to be concerned with questions about how narratives should be interpreted or with elaboration on the narratives through praise."[46] The first category most obviously includes the Pauline corpus and the catholic epistles, as well as the covenantal law portions of Deuteronomy. The second category also easily commends itself as including a number of the psalms and other liturgical material located within the matrix of a biblical story (the canticles of both Testaments). We may be comfortable with this assertion of the primacy of the narrative mode of interpreting Scripture were it not for voices to the contrary.

The vulnerability of this thesis regarding the primacy of the narrative mode of interpretation initially would seem to relate to types of biblical material not obviously related to the Bible's story. The two exceptions most frequently cited are Wisdom literature on one hand and apocalyptic on the other. They stand in seemingly polar relationship to each other within Scripture. The Wisdom material and proverbs in particular "are the product of a culture in equilibrium," while apocalyptic texts "are the literary genres of crisis."[47] Recently, there has been a remarkable resurgence of interest in the Wisdom literature of the Hebrew Scriptures and the New Testament.[48] Here is a body of literature that may have existed prior to the time of the covenantal narratives and independent to them. Most of this material is non-narrative in form and stands in a somewhat vague relationship to the biblical narratives. As observed elsewhere, "Proverbs can be found, interestingly, that may either undergird or undermine specific biblical narratives."[49] Moreover, there are a number of proverbs that are incipient narratives in their own right whose stock characters—the wise, the wicked, the foolish—are described as living out the storied outcomes of their inner being. A significant amount of the Wisdom material serves to reinforce this sense of a followable world in which the righteous may suffer but are vindicated by God, the wicked seemingly prosper but come to tragic ends, and the foolish, . . . well, remain just fools. Interestingly, when these stereotypical plots are called into question— as when the righteous cry, "Why do the wicked live on, reach old age, and grow mighty in power?" (Job 21:7)—the biblical writers turn to a narrative form to deal with these profound questions of theodicy and suffering.

However, for all of the sapiential tradition of Scripture, there is a narrative connection that is inherent in the literary form. William Beardslee identifies the distinctive relationship:

> It is somewhat misleading to speak of the proverb as a statement of a general truth. It is a statement about a particular kind of occurrence or situation, an orderly tract of experience that can be repeated. In this sense, though it is not a narrative, a proverb implies a story, something that happens that moves through as sequence in a way that can be known.[50]

In this analysis of Jesus' use of Wisdom sayings in the synoptics, Beardslee notes a consistent relocation of those sayings from the status of general comments on human life to the story of God's providence and kingdom. The Wisdom sayings are caught up in the story of the Incarnation and of the advent of God's reign.

The other literary form of Scripture that critics have located outside the arena of narrative interpretation it that of apocalyptic. Given a tradition of Scripture so laden with imagery, especially imagery noted for its dire judgment and awesome attending spectacle, how shall we speak of its relationship to biblical narrative? Several considerations can be assembled in response to this good question. First, we note that the images of apocalyptic have their birth within the stories either of the covenant people or else of the powers of the world. That is, as you leaf through the pages of the book of Revelation, a large number of images we encounter are familiar to biblical people—Temple, Mount Zion, the metaphor of the Lamb, and so on. Others derive clearly from the stories of the worldly principalities and powers—images of rulers, warfare, persecution, and symbolic figures standing for earthly kingdoms. Other apocalyptic imagery belongs to its own stock vocabulary of End Times—nature in turmoil, dreaded serpents and dragons, fantastic ornamentation and "a beast" (Rev. 13:1-10). While the narrative location of a portion of the covenantal and worldly imagery may be detected, certainly much of the stock apocalyptic material would seem to be outside any narrative context. However, two factors immediately qualify such a conclusion. On one hand, the entirety of apocalyptic in the New Testament offers "an alternate symbolic universe," offering hope and encouragement to the faithful in periods of great tribulation.[51] On the other hand, a process is at work within Scripture, just as with the sapiential material, of eroding its independent status and reworking its material on behalf of the witness to Jesus Christ. Paul Riceour speaks of an "internal subversion" taking place whereby apocalyptic "is simultaneously employed, transgressed, and upset by its new usage."[52] David

Buttrick provides an excellent example of this subversion of the genre of apocalyptic within Scripture in his analysis of 1 Thessalonians 5:1-11. Here:

> the conventional language of apocalyptic rings out, and the Thessalonians have heard it before—all the talk of night and day, asleep and awake, thief in the night is nothing new. But then, in a single sweeping verse it's blown to bits by grace [Buttrick is referring to verses 9-10]. In the passage, the Bible is busy rewriting itself.[53]

This biblical "rewriting" transpires as the imagery of apocalyptic is "employed, transgressed, and upset" with reference to Jesus and the mystery of the nearness of God's reign.

2. The world of biblical narrative stands in contrast to the narratives of the world and claims a primacy over them

It is one thing to assert that narrative "highlights both a predominant literary category within the Bible and an appropriate theological category for interpreting the canon as a whole."[54] It is quite another matter to claim that the world of the Bible both makes a claim for primacy over the narratives of the world and is, in fact, true. Rising up in opposition to such a radical claim is a chorus of witnesses speaking a language of "pluralism" and operating from an experiential/expressive theological position.[55] Hans Frei identifies this approach to doctrine and interpretation as liberalism's perennial need to ground the particularity of biblical faith in some "shared inner experience" of humanity.[56] For any particular portion of Scripture to be adjudged as true or authentic, in this approach, is for it to be discovered as an instance of some prior category of human experience. Jesus, whether through analogies to other holy or prophetic persons in history, becomes in doctrine and in preaching a representative of this prior, ubiquitous human experience. Therefore, Jesus' particularity and uniqueness in Scripture becomes an embarrassment of riches. As Charles Campbell notes in response to one homiletic example of the experiential/expressive approach:

> Jesus is not a unique subject independent of us, but is rather absorbed into human experience and general "truths" about life; he is not the subject of his own predicates, but is, in fact the predicate of another subject: "human experience."[57]

From this perspective, biblical narrative in general and the character of Jesus of Nazareth in particular have an authority to the extent that they are exemplary of some prior human experience or condition (for example, the universality of suffering, the need for justice, a tenacity of spirit in the face of the world's oppression).[58] The assumptions here: First, some ubiquitous sense of "human experience" named and identified apart from any cultural and linguistic narrative location exists; and second, the witness of the Scriptures to the character of God and Jesus Christ may be significant as regional examples of this prior sense of human experience and general truth.

An alternative, and radical, assertion is that there is no unstoried, neutral vantage point available from which to assess the truth claims of biblical narrative. So, for example, the world may offer a version of the story of Jesus, which celebrates his advocacy of justice and compassion for the poor, but in which he is not risen from the dead and is not Lord of heaven and earth. Such a story may be interesting to explore, but it is clearly now quite distinct from the story of Jesus in the Gospels.[59] Rather, the assertion is made that the Bible invites its hearers to become part of its story, and thereby to have their own stories upset, revised, and redescribed. This is quite distinct from finding our stories within the Bible's stories. What if our stories need redeeming? Most probably, they do. There is a quality to the biblical narratives such that nothing in heaven or on earth remains outside their scope—the God of Israel created all things and in Christ, all things shall be fulfilled. Hence, if the biblical world interprets all of our extrabiblical worlds, along with the "world of our storied self," then there is a sense in which it is able to absorb the universe. The narratives of Scripture offer a world that claims a primacy over the world's stories. These things, the Fourth Gospel claims for itself, are true (see John 21:24). Even without such specific authorial claims, all of Scripture makes the same claim against the stories of the nations.

3. An ecclesial context is normative for interpreting Scripture[60]

To assert the primacy of biblical narrative over the stories of the world apart from this communal context of interpretation would be to admit only one objective and privileged reading of the biblical text. However, it is precisely the communal character of Christian faith—the enduring, diverse community of faith continually living out of the Scriptures—that provides the intended context for the interpretation of Scripture. The biblical story, then, "is not self-referential but rather creates a people capable of being the continuation of the narrative by witnessing to the world that all creation is ordered to God's good end. The church is the necessary context for the testing of that narrative."[61] Individuals and communities outside this community of faith and faithful interpretation may well peer over into the biblical story pursuing a variety of agendas. However, a narrative hermeneutic will insist that Scripture has a vested interest in a community with a variety of material specifications, and the intended and primary location for the interpretation of Scripture is the community of faith in Jesus Christ.

This emphasis on the material specifications pertaining to the community of interpretation is crucial. Once again, we look to the vested interest of Scripture in evoking and sustaining a certain kind of people, equipped with virtues capable of remembering and retelling the biblical story. Lists of these virtues vary from age to age and from ecclesial tradition to tradition. With an interest in proclamation, however, several virtues must be noted among these more extended material specifications of Christ's church:

1. A *lively memory*

One of the essential qualities of a Christian people, African American preachers would insist, is a lively communal memory. The church that is capable of hearing the Word is, ironically, that community within which the Word already dwells. Hence, the Fourth Gospel admonishes the believers to "abide in the Word."[62] Outside the African American church, preachers have a distinctive vocation in these days when biblical narrative remains almost totally eclipsed—the privilege and duty of handing back to the people their own biblical narrative, story by story. Thus equipped, the community will discover a different and much richer way of hearing the Gospel than transpired in experiential/expressive appeals. A lively memory is a glorious virtue, essential for a biblical people.

2. A *persistent hospitality*

The biblical narratives in which hospitality was at the heart of the matter are abundant throughout the Bible. Abraham and Sarah extend hospitality to the three visitors (Gen. 18:1-15); an alien widow offers hospitality to the prophet Elijah (1 Kings 17:8-16); and Cleopas and his companion offer hospitality to the stranger who walks with them from Jerusalem to Emmaus (Luke 24:13-35). In every case, the hospitality offered by faithful covenant people was the essential condition for a bold new vision of the character of God and the mission of God's people. The Scriptures insist on our becoming a people graced with this material specification. Conversely, our most gracious act of hospitality is that of welcoming into our liturgies and our lives the narratives of the Bible.

3. A capacity for thanksgiving

It was for the liturgical movement of the early decades of the twentieth century to recover for the Western Church that making Eucharist is at the heart of sacramental theology and practice. The church has been blessed by the recovery of eucharistic rites and prayers that once again embody a narrative texture. In fact, we have come again to appreciate that thanksgiving in a biblical sense is impossible apart from a narrative rendition of our biblical faith. This capacity for thanksgiving is an essential homiletic virtue for at least two reasons. On one hand, the preacher is freed from the compulsion to say everything—the narrative abides there at the Eucharist and it does "say everything" and "sing everything." On the other hand, the specific narrative at hand will often invite celebration, if not insist on it. There is an intimate connection between a church, in which the biblical narrative has been long eclipsed, and an impoverishment regarding thanksgiving. Preaching the biblical story, however, will invite the hearers to join with beggars and the blind, with outcasts and sinners in that distinctive song of thanksgiving to their God.[63]

Narrative Interpretation and Proclamation

The way back from the eclipse of biblical narrative was by way of a two-pronged attack on the Enlightenment assumptions that undergirded the rationalistic captivity of the Bible. In this prevailing orthodoxy of biblical interpretation, with Buttrick, there existed a "hermeneutic of distillation" whereby each text of Scripture was assumed to be susceptible to ideational redaction. On one hand, the assault on this approach of "slo-cooking" the text was mounted early in the second half of the twentieth century by literary critics and biblical scholars eager to reassert the integrity of biblical narrative.[64] The field of parable interpretation becomes a useful microcosm for observing both the onset and recovery from the hermeneutics of distillation. Counting from Jülicher's 1899 publication in which the "main idea" model of interpretation was first applied to parables, the paradigm persisted through the later work of both C. H. Dodd and Joachim Jeremias.[65] Notice that while the content of the extracted parabolic main ideas differed according to the piety and ecclesial location of the interpreter, the model itself remained unchallenged. (There is an irony here in that a succession of interpreters, each beholden to a hermeneutic that assumed that every parable yielded one and only one main idea, found such a variety of main ideas in the course of their work.) However, the main idea orthodoxy was finally challenged in Amos Wilder's book, *The Language of the Gospels,*[66] in which he first asserted that the parables of Jesus were narrative metaphors. In rapid succession, scholars such as Robert Funk,[67] Eta Lienneman,[68] and John Dominic Crossan[69] approached the parables from a largely shared perspective yielding a remarkable new harvest of biblical insight and homiletical implications.[70] One hundred years after Jülicher, the paradigm has shifted and preachers and other interpreters are discovering the world of the parables and inviting the faithful to discover images of self, church, and kingdom within that world.

The other prong of the attack on the old rationalistic model of interpretation was led by a confederation of narrative theologians, both diverse in their outcomes yet united in their critique of the reigning model. By the 1980s and 1990s, the types of narrative theologies ranged across a new theological spectrum, encompassing theology as storytelling, postmodern phenomenology, postliberal theology, and some liberation and feminist approaches.[71] However, there is this much held in common: An adequate construal of human experience, of Christian community, and of revelation cannot be sustained apart from the narrative of God's dealing with God's people in Scripture. Just as the demise of the old hermeneutics of distillation rendered null and void certain rationalistic approaches to preaching, so, too, the emergence of a vigorous new emphasis on narrativity in biblical interpretation was seen to have immediate and fruitful implications for proclamation in general and homiletic method in particular. In some cases, this return to the integrity of biblical narrative meant the recovery of narrative sermon forms that had endured mainly in the African American homiletic tradition (see chapter 3). In other instances, new approaches to the homiletic plot were informed by literary critical insights into the text, the new narrative theologies, and a renewed interest in the oral-communal language of preaching.[72] However, before turning to those methodological considerations, it is important to underscore the distinctive relationship between narrative theology and proclamation. In any number of theological camps, the exploration of how preaching would be shaped by a particular position is an interesting but optional enterprise. That is, the many "preaching as . . ." homiletic resources offer suggestions by advocates of a certain theological camp who have a particular interest as well in preaching. For example, one publication explored the implications of process theology for preaching with special attention to the passion narratives.[73] This was a fruitful exploration but one not organically related to process theology's central concerns. The same may be said of "preaching as . . ." publications originating from such positions as liberation theology.[74]

On the other hand, an interest in proclamation is not an avocation for narrative theology and interpretation. We have already pointed to the essential communal context of Scriptural interpretation—one of narrative theology's central contributions to the larger homiletical conversation. However, there is a necessity as well that the language of the biblical narrative shape the Christian community in order that it be formed with the virtues sufficient to extend hospitality to its Scriptures, its sacramental life, and to the stranger. This essential formation depends primarily on a preaching that is spoken from Scripture and to the contemporary situation of church and world.[75] Hence follows, with Hauerwas, "the necessity of the sermon as the communal action whereby Christians are formed to use their language rightly."[76] Hauerwas adds:

> The emphasis on narrative, therefore, is not first a claim about the narrative quality of experience from some unspecified standpoint but is rather an attempt to draw our attention to where the story is told, namely, in the church; how the story is told, namely in faithfulness to scripture; and who tells the story, namely the whole church through the office of the preacher.[77]

Compelled by its very insistence on the faithful use of language that forms the community of faith, the preacher gives witness to the Word through the sermon. Proclamation is not an optional interest for narrative theology and interpretation, especially in its postliberal expressions. Preaching, along with the church as context for interpretation, is intrinsic to narrative theology's task and goal.

Preaching Narrative

Just as narrative theology discloses a diverse community of movements and emphases, so, too, narrative homiletic method encompasses more than one approach. However, as we have seen within a variety of narrative models of interpretation, common core is shared methodologically as well. The shared core of method derives from the qualities of a biblical narrative itself—the movement and structure of its plot, the actions of its characters, and the way in which the story is shaped and propelled by setting and location. Implied, too, at the core of narrative preaching is the conviction that "narrative is central to the Bible's own interests in communicating its message."[78] The most compatible approaches to preaching biblical narrative, then, will be methods that retain (or embody) the movement and intention of the narrative text. As Don Wardlaw insisted in *Preaching Biblically*, the preacher's task in preaching biblical stories is to allow his or her sermon to be shaped by that narrative itself.[79] At the same time, every narrative homiletician has an interest in the contemporary import of the biblical narrative—in shaping personal and communal character, in sustaining the community of faith, in directing its praxis out in the world. Therefore, narrative preaching will be seeking strategies for contemporizing the biblical story, or, more accurately, for locating the hearers within the story world of the text. Again, there is no one method for preaching biblical narrative in a postmodern context. Rather, preachers have a suite of methodologies available that can invite the listeners to find their personal and communal location within the world of Scripture's stories. Across the sweep of these methods, however, several necessary competencies for preaching narrative sermons are held in common:

1. Establishing the story

This exegetical skill is a subtype of that of "establishing the text," an exegetical competency long recognized as essential to the task of preaching.[80] However, the preacher of biblical narrative has an especially important initial task in determining the pericope's extent and boundaries. At one level, the issue is that of deciding whether the redactional context of a story will be included in the narrative sermon. Will we attend to Luke's preface to the parable of the persistent widow in which we are told that the story is about constant prayer (Luke 18:1)? And in preaching the parable of the prodigal son (Luke 15:11-32), will the sermon deal with the older son's refusal to join in the celebration in 15:25-32? At times, the lectionary citation will trim off some of the narrative material as in the sons of Zebedee story of Mark 10:35-40—with the omission of the response of the ten and the Dominical saying in 41-45. Given the opportunity to preach a biblical narrative, establishing the parameters of the story to be preached is a frequent challenge.

2. Structuring the narrative plot

Before the preacher decides on the shape and movement of the sermonic plot, he or she will need to sketch out the episodes in sequence of the narrative's plot. Simply put, we will need to spot the scenes of the story and chart them in some helpful form. Perhaps the parables lend themselves most easily to this task since in most cases their episodic structure is readily discerned. So, for example, in the parable of the barren fig tree (Luke 13:6-9), the order of its scenes or *lexies* is as follows:

Without this kind of surface-level structural analysis, the movement and theological intention of the biblical story may remain opaque. Here, in the parable of the barren fig tree, we are struck by the assertiveness of the hired hand in the face of the owner's directive. Also, we now ponder a strange, against-all-odds advocacy of the gardener on behalf of this barren tree taking up space in the vineyard (most always a metaphor for God's people in

There is barrenness in the vineyard.
The fig tree is bearing no fruit.

Says the gardener, "Cut it down!
For three years there is no fruit!"

"Sir," says the gardener, "leave it stand!"
"Give it one more year while I tend it, digging
around it and spreading manure on it."

"Next year, it may bear fruit.
If not, then cut it down."

FIGURE 2A

Scripture). And we come upon the limits of such grace in the loaded phrase, "for one more year."[81] With most every biblical narrative, a similar structuring of the plot's component episodes or scenes is possible. Occasionally, we discover that the intention of the pericope is quite different than it first appeared to be![82]

3. Identifying clues to interpretation

Biblical authors provide the attentive and faithful reader with distinctive clues to the intention of the narrative. These clues may be in the form of certain elements provided in the story that link it to earlier narratives in Scripture. Therefore, we come to recognize certain stories as "type scenes" by virtue of a cluster of elements they hold in common. So when Jesus meets a woman at a well in John 4, we quite readily have our expectations raised that the destiny of God's people will be altered by the encounter—as was the case in other meetings at a well in Israel's tradition. Other clues to a story's interpretation may be disclosed in the intertextual location of the pericope at hand. For example, at the beginning of Jesus' ministry in Mark, there are in rapid sequence a series of actions that are in chiastic parallelism. The sequence is aligned as follows:

a. The healing of Peter's mother-in-law at the house of Simon and Andrew (1:29-31);

b. Jesus cures many who are ill; the demons who are cast out are not permitted to speak (1:32-34);

c. There is a shift in the action—Jesus goes out to proclaim the message "throughout Galilee" (1:35-39);

d. A leper is healed by Jesus, who is cautioned to not speak of it, but he goes out and freely proclaims the word (1:40-45); and

e. At home, many gather around Jesus. A paralytic man is lowered through the roof and is healed (2:1-12).

In the Fourth Gospel, other clues to interpretation are provided by the proximity of various events to one of the three Passovers that organize so much of the plot. Therefore, when the narrator informs us that the Passover was near (as in chapter 2 with its temple-cleansing event and the wedding at Cana), issues of Jesus' "hour" and his being "lifted up" are initially raised. At each Passover, they will be raised once more until the Son of God is raised on a cross and in glory.[83]

Running the Story

By this designation, Lowry invites preachers to construe the sermon's scope and internal structure as quite closely modeling that of the biblical narrative text. The sermon begins, continues, and concludes in alignment with the story text; they are coterminous. One of the most enduring forms of this approach to preaching is found in the African American homiletic tradition and its distinctiveness is examined and celebrated in chapter 3. As a preacher considers running the story with regard to a particular narrative biblical text, there are several considerations that attend to this methodology. In the course of shaping the introduction, the preacher will need to make decisions regarding *reach, trim,* and *point of view*.

By reach, we may speak of the amount of narrative material included in the introduction itself rather than in the body of the narrative sermon. An alternative way of speaking of reach is to raise the issue of the extent of the opening section of the biblical story that will not be expanded into a full scene within the sermon. Material in the introduction of a narrative sermon is often essential to the listener's ability to comprehend and follow the story as it is run. In some stories in Scripture, the introduction's reach is rather short. Certain information is given, usually regarding background to setting or character or both and quite rapidly, the narrator has led us into the story's main body of development, complication, and resolution. The story of Naaman the leper in 2 Kings 5:1-14 provides a rather short reach by way of introduction. The essential information is provided in the first five verses and includes some background on the authority and character of Naaman, the compassionate initiative of the Hebrew slave girl, and the directive of the king of Aram. Running the story, the reach of the introduction needs only to set up the situation, recount the initiative of the Hebrew girl, and send Naaman on his journey with the authorization of the king. Many biblical stories involve only a short reach with regard to their introduction. The parables as a genre fall almost entirely in this category. After a brief exposition, we are at the first scene of the body of the story.

In other narratives in Scripture, the reach is long; more material in the story is encompassed in the relatively brief sermon introduction. In some cases, a longer reach is needed simply because there is more material to develop, which is important to the development of the plot. One factor that necessitates a longer reach is encountered when preaching a pericope out of some long narrative in the Hebrew Scripture. It is necessary, then, to pick up a number of highlights to the dramatic story of Joseph's meeting with his brothers in Genesis 45:1-15, ranging all the way back to plot by his brothers in chapter 37. This is not to imply that the actual length of the introduction will be that much more extensive than, say, the introduction to a sermon on Naaman the leper. However, what is at stake here is the need to reach back at times in an introduction when preaching biblical narrative. Other factors that would be brought into consideration in reaching back to tell the story of Joseph in Genesis 45:1-15 pertain to the relative biblical literacy of the congregation and whether the congregation has been following the account through a series of lessons in worship week by week. (The Revised Common Lectionary is not too much help here. The only lesson related to the Joseph story prior to the reading from Genesis 45:1-15 is the previous Sunday when the narrative's beginning in chapter 37 is read.) In settings where the Revised Common Lectionary is followed, the preacher will need to reach back in the introduction to bring some vital information to the listeners before moving on to the material in 45:1-15.

Another need to extend reach in a narrative sermon's introduction moves in the opposite direction. Occasionally, the preacher will need to reach forward to cover a large portion of the narrative discourse in order to arrive at a beginning of the sermon body later in the biblical text. Here, the preacher scans a number of verses dealing with the opening scenes to arrive at the place where the first scene in the sermon will be developed. Reaching forward is often needed in preaching the longer signs in the Fourth Gospel. When dealing with the story of the raising of Lazarus in chapter 11, a daunting fifty-seven verses of narrative confront the preacher. One strategy, then, is to reach forward by encompassing the material from 11:1 to 11:20 in the introduction. The first scene of the sermon itself would then begin with Martha's poignant words, "Lord, if you had been here, my brother would not have died" (11:21). Other literary considerations also make some reaching forward necessary to running the story. In the Gospel of Mark, there are a number of stories that are intercalated within one another. That is, the evangelist begins one story, pauses at a dramatic moment by introducing another story and after completing the second, returns to the first. Mark 5:21-43 is a textbook example of this strategy of intercalation.[84] If the preacher's interest is in preaching the "story in the middle" (the woman with the hemorrhage in 24-34), there may be the need in the introduction to reach forward through the opening section of the pericope dealing with the plea of Jairus to Jesus concerning his daughter. Again, the strategy of reaching forward in the sermon introduction does not necessarily mean that its length is extended significantly. Rather, it is to speak of the extent of the narrative biblical material that is encompassed in the introduction.

The second category pertaining to narrative introductions is that of trim. Here the issue is quite apparent to anyone who has listened to narrative sermons where every possible exegetical piece of information related to the biblical story is crammed into the introduction. The introduction of any sermon is never the place to put a preacher's exegetical prowess on display. And particularly in narrative preaching, the central function of the introduction is to bring the assembly to a place of communal readiness to enter the initial scene of the sermon. Of course, certain background information may be helpful or even essential to the retelling of the narrative scripture. It is a striking experience to visit Caesarea Philippi on a Holy Land tour and learn of the Hellenistic and Roman religiosity of the place—first dedicated to the god Pan in its Greek period and later to a Caesar in its first-century Roman ascendancy. The niches in the face of the rock cliff over the town are a testimony to the statues of the many gods of these Gentiles over this entire span of Caesarea Philippi's existence. That Jesus brings his disciples to a place where human religiosity and idolatry were so amply on display before asking them the question about his own identity—"But who do you say that I am?" (Mark 8:29)—is a valuable insight to be included in any narrative sermon on Peter's confession. But there is always the temptation to add more and more data related to the town in antiquity and to that Holy Land tour last year—the underground rivers, the grotto in the cliff face, the archaeological excavations, even the signs warning of land mines along the road leading up to the site. What is needed here is some application of homiletical trim, choosing data that will help the listeners obtain a fresh hearing of the story. What is not needed is a bloated introduction that begins to sound more like a travelogue than biblical preaching.[85] Trim also comes into play when the biblical narrative itself embodies more elements in its introduction than can be helpful in any one sermon. When preaching on the deliverance across the sea in Exodus 14:1-31, some modest trim may be needful with regard to the introductory account in verses 1-9. The names of the places and some of the repetitive descriptions may be trimmed down with success while retaining the essential information concerning Pharoah and his intentions. In fact, we trim introductory material within biblical stories almost intuitively. We look for important elements that are essential to the story and leave the other material, perhaps to be used in another sermon on another day.

Point of view in literary studies has provided significant perspectives on the dynamics of biblical narrative.[86] We are now used to stories that adopt the point of view of one of the characters as the consistent perspective for engaging in the plot. However, biblical narrative most frequently employs a third-person perspective with an implied author telling the story to us. Within the story as told, however, other points of view come into play. Most every character offers a vantage point for experiencing the story in a similar but different rendition. Notice what happens when the church elects to enter the parable of the good Samaritan from the point of view of a helpful stranger (Luke 10:29-37). Lessons about helpfulness and neighborliness are certain to be the emphases of a sermon on this text that adopts such a point of view. In fact, the church has become quite conditioned to image itself as such a good Samaritan—a perspective certainly beneficial, but not one that is primary to the parable. Rather, with Scott, Funk, Crossan and others,[87] a compelling case can be made that the primary point of view in the parable is that of the listener's solidarity with the man on the Jericho Road who is robbed, beaten, stripped bare, and left helpless alongside the road. Now, the issue becomes that of the awful prospect of being unable to prevent the mercy and grace extended by a hated enemy. This is not to assert that the parable has only one point of view—a sermon could be construed from the perspective of the Samaritan himself. However, we do raise the question of the issues that are at stake among the various points of view offered in the biblical story.

Running the Story and Our Lived Experience

Once we have settled on an introduction that nicely balances the elements of reach, trim, and point of view, we are now ready to invite the congregation into the body of the biblical story. Now a crucial question of contemporization emerges: At what locations within the narrative do we pause and explore our own lived experience with reference to the text? Several alternative strategies commend themselves for relating the narrative text to the world of the hearers, including contemporizing clues, periodic exursuses, the narrative frame, and modern recasting. These strategies are not necessarily mutually exclusive.

1. Contemporizing clues

As the biblical story is told as a narrative sermon, the preacher need not locate references to the contemporary world within separate exursus systems. Rather, the biblical narrative may be salted with contemporary references and analogies as it is retold in the sermon. It is important, however, that these references to contemporary experience be not simply scattered throughout the homily at random, but placed with some precision where they will strengthen analogy. In a sermon on the parable of the dishonest steward (Luke 16:1-9), the introduction began: *We hear Jesus begin the tale. "There was a rich man," he begins. Okay. We all have images that come to mind—limos, a gated residence, corner office on the top floor of a skyscraper. Rich man. And then Jesus continues: he had a steward. And this, too, evokes images that are familiar. (Think "trusted investment counselor" maybe, or a more lowly official in the investment firm.)* These contemporizing clues were not expanded further; the analogies were salted in the introduction as a way of bringing our world within the biblical world. This use of contemporary rephrasing, Eugene Lowry suggests, "has the effect of saying to the listeners, 'This story is close at hand, not remote and hence difficult to comprehend.' "[88]

2. The periodic excursus

If we have performed that surface level structural analysis of the narrative pericope, we are typically confronted with more scenes or lexies than we can possibly employ. The exceptions here may be with regard to most of the parables in the synoptic Gospels. Many of the parables yield a four- or five-scene structure, in which case most every location within the story may be explored for contemporary implications. So, we may chart the scenes of the parable of the lost sheep (Luke 15:1-7) as follows:

1. Sheep get lost. One of the flock has strayed.
2. Leaving the ninety-nine, the odd shepherd goes after the one that is lost. He searches until it is found
3. Finding the one that is lost, he carries it home with rejoicing.
4. Arriving home, he calls family and friends to join in the rejoicing. The one that was lost is found.

Notice that all of these component scenes of the parable offer themselves for contemporization. An excusus can be imagined as a window that the preacher opens at significant places within the biblical narrative. So, for example, in scene 1, the preacher may develop an excursus that speaks of the way in which sheep get lost in our own contemporary ecclesial situation.

Sheep do have a way of getting lost. We seem at times to be in the business of losing sheep. Just fifteen years ago we had one third more members in our denomination than we do right now. Some go up through confirmation class and then just seem to drift away as teenagers. Others stopped coming when the church was having all that controversy, and they never came back. And others are still on the rolls, but you may see them on Christmas Eve now and then. Sheep get lost. All of the time, it seems that losing sheep is our best talent. We have practiced it for years and years.

Each excursus in a narrative sermon is located within some scene or other and develops that scene's single meaning within the lived experience of the listeners. In other, more extensively structured narrative texts, the preacher will need to choose from among the many possible locations for an excursus, eliminating several while going for others. Remaining with the parables of Luke 15, even if the preacher decides to focus only on the "younger son" portion of the parable of the prodigal son, almost every verse provides the opportunity for an excursus to be developed. One possible arrangement of the excursi locates them at the following scenes of the parable:

1. The younger son goes to the far country. It is a place not at all like home.
2. Reduced to the condition of longing to eat the food of the swine, this son comes to his own "far country" of dissolution and despair.
3. But he comes to himself, resolves to return to his father.
4. He rehearses his script—a plan to return to the household as a slave. Is this repentance, or is he still grasping for control?
5. But his father sees him from afar, runs to him, and welcomes him home. The father dishonors himself to honor his child.
6. So look at the party, a celebration for a lost son come home!

In these more extensively structured biblical stories, the preacher will choose from among a number of possible opportunities to put the story on pause, enter into the contemporary world with the single meaning of that location in mind. The single meaning will be explored with examples and analogies from the lived experience of the congregation. Then, the preacher will reenter the biblical story and continue to run the story until all have arrived at the next location at which an excursus will be developed.

In order to achieve this contemporization, several homiletical skills will be brought into play. First, as mentioned above, the preacher will need to put the running narrative on hold as the excursus is introduced. Just as David Buttrick had detected regarding the need for a closure system for a move,[89] so, too, the running narrative needs to be halted before the excursus is explored. With Buttrick, one of the most effective methods for closing off the story is that of reiteration. Arriving at a location selected for an excursus, we may repeat in paraphrase the single meaning that is to be explored. One approach that does not work well, however, is revealed in well-worn pulpit talk, "Just as it was in Jesus' day, so now it is the same for us." The problem here is actually twofold. First, this one statement is not nearly of enough force to lift the listeners out of a well-told running biblical story and locate them in the present-day world. A more firmly established conceptual is needed here, as Buttrick would say. The second issue concerns the weakness of such stereotyped pulpit prose. People have heard such fond language to the point that its force and freshness is long past. Romantic rhetoric may well evoke a fond sense of nostalgia among some in the congregation (while causing negative reactions among others), but these turns of phrases do not work well at the rhetorical level. And while this particular rhetorical tactic no longer functions, it is critical to design an effective point of entry into the contemporizing excursus. One approach that is employed in African American narrative preaching is the use of a first-person illustration by the preacher. As documented in the next chapter, however, there are some essential qualifications to the use of first-person accounts. The story must be representative of the experience of the listeners. It must serve as a window into the larger issues of the life and ministry of the congregation. Also, the story will be in service of the biblical narrative, neither enhancing the preacher as hero nor elevating the preacher as victim.[90]

Finally, this reference to first-person accounts within an excursus raises the issue of balance between any story illustration used as an analogy to the single meaning in the text. There is a temptation to insert stories into excursi that will take over the congregational mind, making it difficult for the listeners to ever return to the further movement of the biblical story. In such cases, we have more of an embolism than an excursus. Story illustrations that become embolisms have a way of becoming the unwarranted text of the sermon no matter what the homiletic method being employed. The principle here is unequivocal: The world of the narrative sermon will be that of the biblical story. If an illustration hijacks the sermon, the intention of biblical narrative preaching is thwarted.[91]

Once the excursus has been completed—and before it enlarges into an embolism—it is now time for the preacher to shift the congregational focus back to the narrative and pick up the movement of the story that was put on hold just prior to the excursus. The relative weight given to the resumption of the biblical story depends upon the degree to which the excursus has captured the congregation. Let's say that we have decided on an excursus in the John 9 narrative of the man born blind after he was healed and responds to questioners that "the man called Jesus" healed him; but as to his whereabouts, he answers, "I do not know" (9:11-12). An excursus here could explore the varieties of persons in our contemporary world whose lives have had something to do with Jesus, but if they were asked, "Where is he now?" they would have to answer, "I do not know." An example system could be shaped in that excursus—examples of types of people who would give that answer. The point of view would be from the congregation looking out to see these representative persons and to hear in each case, "I do not know." Examples could be the "culture Protestant" or "culture Catholic" who was baptized and confirmed, but lives mostly without any reference to the One into whose death and resurrection he or she was baptized. Other examples could be provided depending on the pastoral situation and the church's area of ministry. Reentering the story line of John 9 will be a relatively effortless endeavor. We simply pick up the story at the next scene as the plot thickens and the man born blind is confronted by the Pharisees because it was a sabbath day when Jesus cured him of his blindness. Other excursi may be more heavily weighted with emotional power and will need a more emphatic reentry into the story line of the text. That next scene (9:13-17) concludes with the confession, "He is a prophet" (9:17). An excursus here could focus on Jesus' prophetic act of healing that precisely does not buy into the disciples' "Who sinned . . . ?" kind of thinking. In the excursus here, that sense of parental guilt, which assumes somebody was at fault when a child becomes ill, could be explored. The point of view could be that of looking down at our sick child, *burning up with fever and feeling so awful. And what pops into our head is a bunch of "If only's" pointing to our guilt. "If only I had done this or not done that, my baby would not be lying here so sick."* After exploring how prophet Jesus cuts through such find-the-guilty-one thinking, we will need to reenter the story's next scene at 18-23. Because the excursus has carried more emotional weight, it is more difficult to bring the listeners back into the narrative. The strategy of repetition is useful here. We build a strong entrance into this next scene:

Well, that didn't go over too well, this business about Jesus being a prophet. The very religious people were not satisfied at all by this answer to their interrogation. So now it's off to his parents. Now it's their turn to be on the receiving end of these questions. And the Pharisees are playing hardball. One strike and you're out, out of the community.

Notice that in these four sentences there is not all that much movement into the plot development of this next scene. We stay near the opening of the scene and invite the assembly to focus once more on the story in John 9. What is the lesson here? We will consider the relative emotional weight of each excursus before we shape our reentry system back into the biblical story.

3. The narrative frame

In the interplay between the biblical story and the contemporary world of the hearers, the preacher has available several strategies that frame the narrative with material developed more discursively. This material, the narrative frame, may be needed in certain situations as a prenarrative exploration of some contemporary issues that set up the context for hearing the biblical story. John Holbert remarks that "such a device might be used if the story is unusually rich in its drama or detail—so rich that the hearer might get lost and thereby lose the thread of its significance."[92] Two additional factors may call for a narrative frame at the narrative sermon's opening: particular pastoral considerations and issues within the biblical text. Regarding the first factor, Eugene Lowry speaks of this strategy as "delaying the story" and adds that the pastoral context for the sermon may provide a compelling need for the story's delay.[93] The problem is named and the issue is allowed to gain complication, and only then is the biblical story introduced as a response to the felt discrepancy in the present situation. The second factor—issues within the biblical text—may argue as well for a prenarrative frame. In a sermon on Genesis 12:6-7 titled, "Divine Appearances and Erecting Altars," William Turner opened with a rather discursive exploration of the relationship between places and events.[94] He invites the congregation to consider how it is when there is an event at a certain place where God meets us and both we and that place are transformed. After this opening narrative frame, Turner begins the narrative of Abram's call to leave his kinsfolk and to set out on a journey with God's leading. Another option regarding the use of a narrative frame involves what Lowry terms, "suspending the story." Lowry describes the process as follows:

> [The sermon] will begin inside the text, run into a problem, and hence require the telling of that story to be suspended while another text provides a way out of the dilemma. Once accomplished, the sermonic process moves back to the central text for the completion of the message.[95]

In this approach, the larger biblical story is suspended (internally framed) by turning to another story in Scripture before returning to the primary text. However, the story may be suspended with a more discursive, analytic internal frame instead of another narrative text. At times this momentary suspension of the story is needed in order to provide the listeners with information essential to an adequate understanding of the narrative. The precedent for this internal framing is in biblical narration itself, especially in the Fourth Gospel. One of the most familiar of these Johannine minisuspensions of the story is in the opening scene of the woman at the well, in which we are told, "Jews do not share things in common with Samaritans" (4:9*b*). When preaching biblical narratives, we may from time to time adopt the same tactic as the narrator of the Fourth Gospel—when a need for some essential knowledge is sensed, we pause the story momentarily and provide it. Of course, we may need more than one brief statement at times in order to inform our hearers of some knowledge essential to their understanding of the story at hand.

The other alternative in suspending the story is to frame it at the end with a nonstory tag. There are occasions when some further material is needed as the biblical narrative comes to its conclusion, material perhaps related to personal or communal applications. In other contexts, we may wish to elaborate the intention of the biblical story in a kind of postnarrative rumination. So, for example, the account of the first sea crossing in Mark (4:35-41) ends with the disciples questioning, "Who then is this, that even the wind and the sea obey him?" (4:41). The postnarrative tag in this sermon could be an extended series of musings on this same question, though now within our contemporary context:

"Who is this . . . ?" Good question, isn't it. Who is this Jesus? Lots of answers floating around today—you read about them and hear them proposed all the time, see the answers in the religious art of the day. Jesus? "A Galilean peasant who tried to speak prophetically to power but was executed for his efforts and his body left out for the dogs." Jesus? "A man who modeled his life after the hero-myth of ancient days, of course failing in that goal at the cross." Jesus? "Part of our American pantheon of 'greats,' right up there with Washington, Lincoln, and Martin Luther King Jr." So for us, the same question, isn't it? Who is this Jesus? Oh, before you answer for yourself, look around at that once-chaotic sea with its wind and its waves. Still as a farm pond just now. Maybe he is the Lord.

What will not be effective in a concluding narrative frame is the addition of discursive material that attempts to tell the congregation what the biblical story means. Rather, a postscript tag may provide "a conclusion that focuses the narrative for the congregation."[96] John Holbert adds,

> By *focuses the narrative,* I do not mean "explains" the narrative. The story is not an extended illustration for a point to be made at the sermon's end. After telling a story, the preacher should never lean over the pulpit and say, "Now, for all of you who did not get the point of the story I have just told you, here it is." That sort of tactic is *not* a part of narrative preaching, as I am defining it.[97]

In her sermon, "Springs of Water Welling Up" (pp. 96-100), Marjorie Thompson adds a concluding frame to her narrative telling of John 4. It is instructive to review that concluding frame with Holbert's cautions in mind. Thompson first focuses the narrative by way of summary. She recalls the three strikes the woman had against her ("She was a Samaritan, a woman, and she had a socially unacceptable personal history"). Then, the preacher turns to our situation, much like that of the woman at the well. The narrative is now focused on the listeners. These commonalities are explored in some depth, concluding with our own longing "for a decisive future revelation that will clarify all things." If we have come to the place where we share our own longings and weariness with the Samaritan woman, then the story is reintroduced, except the point of view has shifted. We are now in solidarity with the townspeople who receive the testimony of the woman and who are invited then to "come and see!" At no point in this concluding frame to her narrative sermon, however, does Marjorie Thompson transgress on Holbert's admonition about telling them what the story means. Rather, the initial identity of the woman is reviewed and a shift is made to our shared spiritual situation with her. Finally, we are invited to hear her witness to Christ and the gracious invitation to come and see for ourselves.

Evaluation

Narrative homiletics is best seen as one distinctive movement alongside others, all indicating that the eclipse of biblical narrative is now passing away. Other movements include those of narrative-based ethics, spirituality, educational theory, pastoral counseling, and aspects of liturgical and sacramental theology. Each of these companion movements share their ideological roots in the recovery of biblical narrative and reflect the clear obsolescence of the eighteenth- and nineteenth-century hermeneutics that had hid biblical story right in front of our eyes. That we can now speak of the narrative center of the web of preaching is a testimony to the vigorous emergence of postmodern hermeneutics in general and narrative hermeneutics in particular. Therefore, we may locate narrative homiletic methods alongside other movements having their root in this new, yet richly traditioned interpretative context. Moreover, these movements, although representing different disciplines, continue to enrich and deepen one another's work. For example, the contemporary homiletician is deeply indebted to the liturgical scholarship that has recovered the narrative mode of the eucharistic prayer. Narrative homileticians in particular are indebted to the narrative ethicists who have recovered the interplay between story, vision, and imagery. These sibling movements provide an environment in which insights are derived, shared, and refined. Narrative homiletics does not travel alone.

Among all of the movements shaping the emergence of narrative homiletics, the role of literary criticism remains a dominant influence. The secular literary critics through the middle third of the twentieth century were especially interested in the dynamics of the novel, the short story, poetics, and folktales. The methods developed with regard to these genres were of immediate relevance to the diverse literature of the Bible and with only a brief but necessary delay, biblical critics were soon applying these methods to the literary forms of Scripture. The emergence of narrative biblical criticism in general and more specialized fields of investigation such as parable studies in particular provided the model of interpretation favored by homileticians who began reclaiming preaching's narrative center. Related fields of criticism—including structuralism and specialized studies in metaphor and irony—were also appropriated by biblical scholars and, consequently, those called to preach. The challenge for narrative homiletics, therefore, became the assimilation of this rich and diverse critical literature and the incorporation of these findings into the emergent methodological approaches to preaching biblical narrative. This complex dynamic of critical influence and narrative method in preaching remains lively and productive.

What has emerged at the center of the web of preaching, however, is a chorus of voices, not always singing the same narrative song. Early in the movement now become known as "the new homiletics," preaching as storytelling seemed the featured solo performance. However, other voices joined in the chorus, and storytelling no longer holds center stage. At the level of interpretation, issues related to foundationalist or nonfoundationalist hermeneutics continue to be argued within the narrative location on preaching's web. Also, much debate persists with regard to the question of experience as a resource or goal for the sermon. Several postliberal homileticians have seen most any invocation of the notion of experience within the sermon as a clear indicator that the advocate is really outside an authentic narrative location. Moreover, some of the adherents of a narrative construal of Scripture are in serious disagreement regarding the consequences of choosing either the element of plot or of character as the centerpiece of their theological program. Simply put, the narrative center of preaching's web is in no way a theological sea of tranquillity. Narrative homileticians seem to contest with one another as much as they engage with colleagues who locate themselves quite distinctly outside the narrative camp.

At the level of method itself, the conversation within the narrative center reflects these issues of theology and interpretation, and includes such issues as the ways and means of contemporizing a sermon based on a biblical narrative. Related methodological questions within the narrative community involve strategies for illustration, issues of the rhetoric of narrative preaching, and techniques for framing the narrative and introducing the biblical story.

Although various homiletic approaches to preaching biblical narrative certainly do differ on these questions of method, all would agree about the profound debt that is owed to the narrative tradition within African American preaching. Alternative approaches for running the story, developing contemporizing excursuses, utilizing rhetorical systems that address mind and heart—these and other strategies have been preserved and refined within the African American pulpit. It may well be said that the vitality and effectiveness of narrative preaching movement remains profoundly dependent upon the faithful preaching of the story of Scripture within the African American churches.

There are as well critiques of narrative homiletics originating from those whose stances are located elsewhere on the web of preaching. For example, those who negatively assess postliberal theology and ethics as advocating a retreat from a public engagement of the gospel will likely have similar suspicions about postliberal narrative homiletics. Other critics point to the debates over truth or meaning within narrative hermeneutics and raise a concern over any fully satisfactory outcome of the conversation. A related concern is that of the adequacy of an approach to preaching that appears to jettison the venerable role of the sermonic theme in favor of some notion of homiletic plot.

Finally, other critics note that the stories of Scripture hardly represent a seamless robe of narrative and revelation. We find, to the contrary, a skein of ideologies and competing claims about God, covenant, and world within the biblical story. None of these controversies give sign of an early resolution. Perhaps the scandal at the heart of these criticisms is that narrative homiletics has claimed for itself a position at the center of preaching's web. That assertion in itself makes for quite a target!

Unable to address the entire range of these internal and external issues in this discussion, it may be useful to select one question from among the former and one from the latter. Within the narrative homiletic community, perhaps no issue is as divisive as that of the plot versus character debate. And from outside the narrative homiletic position, we may profit from some exploration of the question of plot and theme using the categories suggested in the hymn, "Blest Be the Tie That Binds":

1. "Fears Within"

One fault line within narrative homiletics emerges at the intersection of biblical interpretation, theological reflection, and method. Clearly, the two most dominant elements in biblical narrative are those of plot and character (with the other elements of setting, tone, narration, and time also remaining essential). There seems to be a fork in the road of narrative interpretation that involves the two central elements—plot or character—privileged and expanded theologically. For those homileticians who favor the former element, the plot of the narrative, there is typically an appeal to the experience of the preacher and the hearer and an easy transition to the movement and structure of the sermon construed as a homiletical plot. The latter position shows more interest in the element of character, especially as the narratives in the Gospels depict, and thereby convey the presence of Jesus Christ to the assembly through the sermon. Those espousing this trajectory—including most centrally Charles Campbell—insist that narrative must never become an end in itself. "Christians are interested in narrative," Campbell argues with Hans Frei, "only because Jesus is what he does and undergoes, not because of anything magical about narrative form per se."[98] Plot, Campbell might argue, can lead to emphasizing the experience of the listener and thereby lead to subjectivity and self-concern that heads away from a focus on the person and work of Jesus Christ. Particularly as evidenced in narrative preaching's interest in the parables, there is the temptation to view ourselves as imitators of Jesus' preaching; Jesus becomes "a *model preacher* rather than the *one preached*."[99] Finally, Campbell argues that an interest in the imagery embodied within biblical narrative may once again focus the preacher more on the techniques of narrative than the presence of Jesus.

The first response by those on the receiving end of these critiques might be to caution against too radical a distinction between a homiletics of plot and of character. David Buttrick reminds liberals and conservatives that too radical a split between the individual and the social dimensions of the Gospels leaves one with either individuals without a world or a world without selves. Similarly, a construal of biblical narrative that emphasizes either plot or character almost to the exclusion of the other has become an abstraction. The narrative will insist on having its characters and its plot; one without the other no longer yields a story. Likewise, the dynamics of narrative in Scripture will not offer the community of faith solely a focus on human experience or on the presence of God and of Jesus. On one hand, it is rather imperial a stance that judges a parable's shaping and turning of our experience as sermonically inappropriate because Christ is not the subject of the preaching. On the other hand, when a narrative text clearly serves to disclose the presence and power of Jesus, it is a distortion of that text's intention to render it homiletically in terms of inward piety and subjective experience.

Finally, the Campbell critique of a consideration of imagery in relation to narrative overlooks the complex role of the image within biblical narrative.[100] Given the long tradition in the church of the spirituality of the icon, can it not be said that imagery has most profoundly the capacity to bring to the worshiper the presence of Jesus? The question is not whether imagery will belong within narrative preaching, but rather in which narrative does the image finds its home and what vision does the image thereby impart?

2. "Fightings Without"

What can we make of a sermon that appears to proceed without benefit of some theme to provide its unity and direction? From a perspective outside the narrative center of the web of preaching, a sermon shaped by a plot but lacking one cohering theme threatens to place the church on a slippery slope possibly into relativism, and certainly into homiletic chaos. Paul Scott Wilson would concur with most narrative homileticians that a "main idea" model of interpretation is now obsolete regarding biblical stories. However, Wilson would most definitely insist that any biblical narrative will yield some limited, appropriate collection of themes and that one task of the preacher is to identify which of that collection will serve the particular sermon that is at hand. If Paul Scott Wilson directs his concern from one side of the web of preaching, David Buttrick would argue from the other that while no narrative in Scripture can ever be reduced to a single theme, each of the moves of the sermon should be able to be articulated as a simple conceptual statement (i.e., as a theme). However, from Buttrick's side, the structure and dynamic of the sermon is provided through a plotting of these moves with an eye toward intention. The unity of the sermon, Buttrick would insist, is a by-product of a carefully shaped sequence of moves intending to form in the consciousness of the listeners. In a similar fashion, narrative preachers are familiar with a way of preaching that is mobile, episodic, and fraught with intention (the plot wants to take us somewhere or show us someone). Therefore, the strategy of running the story is no more dependent on a theme to provide overall unity in preaching than in other narrative forms. Certainly thematic material will be encountered along the way, but it is the action of the characters and the movement of the plot that holds things together. In real preaching in real-life churches, narrative homileticians along with David Buttrick would counter, it is usually a lack of control over point of view and an overdependence on discursive, talk-about material that confuses the listeners. Narrative preaching will not abandon themes along with that conceptual material. However, the sermon will follow along a plot in most cases very much like the plot of the story that is in the Bible in the first place.

Springs of Water Welling Up

Marjorie J. Thompson

John 4:4-42

It all starts off innocently enough. Jesus is thirsty and asks for a drink. If the woman had drawn him water and asked no questions, there would be no story to tell. But the situation invited questions. For all kinds of reasons, this was no ordinary interaction.

First of all, Jesus was a Jew and she a Samaritan. Between them lay a huge cultural rift. With a history dating back seven hundred years, it is small wonder that the woman was startled, even suspicious. Jews considered Samaritans—along with their eating and drinking vessels—to be unclean. The woman naturally assumed that any Jew would disdain her as a religious apostate—morally inferior and ritually impure. The shock and incredulity expressed in her question are quite understandable: "Why would you, a Jew, ask me, a Samaritan, for a drink?"

But their ethnic difference was not the only barrier. The gender divide was equally formidable. One rabbinical law stated that a man was not to talk to a woman in the street, even if it was his own wife! And it was simply unheard of for a rabbi to speak in such a familiar way with a woman in public. Toward the end of the story, we see the disciples more disturbed that Jesus was speaking in public with a woman than that he was conversing with a Samaritan.

Jesus seems oblivious to all such conventions. Fully aware of who she is and who he is, he asks her for a drink from that "unclean vessel," her water jar. (Certainly he gets her attention with that request!) And after her amazed response, he teases her curiosity further by turning the tables on her: "If you only knew what God is offering . . ." Wait a minute; who's offering what here? With magnificent irony that is clear only to Jesus (and to us, of course), the Author and Fountain of Life asks for a simple drink, then says cryptically: "If you only knew who was asking, you would have asked him, and he would have given you living water."

It seems that Jesus perceives some kind of thirst in this woman—a thirst that far exceeds his own, even if she herself is unaware of it. How might Jesus know this woman is thirsty, and what kind of thirst does he perceive? One clue lies in the hour of the day. The blazing heat of high noon was hardly the time most women would undertake the physical rigor of hauling around large, full earthenware jars. No, the hours for drawing water were in the early morning or late afternoon; and these were gathering times for the village women to laugh and natter, share news, and no doubt spread a little gossip.

Our second clue comes a bit later in the story, when Jesus directly intuits this woman's marital history. She had been married five times and now lives with someone to whom she is not married. Even in today's more permissive moral climate, we tend to wonder about the character of a person who's been married more than three times. Apparently three was considered the legitimate limit in Jesus' day. Five husbands were beyond the pale. And in that culture, for a woman to live with a man outside of marriage was about the equivalent of being a prostitute.

Not if you were a prime target of village gossip—if you knew people were snickering and clucking their tongues at you behind your back—you, too, might choose to suffer the intense heat of the day to avoid meeting your peers at a popular watering hole. This woman was no doubt desperately thirsty for personal acceptance and social healing. Yet, like people who have been starving too long, she didn't seem able at first to take in what Jesus offered; indeed, she resisted his words in several ways.

Psychologists know that one of the simplest ways to resist someone's words is not to understand them. The woman does this by seizing on the literal meaning of Jesus' words whenever possible. The first literalism is "living water," which the woman takes to mean flowing or moving water that would be found in a deep well source. "Why the man doesn't even have a bucket. Who does he think he is, a challenger to Jacob himself?" (Jacob, by the way, was a common ancestor for both Jews and Samaritans.) Then, when Jesus reveals a tantalizing bit more about what he means by living water, the woman again grasps at the literal possibilities. If he is talking about some kind of magical water that will quench her thirst permanently, she's game, whatever it is. There were, after all, several reputed magicians wandering around Palestine in those days. She says in effect, "Sure, give me some of your potion so I won't have to get thirsty and trudge out here every day." What a relief it would be not to have to remind herself in this daily trek of what an outcast and loner she is.

At this point, Jesus throws in what seems a complete non sequitur: "Go call your husband." What has that to do with anything? This, I suspect: As soon as the woman asks Jesus for what he is offering—even if she doesn't understand it—Jesus puts his finger precisely on the source of her thirst. The seeds of her social and emotional pain are somehow to be found in her history of serial marriages.

Now a second form of resistance to Jesus' words surfaces. The woman understands him all right. She'll even give him a truthful response—sort of: "I have no husband"—the kind of half-truth that's probably intended to veil a larger truth. This conversation is definitely getting too personal for comfort. But Jesus keeps his light on the sore spot, opening her wound for both of them to see; no healing can occur if the woman tries to hide from the reality of her life. In a quite lovely way, Jesus affirms what truth there is in her response: "What you have said is true." Then he goes on to reveal that he knows her fully: "You have had five husbands, and the one you now have is not your husband."

There is no need for us to hear a cynical or judgmental tone in Jesus' words. While not afraid to confront what needs confronting, he is also, I suspect, genuinely sympathetic. In Jesus' day, only a man had the power to divorce. According to Jewish statutes, a man could divorce his wife for the most trivial reasons, and could effect it merely by saying three times, "I divorce you!" Those laws could not have been much different in Samaria. In traditional cultures, the laws are not so different even today. Who knows why this woman was considered so undesirable a wife? Perhaps she was too feisty, too strong willed. Maybe she asked too many questions. My impression from this story is that this woman had a mind of her own. She certainly doesn't come across as a wallflower with Jesus.

Which brings us to a rather interesting part of the story. How are we to interpret the woman's response when Jesus reveals that he knows her so personally? We all know how vulnerable and embarrassed we can feel when someone seems to be able to see right through us. Wouldn't it be quite natural for the woman to gasp inwardly at the shock of exposure, swallow hard, and then leap nimbly from the uncomfortable realm of personal issues to the safety net of theological argument? "Oh, I see you're a prophet! Well, let me ask you about this burning theological question. Our ancestor worship here, while your people say . . ." Was it a real question, or an evasion?

On the other hand, it is possible that the woman's religious question was indeed real and vital to her. Studies have shown that when people encounter someone with apparent prophetic or clairvoyant abilities, they often ask the big questions of life, those that are the deepest and most perplexing to them. After all, if I've discovered someone who can tell me true things about myself that they have no natural way of knowing, then perhaps they can also give true answers to my deepest religious questions.

Which was it—an evasion of the painful personal realm, or an authentic religious question? We really don't know. Maybe it was a bit of both. What we can see is that Jesus presses no further on personal matters. It is enough for her to know that he knows her—all of her—and yet still respects her enough, accepts her enough, to remain in conversation with her. Indeed, to engage in full theological conversation with her. Here we need to remember that women received no formal religious education in that culture, and were never directly taught by rabbis. Jesus treats her question seriously. Perhaps he is the only man who has ever treated her religious questions seriously.

So Jesus speaks to her of God; of the need to worship God not on this mountain or that, but in spirit and in truth. The place for worship is a heart open to truth. This woman has already learned something about truth. Jesus has helped her to acknowledge fully the truth of her own life. In the process, she has learned more the truth of who Jesus is. He has gone from ethnic Jew to prophet in her sight. Still, all this theology of spirit and truth seems just a little heavy to deal with for now. She responds by saying in effect, "Look, I know the Messiah is coming, and when he does, he'll explain everything we need to know."

Now come the words that will change her life, and through her the life of an entire village: "I who speak to you, I am he." (Actually, the Greek text simply says, "I am," echoing God's words to Moses.) It is as if light cleaves into her partly opened heart. This thirsty Jew who has become an unnerving prophet is now revealed—could it be?—as the Messiah himself.

In the parched landscapes of the southwest, the dryness creates great cracks and fissures in the earth. Torrential rains simply run off, further eroding the land. But a gentle steady rain brings forth green plants that help to heal the eroded soil. Jesus' persistent interaction with this woman is like a steady, gentle rain for her parched soul. And the woman, persistent in her own way, has been able to receive.

Springs of living water are already welling up in this woman of Samaria. How do we know her thirst is assuaged? She, who once went out of her way to avoid public exposure, now runs directly into the middle of town, crying out, "Come and see a man who told me everything I ever did!" Can you hear the townsfolk mutter, "Someone finally told her, and she's crowing about it?" But the sudden transformation of such a reclusive, self-protecting figure seems to have an arresting effect on the villagers. Dear me! Witness to God's truth can come from the most unexpected people. Yes, the townsfolk see something so changed in this woman that they are willing to believe her words enough to go check out Jesus for themselves.

This woman began with three strikes against her: She was a Samaritan, a woman, and she had a socially unacceptable personal history. Jesus' way of relating to her canceled every strike, transcended every human barrier. We will never know her name. But in some way, I think, we know this woman from two millennia past, don't we? Aren't we, each of us in our own way, deeply thirsty for some kind of relational, emotional, spiritual healing— thirsty for a wholeness we can only find in God? Don't we often live more easily at the surface of life, preferring literal understanding to the deeper riches of the spirit? And surely we, too, draw on subtle and devious defenses, sometimes using half-truths to obscure the full reality of our lives from one another and even from God, if we can. Yet at the same time, we also ask our deepest, most authentic questions of God, and sometimes grow weary of trying to understand the answers we seem to be given. Like this woman, I suspect that we, too, wait for the decisive future revelation that will clarify all things, instead of opening our eyes to the Lord at our side in the ordinary events of daily life—events as simple as offering a drink of water. Thank God the risen Christ continues patiently to communicate with us—inviting, challenging, correcting—yearning to transcend every barrier we erect against the healing intimacy of his love.

The woman of Samaria invites us, along with her village companions, to "come and see" the one who knows us as we really are, and still accepts us, still engages us in a living dialogue. We can't just take her word for it, though. Each of us is called to faith out of our own experience of the Lord of life. He won't give you a sales pitch. Neither does the woman of Samaria. Only an invitation: "Come and see!" But if we do respond, then along with those townsfolk of Samaria, now we hear Jesus for ourselves and know that he really is the savior of the world. So come and see.

CHAPTER 3

Narrative Preaching in the African American Tradition

"From the Beginning . . ."

When James Weldon Johnson felt called to put into writing the oral art of African American folk preaching, his first recorded sermon was on the Creation. The story of creation was precisely that, a narrative of creation's early season when God:

> Like a mammy bending over her baby,
> Kneeled down in the dust
> Toiling over a lump of clay
> Till he shaped it in his own image.[1]

There are implications here for both the interpretation of Scripture and the methodology of preaching. In the African American church tradition, it is the biblical story, the narratives of the Hebrew Scriptures and the Gospels, the books of Acts and Revelation, that are the foundation of the faith. Likewise, when an African American congregation considers a pastoral transition, a narrative capacity in preaching is essential. "In black churches, the one who preaches the Word is primarily a storyteller," remarks James H. Love. He adds, "And thus when the black church community invites a minister as pastor, their chief question is: 'Can the Reverend tell the story?' "[2] Therefore, David Buttrick comments:

Many persons have noticed that African American preaching often works out of a large narrative sense. . . . Although the story of the exodus is especially significant to the black community—the paradigmatic narrative of an enslaved people—even the exodus account is held within a wider story, a story that begins in creation and ends in a vision of God's "Holy City."[3]

Preaching in the African American tradition is narrative preaching. It draws upon the stories of Scripture and insists that the preacher both know and tell the story.

To be bold to preach within the African American church—or by the Spirit's leading, to be compelled to preach—is to know the biblical story and, more profound, to be formed by it. If the sermon is to be an event that authentically creates an experience of the Word within the community, that Word must first become internalized within the preacher. Here, the art form of the sermon is dependent upon the spirituality of the preacher along with that preacher's capacity to employ the rhetorical and methodological skills of the black church tradition. Warren Stewart, therefore, observes that preaching "when the Word is internalized by the preacher, becomes a *living* experience first to the preacher and then to those to whom the message is directed."[4] Before the preacher masters the art of telling the story in the congregation, the story must come alive within the preacher's own life; the congregation's experience of the living Word has as a necessary precondition the preacher's ongoing encounter with that same living Word. Stewart states the appropriate sequence as radically as possible: "In order to create an experience with the Word, the preacher must become the Word-incarnate, at least to some degree."[5] Only then can the sermon become an act of creation, not *ex nihilo*, but out of the stories that embody the Word, the personal and communal experience of both preacher and congregation, the rich oral tradition of the African American church, and, of course, the work of the Holy Spirit.

"A People . . ."

Just as the preacher's own experience of the Word is essential to the art of creating the sermon, so, too, is a thorough knowledge of the experience of the listeners. That homiletic empathy is a necessary precondition for any faithful preacher of the gospel, but within the African American church, the preacher will never forget the inherently communal character of the congregation and the factors involved in their personal and communal formation. This caveat almost goes without saying within the African American church, but for European American Christians, such a communal context for preaching may not be discerned because of the individualism present within the majority culture. There is a fit between the biblical witness, with its strong communal fabric and the oral art of preaching within the black church. In fact, the distortion emerges when an individualistic reading is imposed upon texts that address communities and that invite the community to find its home within the narratives of Scripture. The approach to first-person illustrations within the sermon is one readily identifiable location where the respective models of interpretation may be seen. In sermons preached within majority churches, a first-person illustration will normally fail in its intended purpose of supporting some "point" or single meaning. Rather, the first person anecdote will usually result in illustrating the preacher, typically construed as "hero" or (in this age of the triumph of the therapeutic) a "victim." Therefore, homileticians like David Buttrick call for a total ban on first-person illustrations in preaching. The warrant for their use is either in error—they do not function as intended—or wrong-headed—our purpose in using them is not to appear "real" or "authentic" to our listeners. However, David Buttrick's dictum regarding first-person pulpit prose does not extend with the same force within the African American church situation. Two factors must qualify the issue. First, with regard to the person of the preacher in the black church, the symbolic role he or she assumes within the community remains invested with greater authority and honor. Second, the African American preacher will likely not squander that authority and honor with regard to the use of first-person illustrations. Instead of trading on the idiosyncratic, the wise African American preacher will provide personal illustrations that are representative of the community's experience. However, notice that all of the competencies of black preaching involve an art form that is both oral and communal.

"Formed by African and American Experience . . ."

In his excellent essay, "A History of Black Preaching,"[6] Henry Mitchell traces the "fusion" of two cultures that shaped the black preaching tradition. These two streams, one West African and the other Euro-American, both provided essential contributions to the shape of black preaching. From the West African tradition came the strong sense of the communal, the social role of the community's leaders-as-speakers, and the oral tradition of culture upon which generations of preachers were to draw. The communal setting of West African traditional religion, according to Mitchell, made possible the emergence of a black church on American soil. In fact, those communal patterns of West African culture and religion "were a kind of prefabricated *koinonia*, which emerged first as a form of indigenous underground Black church." [7] On the other hand, the formative experience upon American soil of these African peoples was one of slavery, with its brutality and its oppression. No interpretation of the African American preaching tradition can be achieved without pausing to remember those who were torn from their native soil, toiled over American soil, and were buried in it, all the while enduring the horror of slavery. Of course, that horror was then succeeded by generations living with Jim Crow, the normalcy of discrimination, by the persistence of racism in the American national fabric.

At the same time, other aspects of the Euro-American society and religion entered into this process of fusion. The Bible itself is welcomed into the African American community, an acculturation, W. E. B. DuBois noted, resulting in the black church becoming Christian.[8] Other factors contributing to the fusion of the two cultures for Mitchell included the impact of the First Great Awakening and the preaching of George Whitefield. Here, a decisive break was made from the formalistic, cold preaching that preceded it. The First Great Awakening showed African Americans a kind of preaching that appealed to the emotions as well as to the intellect and was passionate to bring the gospel of Christ. Notable, too, was Whitefield's interest in bringing the gospel to all persons of whatever race or station. The two elements came woven together—the appeal to the heart as well as the mind and the appeal to all sorts and conditions of people. Henry Mitchell notes:

> Whitefield preached up and down the Atlantic seaboard, starting in Savannah, where he both preached and founded an orphanage. In the crowds that swarmed his often-outdoor meetings, there were sure to be many Blacks. It is well known that Whitefield's style influenced thousands, in a movement that greatly democratized the pulpits and platforms of the colonies. It included the previously rejected White males without education, White women, and Africans.[9]

In the Great Awakening, an expression of Christian faith that spoke to the whole person touched and attracted African Americans, both by virtue of its appeal to reason and emotion and the message of God's Word to the downtrodden. George Whitefield built a bridge over which the gospel "could travel to a spiritually hungry and brutally oppressed people from Africa."[10]

The American experience of African people, then, was one of all sorts of contradictions and polarizations. The same Savannah, Georgia, that was the site of Whitefield's fervent preaching was also a key port in the slave trade.

The same society that delivered Christian faith to Africans in America also enslaved large portions of that people. Henceforth, there would persist a wedding of African and American in the souls of this people, at once a marriage and a divorce. DuBois himself pondered this binary experience, this "felt two-ness" that led less to a fusion than to a persisting struggle if not war. However, the "dogged persistence" of a people, partly African and partly American, led to "a kind of consciousness that makes for 'creative marginality.' "[11] Evans Crawford speaks of this binary experience as a process of "biformation," or "a shaping of identity, perspective, and expression that flows from being both African and American."[12] Within the medium of this "felt two-ness," the musicality of black preaching took root and grew. But it would be only a half-truth to see African American preaching solely as a product of this biformation. The other side of the coin is that the African American homiletic tradition is one of the most effective and persistent environments within which this biformation continues its highly creative fusion.

"Sang the Word"

One unique gift to the world of this fusion of African and American experience is the tradition of preaching in the black church. It took root and blossomed with an inherent musicality. To study this tradition is to come to appreciate that the conventional elements of homiletic analysis do not provide an adequate grasp of the communal event of this preaching. So Evans Crawford discloses his interpretive stance:

> Instead of the more common homiletical concepts—outline, development, exposition, structure, and so forth—my language will reveal a musical understanding of the way sermons are *heard* and the oral response they awaken in listeners, who in turn are *heard* by the preacher and one another.[13]

We do well to heed Crawford's insight. Any adequate interpretation of the African American preaching tradition, especially one interested in elements of method, will begin by attending its distinctive rhetoric best described as a "homiletical musicality."

Elements of a Homiletical Musicality

As implied by Evans Crawford, the homiletical musicality of African American preaching is much more a duet involving preacher and people than a solo performance. Each of the elements of this art form serves a distinctive role in supporting the dialogue of preacher and listener. Therefore, it is not the case that the dialogical characteristic of black preaching can be construed as one rhetorical element alongside others. Rather, it is a persistent thread that weaves together the various rhetorical devices into one song of the Word. Each of the discrete elements in this homiletic musicality, then, will be assessed with regard to its function in sustaining the dialogue that is black preaching. At the same time, we will keep in mind that the elements of this art form's musicality have as their location a strong communal context within a people of faith biformed as African and American. Olin P. Moyd lists the elements of oral style that constitute this distinctive homiletic musicality:

> Rhetoric, repetition, rhythm, spontaneity, tone, chant, cadence, melody, drama, and epic are distinguishing elements in the African American preaching style.[14]

Our strategy will be to combine some of these elements and break others into subgroupings. We will analyze the elements of style sustaining a homiletic musicality form by focusing on: rhythm, melody and "the hum," call and response, and climax and celebration.

1. Rhythm

William E. Pannell attributes this element to the distinctive manner in which "the emerging African church on American soil . . . blended and formed a new style of communication, a blend of Christian content and African rhythms of speech."[15] While the rhythmic qualities of black preaching are most notable in the performance of various rhetorical systems, those devices Moyd designates as "epics," the traditional sermon in the black tradition rarely loses its rhythmic sense. There is a cadence to black preaching that has to do "with intentional timing in the use of words, phrases, and sentences."[16] Majority culture preaching, for example, may lament that "persons simply do not come to church or Sunday school like they used to." A black preacher, though, may sing that "folk complain that Bible study on Sunday morning is too early, and Bible study on Wednesday evening is too late." Even a word itself may be chosen to exploit its inherent rhythmic character. While it is the case that the wise preacher will heed Henry Mitchell's admonitions regarding the use of a familiar preaching vernacular, precisely this norm allows the preacher to break from it by way of salting the discourse with a "big word" now and then. And most typically, when the big word is injected into the vernacular sermon, it is cued to the hearers by an intensified rhythmic pronunciation. So in a sermon on 1 Thessalonians 5:1-11, we might hear the preacher speak about the day of the Lord coming like a thief in the night (5:2). "Now the theologians have a word for this—es-cha-tol-ogy. Eschatology, they would say . . . all about God's last things in Jesus. But we might answer the theologians that we know about eschatology as well. It has to do with when the roll is called up yonder, and what glories we shall see when we are there."

The rhythmic element in black homiletic musicality, then, may be heard on a micro scale as a phrase or even a word is shaped with "vocal percussiveness," to use Jon Michael Spencer's apt description.[17] The African American preaching tradition described this rhythmic device colloquially as "hitting-a-lick" (a term adopted later on within the idiom of jazz and blues musicians). On a broader scale, a variety of rhythmic variations are achieved in "epics," rhetorical systems designed to move the listeners and evoke a response. For example, Spencer observes that "one of (Martin Luther King Jr.'s) favorite literary "licks" consisted of parallel syntax with similar word endings, which resulted in a rhythmic cadence."[18] So King delivered the following "epic" in his sermon, "The Drum Major Instinct":

> Yes, if you want to say that I was a drum major,
> say that I was a drum major for justice;
> say that I was a drum major for peace;
> I was a drum major for righteousness.[19]

However, the rhythmic expression of black preaching is not limited to literary licks and vocal percussions, it is embodied as well. A number of African American homileticians have drawn attention to the way in which a preacher in the black church will drum out the beat or accentuate the off-beat rhythm of the sermon by tapping on the pulpit. The audible rhythms of the sermon may then be accompanied by a more visible expression as the preacher walks to the beat or gestures the rhythm through other bodily movements such as a nodding of the head or a swaying of the torso. Again, on a Saturday night, these motions may be observed as a crowd listens to a blues or gospel singer or instrumentalist, likewise embodying the rhythms of the song. "It is evident," Spencer notes, "that rhythm is not only heard, it is also observed as the momentum of preaching picks up."[20]

2. Melody and "The Hum"

A worshiper who is new to preaching in the African American tradition will soon notice one distinction that sets this preaching off from that found in most Euro-American churches. There is most likely a tonal quality to the preacher's oral delivery; the sermon almost seems sung. That this remains the case in many, if not most African American churches, testifies to the strength and persistence of an oral tradition having its roots in African soil. Olin P. Moyd identifies tone as one of black preaching's essential elements. Therefore, we may speak of "the African nonmaterial cultural survival that gives the sermon a kind of singing quality." Moyd continues:

> That tone—"tuning up"—or melodic quality in African American preaching gives the sermon a congregational dimension. It is a type of "tuning" that gets the congregation involved, and the sermon is no longer the presentation of the preacher. It is the song of the congregation and the preacher is the lead soloist or the lead singer.[21]

In fact, this intoned quality of preaching in the African American church has become a shorthand way to refer to this preaching tradition in general. It is the worship of a people who hear and participate in "the hum." Evans Crawford, then, is on solid ground when he titles his book of preaching in the African American church, *The Hum*.[22]

The biformation of the black church is readily apparent in the songlike quality of much of its preaching. On one hand, the tonality of black preaching is rooted in the songlike recitals of African storytelling. Moreover, as Spencer notes, "there are also commonalities between the melodic style of black preaching and West African folksinging."[23] On the other hand, the experience of slavery provided the social location for the birth of the spirituals, themselves derived both from African musical idioms and the rhetoric and content of early African American preaching. Spencer helpfully observes that just as in the African storytelling tradition, any recital will rarely be sung throughout. Rather, the storyteller will break into chant that is "a more economical method of declamation."[24] Energy is achieved and along with greater clarity when a chant replaces full-blown song. However, such chant, this intoning of the sermon, nevertheless remains a kind of singing. So, Spencer's analysis of hundreds of sermons preached in traditional African American settings reveals a subtle but sophisticated musicality:

> The principal melodic mode employed by black preachers in their "tuning" is the pentatonic, a scale common to African folk song and traditional black spirituals. From the tonic, the ascending intervals of this scale are a minor third, two major seconds, and another minor third. With a heavy emphasis on the tonic (reciting tone), many of these modern spirituals employ only a portion of the scale . . . (while other sermons) are much more melodically flexible in their use of the entire pentatonic scale.[25]

Fully notated, an epic or rhetorical unit of a sermon in the black church tradition would appear as follows on page 112.[26]

3. Call and Response

There is a sequence inherent within the African American tradition of preaching that moves from the biblical story to that oral event of the sermon by way of dialogue and congregational response. The biblical Word is restored to an acoustical affair in the event of preaching, and, empowered by the Holy Spirit, the experience in the text becomes the experience of the preacher and of the listeners: "The Word that has been received, deciphered, and translated into the common language of the people is to be shared horizontally in dialogue with those to whom the message is directed."[27] The participation of the people is essential to the task of proclamation; there is a necessary "word back" from the people that is crucial in proclaiming the Word. The priesthood of all believers is manifested in this dialogical character of the African American sermon. And since the Word is preached by way of an oral and communal art form that is inherently musical, the word back is also to be understood as belonging to this homiletic musicality. Crawford speaks of this "call and response" as "a striking example of the musical richness of life in Christ [that] is the antiphonal response of the listeners to the preacher in congregations that practice participant proclamation."[28] So the oral event of preaching is bi-directional within the black church tradition, with both call and response sharing in the music. Therefore, it is more accurate to speak of the African American sermon as an antiphon than as a solo.

The dialogical preaching of the African American church is a remarkable liturgical achievement. It is precisely *leitourgia,* the "work of the people" along with the work of the preacher and, of course, the Holy Spirit. However, a number of black homileticians have invited a more nuanced assessment of the sermon as dialogue. They observe that the participation of the listeners can be verbal or nonverbal, cognitive or emotional, "talk back" or "feel back."

You're Not Great by Your Own Might

JON MICHAEL SPENCER

I pressed you to my bos-om and I plant-ed my kiss up-on ya, and I spoke to ya and bade you live. You're not great by your own pow-er. You're not great by your own might. But you're great be-cause I cared for ya.___ You're great be-cause I love ya and gave you my name. I gave you my law to be in your midst, to show you the way of truth and of right-eous-ness.

From *Sacred Symphony: The Chanted Sermon of the Black Preacher* by Jon Michael Spencer. Copyright © 1987 by Greenwood Publishing Group. Reproduced with permission of Greenwood Publishing Group, Inc., Westport, CT.

Moreover, any stereotyping of the verbal response of the congregation should be avoided: "The issue is not necessarily *how* the audience participates, because various congregations within the same cultural group may express their participation in a multitude of ways, depending upon the occasion, the message, and the preacher."[29] What is crucial is to understand that dialogue is at work in the homiletical musicality of African American preaching. However, there are several distinctions that can be made among the varieties of dialogue that occur within these diverse occasions, messages, and preachers. First, Henry Mitchell has observed that the dialogue of the black sermon "may be audible or silent—involving physical or body language and/or mental response."[30] The word back from the listeners may well be audible, drawing on the rich tradition of stock responses such as "well," and "Help 'em Lord." Moreover, the word back may be an answering "new word" drawn from the rhetoric of the biblical text and the sermon itself. For example, in a sermon on the prodigal son (Luke 15:11-32), an African American preacher focused on the older son's way of leaving home and concluded an epic with the line, "but he wouldn't come in." Without missing a beat, the congregation took up the antiphon, becoming somewhat like the chorus in a Greek tragedy!

On the other hand, as Mitchell observes for us, there are nonverbal responses of the congregation as well. Some are bodily actions that fit hand and glove with the verbal antiphons and may include clapping or other embodiments of the antiphonal musicality. On other occasions, the emphasis will be on silent gestures and body language. Evans Crawford speaks of these nonverbal responses as feel back, and suggests that the current trend may well be away from the verbal feed back and more toward this feel-back type of response. If this trend continues, Crawford notes, "then preaching now should not necessarily be geared toward cultivating a return to old patterns, because for some they perhaps have had their day."[31] However, Crawford opts for a strategy of shaping the trend so that audible feedback as well as bodily and emotion feel back have their place in the call-and-response dynamic of the sermon. For one thing, "the preacher needs the laity's 'bold particularity' to remind preachers that they are not gods but persons who themselves need to be spoken to as hearers."[32] One other important role is served by the verbal as well as nonverbal responses of the congregation. Since the dialogue of the sermon is a two-way avenue, as Crawford has noted, it is sometimes the people who are doing the calling and the preacher who may assume the role of the responder. The word back has the capability of shaping the sermonic word by way of intensification (in which the preacher is invited to probe more deeply at a given location) or even redirection. By virtue of a "call" from the people, "the pastor may even redirect the journey of the sermon in response to the people's reactions to the sermon."[33]

4. Climax and Celebration

In the living progression of call and response, both preacher and people finally arrive at celebration, at a "glory hallelujah!" Just as a classical piece of music will move toward a climax and expressive conclusion, so, too, will the sermon. Theologically, as Mitchell insists, the note of grace and celebration needs to be the goal toward which the sermon points because the Word is good news. Given this centrality of the gospel, Mitchell adds, "it should be apparent that the traditional sermons of Protestant orthodoxy have been entirely too judgmental, critical, and characterized by bad news."[34] There is another, anthropological reason for this emphasis on celebration. Once more, Henry Mitchell touches the vital note:

> Knowing that emotion is inescapable, the preacher must weigh each homiletical move for impact or effect, making sure that, so far as is in his or her power, the emotional involvement and suspense ascend progressively, to the final celebration.[35]

Mitchell understands communal celebration as the vehicle in preaching within which the compelling logic of the message is reunited with deep emotion, which only can lead to deep motivation. Hence, he speaks of this fusion of affect and cognition as an *"ecstatic reinforcement* of the truth portrayed and the growth sought."[36] The gospel demands such celebration, human nature needs to rejoice in the truth, and lacking it, the sermon may slide into bad news and scolding.

In order to achieve this finale of celebration, the art of homiletical musicality has a number of riffs and epics at its disposal. Once again, Mitchell is our indispensable guide. He notes that "authentic celebration requires poetic license; the task demands the free flow of joyous emotion."[37] Therefore, the rhetoric of celebration may exhibit more hyperbole than elsewhere in the sermon; its rhetoric may shift to poetry or testimony (from the community and not autobiographical). Such shifts in sermonic rhetoric will also signal closure for the congregation. Here, not much new information is added to what has previously been said. The emphasis now is on achieving the behavioral purpose of the sermon rather than on adding new insights regarding the message itself:

This heightened rhetoric *belongs* at the end, and it is not useful in the more logical and detailed communication in the body of the sermon. Embellished language is more suitable for the expression of deep feeling, or the symbolic projection of those things which surpass understanding. They do not negate reason; they simply go beyond the places we are capable of venturing to with logic.[38]

From such a perspective, the sermon's climax and its celebration are coterminous. They will come finally as the community joins with the preacher in a festive finale.

This exploration of celebration and climax must reflect two qualifications if it is to be fully understood. Cognizant of this homiletical finale in African American preaching, it now needs to be nuanced in order to be fully appreciated (and preached). First, the emphasis on celebration as the sense of the ending should not detract from our noting other occasions of festivity within the body of the sermon. Among James Earl Massey's classic statement of the five main characteristics of the black sermon, his second feature is that "the sermon is festive." While the fifth deals with "a climax of impression."[39] There is a sense in which the black preaching tradition is inherently festive, precisely because of the circumstances the world has piled upon the African American community. Once more, the homiletical interpreters of the tradition assist in understanding this distinctive flavor of festivity. It is a bittersweet flavor, sung in the blues and preached on Sunday: "It majors in the celebrative aspects of faith even as it sings of the troubles nobody knows."[40] Crawford adds concerning this "trouble-glory" fusion:

> festivity comes to preaching more in terms of context than content. It is part of the congregation's orientation, a predisposition that they bring to the hearing of sermons, and provides a heightened sensitivity to the festive element that is already present in biblical stories.[41]

Elements of the festive, then, will be woven within much of the body of the sermon. The preacher and people will journey with the story, for example, taking time to see the ironies in the Pharisees' questioning of the man born blind along with his increasingly skilled apologetics in response (see sermon, "I Was Blind, but Now I See," pp. 145-50). The preacher and the congregation will enjoy these occasions of irony and insight within the sermon. Even if bitter sweet in flavor, the festive note will be heard from time to time throughout the sermon and not just reserved for the celebration at the end.

The second qualification of the norms of celebration and climax extends the previous insight to its fulfillment. Celebration is not only a location, an essential "sense of the ending" of the sermon, it also permeates the entire event of preaching. Particularly called into question is any rigidity regarding the location of the occasion of celebration within the sermon. It may occur almost at any time! So Olin P. Moyd first agrees that "it is true that climax might be the ending portion of the sermon in which phrases and sentences are presented in ascending order in rhetorical forcefulness." However, Moyd extends the argument:

> My position is that ending is not the only point of celebration in "good" traditional African American preaching. If celebration means the ecstatic talking and hearing and involvement in the story, then, in most African American sermons, the celebration is interspersed throughout, with greater intensity toward the end. When the African American preacher engages in narration and storytelling with imagination and glorification at several places throughout the proclamation, the preacher and the audience are drawn into an identification with the biblical characters in the story, and the historical event becomes an existential event. Thus celebration is the natural response.[42]

Hermeneutical Bass Notes

The church asks the question, "Can the Reverend preach the story?" because at its foundation, preaching in the African American tradition construes Scripture as a narrative. As noted earlier, "the story" that is expected of the Reverend is the biblical story, extending in its sweep from creation (see "The Creation" in *God's Trombones*[43]) through to the ascent up Jacob's ladder to the heavenly city (see "Uncle Walsh's Funeral"[44]). As with other forms of narrative hermeneutics, the African American preaching tradition certainly acknowledges all of the other literary forms of Scripture and is comfortable with preaching them all. However, it is the biblical narrative that is the deepest bass note of preaching in the African American church, especially as it is centered in the Exodus and in the ministry, suffering, death, and resurrection of Jesus. The challenge, of course, in any approach to interpretation is to articulate the vehicles through which the biblical Word becomes a Word for the congregation in the event of proclamation. Here, the African American sermon depends on a complex of highly sophisticated elements. Each element supports the other and it is rarely the case that any is absent as the sermon takes shape and is preached. Eugene L. Lowry proposes three elements that

serve a hermeneutical function within African American preaching—
"Word/world juxtaposition, transconscious connection, and biblical narration."[45] We will arrange Lowry's sequence differently, revise his terminology
somewhat, and add two other core elements—the unique role of the preacher
in African American preaching and the importance of the liturgical and sacramental context of preaching. We will begin, however, with the biblical foundation, the centrality of Scripture, of God's story, to the sermon event.

1. The Biblical Foundation

Warren Stewart makes a striking claim regarding the foundations of
preaching: "Hermeneutics in preaching does not begin with the text but with
the Author of the text." And he adds that "the first question that the biblical interpreter must ask is not 'What does this text mean to me?' or 'What
did this text mean when it was originally written?' but *'Who is God?'* "[46]
According to Stewart, the qualities of the Author of Scripture that are most
prominent are: the omnipotence of God; the passion of God for the oppressed
where God comes as a liberator; and God is personal, caring, and self-giving,
best revealed as "warm Personality, intimate Father, and self-giving Son."[47]
Hermeneutics, then, begins with a doctrine of God obviously drawn from
Scripture, yet methodologically prior to the interpretation of any specific
text. Yet this approach in no way diminishes the role of Scripture in African
American preaching; to the contrary, it tunes the ears of preacher and people
to listen for God's Word as Scripture is read and proclaimed. That preaching
will draw on the text of the day in order to proclaim God's Word is more a
norm held in common than an articulated doctrine. Yet most every commentator in and of the African American homiletic scene positions the text at the
heart of the sermon's warrant and authority. These commentators, moreover,
articulate a doctrine of the Word of God that is embodied within the biblical text as well as addressed to the present-day hearers.

We are not likely to read essays, therefore, within the writings of African
American homileticians and preachers suggesting that the Bible is "not that-
which-is-preached."[48] God's Word that created all things is available as a saving, comforting, and liberating Word as the Scriptures are faithfully
proclaimed. Therefore, the entire sweep of the biblical narrative is available
for preaching. The three central qualities of the Author of Scripture do not
exempt portions of the biblical witness (nor an entire Testament). African
American preaching has retained a balanced approach to both Testaments
through a time when Euro-American preachers largely ignored the Hebrew
Scriptures). Rather, the preacher is admonished to preach the whole counsel

of God (Acts 20:27). Even when the majority church ignored the biblical witness to justice and God's passion for the poor and the oppressed, African American preaching "has always striven to incorporate the whole counsel of God, including salvation from sin, but also the hope for freedom, justice, and redemption."[49] God's Word is a biblical Word, revealed centrally in the narratives of Scripture, but offered throughout the whole counsels of God. It is a Word, moreover, that is meant to be experienced in the here and now. Hence, "it is believed by the preacher and the receiving audience, that God speaks a direct word, to a direct audience, for a direct purpose."[50]

2. The Preacher As Hermeneut

This question of the immediacy of the Word as an experienced Word of comfort, of troubling, and of freedom raises the issue of mediation, of the ways in which the ancient text is bridged to the present situation of the hearers. More than any specific church tradition, or even the church's tradition of teaching and interpretation, it is the preacher who mediates the Word. The preacher is not only the interpreter of the Word, but also the one who is placed in a mediating position regarding how the congregation experiences that Word. Put simply, the preacher must experience first what later will be experienced by the congregation. Therefore, Stewart instructs that "the first step in internalizing the Word to be preached begins with the preacher him or herself."[51] Stewart continues:

> The preacher must become intimate with the particular scriptural passage that he or she seeks to interpret. Through *empathic application* the preacher takes on the roles of the different character(s) in the passages or those to whom it was originally directed. The ancient story becomes his or her story.[52]

Perhaps no author has underscored this hermeneutic function of the preacher in first experiencing the text in all its rich saving, consoling, and liberating dimensions more than Henry Mitchell. Beginning with his seminal work, *Black Preaching,* Mitchell has emphasized the importance of the preacher's initial experiencing of the message and experience of the text. There must be an "eyewitness" quality to preaching, Mitchell insists, a sense of immediacy concerning the experience of the event of Scripture. And Mitchell further notes, "one cannot generate a rerun of an experience one has never had personally nor appropriated."[53] This capability to generate a rerun of the biblical experience involves several competencies required of the preacher-as-hermeneut. First, as stated above, the preacher must know the story; that it, there must be a "knowing" of the biblical narrative that extends deeper than the ability to quote chapter and verse. Perhaps the best way to translate this need to know the story is to say that the preacher must find himself or herself as present within the story. Otherwise, the preacher could never come to a service of worship, for example, and announce, "I see Ezekiel ascending to heaven in a chariot of fire!" Second, the preacher must internalize the entire biblical story, including not just favorite and easy texts, but also the challenging and even terrifying ones as well. A frequent expression for this engagement with difficult texts—and with the darkness of present-day experience, as we shall see—is that of "riding the terror." While an African American congregation will expect to be invited to beloved and familiar scenes in preaching again and again, the people will also expect to be taken to unfamiliar places and be provided new and unexpected insights into stories that are so beloved. Third, the preacher's relationship with the text will be neither capricious nor incidental. Rather, there will be a providence that is at work linking *this* particular text with *this* preacher for *this* occasion. As with perhaps no other homiletic tradition, therefore, the call of the preacher—the call of God and the anointing of the Spirit—is of central hermeneutical importance in the African American church. To put the issue in the negative, if the Spirit of God has not led a man or woman to preach on a particular text at a particular occasion, then that person should really refrain from the pulpit until a more providential season.

3. The Congregation As Resource and Need

The lived experience of the congregation is another essential component in the hermeneutical process within the African American church. Once again, it is crucial to echo James Earl Massey's words regarding the communal characteristic of the black sermon. Massey relates this communal characteristic to two central aspects of the sermon—"function and festivity."[54] The former aspect serves to keep the biblical Word focused on the experience of a *people*, their endurance, suffering, and achievements. This function of the sermon, then, will shape the preacher's hearing of the Word of Scripture as the preacher locates himself or herself within the experience of both the gathered congregation and the African American community at large. This communal experience is a rich resource for the preacher as a hermeneutical location. And ironically, the communal experience that first serves as a resource for interpretation is the evil that results in so much suffering. As Frank Thomas observes:

> The existential plight of African American people forced the preacher and the people to move beyond sin, evil, and suffering as primarily intellectual concepts and philosophical categories. African Americans interpreted their experience of slavery, segregation, and racism as evil that was deeply and concretely experienced in their bodies, emotions, and thinking. The reality of evil was seen, felt, heard, and touched.[55]

Here is one clue to the bodily, affective, and emotive quality of preaching in the African American tradition. The Word is directed to a people who have experienced evil and suffering concretely. Evil, as Thomas indicates, has been "felt, heard, touched." On the other hand, this need to reach the bodily and the cognitive level of the hearers also gives African American preaching its distinctive insistence on the connection between grace and celebration. The gospel needs to be experienced as deeply as evil and suffering and not remain at an intellectual level of abstraction. "The assurance of grace," Thomas affirms, "must be seen, tasted, heard, felt, and touched."[56] The congregation's experience, then, is both resource and need for the preacher in the work of interpretation. That lived experience is individual and communal in its ongoing struggle with evil and its encounters with grace. And the evil and grace of the African American experience touch the emotions and the intellect, the body and the soul. The preacher will look to a Word from the Lord that encompasses these spans of human experience. Of course, only a story is capable of spanning these distances.

The communal character of the listeners, the insistence on a lived experience of the biblical message, and the narrative hermeneutic foundation come together for Henry Mitchell in his notion of a transconscious level of communication. A people are drawn into community by a collective, transconscious apprehension of a shared story and a shared tradition. However, in order for communication to be effective at a level where deep cries out to deep, the sermon will need to speak to the whole person and to the whole community. Such address, then, will have a necessary rationality about it; in fact, Mitchell notes, "The very formulation of faith into an utterance capable of being communicated and understood requires language as a tool of *rational* expression."[57] However, transconscious communication must speak to other aspects of the whole person and community as well. There are intuitive and emotive aspects of consciousness that are more the abode of faith than the rational mind itself. Mitchell distinguishes between emotional or intuitive consciousness—that sector of the personality in which faith is born and grows—and the transconsciousness that reaches across the listeners, uniting their contemporary experience and their apprehension of the biblical experience of faith. Both are resources for the preacher. He or she will need to shape his or her language of preaching to reach deep within the soul, touching the emotive and the rational, and rhetoric will need to be spoken to a people who share transconsciously their lived experience and the stories of Scripture. In all of these levels of communication, Mitchell calls for an experiential encounter—"a homiletical plan in which the aim is to offer direct or vicarious encounters with and experiences of truths already fully certified as biblical, coherent, and relevant."[58]

4. The Liturgical Context of Preaching

Often overlooked by outsiders is the powerful role that the entire event of worship plays in African American preaching. Although it is usually not couched in such a way, preaching is a liturgical act within the black church. By that statement, several affirmations are proposed: First, that like the sermon itself, the communities entire service of worship will involve the full range of human experience—the cognitive, the emotive, the sensate, and the bodily. Second, preaching as a liturgical act is demonstrated in the call-and-response pattern of the sermon. The African American event of preaching is as deeply responsorial as an ancient litany of the church; preacher and people both enter into the ritual enactment of the sermon. Third, the sense of call is extended inevitably from preacher to entire worshiping community. That is, as the preacher informs the congregation that the sermon's text and warrant are from God, the people are by extension caught up in the providence of this particular Word from the Lord. The providential sense of the sermon ripples out into the entire service of worship. Melva Costen recaps these themes and captures well this interplay of worship and preaching with the black church:

> The preached word, presented so that it is heard and experienced, allows one to know that "there *is* a way out of no way," and frees worshipers to celebrate this fact with the preacher. The word from the Lord is heard with the ears of one's total being, and it is experienced in the poetic flow of the preacher. The word elicits holistic responses that may begin in the gathered community, and will continue with worshipers as they move into the world.[59]

Costen's term "holistic" is an apt description of faithful preaching within the African American church. It is holistic in its use of Scripture, in its involvement of the preacher in the act of interpretation, and in the experience of the community. Moreover, the sermon is holistic in its relationship to the entire liturgical drama. We may identify several perspectives that function to connect the sermon with the broader liturgical experience. First, since the African American sermon is so rooted in the biblical Word, there is living tissue connecting the reading of Scripture and its proclamation. The connection is likely to extend to other acts of worship that reflect the text—hymns, anthems, special music, and the prayers. Second, there is continuity in the dynamic of call and response that extends out from the sermon to encompass much of worship. Prayer times also will be deeply dialogical, with the congregation feeding back and feeling back to the pastor as she or he prays. The congregation may well share in a dialogue with the choir as a spirited song touches the worshipers' souls. Third, the note of celebration not only is a characteristic of the African American sermon, but also permeates the sequence of liturgical acts as the congregation joins in prayer and praise. In order for worship to be holistic, it must range through the gamut of human emotions as led by the Spirit. Worship will involve "intuition and emotion, as well as logic."[60] Still, the sermon will embody celebration and thereby infuse the rest of the worship with its joy and its grace. Mitchell comments:

> Whole liturgies need to be reconsidered in artistic terms, and this applies especially to the sermon. Although no one should overload the preaching role and expect it to generate miracles, it is a fact that the sermon is the facet of worship over which the minister has the greatest and most direct control. And the acceptability of celebration is more likely to be won here than anywhere else, albeit subtly and by no means in confrontation.[61]

Fourth, the sermon and the rest of the liturgy may intertwine in certain churches and occasions as the call-and-response pattern exploits its musical grounding. "This verbal call-and-response African form can easily evolve into a musical dialogue, sometimes with the aid of a skilled organist or pianist."[62] Finally, there is a special connection between preaching and the observance of the Lord's Supper in most African American church traditions. The preacher is keenly aware of the fulfillment of the worship and solemn celebration in the Holy meal. As William B. McClain notes:

> Preaching is always a very real and central part of the celebration of the Eucharist. In the black church it is, in fact—and by good intention—Word and Sacrament. It is preaching, not meditations or "sermonettes for Christianettes" or merely even short homilies, but the preaching of the Word with preparation and passion. Any pastor of these African American churches needs to know that his or her best sermon of the month ought to be prepared and preached on Communion Sunday![63]

Elements of Homiletical Performance

Biblical scholars and literary critics have identified a persistent quality of narrative texts. There is a sequential movement of the plot, advanced through a series of scenes or *lexies*. Preaching that is narrative in quality will similarly reflect this episodic character, moving from one location to the next in a followable plot. Likewise, a jazz or blues piece will typically involve a statement of the theme followed by a series of variations and complications, leading to a final resolution and celebration. Eugene Lowry relates his explorations into the narrative homiletical plot to his experience as a jazz pianist. Two dominant factors, pain and grace, are expressed at the keyboard, he reflects, through a sequence of complicating motifs and resolutions.[64] Before turning to the homiletical plot, however, we will focus first on the basic unit of the sermon and its design and variations. Described as a "generating unit," "formula," or, with Buttrick, a "move," each of these components of the sermonic plot share a number of distinctive qualities and compositions.

1. The "Unit" of the Sermon Plot

Each formula of the African American sermon is a more or less independent unit of language that is nevertheless located in a narrative sequence and connected thematically to its adjacent units. These formulas also embody specifically biblical, Christian themes and images along with contemporary, worldly examples. And each formula will most probably weave together abstract and conceptual discourse with concrete and image-laden speech. Gerald Davis summarizes these components of the sermonic unit or formula:

> The body of the African American sermon is constructed of independent theme-related formulas. Each unit of the formula develops or retards a secular and sacred tension and moves between abstract and concrete example. Each generated formula is an aspect of the "argument" of the announced theme and advances the discovery and examination of the theme.[65]

Let us notice, then, that these units or formulas are serially ordered; that is, there is a homiletical plot. Each also serves to propel an overall sermon theme through a sequence of alternations, reversals, and restatements. As Henry Mitchell has observed, these units—with Buttrick, he names them "moves"—are the "principal stages of action, like acts of a play."[66] Yet at the same time, according to Davis, there is an independence to each unit and a referential function. Regarding the former trait (its independence), each unit more or less stands on its own, with its own theme, elaboration, inclusion of secular material along with theological reflection, and component rhetorical systems. With regard to the latter (its referential quality), each unit is referential; it is "an intense encapsulation of those techniques and considerations more expansively employed in the performance of the whole sermon."[67] Davis adds, "the referential unit of the African American sermon is an independent narrative unit within the larger sermon performance."[68] The exception to Davis's rule, or at least a significant qualification, is that when the biblical text is fully narrative, the units become less independent (and therefore more dependent on the sermon's plot) and are diminished in their referential character.

The unit or formula is developed through a braiding of conceptual, thematic material with images and examples from the world of the listeners. In this respect as Mitchell has noted, a unit within the body of an African American sermon is constituted much in the way David Buttrick describes a move. There is a single meaning—a theme—that is stated and explored and then imaged out of the lived experience of the congregation. Also intertwined are material from the Scripture and living tradition of the church along with material drawn from the larger, and mostly unbelieving, world. While perhaps not drawn as tightly as the Buttrick specifications, each unit of the sermon will contain conceptual material related to its theme (Davis) or "movement in consciousness" (Mitchell). In a sermon titled "Little Ships" based on Mark 4:35-41, the Reverend Lymon Gaines[69] introduces a new unit in his sermon with the following, Buttrick-like opening system of language:

> Now the ship has a destination. Its destination is to reach the other side. And that's another thing the church should be busy doing—helping people reach the other shore.

As Davis has observed, the narrative unit will have a thematic quality, in this case related to the church/ship serving to carry people across the sea. Once the conceptual has been stated, the preacher is then free to expand on that thematic material, analyzing it from a variety of perspectives, and then imaging it, perhaps with an accompanying rhetorical system. However, it will typically be the case that the conceptual will lead off the unit. Even in a sermon that is narrative in its homiletical plot ("running the story," as Lowry puts it), the theme or conceptual will be provided to the listeners.

Once the conceptual, thematic statement has been provided, the preacher then proceeds to the body of the unit. There will be in most cases an elaboration of the theme, often shaped into a rhetorical system that conveys a sense of meter and rhythm. So, immediately following the opening of the move quoted above, Lymon Gaines continues:

It should bring people to sainthood,
the lost over to the "I'm found" shore,
those who are weak to being strong,
from being unholy to being holy.
The church should always be progressing, moving from the shores of carnality to the shores of spirituality.
It should be in the business of preparing folk to move from time to eternity.
We are pilgrims here on earth; just passing through.

Now while the congregation may experience this formula as a rhythmic set piece, a glance at the lines the Reverend Gaines assembles quickly discloses a variety of metrical lines. Gerald Davis studies this rhetorical system and concludes that "the most important characteristic[s] of the African American sermonic formula are the groups of irrhythmic lines shaped around a core idea."[70] Interestingly, the lines sound regular and rather metrical even though the words do not provide such regularity and meter. However, even though the actual text of the formula is irregular, "like blues performers and rhythm and blues performers," the African American preacher produces "a phrasing structure that to the listener seems regular and consistent."[71] This technique, termed "syllabic increase" by Davis, is "sometimes known as 'worrying' a line, or the elongation of a word through creative syllabization."[72] Through these and other oral techniques, the irrhythmic structure of the formula is conveyed as regular, metered. The effect is one of increasing intensity and emotive impact. And given the conveyed sense of build and intensity, it becomes important to close off the formula by breaking that sense of regularity by a tag line that either shortens the meter or extends it. In either case, the somewhat hypnotic oral beat is intentionally broken at the end. (Notice that Lymon Gaines breaks the set through lines that embody both strategies—two lines extend the number of syllables while the last shortens the beat and thus provides the sense of the ending.)

Within the course of developing the sermonic unit or move, the preacher will turn to the task of evoking what Henry Mitchell refers to as an "eyewitness" stance by the hearers. The preacher will need to supply the details that are both essential to the homiletical plot and crucial to helping the listeners "get aboard and find identity in the action."[73] Davis refers to these "secular" elements within the move as "exemplums." They are "a customary part of the

African American sermon" and share a number of qualities.[74] These mostly shared qualities, Davis lists as follows:

1. Primary concern of exemplum is to anchor, give force and presence to reality;
2. Narrative tense is present perfect, fixing the event in the immediate past;
3. Absence of introductory formulas;
4. Time and place are important markers; and
5. Narrative beginnings frequently marked by change in tone; closure not usually provided within the exemplum.[75]

In the sermon, "Little Ships," Gaines develops a series of "little ships" that church members are tempted to board, but that will not safely transport them to the other shore. These little ships are symbolic of churches within the church revealing that "everybody in the church building is not in the same boat with Jesus." A series of examples is developed that includes this exemplum:

> There is another group we find that makes up a little ship. They are the do-nothings. They are the ones who come along for the ride. They are like the flea and the elephant that walked side by side over the bridge. After crossing, the flea said to the elephant, "Boy, we sure did shake that bridge!" These members ride the wagon while others push. They criticize while others try. They are as light as a feather in the balance, and then cry, "Boy, look what we did!"

While Davis refers to these examples within a sermon unit as the secular component, it is clear from the examples provided by Gaines that they may be drawn from the churchly and the worldly experiences of the congregation. While Gaines's example system concerning the little ships is not composed of fully narrative illustrations, most all of Davis's proposed qualities listed above are to be found. Time and place may seem a bit less clear in the Gaines example, yet those qualities are simply more latent than explicit. The place of the example is in the church building, with an implied, more concrete place being within the hearing of the sermon. The time of the example is an ongoing present in which the kind of sniping and criticizing mentioned in the example are found. Whether developed as a fully narrative illustration or given in an example or example system, the goal is the same—the exemplum "must be recognizable in terms of the quality of the lived experience of African American congregations."[76]

The sermon unit or move, then, is the episode within the sermon plot that is developed with a narrative logic and designed as "movements in consciousness."[77] The unit will articulate and expand upon its theme or conceptual, and there is the possibility that the thematic statement will be shaped into an irrhythmic rhetorical system. As Davis insists, there will be a balance of sacred and secular elements within the unit, the former typically being the principles and their elaboration and the latter being the illustrative material or exemplums. While we may quibble over Davis's terminology, the unit's ability to function as a movement in consciousness is dependent on this interplay of conceptual material and real-life examples and stories. Notice that either the thematic material or the exemplums may be shaped into a formula or rhetorical set whose conveyed sense is rhythmic but whose actual meter is irregular. Not every unit or move will employ a formulaic structure. However, it is more likely that this device will be used when the sermon finally arrives at its celebration. In addition to the formal examples, other devices available to the African American preacher to enhance the lived experience of the unit's theme include various epics, as noted by Olin Moyd. Epics "are citations, roll calling, lines, brief sayings, narratives, and stories regularly employed in preaching to drive home a point or to clinch the theological task of God's action."[78] Other possible epics include reciting lines from a hymn or other poetry, spirituals, and sacred or secular (gospel) songs. While Moyd's listing overlaps somewhat with Davis's construal of the exemplum, the insight is clear. An African American preacher has a wonderfully diverse rhetorical palette as he or she considers the ways in which the Word is to become incarnate within the listeners.

2. The Homiletical Plot

Whether the sermon is based on a story or another type of biblical literature, there will be a plot whose essential quality is narrative. The plot consists of a sequence of units or "scenes" that will lead to celebration by way of complication and resolution. The sermonic plot is serially ordered, a "this" leading naturally and compellingly to a "that." Hence, as Davis puts it, "for the most part, a 'sequence of events' is the sine qua non of the referential formula of the sermon."[79] The individual units that comprise the body of the sermon are designed to be easily followable, a series of episodes that want to effect something within the hearers' consciousness (Mitchell and Buttrick). Hortense Spillers sums up the narrative quality of the African American sermonic plot:

The thrust of the sermon is passional, repeating essentially the rhythms of plot, complication, climax, resolution. The sermon is an oral poetry—not simply an exegetical, theological presentation, but a complete expression of a gamut of emotions whose central form is the narrative and whose end is cathartic release.[80]

Each unit of the sermon's plot, then, will be ordered by the preacher so that the audience will be able to proceed to the next move or scene. Since the fundamental structure of the plot is narrative, a number of genres may be used to advance the plot. Almost every commentator agrees, however, that the plot will finally arrive at a place of celebration. These narrative elements include the following:

A. Narrative location

A story has a location, or some, or many. A prerequisite to having a point of view is the awareness of where you are within the story. Given the complexities of African American narrative preaching, it is the wise preacher who first "locates" the congregation before inviting some point of view or other. Perhaps the congregation this morning is at the sea, with the expanse of water dead ahead and Pharaoh's horsemen and chariots closing in from behind. Perhaps another morning, the congregation finds itself located within Jerusalem as a messenger hastens to tell King David of the battle against the forces of his son Absalom. At an evening service, it may be on the Emmaus road or huddled in a room behind locked doors. In Gaines's sermon "Little Ships," the congregation's place was clear. Their vantage point for considering all of those pathetic little ships as well as the location of their Lord was from within "the old ship of Zion."

Of course, a primary means of providing the congregation's location within the sermon is by the preacher locating himself or herself in relation to the plot and the story. The representative character of the preacher in the African American church provides a unique opportunity for the congregation to experience the story alongside the preacher. There is a tensive and dynamic imaginative play between preacher and people here—an adventure of the Spirit in which the congregation extends permission for the preacher to locate himself or herself somewhere important and take the congregation along. This is the necessary precondition for the dexterity regarding various points of view. "Therefore," Warren Stewart Sr. concludes, "it is not anything new to hear a Black preacher say, 'I saw John on the Isle of Patmos early one Sunday morning,' or 'I was in the Spirit on the Lord's Day.' "[81] Of course, it is a close distance from the homiletical self-locations mentioned by Stewart to an outright character sketch by the preacher.[82] In actually adopting the role of a biblical character or other historical (or fictional) person, the situation shifts somewhat. Now, the congregation becomes an audience as well, and some of the canons of theatre may begin to apply to the sermon.[83]

B. Point of view

One of the abiding virtues of preaching in the black church is the care with which so many preachers shape the focus of the listeners toward the characters and events of the sermon. If narrative location serves to ground the place *from which* the congregation will experience something or someone, the point of view is the distinctive perspective *through which* the experiencing is achieved. Therefore, while running the story, a preacher may well employ gesture and inflection to indicate the point of view for the hearers. A certain character in the story, then, may come to be positioned to the preacher's right hand, while a crowd may be gathered off the left. In one sermon, the older son who stood angrily out in the field while the household rejoiced in the prodigal's return was located to the preacher's left, over in the middle of the chancel. The preacher established that point of view on behalf of the congregation, spoke to them about him, entered into a dialogue with him, and concluded with a rhetorical system about him using the tag line, "But he wouldn't come in." Needing no cues, the congregation picked up on the persistent refrain throughout the formula set. In the sermon "Little Ships," Gaines, while running the story, provides congregational perspectives for viewing the various follies attempted by the little ships. Then he shifts the point of view quite deliberately by adding, "Look at Jesus over there in the hinder part of the ship, lying on the wet deck, asleep on a pillow."

Point of view serves also to modulate the level of emotional intensity within the sermon. How near or far away the image is experienced qualifies its emotive power. David Buttrick employs the camera model of imaging and speaks of focal distance as a way to establish the distance from the congregation's homiletic location toward the experienced person, object, or occurrence.[84] Since the preacher is addressing an emotive and a cognitive consciousness (with Mitchell), the African American sermon will seek to create "an emotional-intellectual experience among those who hear the Word preached."[85] Notice, however, that this is decidedly not to advocate an anti-intellectual emotional experience. The employment of points of view that evoke strong emotional response in every case in the Lymon Gaines sermon, "Little Ships," have their location within units whose thematic statements have been strongly drawn as well. In fact, there is a correlation here. The more

129

intense the emotional quality of the point of view, the more emphatic the conceptual context is likely to be established by the preacher! Among a variety of methods for achieving this control over the emotional aspect experienced Word, this careful use of "focal distance" is of crucial importance. So, in Gaines's sermon, the congregational point of view, as we discovered, is from their location in the big ship with Jesus. Therefore, the point of view toward the follies of those attempting the crossing in the little ships is at some distance emotionally. We look over the water, assess their lack of faith and community, and anticipate the outcome of their attempted voyage:

> You ever wondered what happened to those people who joined your church a few months ago or a year ago? They were a part of those little ships, and when the storms began to rage in their lives, some got lost while others were driven back where they came from.

The emotional distance is established by our narrative distance from those tiny crafts and their passengers. On the other hand, the focal distance portrayed later in the sermon is near at hand, literally within the big boat, as the disciples, too, begin to fear in the face of the storm. Since our narrative location has been established as with those disciples and as among them, their fear is our own. Therefore, all of us disciples are called to the point of view that beholds Jesus asleep in the stern of our big ship:

> Oh my brothers and sisters, a sleeping Christ is not a dead Christ. Though asleep, he forgets not his disciples. When he sleeps, he does not sleep. "He that keeps thee will not slumber," says the Psalm. "Behold, he that keeps Israel neither slumbers nor sleeps." Jesus was in the hinder part of the ship. This is the place for the pilot. Although he was asleep at the helm, he was still in control. Jesus got up and rebuked the storm. He said, "Peace, be still!" And the winds and the waves obeyed his will.

With the other disciples, our focal distance to our Lord is one of intimacy—we are all in the same boat! It is a life or death matter who is in that hinder part of our ship. It is the Lord.

C. Variations on the theme

In a typical jazz performance, the musical theme is stated, embellished, and then improvised through the various instruments in the combo or band. (Finally, the musicians may "bring it all home" in a finale of celebration.) In those cases where the biblical narrative is not exercising a strong control over the homiletic plot, this "variations on a theme" approach is at home equally in a stirring jazz performance or a stirring African American sermon. In the sermon, "there is an initial statement, a motif or core element, in which all of the characteristics of the ideal form of the event are concentrated," observes Gerald Davis.[86] This motif then is explored from various perspectives yielding a plot that progresses yet is experienced as somewhat circular. Just as in the jazz performance, there is a movement forward as each voice explores and expands the theme, so in the African American sermon, the motif is both advanced, yet revisited. There is a repetition in this playing with the motif that is one of the four R's of black preaching, depicted by William B. McClain as "rhetoric, repetition, rhythm, and rest."[87] These elements, Eugene Lowry notes, "are strategic sequencing strategies that serve as cues for delay and anticipation."[88] Important to recognize, however, is that the strategy of repetition as the motif is reinterpreted and expanded is nevertheless a narrative strategy in preaching. It is a feature of oral narration—encountered in the Gospels, for example, in the device of chiastic parallelism—and in the oral tradition of black preaching.

To return to our sermon example, "Little Ships," Gaines is shaping the homiletical plot according to the narrative text of the sea crossing in Mark, yet a closer examination of the sermon discovers that the preacher first establishes that storm motif as early as the introduction and then in the course of the sermon, returns to the context of the storm at two other crucial points. After exploring the varieties of people trying the crossing in the little ships, the storm is imaged to their despair and, for some, their destruction. Then, after the congregation is located in the big ship with Jesus, once more the motif of the storm is developed, this time with an outcome that invites celebration. However, a closer examination of the homiletical plot of "Little Ships" discloses that Gaines has actually presented the motif a third time in the body of the sermon, this time, as the jazz musicians call it, "inside out." This contrapuntal motif is explored as Gaines reflects for the listeners that "before Jesus was in the ship, there was no storm." He continues:

> This reminds me of the words of Jesus when he said, "In me you might have peace, but in the world, you shall have tribulation." If you want the devil to be mad with you, then come on over to the Lord's side.

The motif is presented inside out—if you are having peace in the world, then you are not in the big ship with the Lord! Finally, the repetitions lead to a crescendo, "growing, swelling, until finally bursting into celebration."[89] The motif is finally set aside, its themes are resolved, and the preacher is invited to range freely in celebration.

D. Celebration: "Bringing it home"

"Finally, the motifs are set aside and the musicians lose themselves in a climax of celebration." This apt description of a spirit-filled jazz rendition is immediately applicable to preaching in the African American church as well. James Earl Massey concludes his listing of the five characteristics of the black sermon with this statement: "Finally, black preaching is intended to produce a climax of impression for the hearer."[90] With some exceptions, the sermonic climax and a finale of celebration go together. Olin P. Moyd observes, however, that the sermonic climax/celebration may happen at locations other than the ending. Based on this analysis, he concludes that "the meaning of celebration as climax advanced by my mentors and model preachers must be reexamined and extended."[91] Hence, the primary viewpoint on celebration's necessity in the sermon deals with the trajectory of the homiletical plot. The sequence of motifs is not literally circular in meaning and experience. Rather, it is better to speak of a spiral here. Lowry is on target when he describes the repetitions as "growing, swelling, until finally bursting into celebration." If the motifs have been shaped with a heightening tension and narrative development, then a climax is the natural outcome of this journey with the Word. Being eyewitnesses of the biblical story means that the resolution of the good news occurs both within the text-as-preached and among the listeners-as-participants. Frank A. Thomas therefore states that "the sermon is experiential encounter, to the extent that the Bible is taking place in the midst of congregational life, and the people are included in the unfolding drama."[92] A good jazz rendition explores a sequence of motifs, there is a growing tension in the interplay, and the ensemble finally reaches a climax appropriately described as a celebration. This template applies to the African American sermon with remarkable ease.

There is another perspective on the imperative of celebration in black preaching related to the role and person of the preacher. As in few other homiletical traditions, the preacher is burdened with the vocation of "riding the terror" as the representative of the people and, through his or her divine calling of God. Therefore, a constant refrain of African American homileticians is that the preacher must experience the Word before that experience can come alive for the congregation. Henry Mitchell, who has articulated this principle again and again, puts it directly: "Yet the experientially involving sermon must come from a preacher who has already tasted and experienced the Word of God, and shows a pleasant countenance because of it."[93] In other words, there is an opposite side of the coin to that task of riding the terror, which is knowing the joy of the gospel. If the preacher first tastes and experiences that the Lord is good by living within the Word, then showing "a pleasant countenance" may well be a profound understatement. Perhaps Mitchell would do better to say "show a countenance that radiates the light and fire of the Divine." In either case, that which the preacher first experiences will then become the stuff of the sermon. If the encounter with the Word leaves the preacher with a pleasant countenance, then the congregation, too, may well share in the joy. If the preacher has come to a place where he or she can rejoice, "I have been to the mountaintop," then the congregation may well be invited to rejoice with Martin Luther King Jr.:

> Like anybody I would like to live a long life. Longevity has its place. But I am not concerned about that now. I just want to do God's will. And he's allowed me to go up to the mountaintop. And I've looked over and seen the promised land. I may not get there with you. But I want you to know tonight, that we as a people will get to the promised land. And I'm happy tonight. I'm not worried about anything. I'm not fearing any man. Mine eyes have seen the glory of the coming of the Lord.[94]

The congregation joins with the preacher at the mountaintop, sees the promised land, and a proleptic celebration is the only appropriate outcome of the shared experience of the Word.

With this insistence on the primacy of the preacher's experience of the Word—knowing the joy as well as riding the terror—the role of the African American preacher is inevitably altered. The preacher will facilitate the place of celebration in the sermon in his or her role as "conscious celebrator." Put positively, the preacher's vocation is fulfilled as the listeners are invited to join in the experience of celebration already encountered by the preacher. Put negatively, "your preacher can't preach" means that the preacher does not know the story; it also means that the preacher has not already experienced its good news. Employing the image of baptismal waters, Thomas puts it nicely:

> Therefore, the preacher is the first into the waters of celebration, and invites the congregation to wade in as well. Based upon the preacher's experiential invitation, several accept, and celebration becomes a contagion that spreads until we find many members of the congregation in the waters. Celebration usually will not occur if the preacher/designer/catalyst does not celebrate and wade in first. As we stated earlier, if the preacher does not experience celebration in the preparation and delivery of the sermon, then in all likelihood the people will not experience celebration either.[95]

This "first in the water" mandate to the preacher, then, qualifies the homiletical vocation, the call. The preacher stands before the people as the conscious celebrator. If that calling is to be fulfilled, the sermon will come to a crescendo of celebration. Two kinds of knowing are presupposed in order for this calling to become fulfilled. The preacher will have experienced the good news first, will have waded in the waters of celebration prior to inviting the people to come along into those joyous deeps. Second, the preacher will bring a more practical knowledge of the principles of the sermonic celebration. Both elements are essential.

Frank Thomas has explored the question of the principles of celebration design, concluding that five fundamental guidelines persist: "avoidance of new concepts, contagious conviction, affirmative themes, focus on the theme, and timing of impact."[96] The five elements invite further expansion.

1. Avoidance of new concepts

Frank Thomas says, "New cognitive ideas do not belong in celebration, because it is difficult to celebrate and digest new cognitive truth at the same time."[97] Noting that consciousness cannot simultaneously embrace emotion and process new cognitive information, Thomas cautions the preacher to avoid the temptation of introducing new concepts once celebration has begun. To do so, he notes, is to redirect the congregation back into the main body of the sermon once more. New conceptual material will inevitably "shut down the emotional flow."[98]

2. Contagious conviction

Celebration cannot be manipulated if it is to be authentic good news. There needs to be absolute integrity in the preacher's vocation as the first to wade in the water. With that conviction, the preacher's own celebration becomes contagious, and others are invited in. There needs to be a "gut conviction" that shapes and moves the process of celebration. However, in order for the experience of celebration to infect the congregation, a participatory and intuitive link must exist between preacher and people. Therefore, "with intuitive connection, conviction intensifies and becomes more contagious, until others are infected."[99]

3. Affirmative themes

Examples abound of rhetoric that stirs the emotions by stereotyping others and deriding them and their beliefs or actions. Adolf Hitler, of course, was the twentieth century's most horrible (and perhaps most gifted) representative of this school of vilification and derision. Unfortunately, the model persists—in talk show rants, in our nation's "politics as usual," and, most lamentably, from time to time in the American pulpit. Thomas is on target, therefore, when he cautions that "not all deep feeling and conviction is celebration; some is vicious and mean-spirited."[100] True celebration will be rooted in the great themes of Scripture, which are always affirmative and build up rather than tear down. Love, forgiveness, mercy, healing, grace—these are the themes that authentically give birth to celebration. If there is a word of judgment or helpful criticism, Thomas adds that it belongs earlier in the sermon: "In the final stage of the sermon, there is only room for a genuine and sincere invitation to the healing, forgiving, and reconciling grace of God."[101]

4. Focus on the theme

Within the African American church, Thomas notes, there is "tremendous pressure to close the sermon with a powerful crescendo."[102] Given such pressures, a temptation emerges for the preacher to manipulate a celebration rather than letting it emerge naturally out of the truth of the biblical text and the sermon's theme. That this temptation exists in the first place is a testimony to the enduring expectation of African American congregations that the sermon will finally come to a place rich with emotion and good news. Thomas admonishes preachers, therefore, to do the hard work of mining true celebration from the Word rather than using "tried-and-true celebrative standbys, such as a story of conversion or deathbed healing, or 'taking people by the cross' (the Calvary-Easter narrative)." [103] The hard work of mining celebration is fulfilled when the themes of the sermon come to a climax that erupts in the experience of the good news.

5. Timing of impact

Two habits can defeat true celebration. On one hand, the preacher can give away the sermon's climax prematurely and thereby render null and void any climax of emotion at the sermon's ending. Giving away the suspense prior to the sermonic climax removes the motivation for listening to the remaining material. "At every point in the sermon, the materials should be structured to maintain suspense that moves upward at resolution to celebration."[104] On the other hand, the preacher can introduce issues into the introduction or body or the sermon but leave them unresolved and unexplored. The outcome of this practice is that the hearers will remain focused on those tension-producing issues to the detriment of celebration. The climax of the sermon is its natural unfolding and resolution of the themes presented thorough the body of the sermon: "Unresolved issues create unplanned suspense that breaks down the upward flow and diminishes intensity in celebration."[105] Avoid these two bad habits, Thomas admonishes, and replace them with a seasoned sense of narrative timing, dealing with evil and hurt, yet ordering the sermon to conclude with God's grace notes of good news.

> This means that we take the suspense of the bad news seriously, but underneath the bad news is the melody of the gospel. The bad news hurts, the bad news makes us cry, the bad news gives us grief and agony. But the gospel resolves the suspense, and at the point of celebration, this melody moves from the background to take center stage. Though particular notes and measures may be harsh and discordant in the sermonic symphony, only in celebration does the gospel melody develop into full crescendo, and in that crescendo all doubts are settled and all fear is gone.[106]

Introductions and Conclusions

Introductions: Establishing the Song

The traditions passed down from preacher to preacher in the African American scene admonishes concerning introductions, "start low." Based on what has just been explored regarding climax and celebration, start low may be roughly translated to say, "Preacher, you do not yet have at your sermon's introduction enough development of the theme to undergird celebration, nor have you created a sense of narrative suspense sufficient to be resolved in any kind of homiletical crescendo." However, the introduction of any sermon is crucial to its performance and especially so in the African American tradition. Several functions of the introduction the black church holds in common with most every approach to preaching. First, the preacher will need to speak long enough to be heard. While David Buttrick formally states this principle, it is intuited by most preachers in many ecclesial and ethnic traditions. The days of one statement theme sentences right at the opening of the sermon are mostly in the past. A preacher starts low, inviting the hearers to tune in to his or her voice, a tuning that is needed even when the preacher has a long tenure within the congregation. Also, the introduction functions to gather attention from the many diverse points of view held by the congregation as the sermon begins. In some instances, the preacher will come right out and ask for a hearing, beginning, as it were, with a "Prayer of Humble Access." The introduction to the sermon will serve to invite the listeners to tune in the message; it will also begin the task of focusing congregational attention on the matter at hand.

"The matter at hand" will typically involve one or more of the following elements as an opening gambit: scriptural text and divine sanction for the sermon, personal and communal experience, and sermonic theme.

1. Text and sanction

It will be more likely that the preacher begins with the text. By virtue of the close connection we have seen between the authorization of scriptural warrant and call to preach, the introduction may seek to explain or interpret the rationale for the text of the day rather than begin more immediately from within the text. Both approaches may be found in ample variety within the preaching of the black church. In the sermon "Little Ships," Gaines takes up both tasks in sequence, first by asking for a hearing and then by setting the scene of the biblical story. His first sentences speak of the familiarity of the story of the sea crossing and how it has rooted itself in popular devotion and hymnody. He then petitions, "As popular as the text may be, please allow me this opportunity to try and glean from its fields." This "prayer of humble access" also serves to align the preacher with his or her people. There is a call here that invites a response much as the celebrant's dialogue at the Eucharist invites "Let us give thanks to the Lord our God," with the people ratifying that call as they respond, "It is right to give our thanks and praise." The intimate relationship of textual attribution and divine call to preach, Gerald L. Davis notes, serves "to intensify the nature of the Godly sanction that attends the sermon performance."[107]

2. Personal and communal experience

Second, the preacher may begin with an incident out of his or her personal experience or taken from the congregation's lived experience in the world. Regina Anderson begins a sermon titled "Faithful Mothers: Stewards of the Spirit" by tapping into the cultural experience of the community:

> More often than not, an African American celebrity—whether an athletic hero, Emmy award winner, or recipient of some signal honor—will begin the acceptance remarks by thanking "God and my mama."[108]

Notice that Anderson relates a series of experiences common to the community and to the preacher. The point of view, however, is direct—the congregation is invited to witness the succession of African American celebrities all giving thanks to their mothers. A related tactic is to access the communal experience of the listeners through a first-person example in the introduction. Here, the "currency" extended to the preacher as a representative of both God and the community is traded upon. For this exchange to function, though, the preacher's experience related in the introduction will need to be almost immediately recognized as one shared with the congregation. In one sermon, Bishop Leontine Kelly spoke of her experience as a seven-year-old child sent to explore the hidden recesses of the cellar in her family's parsonage at Calvary Methodist Episcopal Church in Cincinnati, Ohio. The family had discovered that one dark place opened up into a tunnel, a tunnel that was one vital passageway on the Underground Railroad for escaping slaves. Bishop Kelly then proceeds to describe her venture into the tunnel and reflects on that experience in her life.[109] Here, a profound childhood experience is at once recognizable as the community's experience as well. The preacher's experience is also her family's experience, her church's experience, and a core experience that continues to shape the African American people.

3. The theme

A third approach to the introduction is by way of the statement of the sermonic theme. Typically, this statement will be one of the great themes within the African American culture and church tradition.[110] One of these "great themes" is the Providence of God, and we find this thematic statement at the opening of a sermon by Henry Mitchell:

> I want to talk to you this morning about an interesting thing, and I say interesting because in Black culture the Providence of God is far and away the most popular doctrine. Most people might not know that they had a doctrine and certainly there's never been such a thing as a popularity contest about doctrines. But there is no mystery about why this is so popular both in Africa and in Afro-America. This is something I have stumbled upon in recent years and, in fact, am in the process of writing a book about: these doctrines, these affirmations keep people alive.[111]

It is also the case that these approaches to the introduction will frequently intertwine two or more of these opening gambits. The first-person reference is at play in Mitchell's thematic statement, for example, and the invocation of a homiletic "Prayer of Humble Access" offered during an introduction that begins within the text links the Scripture with the person and the vocation of the preacher. In one remarkable introduction, Ella Pearson Mitchell combines most every element surveyed—text, "humble access," personal and communal experience, and thematic statement:

> This morning I invite you to consider these words of Scripture from Luke 7:48, "And he said unto her, 'Thy sins are forgiven.' " Our theme is "God's Call to Reclamation and Restoration." In keeping with the thought of reclamation and restoration, let me share with you the complaint of a man who is desperately in need of restoration, now that he has been reclaimed. I read his appeal on behalf of the African American prison population in a great Christian magazine called "The Other Side." He wrote of the painful plight of African Americans in jail—in the big house. Some of what he said is already well known.[112]

Theme, "humble access," personal and communal experience, and biblical text are intertwined within one well-focused introduction. Within the African American homiletic tradition, the sermon may be introduced by means of one or more of these elements. There is one qualification that must be attached to the strategy of employing a theme-based introduction. Rather rapidly, this discursive element will need to be connected to the text *and* to the lived experience of the listeners. Or, to put it more vividly, the preacher will soon need to shift from "the 'cool' world of stated doctrine to the 'hot' environment of everyday application of doctrine to experience."[113]

The Conclusion: "Bringing It on Home"

Most of what can be said about the conclusion of an African American sermon has already been explored under the category of celebration. The dominant approach to the sense of the ending is that celebration and climax occur together. Henry Mitchell speaks for this majority view when he concludes, "We in African American tradition have cultural roots that demand that a sermon end in a celebration."[114] However, more recently, a strongly argued minority position has emerged, namely, that celebration and climax are not to be construed as synonymous. If celebration means "ecstatic talking and hearing and involvement in the story," Olin Moyd insists, "then, in most African American sermons, the celebration is interspersed throughout, with greater intensity toward the end."[115] Moyd then concludes,

> It is true that climax might be that ending portion of the sermon in which phrases and sentences are presented in ascending order in rhetorical forcefulness. Climax ordinarily means, "the final and highest point or the summary explanation among a number of points in the sermon with significant

intensity." However, this might or might not be the point of highest celebration of the preacher and the audience.[116]

Perhaps James Earl Massey stated the issue in terms that encompass both
positions: "Finally, black preaching is intended to produce a climax of
impression for the hearer."[117]

Whether adopting the stance of the majority with Mitchell or Moyd's
minority position, all would agree that the conclusion embodies certain
virtues and abstains from certain vices. Among the latter, there is a wide-
spread consensus shared among the larger homiletic community as well that
the preacher should not introduce new ideas at the sermon's ending. There
needs to be a rather single-minded and single-hearted focus during the conclusion. Introducing a new idea will most likely deflate the sense of celebration and defuse the ecstatic dialogue between preacher and people. Then,
too, the college of African American homileticians will agree that there
must be some constraint regarding closure at the sermon's ending. Gerald
Davis speaks for a wide range of commentators when he observes that "closure is rarely found at the end of the African American sermon, . . . the sermon's energy carries into a time-space well beyond the limitations imposed
by the performing place and time."[118] Put simply, the sermon's function will
spill out into the arenas of life beyond the doors of the church. On the other
hand, two positive qualities will mark the conclusion of most every sermon.
First, the language of the conclusion will be concrete and immediate. This
is not the time for further argument for a position argued earlier. As a time
of celebration, the language will shift more to the emotive and the rhetorical shape of the language generally will become more cadenced, more reiterative. Second, to the extent that the African American sermon spirals in its
performance and plot (thereby constraining closure), the conclusion will
pick up ideas and images developed earlier in the sermonic body. These
embodied virtues are quite evident in Gaines's conclusion to his sermon
"Little Ships":

Paul tells us, in Acts 27:31 that "Except these abide in the ship, you cannot be saved." It's the ship which is the church, where the Lord brings and
keeps his people in fellowship with Himself by His Spirit and His Word.
It's the ship where we hear the preaching of the Word and partake of the
sacraments. It's the ship where you receive all the promises of God and the
forgiveness of sins. It's the ship where we can be edified, built up, taught
the Word, and strengthened. It's God's training facility for making fishers
of men. This ship has a name. It's called the "Ole Ship of Zion." And Jesus

is its captain. When you look at the ship's records, you'll find that it has landed many a thousand.

Avoiding undo closure is evident in this conclusion—the function of this ending is to locate the hearers onboard the "Ole Ship of Zion," to build them up in faith, and again to extend the promise of glory. The rhetorical system is one of intoned cadence that gives the impression of symmetry, yet is really composed of irregular phrases. The image of the ship is repeated, yet each line picks up yet another subtheme from the sermon. Its force is certainly not limited to the here and now of the worship event. Davis has the last word: "The power of the performance moves well beyond the walls of the auditorium or the church." He adds that the force and value of this performance "may well be carried into the days and weeks following the actual performance as those who experienced the performance, or those who heard reports of the performance, discuss it, evaluate it, and relive it."[119]

Evaluation

African American narrative preaching has so much to commend itself that it is difficult to know where to begin. We may be instructed by the methodology of *Fulfilled in Your Hearing*,[120] which begins its consideration of the ministry of preaching with the assembly, the congregation. Here, it is to be celebrated that a most communal, yet profoundly personal context for interpretation abounds whenever African American Christians gather for prayer and praise and to enter into the dialogue that is proclamation. Henry Mitchell's label for this communal yet personal context is the "transconscious" communication among preacher and people. Evans Crawford's insight into the binary character of the community's experience of the event of proclamation is also instructive. At once African and American, never far from the memory and present experience of suffering yet abounding in hope and joy, this "trouble/glory fusion" is a remarkable location for a listening for the Word of God. The community's experience brings to the preacher both need and resource, woven together by a tradition of ritual action, song, prayer, and preaching. Such a deeply communal context for interpretation and preaching avoids the Scylla of American individualism and the Charybdis of what Edward Farley terms "social-ism" (the hermeneutic that construes institutions as most real and redeemable). The resource of the community, its diversity, its gifts and tradition, and especially its suffering, is essential to the genius of African American preaching. The preacher, then, goes to the text with the community's experience in mind. God's Word will be addressed in a manner that is both profoundly personal and communal.

The second element in the homiletical triad in *Fulfilled in Your Hearing* is the role of Scripture and the nature of biblical interpretation. Here, too, we have an abundance to celebrate within the African American preaching tradition. First, we have noted the centrality that a narrative sense of Scripture has within the African American church. "Can the Reverend tell the story?" is the central question of the congregation. The searched-for response is, "Yes, the Reverend knows the story." Also to be celebrated is the place the biblical text has in the sermon, both regarding its authority that warrants the sermon and its content that gives impetus to the sermon's narrative plot. We have observed the frequently employed protocol within the introduction of an African American sermon whereby the congregation is petitioned to allow the preacher to lay a text before the church for consideration. The implied response of the people is to warrant the use of a particular text. However, both preacher and people are engaged in a ritual that honors the essential role of both and honors God whose authority is reaffirmed each time the ritual is played out. There will be a Word from the Lord that catches up both preacher and people. It will be sung by all.

The role of the preacher is the third element in the homiletic triad. That role assumes several essential competencies. We have already noted the competency regarding a knowledge of the story (both in the megasense of the sweep of the biblical drama from creation to the Day of the Lord and in the microsense of the specific text for the occasion). However, the preacher will also be expected to know his or her people, their joys and triumphs along with their struggles and suffering. Before the preacher can speak from the text and to the life situations of the hearers, there is a need for the preacher first to "ride the terror." Put simply, the African American preacher must have experienced the message before proclaiming it to the people. The sermon will of necessity become a dialogue, involving a call by the preacher and a response by the people. The latter may come by way of vocal and musical feedback or, at a deep soul-level, through congregational feel back. Either way, the event of the sermon will involve a dialogue. The preacher will also be expected to possess and demonstrate competencies related to such rhetorical resources as rhythm, pause, and the hum. (The employment of these elements of African American musicality, however, will vary from congregation to congregation.) And since the normative African American sermon will embody celebration at some point—usually at its ending—the preacher will be capable of authentically inviting this communal catharsis and rejoicing.

There is a similar intensity and passion within the African American preaching tradition with regard to the ample presence of good news as in Paul Scott Wilson's "sermon in four pages." It is to be celebrated that authentic celebration will most likely come to center stage at the sermon's end within the African American sermon.

The question of homiletic method comes into focus at the intersection of the biblical text, the assent and resources of the people, the preacher's own experience of the message, the rich rhetorical tradition, and the liturgical setting. We have noted that commentators on the African American sermon speak of its narrative quality, composed of a series of units or moves leading to celebration. These units in the episodes of the sermon are described in much the same manner as moves within the Buttrick system. There are typically opening and closing systems that establish the meaning or theme of the unit and a variety of strategies for developing the unit's internal material, including exemplums, formulaic structures, and epics. Also noted is the careful way in which biblical and contemporary experience is sharpening through point of view, primarily imaged from the congregation's perspective. Whatever strategies are adopted as the preacher shapes each unit, the entire experience is conceived as a dialogue. There will be a call and some form of response is invited. Finally, in most cases, the sequence of units or moves will culminate in celebration. Frank Thomas's principles for celebration (see pp. 134-36) are rewarding admonitions for any preacher who turns to naming and celebrating grace and he mines them from the rich depository of the African American preaching tradition. These elements of homiletic method are sufficiently diverse to offer the preacher and people a remarkable diversity of strategies for shaping the sermon. Yet the old advice remains the best:

> Start low; go slow,
> Go high; strike fire.
> Sit down.[121]

In the way of cautions and critiques, we may point to one concern within each of our three categories—the congregation, the Scripture, and the preacher. Each of these concerns, ironically, comes into focus precisely by virtue of the amazing strengths of the narrative tradition of preaching in the African American church.

1. The congregation

The communal context of preaching in the black church remains one of its most central, enduring qualities. Thomas speaks of the congregation as resource and as need in the pastor's work of interpretation. The resulting sermon could become unbalanced if the pastor attends only to one or the other of these companion qualities of congregational experience. An all-resource sermon could bypass a theology of the Cross (unlikely given the past and present suffering of the community). More likely might be the temptation to weight the sermon mostly toward congregational need, thereby diminishing the assurance of grace. (Here, the dynamics of celebration remain the needed corrective of any imbalance.) At times dipping more deeply into the congregation as resource and at others ladling up the deep need of the community, the African American preacher will be attentive to both aspects of the lived experience of the people.

2. The Scripture

The concern here emerges out of an appreciation for the vigor and strength of African American narrative hermeneutics. There is a compelling rationale to an approach that grounds all of Scripture in the drama of the biblical story. The underside of this central virtue of interpretation is that other, non-narrative texts may not gain as full a hearing as narrative ones will certainly receive. If distorted in usage, the motto, "Preach the Story" can function more as a principle of Scripture selection, "Find the Story." It is one thing (and a good thing) to affirm the homiletical canon of the African American church as primarily composed of the narratives of Old and New Testaments along with the prophets and the book of Revelation. It would, however, be an impoverishment for the preacher to remain within this canon to the exclusion of other biblical literature.

3. The preacher

There are several capacities expected of the preacher that are essential to the achievement of the African American dialogical sermon. First, the preacher is expected to know the story. At one level, that expectation deals with a thorough knowledge of the biblical narrative from the Creation to Parousia. However, we have been instructed by Henry Mitchell and others that this knowledge of Scripture must be of a biblical kind of knowing—deep, intimate experiencing of the Word. A faithful preacher, Mitchell insists, is one "who has already tasted and experienced the Word of God."[122] That deep experiencing of the Word may, in some cases, call for "riding the terror" while at other times it may be a soul-deep savoring of the joy of the gospel. In any event, the preacher must know the story.

The preacher will also need knowledge of the rich rhetorical tradition of the African American church. To preach the story involves expectations around competencies regarding the use of oral, communal language, the wide variety of epics and exemplums handed down by the tradition, and a freshness of insight into contemporary situations. The challenge comes to the preacher so gifted and immersed in such a tradition regarding possible manipulation. Ironically, it is precisely those preachers and traditions that are most rhetorically sophisticated who have the most temptation to misuse these skills and gifts. It has been interesting to overhear the conversation within the guild of African American preachers regarding the inappropriate as well as effective uses of the rhetorical riches they have inherited. However, the criticism here loses its force if the alternative that is implied is to remain innocent of the ways in which oral, communal language can function and fail in the sermon. Such a critique, directed to David Buttrick as well, assumes that the preacher is relieved of an ethical responsibility for his or her pulpit language if there is an innocence of how that language functions. Both Buttrick and his African American colleagues in homiletics would respond that it is far better to risk the possible misuse that comes with a rhetorical savvy. Attempting to avoid the problem by a studied ignorance of the ways in which language functions in proclamation does not let one off the hook regarding the virtues of the preacher. Far better, then, to ride the terror that comes with such knowledge—whether taught or caught—than to avoid that ride by maintaining an innocence of the rhetoric of preaching.

"I Was Blind, but Now I See"

Maurice J. Nutt, C.Ss.R.

John 9:1-41

This morning we come to a passage in the Scriptures that enables us to have a keen insight on what being a Christian is all about. In John 9, we hear of a man born blind. We hear of a man who doesn't have a name—he is unidentified. I don't know, my brothers and sisters, if you understand the plight of being born blind. Being born blind, that means that you didn't lose your sight. It didn't mean that you lost it gradually, but you never had it in the first place! Never seeing the light of day. Never seeing your parents' faces. Being born in absolute darkness. Not seeing a thing. Scripture tells us that this is the only miracle in the New Testament where someone is healed having been blind from birth.

145

Brothers and sisters, Jesus was going through a town, and the disciples, while walking, noticed this blind man. They knew who the blind man was; they were accustomed to him. They would see him day in and day out, and seeing him there once more, they posed a question to Jesus. Was this man born blind because of a sin he committed or was it the sin of his parents? You see, some of the Jewish people equated suffering, pain, and blindness with sin. If you were born with a disability or an illness, they began to question and say, "Oh, you must have done something wrong!" They began to question and say that he must be living a sinful life or someone in his family, his parents must have lived a sinful life and that's the reason God had cursed him. Jesus made it clear. This man was born blind not because of a prenatal sin, meaning before he was born. How could somebody before they were even born be in sin? How could somebody before they came from their mama's womb know how to reject God the creator, the One who knitted them in their mama's womb? Jesus said, "No, it wasn't his parents' sin or his sin." It's the fact that God wanted His glory to shine. It's that God wanted to be known, as the only one who can heal. So he was born blind—let me break it down for you—he was born blind so that God might restore his sight. He was born blind so that God might bring a miracle into his life and give him the holy wholeness of good health.

You have to go through your trials, you have to experience some tribulations, some hardships, for God to be able truly to deliver you. You see, you have to have a need for deliverance to truly encounter the Deliverer. If everything is going just fine and dandy for you, you have no need for a deliverer. If you had everything going just wonderful for you, God could not move and work in your life. Brothers and sisters, we need someone to deliver us. And in order to call upon someone to deliver us, we need to be delivered from something. Church, I want you to talk to yourself this morning. Say to yourself, "I need to be delivered."

While Jesus was among his disciples, he told them, "While I am in the world, I am the light of the world." The Bible says, "While he said this, he spat on the ground and made mud with his saliva." It was the belief of the Jewish people that the spit of people of influence—teachers, rabbis—contained the essence of their life. I just want to teach for a minute. Jesus took the essence of all that he was and he mixed in that dirt and smeared it in the eyes of the man born blind so that he might see. Jesus told him to go and wash himself in the Pool of Siloam. He went to the Pool of Siloam, which means "sent." Jesus told that man born blind to take himself to the water.

"Go wash yourself in the pool," Jesus said. The man born blind went and washed himself in the Pool and was able to see.

You know, Christians, we often say that we've got to go to the water. We ask the questions, "Have you been to the water?" "Have you been baptized?" "Have you been down to the Jordan stream?" He sent him to the water and once you go to the water—I wonder if I got a witness? Once you have been to the water, I don't care what you went in with, you're going to come out different. You're going to come out changed! This man born blind came back able to see!

You know, brothers and sisters, everybody don't rejoice in your blessings. Everyone in town knew of this man sitting on the side of the road begging. They said, "Isn't that the one who was born blind?" "Is that not he?" Some said, "I think it is." They looked at him real good and said, "I think it might be him." "The last time I saw him, he couldn't see and now he has his eyes wide open." You know, brothers and sisters, people don't like us to change. People don't like us to gain a blessing. There are some folks who know you well and will not rejoice in your blessings. The Pharisees began to ask what happened to him. So they brought him to the Pharisees and he told them that a man they called Jesus took some mud and smeared it on his eyes. He told them that he was blind but now he could see. The Pharisees told him that this man must not be from God because he performed this "work" on a Sabbath day. You know that we can get so caught up in rules and regulations that we miss our blessings!

A man not able to see has received his sight and there is no rejoicing about it, there's just persecution. Now that his sight was restored people began to judge and question him. They continued to interrogate him. They asked the man born blind, now able to see, "What do you have to say about him since he opened your eyes?" He said, "He's a prophet." If you really want to find out what someone really thinks, you ask a blessed person! If you want the true truth, you find someone who has met Jesus by the cleansing of their sins, some-one who has been delivered, someone who has been brought out of sickness and pain. If you really want a true testimony, this healed man said, "You don't really want to know what I think; because I'm going to tell you what I think. This man is a prophet!"

The Pharisees did not believe that he had been born blind, so they said, "We're not going to ask him any more questions." The Pharisees said that they were going to summon his parents. They brought forth the man's mama and daddy and asked, "Is this your son?" They answered, "Yes." They asked if he was born blind and they answered, "Yes, he was blind at birth. Now he is able to see, but who healed him we have no idea." They agreed that this was their son and they knew that if they said anything more they would be kicked out of the synagogue. So they said that they were not going to answer directly. "Our son is old enough to speak for himself," they said, "ask him." So a second time they questioned him. They told him to give glory to God and give praise to God. They said that Jesus was a sinner. The man born blind said, "If he is a sinner, I do not know. I am not here to judge. But one thing I do know. Before I met this man named Jesus, before he changed and set me free, I was lost and living in darkness. I've got only one thing to say to you. This one thing do I know—I was born blind, but now I can see."

Now the Pharisees kept questioning the man born blind such that he finally shot back, "I believe that you want to become one of his disciples too. You keep questioning me about this Savior named Jesus. You keep interrogating me about who he is. Is it that you want to follow him, too?" You know, there are a lot of people who will persecute you for following the Lord. They will put you down for going to church every Sunday. But then, let something happen in their lives, you will be the very first person they call to lift them up in prayer. They will call on a Christian and ask what keeps you so faith-filled. What is it that helps you out of your burden and despair? What is it that you've got and I don't have? They want to know what you know and whom you know! You know that it is your deep faith that keeps you steadfast in following the Lord. And so they came to him again. They said that they followed Moses because they know that God spoke to Moses, they do not know where this Jesus came from. But this blind man knew God's Word. He didn't know much about theology or philosophy; he didn't know how to argue, and he wasn't great in debate. But he said "I know this much, a sinful man could not have done for me what Jesus had done."

Church, if we look at Job when he was speaking of the hypocrite, he said, "Will God hear his cry when trouble comes before him?" And the psalmist David said, in Psalm 66, "If I had cherished iniquity in my heart, the Lord would not have listened" (v. 18). The Word from Ezekiel says, "though they cry in my [ears] with a loud voice, I will not listen to them" (8:18). Jesus was not a sinner because he could not have performed this miracle. God would not have heard his prayer. For those who live in righteousness, the Word says, "The eyes of the Lord are on the righteous, and his ears are open to their cry" (Psalm 34:15). David also sings, "He fulfills the desire of all who fear him, he also hears their cry, and saves them" (Psalm 145:19). Proverbs instructs that "the Lord is far from the wicked, but he hears the prayer of the righteous" (15:29). Through our scripture reading this morning, I believe that there is a new definition of being a Christian: "I was blind, but now I see." Christians are those who come to a place in life where they do not want to live on in blindness.

The Pharisees got so upset with the healed man that they told him he had to worship their God and he let them know that he was going to worship the One that did something for him. They kept verbally abusing him until he couldn't take it any more. You know, sometimes folks will get on your last nerves! It is a shame that there was no rejoicing with the now-healed man. He told them that Jesus was not a sinner but a healer, and the Pharisees got so mad that they bodily threw the healed man out of the synagogue.

The blessing is found in our next verse. When you are cast out . . . (come on now, you didn't hear me). When you are cast out, . . . when you are kicked out, . . . when you are put out, . . . What did the Word say? "Jesus hearing that he had been expelled, he came looking for him." Church, when you have been put out, God will bring you in. When you have been left out and kept out. . . . (Have you ever been put out? Do you know what it means to be rejected?) There's a song that says, "If he has to reach way down, Jesus will pick you up." And he picked this man born blind up and asked him, "Do you believe in the Son of Man?" And the man answered, "Well, who is he so that I might believe in him?" When someone does something so wonderful and great for you, you don't have to ask for any further qualification about that person. Jesus told him, "You are looking at him." And all of a sudden that man began to worship Jesus!

You see, worship and praise are for a purpose. If you come here every Sunday and don't have a purpose, you are not authentically praising God. If there is no reason for your praise, you are not giving God all the honor and glory. Praise in its sincerest form means because of God's goodness, virtue, and deeds, I have cause to praise him. The healed man could have said, "I can see now that the One who did something for me, the One who turned my life around, the One who changed the way I used to be, and gave me new vision and insights is indeed a prophet." Praise has a purpose.

Jesus said, "I have come to divide the world." Those who think they see really don't see. And those who are blind and are in need of me shall see. It is only when we are able to confess our blindness and our need for deliverance that we are healed. A man born in darkness—who never thought he would see the light of day—was made to see. I pray that we stop making excuses and confess our need for a savior. And yet, this scripture verse, in my mind, is not yet complete. People had beaten this once blind man down and they had interrogated him. They brought his Mama and Daddy in. They had kicked him out of the synagogue. They doubted him. They did not celebrate with him. One thing is missing. I don't know that if two thousand years later, if anyone ever celebrated with the blind man but who now can see. I wonder if he ever had a victory party to celebrate what God had done for him? I think this man deserves his just due, don't you? I think we ought to celebrate what God has done for this blind man. He never ever had a party. We don't know if he ever celebrated with his friends. So I would like to issue an invitation right now: "The pastor and saints of this church request the honor of your presence. We cordially invite you to a victory party. We cordially welcome you to celebrate with a man born blind in the ninth chapter of the Gospel of John." He never had a party to celebrate the goodness of God in his life. It's never too late to praise God for what He has done. It's never too late to lift up praise for this healed man. Brother, you're not alone any more! We recognize God's goodness with you. So let's get this party started as we stand up from our seats and praise God by singing, "I'm so glad Jesus has lifted me." If you have not rejoiced for what the Lord has done for you in this life, this is your party, too! Amen. (Music, dancing, and rejoicing)

CHAPTER 4

Moves and Structures: The Homiletics of David Buttrick

Hermeneutics

The assumptions about interpretation do not remain hidden very long. Our hermeneutics can be flushed out quite easily. Watch a collection of preachers gathered for a workshop on their trade, having come to an event perhaps entitled "Breaking Open the Word." The preachers assemble, registration is completed and "Hello I'm ———" nametags have been filled out and affixed. David Buttrick is the guest facilitator for the event and he means to get to the hermeneutic assumptions in short order. He distributes a sheet of paper with a biblical story printed out, perhaps one of the familiar Gospel lessons about Jesus. "OK," Buttrick begins, "it's coming up on Sunday and here is the text we have decided to preach, or we bump into this text in the lectionary for the coming Sunday." Then, the teacher asks his students this question: "Now what is there about this story that we spot as preachable?" He adds, "I'll just jot down your findings on this newsprint over here."

Now assume that the printed-out narrative being studied by the preachers is Luke's story of the paralytic in 5:17-26. Watch what happens next. There is a brief pause and then one participant speaks up: "The text is about forgiveness. Jesus says to the man, 'Your sins are forgiven.' " Soon, other phrases are added on the newsprint: "Stand up and walk," "Helpful friends," "The power to heal," "Giving God the glory." One colleague speaks up and notes that she would preach on the feelings the paralyzed man has as he is being

151

lowered down from the roof and how we feel like that when we are in situations we cannot control. Her colleagues murmur in assent. "Fine," Buttrick mutters, looking at the list on the newsprint. "But watch what has happened. We have treated the story of the paralytic and Jesus as a still life painting, and we have assumed that we can take one component of the whole composition, extract it from the scene, and reduce the painting's meaning to just this one part." Buttrick then turns to the gathered preachers and says, "Now we did not invent this hermeneutic of distillation. It's been around since the Enlightenment. Problem is, we have taken a wonderfully rich story and reduced its meaning to a thematic of some sort. Distilled out some topic that sounds an awful lot like a sermon title, and that is what we will now preach on Sunday. But look what has happened. We have just eliminated the story's form, its plot and characters, and its movement in our hearing. What biblical scholar today would agree with us that meaning can be detached from the form of a piece of Scripture? No one." And so begins the workshop on preaching with the revealing title of "Breaking Open the Text."

While the workshop's participants are trying to recover from this traumatic challenge to their models of interpretation, we have time to expand more fully on David Buttrick's critique of the hermeneutic of distillation. The assumptions underlying this reflexive approach to preaching biblical texts are easily spotted:

1. That content can be separated from words.
2. That content can be translated from one time-language to another without alteration.
3. That such content can be grasped as an objective truth apart from particular datable words.[1]

The result is like a kind of shell game, Buttrick argues, in which preachers search for a (usually) propositional truth within a text, a kernel within a shell. Problem here is this: "If we toss aside the first-century context as a shell, we then reduce Christian faith to a series of propositional truths (in *our* language) so that it is no longer what the New Testament means by faith at all."[2] Actually, there are several versions of this shell game approach to the meaning of a biblical text, different ways to construe just what kind of kernel the preacher is supposed to be after in the first place. Our hermeneutic of distillation, after all, looks for several things it wants to distill from the text. While the hermeneutic assumptions remain constant, interpreters have sought for a variety of kernels hidden beneath the shell of the text.

The hermeneutic of distillation, Buttrick instructs, will usually manifest itself within one of several models of interpretation—a rationalist model in which the hidden kennel under the text is some sort of ideational payoff (a main idea, for example); an experiential model in which contemporary human experience is paralleled with that of persons in Bible times; or a model locating a perennial faith experience as the element held in common between our own age and that of the Scriptures.[3] The distinguishing characteristics of these alternative models as well as the core assumptions they hold in common are perhaps best seen in modern parable interpretation. Over the span of the preceding century, the dominant approach to ascertaining the meaning of a parable with reference to preaching has been Adolf Jülicher's dictum that a parable must have one and only one main idea.[4] Offered a parable for analysis, our group of preachers mentioned earlier would most likely begin the quest for a main idea, though all of the shell game models Buttrick identified would come into play. Consider the parable of the talents in Matthew 25:14-30, for example. Each of the positions first assumes the parable itself to be a shell under which a (different) kernel of meaning is to be found. While the main idea adherents have detected any number of main ideas—which in itself is somewhat ironic—the conventional homiletic wisdom around the fall stewardship season is that the parable is about using our talents, the gifts God had entrusted to each of us. In this take on the parable's main idea, the story itself becomes an illustration from the gospels of Paul's message concerning spiritual gifts in 1 Corinthians 12:1-11. So we see church signs amidst the fall foliage with sermon titles like "Using All of Our Talents" and "Even You Have a Talent!" Those committed to finding experiential kernels under the shell of the parable may write sermons entitled "How Anxiety Keeps You from Sharing." And preachers fond of the kernel of a perennial faith might jot down a homily that speaks of the risk of faith, perhaps quoting extensively from Bultmann and Tillich.

A collection of pitfalls lie in wait for every interpreter who plays a shell game with a biblical text.[5] For those whose quest is for an ideational payoff, a rational proposition underlying the text, initially Buttrick notes this: "The beauty of a distilled topic is that you have no decisions relating to the scope of the text and, in addition, no exegetical homework."[6] Furthermore, as Buttrick noted earlier, meaning is inseparable from form and context; it cannot be exported from one culture to another, from one language to another yet remain the same. Take the conventional pulpit wisdom regarding the parable of the talents. Typically overlooked in the search for a main idea about "Christian money management" or some other theme-based approach are such considerations as the grandiosity of the entrusted monies in the first place. A talent, according to Bernard Brandon Scott, was a silver coin weighing in at about sixty pounds and was equal to six thousand denarii.[7] Even the one-talent fellow was entrusted with mind-boggling abundance! Overlooked as well by the distillers of topics is the way that the parable's plot brings the audience to a location where they must decide on the truthfulness of the third servant's image of the master. Is he such a harsh taskmaster? If so, how, we might ask, are the first two servants able to risk such immense riches with creativity and freedom? But, we only arrive at such a question by following along with the parable, entering its narrative world. In any event, it rapidly becomes apparent that the parables do not yield single truths or teachings.

The parables of Jesus, Buttrick concludes, "were systems of language characterized by movement that could work transformations in the consciousness of the listeners."[8] The statement is carefully drawn here; each term projects the preacher further away from the old hermeneutics of distillation and toward a postcritical approach to preaching. We shall look at them in turn.

1. Systems of Language

With the advent of literary-critical approaches to Scripture, we have come to discover the Bible as a remarkably diverse collection of literary forms: narratives, parables, poetry, epistolary writings, prophetic poetry and prose, Wisdom sayings, apocalyptic, just to point at some of the more obvious. Each of these systems embodies its own grammar, its own logic within which its meaning and intention are disclosed. Therefore, the rationalist shell game of looking for a distilled thematic as the text's payoff errs in several ways. First, the shell game errs by its inattentiveness to the distinctive language of the text, the structured way in which it generates meaning and understanding. Form is not simply ornamental and the structure of a text cannot be separated from its meaning! Second, the shell game makes the fatal assumption that meaning lurks somehow behind the text—in its main idea or perhaps in a perennial human experience—rather than in the structured system of its enactment. As a corollary at this point, Buttrick notes that while much has been gained through the historical-critical method, "it is nevertheless the case that preachers do not preach *about* the Bible, they declare the gospel *of* the Bible."[9] Third, the shell game fails in its selectivity—the interpreter is drawn to a verse or perhaps only a phrase within the biblical pericope. If meaning and intention are functions of a component literary form, then isolating one fragment of that unit renders its meaning ambiguous or worse. Texts are systems of structured language designed to function in accordance with the protocols of the particular literary form. Bypass that form to get behind the text or to break the text open and its function is rendered null and void.

2. *Characterized by Movement*

There is a sequential movement within the structure of a biblical text. A narrative text, for example, will embody a series of scenes or locations that assemble into a plot. David Buttrick likens this episodic quality of a text's movement to the way a filmstrip projects now this, then that picture onto the screen. (We are not speaking here of a random series of images derived from a jumbled collection on a slide projector carousel.) The elements that comprise a text's movement, put simply, include the sequential series of single meanings together forming a plot. In narrative texts, obviously, a narrative plot is the result of this intentional sequence of scenes. Returning to the parables for an example, the barren fig tree in Luke 13:6-9, we may spot quite readily its plot and component scenes:

A. "A man had a fig tree planted in his vineyard; and he came looking for fruit on it and found none.
B. "So he said to the gardener, 'See here! For three years I have come looking for fruit on this fig tree, and still I find none. Cut it down! Why should it be wasting the soil?'
C. "He replied, 'Sir, let it alone for one more year, until I dig around it and put manure on it. If it bears fruit next year, well and good; but if not, you can cut it down.' "

As Buttrick observes following a similar exercise in spotting the surface structure of a biblical text, "We have here a language intending toward and intending to do."[10] As a number of parables scholars have observed, the vineyard image introduces the ecclesial context for the parable; throughout the Hebrew Scriptures, "vineyard" is a metaphor for Israel, for the covenant people. The first two scenes (A and B) comprise a unit—the owner of the vineyard comes seeking fruit from a fig tree planted there. For a third year now, the fig tree remains barren. The response is final and understandable. "Cut it down" announces the owner of the vineyard. What follows in C is surprising and constitutes a reversal of authority and, potentially, of outcome. The vinedresser responds, "Sir, let it alone." The verb is forceful and multivalent, connoting not only sending away, but perhaps forgiving as well. Then, the gardener announces his own program, again through forceful verbs—he will "dig" *(skapsō)* and will "throw" *(balō)* dung around the fig tree. Whether through simply leaving alone the barren tree or forgiving it, the owner of the vineyard recedes from the story. Actively in charge is the lowly gardener, caring for the tree with intensity and persistence. Of course, Luke's theology of the year of the Lord's favor echoes at this point, adding urgency to the demand for fruitfulness. But for now, the fig tree will receive this undeserved care in hope of a future fruitfulness.

By way of such a surface analysis of the structure of the passage, the parable's plot is discerned and its intentions are discovered. The hearers are first invited to share in the worldview of the owner of the vineyard: Barrenness is not to be tolerated but "cut down." Notice also regarding point of view that the perceived barrenness is at some distance. How close does the owner need to advance to detect an absence of figs? The theological foundation of the world of the owner is one we are invited initially to affirm and claim as our own. A lack of fruitfulness within the community of faith is to be identified, indicted, and judged. And since our point of view has become that of the owner, we locate ourselves alongside the judgment seat of authority and power. The profound reversal calls all of the above into question. A gardener speaking with authority, a closing of the distance to the offending fig tree (digging and throwing are rather hands-on activities) and an obvious compassion for the fig tree irrespective of its dismal performance. Invited into this vinedresser's world of grace, we are invited as well to abandon the worldview of the owner and adopt another best described as the kingdom of God. Moreover, our point of view after the reversal remains somewhat destabilized. On one hand, we are invited to come near in compassion and caring to this barren fig tree; on the other hand, we might even risk now an identification of ourselves with the tree and its barrenness. Throughout the structure of the parable, then, a sequence of episodes is designed that anticipate reversal and relocation. We may speak of these outcomes as the intention of the pericope. And once again, extracting any theme or main idea to turn into a rationalistic sermon violates the plotted intentionality of the parable. Only by way of the parable's plotted logic does its intention emerge with force and with invitation.[11]

3. In the Consciousness of the Hearers

For Buttrick it is crucial for preachers to comprehend how the consciousness functions within biblical texts. Among the central characteristics of Buttrick's category of consciousness, several qualities are repeatedly rehearsed for the preacher. The consciousness within which biblical texts intend their performance is communal rather than individual, is dual in encompassing both the world of Scripture and the world outside the biblical narrative, and is subject to profound shifts and alterations. With regard to the communal nature of the hermeneutic context of consciousness, Buttrick asserts (rightly) that "virtually everything in scripture is written to a faith-community, usually in the style of communal address."[12] Conversely, "texts do *not* address individuals in individual self-awareness."[13] David Buttrick devotes considerable energy to advancing this insight. He is aware that with "the triumph of the therapeutic," preachers are most likely to twist the biblical text's communal language into a personal, even private language for the believer-in-isolation. He notes, to the contrary, that most texts in Scripture use a communal form of address to the hearers—the majority of the "you's" encountered in the Bible "should rightly be translated into 'Southern' as 'you all's.' "[14]

A second quality of the consciousness reflected in Scripture, in addition to its communal character, is its double nature. By this duality, Buttrick means that biblical texts address a consciousness "of being-saved in the world."[15] Perhaps "binary" becomes a better term to describe the relationship between the consciousness of being-saved in community and worldly consciousness that comes so easily to mind. By binary, we mean that neither of the two polarities is dispensable; they remain held together in tension. Listen to Buttrick's description of this tension of the two aspects of consciousness addressed by the text:

> Thus texts addressed to double consciousness cannot properly be truncated so as to speak either of humans in human awareness or to the saved in a one-sided consciousness of being-saved. We are a bifocal people and biblical language speaks to our bifocal consciousness. Therefore, it will be inappropriate to interpret the Bible through some available secular hermeneutic such as Jungian psychology or capitalist ideology. . . . On the other hand, a so-called holy hermeneutic may be equally devastating, and obscure the sweet complex earthiness of many, many biblical texts.[16]

One implication of this need to hold in tension the two forms of consciousness as we interpret Scripture is that, as we encounter texts that appear to address more one than the other, most always that other is implied. This bifocal consciousness is implied even in texts that appear unequivocally churchly or worldly. We note, for example, that in the miracle of the loaves and fish in John 6—one of the few events in Jesus' ministry shared by all four Gospels prior to his passion, death, and resurrection—a sign is provided regarding Jesus' identity as the new

Moses and as Son of God. Also implied in the narrative is our capacity to rightly see the hungry poor who lack even those meager gifts of barley loaves and fish. Buttrick concludes: "We are suggesting that scripture be read by double consciousness—a consciousness of being in the world and a consciousness of being-*saved* in the world."[17]

A most important third aspect of Buttrick's notion of consciousness is that it does not remain fixed. We do not share in the worldview and language that shaped a first-century biblical consciousness. At a macrolevel, we can speak of an entire age as sharing in a common consciousness, for example, "the medieval European age." That distinctive human consciousness endured for long centuries before breaking up at the time of the Reformation and the Renaissance. Our particular location is at the breakup of another age with its enduring consciousness—that of the Enlightenment with its rationalistic anthropology and its Cartesian dualism of subjective and objective realities. When we look at these eras such as our own (a between-the-times kind of place), among all of the symptoms of the breakup of culture and social consciousness, a dramatic shift in language is perhaps most obvious. It may not be precise, however, to speak of these profound shifts in language as only a symptom of the shift in social consciousness. When language undergoes some major dislocation, the structures of consciousness inevitably will undergo change as well. Noting that worldviews are embodied in language, Buttrick asks, "So what's going on in the world today?" Answer: "Why, a whole wide world is changing its mind."[18]

Preaching during such times that are changing is a vocation fraught with challenge. Given the linguistic component of these shifts in human consciousness, the problem of the language for preaching is more critical now than any time since the Enlightenment.[19] Just within the last half-century, for example, our social vernacular has lost easily more than one third of the words that were in common usage well into the twentieth century. Moreover, language has now begun to enlarge once more, our consciousness being shaped these days by new words that are more imagistic and metaphorical as well as more technical. We are called to preach at a most interesting time, when the language that shapes a world in consciousness is in rapid, profound change. Again, Buttrick states the challenge: "We must find a way to preach in a world that is changing its mind."[20]

Structures and Moments of Consciousness

We do not move directly from text to sermon, at least not within the homiletic of David Buttrick. If his notion of consciousness functions in the ways we have traced, then personal and communal consciousness becomes the essential middle term between the text and then sermon. Additionally, preaching itself serves a mediating function, and its mediation has much to do with the structures of consciousness within which the sermon is embodied. Therefore, Buttrick concludes:

> Preaching, we have said, is mediation. Preaching mediates some structured understanding in consciousness to a congregation. Therefore, preaching is speaking related to *understanding.* The language of preaching will tend to imitate phases of understanding in consciousness.[21]

In order to grasp the ubiquitous hermeneutic role that is played by human consciousness in preaching, Buttrick suggests three component phases or "moments" of consciousness that in turn mediate the event of preaching. The three moments include the modes of immediacy, of reflection, and of praxis. Before we explore each in its distinctiveness, however, it is important to recall what all three stages hold in common. First, all of the moments will mediate some structured location in consciousness. The biblical text will be read or heard within one of these structured fields of understanding. The sermon itself will likewise be located within one (or more) of these modes of consciousness. The particular method, and language, of the sermon will intend toward one of these moments in the communal consciousness of the hearers. Finally, the congregation will hear the passage of Scripture in contemporary consciousness and not with a past-tense "far away and long ago" point of view.[22]

Immediacy

In the mode of immediacy, the field of understanding evoked by the biblical text becomes for the preacher the moment in consciousness within which the sermon will be preached. Again recalling the mobility and sequential quality of most biblical texts, the sermon can be plotted rather immediately to conform to the text's own plotted intentionality. So, for example, given our analysis of the plot and intention of the parable of the barren fig tree, a sermon could be shaped that follows the same trajectory. The sermon could move first through the field of understanding represented by the owner and then in a shift in consciousness to the field of understanding reflected by the vinedresser. A homiletic plot, then, may well follow the order of the scenes in the parable with little alteration in order that the parable's "intending to do in consciousness" is faithfully rendered in our preaching.[23] However, the preacher is not constrained to follow the actual sequence of plotted structure in the pericope. Some rearrangement may be necessary for several reasons, including issues of rhetorical clarity. However, what happens in sermons that operate in the mode of immediacy is "that passages are allowed to exert their *intentional* power on congregational consciousness."[24] A sermon imitating the performative intention of the parable of the barren fig tree may be designed with the following sequence:

A. There is barrenness in the vineyard. God's people are bearing little in the way of fruitfulness. Oh, we were put in the vineyard to be fruitful. Look around at the church, though. Barrenness in the vineyard, that's what you see.

B. Faced with all this lack of fruit, it's natural to hear the words, "Cut it down!" A familiar response here: see a lack of fruitfulness and you want to cut it down. We do it with each other; do it with ourselves.

C. Then comes the surprise—a word of grace comes to God's people. "Let it stand," the voice insists. Look, undeserved clemency, that's what we are getting here. A new season for becoming fruitful, for becoming God's people of abundance.

D. Now comes the conditions of this new season—caring, encouraging, disciplined love—all designed to build us up in Christ, bearing much fruit. Then, too, we are as much gardeners as we are fig trees. So we turn to each other with the same loving care.

E. Still, there is an end to this new season of grace. God will have a people of fruitfulness. "If after a year . . ." comes the warning, "if after a year . . ." What a gift, this season of grace! But will God find us fruitful at its end? Maybe we should start bearing fruit pleasing to God this very day.

Preaching within the mode of immediacy, then, is marked by several distinctive characteristics. First, this mode assumes a prior analysis of the surface-level movement and structure of the biblical passage. There is an "intending to do" in consciousness that is disclosed by an alert, informed attention to the pericope's plot. While the parables and other biblical stories yield their plotted attention through a narrative kind of "logic," Buttrick is quick to add that other literary forms of Scripture have their own distinctive plotted language, also "intending to do" in consciousness. Put simply, we may preach in the mode of immediacy in a variety of literary forms and are not restricted only to such obvious narrative forms as the parables. Second, the preacher is now provided with the opportunity to design a homiletic plot that evokes immediate consciousness: "the design of the sermon will travel as a series of responses to the text in which analogies of understanding form."[25] Consequently, in our mode of immediacy plotting of the barren fig tree, the location or move related to the dynamic of cutting down any perceived barrenness may evoke a number of analogies within the lived experience of the congregation. For example, in a sermon on this text, I imaged the "Cut it down" move with reference to a classmate of my daughter (then in elementary school). Daughter Catherine came home quite worried about her friend, a lovely, bright child. "I'm just a big fat pig," the friend had proclaimed. In spite of arguments to the contrary, that ugly self-image remained. "Isn't it strange," I said in the sermon, "when we feel a terrible barrenness deep down inside, we cut ourselves down."

What occurs when preaching in the mode of immediacy, then, is that the intentional force of the biblical text is replicated in the consciousness of the hearers. Essential to the achievement is a keen assessment of the text's plot and intending to do along with a skill in shaping a homiletical plot that will travel in consciousness and imitate the text's intentionality. Also essential is the alignment of a series of moves that may flow quite naturally in the hearer's communal consciousness. Moves that do not follow naturally as thought progress easily from this-now-to-that will defeat the ability to follow the sermon's plot and render any intending to do null and void. Buttrick notes that the moves comprising a sermon's plot, in whatever mode, will follow each other quite easily if read in sequence.[26]

Reflection

Another form that consciousness takes is that of reflection. Here, the situation implies some distance from the text; we are, Buttrick notes, "standing back" or "considering."[27] This distance means that we are no longer conforming our sermon's structure and movement to the structure and movement of the text. Therefore, several distinctive characteristics mark preaching in the mode of reflectivity and distinguish it from the mode of immediacy:

1. "We are considering a field of meaning in consciousness configured by the text or situation."
2. "We may be extending the field of meaning to cover (better, overlay) areas of experience, forming by analogy ever-wider connections."
3. "We now tend to view our structured understanding in terms of an objectified model of ourselves in the world."[28]

These distinctions of the mode of reflection are best understood as we shape a homiletic plot related to (but not based immediately upon) another text of Scripture, in this case, Mark 9:33-37. Here, the situation involves an argument among the disciples, with Mark interjecting that they were in a dispute over who was the greatest. Perceiving this debate, Jesus announces: "Whoever wants to be first must be last of all and servant [*diakonos* here, and not *doulos*] of all" (9:35). Then, taking a child, putting it in their midst and taking it in his arms, Jesus then adds, "Whoever welcomes one such child in my name welcomes me, and whoever welcomes me welcomes not me but the one who sent me" (9:37). Given that the image of a child is central to the intent of the passage, it is noteworthy that "child" already has literal and metaphorical meanings in the text. Literally, a collection of first-century Jewish men discussing greatness among them would have an implied least-ness ascribed to women and especially to children. The figurative use of child was already present in the Septuagint's translation of Isaiah 53:2 and functioned as the equivalent of the suffering servant. Within the New Testament community, the term "child" had also come to be associated with those new to the faith and of fragile faith. Hospitality, it seems, cannot be extended to Jesus without also being extended as well to those like the child who are "last of all." A sermon operating in the mode of reflection may consider this pericope and plot the following moves:

A. "Who is the greatest?" the argument goes. The disciples argue about greatness. Of course, not much has changed. God's people strive for position, with one another and with the world. "We're number one" is a game we Christians still play.

B. And the rule of the game is this: You know when you're at the top when you hang around with all the other VIP's, the in-crowd. Maybe that's why our church leaders like to get invited to the White House, why we feel so good when a celebrity "gets religion."

C. Now listen to Jesus' words—"last of all," "servant of all." And worst of all, there is that child the Lord puts there in the middle of the those squabbling disciples. For those Jewish men, it was to be shamed to have this much to do with children. And Jesus adds: "Whoever welcomes one such child welcomes me." What a strange way to become great—become a servant and welcome those who are least!

D. Now comes the question for those of us who really do like children. The question goes like this: Just who, now, is Jesus going
to take and embrace and put in our midst and say, "Whoever
welcomes this one welcomes me"? We should know by now that
it will certainly *not* be one of the in-crowd. No, it will be one of
the "outs" that Jesus will embrace and put in our midst and say
"Welcome me, welcome this little one."

E. So maybe it's time to put away this arguing, and bickering
about greatness. Servants, that's who we are. And how about
this, let's surprise Jesus by welcoming these little ones now. Of
course, do that and we'll welcome Jesus too.

Notice in this sermon related to Mark 9:33-37, the structure and sequence
of the passage are not determinative of its actual plot. We have picked up segments of the Markan text, but several of the moves (B and E particularly)
function as reflective moments in congregational consciousness. "The movement of a sermon in the reflective mode of consciousness is movement around
a structured field of meaning," Buttrick observes, "a moving from one contemporary meaning to another."[29] In the case of our sermon on Mark 9:33-
37, that structured field of meaning is one of surprised reversal in which the
world's notions of greatness and insignificance are turned upside down. (The
sermon plot builds in the surprise of this reversal and then turns the tables,
inviting the congregation to "surprise" Jesus!) This text functions much like
the parable of the good Samaritan with regard to reversal and point of view.
It is always the hearers who are reversed and who are subjects of the dynamics of the reign of God. Therefore, the careful preacher will not select from
among the hearers' list of "most favored victims," that is, invite a liberal congregation to receive a homosexual person or an evangelical community
receive a poor, persecuted Chinese Christian. No, just as with good
Samaritan, the field of understanding is always reversed for the hearers.
Therefore, sermons preached in the mode of reflection "may differ according
to the fields of lived experience that we align with structured meaning in
consciousness."[30]

Praxis

One set-piece sermon pattern can be found most frequently in the evangelistic preaching of, for example, Billy Graham. The pattern begins with
some aspect of the world's fallen state, usually an issue of heightened social
consciousness, whether crime, drugs, and violence; unwed mothers and

fathers; or the evils of gambling. Typically, the next stage in the sermon, following some in-depth analysis of the problem or topic, is to lift up some portion of Scripture as God's response and answer to the crisis. Following an exposition of that biblical response, a concluding section will follow, in which the hearers are invited to turn from the worldly, fallen state of affairs and live out the gospel. The difficulty with this sermon strategy, for Buttrick, is that it will be both artificial and misleading to apply some scriptural text immediately to a contemporary problem. The issue here is that the preacher has developed the problem within a worldly hermeneutic and then applied a biblical text. "Worldly readings of situations" Buttrick cautions, "will invariably lead us to wrong scriptural analogues."[31] He continues:

> Instead, we move from a situation to a structured field of meaning which may or may not recall scripture. Thus, we do not turn from a situation to the immediacy of scriptural language without moving through reflective consciousness. And, of course, we may not think our way back to a particular scripture at all.[32]

That we may not think our way back to a particular Scripture at all may well be off-putting to many preachers. Therefore, we will need to sketch out Buttrick's understanding of preaching in the mode of praxis with some precision.

The mode of praxis emerges as a moment in personal and communal consciousness when consensus has broken down and inherited solutions no longer functioning in a changed context. In more "normal" times, we tend to act out of a prereflective approach—"This is the way we do thus-and-so"—or out of a postreflection as these usual ways of acting are simply reenacted. Take, for example, the issue of the decline in membership in the formerly mainline denominations. A congregation may somewhat oddly continue its activities and belief system shaped during the 1940s and 1950s through decades of subsequent decline without much of any significant alteration. We may say that their prereflective habits have not undergone much change and their postreflection consists of simply reenacting "what we've always done here." (Even more oddly, we may notice that for some extended period of decline, the congregation and the denominational hierarchy will actually intensify its prereflective habits and postreflective enactings!) The mode of praxis emerges when the situation intensifies to the point that people begin to question their identities. This questioning may begin at the same time that commitments to outworn habits and solutions remain strong. Put simply, the conflict between the worldly way of thinking and that of the being-saved community has become intense. And when issues of identity are raised in such a conflicted context—when the community deeply questions what it should do—it turns "to search memory for some 'light' in which to walk."[33] The mode in consciousness Buttrick labels "praxis," then, involves the following moments:

1. We read a situation in which a worldly hermeneutic has raised the question of our in-action lives.
2. We take the situation into a Christian hermeneutical consciousness between symbols of revelation and our awareness of being-saved in the world.
3. Within the Christian hermeneutic we search for an analogous field of meaning through which we may view our situation.[34]

It is that second moment in consciousness that is crucial for Christian preaching in the mode of consciousness. Again, given the tendency to assume the fix of the situation is susceptible to a worldly logic, true praxis is thwarted if the situation is not relocated to what Buttrick refers to as a "Christian hermeneutical consciousness."[35] Also, we note with Buttrick that the turn to this "Christian hermeneutical consciousness" may not involve a turn to any particular text of Scripture. Rather, the turn is to a structured field of meaning shaped by Scripture and perhaps "built into memory by preaching."[36] However, for Buttrick, preaching in the mode of praxis will neither begin, "My text for today is . . ." nor develop a contemporary problem and then respond, "The Bible says. . . ."

In place of a problem-solution pattern to the sermon, then, in the mode of praxis, an analysis of the problem will force the preacher and people into a different location where the worldly construal of the issue is left behind. Here, within the Christian hermeneutical consciousness, the issue is, as it were, reframed and the story and living symbol Jesus Christ recalled. What then remains within the mode of praxis is for a theological structure of meaning to be articulated within which the situation is viewed. (Buttrick adds that this latter process normally proceeds on the basis of a structural similarity between the problem and the theological field of meaning.) A sermon structured within the mode of praxis and speaking to the issue of addiction, to select a prevalent pastoral concern, may follow Buttrick's sequence through a series of moves:

A. There's one place where the world is of two minds—addiction. Name whichever one you want, you always get a mixed message. Take the cigarette industry and its addictive products. For years, we heard two messages from our government. On one hand, there was the little message on the box that smoking was harmful to your health. On the other hand, while the Surgeon General was raising those warnings, other parts of the government were helping raise the tobacco crop through huge subsidies. Now, there is a proposal to tax smoking products and use the money to help support child day care. Now there's a contradiction—stop smoking and you deny day care to a young child!

B. But wait a minute, what about the gospel here? Is our faith of two minds on being addicted, too? Look at how Jesus related to people; at every point he opposed and overturned any power that held them bondage. Oh, that power could be a system that assigned the category "outcast" or "unclean" to folks who were lepers or held in bondage by what the Bible names "an evil spirit." Or the power that enslaves us to sin and death. Didn't Paul announce that in the Cross, its power was overturned? And back in Egypt, when the Hebrews were enslaved by Pharaoh, was God of two minds on their freedom? No, through Moses, the single-minded word of God was spoken: "Let my people go!" Made in God's image, God wants us to live in freedom, not enslaved or held in bondage by any earthly power.

C. So maybe that means we need to be a single-minded church on this addiction business. Check out where we're like the two-minded world. The trustees may well have to check that mutual fund we own. Would it surprise us that we own stock in a couple of companies whose profits are mostly from cigarettes? Just maybe we're a bit double-minded when all we serve at the fellowship time after church are snacks that are so good but crammed with sugar and fat. We can become addicted to those foods, too. And up at the (presbytery/conference/district/diocese) level, ever notice how much turnover there is? "Burnout" is the buzzword you hear a lot. Could be the whole organization is addictive. Now that would be a double-minded message on addiction, wouldn't it?

D. But it begins right here, with us, this healing—become single-minded about God's gift of freedom. Maybe our spiritual life retreat this year needs to be on addictions and the image of God. And it may well be that we have some call of God to take this word out to a world crammed with addicted folks. But first of all, it begins with the question of our own soul-health. And maybe an opportunity to open ourselves to the cleansing, healed refreshment of the Spirit.

Several aspects of our sermon plotted in the mode of praxis should be noted. First, in keeping with Buttrick's identification of the typical stages of "thinking in praxis," we began with a situation—addiction—as read by the world. We labeled this worldly approach to addictions as being of two minds. The next stage (move B) is where the situation is brought into "Christian hermeneutical consciousness where an awareness of being-saved in the world grasps symbols of revelation." With Buttrick, the move did not turn to any specific biblical text, but explored contemporary Christian consciousness regarding freedom and bondage. The hearers will be invited to bring to overt memory the symbols of the Exodus and the Resurrection as well as some words of Paul and events and sayings from the ministry of Jesus. What we did in move C was to recognize the in-the-world state of our Christian community and in so doing, cycled back to Buttrick's first stage of praxis thinking. It is important to note here that such shifts in the sequence of sermon plots may be made within any of the three modes—immediacy, reflection, or praxis. We may shift around the scenes while tracking a biblical narrative in the mode of immediacy, or we may play with various alignments of reflective moves in the homiletical plot. Here, we returned to the first stage of praxis consciousness, but with a new focus on addiction within the community of faith. In all cases, however, two considerations dominate homiletic strategy. First, the congregation must easily follow the sequence of moves within any mode; they must be designed to travel in communal consciousness much as thought forms naturally. Second, since method in preaching is organically connected to theological considerations for David Buttrick, we cannot so adjust the sequence of moves that something other than the gospel is preached. (Note: A musical example might help here. It would be both odd and opposed to the gospel to sing Luther's hymn, "A Mighty Fortress Is Our God," beginning with the last verse and ending with the first. That is, the hymn's intention is not to lead the congregation to conclude that regarding Satan, "on earth is not his equal"!) Given these two overriding criteria, it is essential that the moves of the sermon's plot, whatever the mode, form successively in the consciousness of the hearers. For one move in a sermon plot not to function will jeopardize the first criterion regarding the followability of the sermon's movement and structure. Intention will be compromised if the congregation cannot track the moves in succession. Moreover, if the sermon's plot is garbled with one or more of the moves becoming lost or strayed, the theological field the sermon intends probably will become distorted.

An example of how the theological intention of a sermon is distorted by the congregation's inability to track the sequence of moves involves the frequently employed strategy of "then—now." A bit of Scripture is developed (usually in a past-tense voice) followed by a somewhat related contemporary experience rendered in present tense. Almost invariably, the present-day situation is brightly imaged and illustrated while the biblical situation is merely referred to at some distance. The back-and-forth sermon structure presents too many shifts in consciousness for the congregation to follow, and the concretely imaged contemporary references will often mean that the biblical text and its moves drop out of consciousness entirely. Theologically, this often leaves a congregation only with some rather vivid reminders of the darkness of today's world, but with no good news at all! Again, the rhetorical and methodological strategies in our preaching invariably present serious theological considerations. Most centrally, however, we will need to learn how to shape a move within our sermon's plot in order that it form in communal consciousness. Move theory and praxis, for Buttrick, is a necessary competency for those of us called to preach.

The Science of Moves

The building block of any sermon, for David Buttrick, is the move, a module of language designed to form in consciousness and articulate some single meaning: "A sermon, any sermon, will involve a sequence of subject matters—simple meanings—arranged in some sort of structural design."[37] These single meanings will be developed into a move, that module of language designed to form in communal consciousness. At present, the rhetorical situation demands a great deal of the effective preacher. Right off, there is the issue of span of attention. A single meaning, some idea simply put, will take about three minutes to form in the consciousness of the hearers. However, remaining with the same idea for more than four minutes will evoke boredom and drifting. In this respect, a communal rhetoric differs considerably from one-to-one speech. In the latter, for example, several ideas that range across a number of contexts can be spoken and heard with ease. In the oral/aural context of preaching, it is as if we speak and hear a different language, each with its own purpose. Buttrick adds:

> While public address cannot present as many ideas in a short time as can one-to-one talking, it can achieve depth and formational power impossible

in the rapid linear movement of everyday conversation . . . when public language is shaped with technical proficiency, it can have awesome formational power in human consciousness.[38]

We repeat Buttrick's definition—a move is a module of language designed in such a way to form a single meaning within communal consciousness. We also recall Buttrick's earlier assertion—the plot of a sermon will be composed of a sequence of moves shaped to proceed in consciousness much as thought naturally occurs.

Opening and Closure Systems

Since each move is defined as attending to a single idea, we may recall a past day in homiletics when the opening theme sentence was argued as the best and only way to begin. These theme sentences were usually expansive discursive propositions, later to be argued and illustrated. Buttrick is quick to explain that a move will not open in such a manner, and for several reasons. First, and most obvious, even though a move will attend to a single meaning, that idea is not to be construed as a point to be argued. Moves will succeed only as they form in succession within the hearing of the congregation. What holds the sermon together is its structure and movement designed to form within one of the modes of consciousness, not a main idea or sermonic theme. Second, theme sentences will not function to open a move because groups of listeners do not really hear the first sentence of a section of discourse. Rather, the opening statement of each move will state the meaning at hand in simple, direct speech with intentional repetition. That is, the opening statement of a move is composed of several sentences that essentially say the same thing in somewhat different ways. Finally, the opening statement of a move cannot borrow the theme sentence of the past because their purposes so radically differ. The theme sentence aimed for expansive inclusion; no part of the sermon should be outside its scope. The opening sentences of a move, however, are restrained to form only that single meaning within the hearing of the congregation.

By way of illustration, let us assume that we are working on a sermon on 1 Corinthians 12:1-11 and have decided on a plot in the mode of reflectivity that begins, "We are all gifted by God." Our first move's opening system will need to state that single meaning through a series of rather simply constructed sentences, each not adding much new information to the one prior to it. The move may begin as follows: "We are all gifted by God. Every Christian, gifted; equipped for Christ's service. We may not always know what our gift is, but it is there, waiting to be discovered and used." What this rhetorical unit is doing in the hearing of the congregation, Buttrick notes, is allowing the hearers to tune in to the single meaning that will be expanded and explored in the move. This tuning in takes more than just one statement, Buttrick adds. Consequently, an opening system composed of just the first sentence—"We are all gifted by God"—will not work. On one hand, there needs to be reiteration in the form of several statements, each one not adding much new material and each rather simple in organization. On the other hand, to expand the system in size by adding, say, another three or four sentences of similar content and structure would also defeat the purpose. In this case, the hearers would become restless and their attention will start to wander.[39]

In addition to providing for an initial attentiveness within the hearers, the opening system of a move will also perform other functions as well. There will be a connective logic within the sermon's plot as the moves lead the hearers from "this" to now "this." A simple connective strategy may be seen in a sermon in the first two moves of a sermon on 1 Corinthians 12:12-27. Buttrick labels such closely connected moves "a set": "We are 'many members.' Paul is right. Just look at us, how different we are," and "Problem is, our differences just reflect those in the world. Look at how we separate ourselves from one another—by race, doctrine, and class—well, you name it. We are 'many members' and it's hard to see what we all have in common." In this example, the connective logic is a two-move set that begins with Paul's image of many members and then adds an awareness of how intractable our world-based divisions really seem. In addition to establishing the connective logic between moves, an opening system also sets the mood for the move and builds a perspective for the move within consciousness. Regarding the former issue, the mood, our language will shift even within the parameters necessary for the opening statement to focus congregational attention. So, for example, a move dealing with anger within the congregation will employ language that itself will snap and snarl. A move relating the joy of finding the lost in one of the three parables in Luke 15 will use a language of rejoicing in its opening statement. The mood of each move is already being established in the opening system's choice of words. With regard to the perspective of a move, consider once more that for Buttrick, the preacher is using language to form meaning within the congregational consciousness. Since consciousness can orient meaning in a variety of modes—just think of how memory involves a distinctive kind of consciousness—the opening statement serves to locate the perspective of the entire move. So, in a move involving memory, the opening system might begin, "We can all connect with Jesus' words that we must become like a child. We were children once, remember? The way we once saw the world as fresh and pure, and felt ourselves new and really excited about good things." To conclude, the opening statement of a move must function primarily to focus the congregation's attention on the single meaning that will be developed. Additionally, however, that same brief rhetorical unit will serve to establish some connective logic between the moves, to begin to color the mood of the move, and to shape the perspective of the move within congregational consciousness.

Every move will need to have a way of ending that will tie off congregational attention to its meaning in order that the preacher can begin with some connective logic a new move. If the idea of a move is simply left unconcluded, it will persist in consciousness, thereby jeopardizing the hearers' ability to take up consideration of some new meaning. (Incidentally, this is one explanation of why congregations become so garbled in their ability to track a sermon organized around a lengthy series of points. Without much attention to a closure system, the preacher assumes that to enumerate a new point is to automatically close off the previous one. So when the preacher announces, "My sixth point is . . . ," hearers may remark to themselves, "Six? I though we were on four.") The strategy for the needed closure system is straightforward: "Forming closure will always involve a return to the idea of the statement with which the move began."[40] At its simplest, the closure can be a copy of the opening system, verbatim. Even as we shape a slightly different way of stating the opening's meaning in the closing system, the same protocols remain. The language will need to be rather simple and especially the last sentence of the closure will need to itself be "a terse final sentence."[41] To be avoided here: compound sentences, sentences with numerous clauses, and sentences that end with a strong participle (these will convey a sense of continuing action, or questions, Buttrick notes). However, there are a number of ways to nuance this needed reiteration of the opening's idea. The preacher can build a rhetorical system with certain rhythmic characteristics, usually progressing from a more complex sentence to that final, terse one. We might conclude the move on many members: "Well, here's who we are, we're 'many'—many denominations, many churches, many congregations. Even gathered here, we are many."

The Body of the Move

Within the time frame of three or four minutes, the preacher has the opportunity to design a module of language that will form in communal consciousness and function with regard to the interconnection of the sermonic plot. The move itself, apart from its opening and closure systems, attends to several basic aspects of the way thought occurs in consciousness. By describing a move as pertaining to a single meaning or idea, Buttrick is indicating that some theological thinking will be the very stuff of which the move is comprised. Thus, in a move dealing with the kingdom joy of, say, the parable of the lost coin, the preacher will be about some theological reflection on the extravagance of the celebration in comparison with the worth of the coin that has been found. Friends and neighbors—the whole village?—are invited to join with the woman in this rejoicing over the lost being found. (In a reflective mode, one could ask whether the ensuing party cost far more than the worth of the little coin!) Theological reflection on this move related to rejoicing could also focus on the quality of the worship within the congregation—filled with much joy?—or on the connection of that celebration to wider meanings of God's reign and, indeed, the whole creation. There is much to consider, theologically, in such a move. Not all of our insights will make their way into the move given the three- to four-minute temporal parameters. However, the meaning of the move will be expressed through such theological reflection.

As we explore aspects of this kingdom joy, notice that you may be having examples to the contrary come to mind. We focus on the communal character of kingdom joy in finding the lost and our culture's individualism intrudes, both on the joy and on our work on the move itself. We may also become aware of how churchly piety may mitigate against outright joyful celebration. It is important to take notice of how consciousness works in this regard. Our life as Christians, living at once in the being-saved community and in the world, is thereby ironic and laden with oppositions. As we develop the idea of the move, then, we will need to recognize the oppositions that emerge regarding the invitation to kingdom joy. Buttrick provides a list of locations for such oppositions, including: our own human sinfulness, oppositions built into the culture worldview, those that originate in the ever-changing cultural values and "lifestyles," current social attitudes, and various religious distortions.[42] (The last of Buttrick's list, the religious distortions, could explain the strange dissonance between the joy of the woman in Luke 15:8-10 and the often dour restraints of our liturgical piety.) Preachers will need to identify and interpret the oppositions—from whatever source—that are spawned from these various locations. Homiletically, we will need to come up with strategies for dealing with them and their potentially adverse effect on the move.

We noticed that some oppositions came to mind as we were reflecting theologically on the meaning of the woman's joy in finding the lost coin. From such an awareness, we have concluded that oppositions to the move will also lurk in the consciousness of the hearers. Similarly, as we reflected theologically, we may have had some images of this joy come to mind as well. Perhaps we are reminded of a recent festival in the congregation's liturgical life when some intimations of kingdom joy really did seem to burst free of convention. Or we may have remembered a worldly occasion where a people's joy became a sign of God's reign (the celebrations in Poland or South Africa, for example, as old systems of oppression crumbled into dust). What is happening here is that the meanings we are exploring have a way of becoming concrete in particular images. We now build this insight into our homiletical method, according to David Buttrick. "Homiletical thinking is always *a thinking of theology toward images*."[43] Buttrick adds:

> We know that in preaching any idea, we will have to image. Ideas without depiction are apt to be abstract and, oddly, enough, unconvincing . . . we will have to find some way of picturing what it is we are talking about; we must turn to lived experience.[44]

Where we turn to find the images of lived experience is not a difficult question. We turn to the social world out there and to our own self-awareness. For a move to form and be retained in consciousness, it must be imaged; the source of the imagery is the social context of the listeners and their human self-awareness.

Strategies for Interaction: Theological Thinking and Opposition

Theological Thinking

The internal composition of a move is organized in such a way to form in the consciousness of the listeners with regard to its meaning and its location in the homiletical plot. A major element in the discourse of the move will be its logic that reflects the theological reflection done prior to the shaping of the actual sermon. "We are presenting a single idea," Buttrick states, "but doing so in a strategy that probably involves a number of parts, namely subordinate gambits of thought."[45] As we have reflected on the kingdom joy that comes as the lost is found, several dimensions to this joy may well call for attention in sequence. We may invite the congregation to recall moments of joy that were quite individual in sequence. We may invite the congregation to recall moments of joy that were quite individual in their expression, followed by a focus on the inherently communal character of joy within God's reign (all the friends and neighbors who are invited to share in the joy). Preaching at the Eucharist also invites the assembly to experience anew in their Holy Meal the joy of Christ's presence and the glory of God's reign when we feast together in the heavenly banquet. The elements, so far, that compose the internal structure of the move involve three units that focus theological reflection—on the distinctiveness of deep personal joy, its communal expression, and its eucharistic fulfillment. Already, an internal logic to the move's development of the single idea related to the woman's joy-in-community is taking shape. This is all in accord with Buttrick's insistence that "every move in a sermon will require a thinking through of how we present material, what kinds of material will be chosen, and how such material will be designed in view of theological understandings and our common cultural mind."[46]

Opposition

We noted, too, that oppositions began to emerge within our own consciousness even as we were considering the theological content of the move. And we easily came to agree that if we preachers find oppositions emerging as the material is heard, so too, will an entire congregation. Here is where Buttrick's emphasis on strategy comes to the forefront of our homiletical reflection. First, let us assume that there will be moves in our sermons in which not much of any significant opposition will be confronted as they are preached. In most of our communities of faith, a move whose idea relates to praying for members who suffer illness and hardship will have such minimal opposition that no strategic gambits need to be designed into the move or the sermon. (Nevertheless, even such a seemingly uncontroversial idea may in fact evoke strong opposition in some congregations if one of the members has contracted HIV positive, has come out as homosexual, and is living with AIDS.) However, if we have concluded that enough opposition (sufficient resistance to the idea) abounds, the reception of the move is in jeopardy, there are several alternatives available to the preacher. Two of the strategies occur within the move, while a third involves the shaping of another entire move. In every instance, however, a series of protocols obtains regarding the use of "contrapuntals" (Buttrick's term for the homiletical acknowledgment of opposition). We may summarize these conventions as follows:

1. A contrapuntal becomes the prescribed strategy within a move when opposition within the hearers would distort or delete the move's statement. Speaking of the opposition, then, tends to "let off steam" (Buttrick's phrase) in order that the move's statement may be received.

2. Since the primary task of the move relates to its statement, its idea or single meaning, the contrapuntal must be restrained in its development. "A contrapuntal may never exceed the time given to a development of the statement, may not have brighter imagery, or be illustrated."[47] The preacher who is wise enough to spot oppositions to a sermon's moves will also need the wisdom to employ contrapuntals with prudence and control.

3. Since the purpose is to *acknowledge* congregational opposition but not to *reinforce* it, a contrapuntal will not be located in the midst of a move's development. Rather, the preacher has two options available within the move—the contrapuntal may be placed immediately following the opening system and initial presentation of the statement or immediately prior to the closure system.

4. If the congregational opposition to the statement of the move is judged to be too intense to be dealt with within that move, Buttrick allows that an entire successive move may be devoted to the opposition. Such a strategy, however, is infrequently the case, but it is available to the preacher if needed.

With an eye for how the theological statement along with its analysis interacts with possible contrapuntals, we might provide several alternative scenarios. Imagine, for example, that the initial move in a sermon on the Prologue of John involves the statement, "The world is a world of darkness." And let us suppose that the logic of our theological development of the move is to invite the congregation to "look deep down inside ourselves, look at the darkness down there" and then a shift to "look around you, look at the darkness out there." Each of these perspectives then will need to be appropriately imaged (our next task in move development) out of the lived experience of the congregation. However, as we are developing the statement, "The world is a world of darkness" into the full content of the move, we will need to become aware of oppositions to that statement and to the "deep down inside" and "out there" dimensions of the world's darkness. Is there more resistance to hearing about our own dark corners of our souls, places labeled "unforgiven"? Or will the congregation have more opposition to hearing about the darkness in the world, especially as we image it quite concretely? Let's assume the latter—imagining our auditors as a suburban, predominantly white affluent congregation. In order to acknowledge the opposition that has emerged in the course of the development of the move, a closing contrapuntal will need to be devised. Perhaps we could point to a recent event involving the youth of the congregation that showed some glimmers of light in the world's darkness. Our end-of-move contrapuntal, then, might go as follows:

"Thank goodness there is some relief from the darkness now and then. Just last Friday night, many of us gathered at the high school for the (musical production/athletic event/honors awards). There were some really proud parents! But as it came time to leave, we walked by all those bulletin boards with the messages about drugs. Yep, darkness, right here at Northern High, too."

What Buttrick would caution, here, is that we go no further in imaging the contrapuntal. We may be tempted to brag at length about the positive evening at the high school, especially if several of the stars of the musical production were members of the congregation. But recall the purpose of a contrapuntal—it acknowledges, and thereby moderates, the congregational opposition to the statement of a move. It should not, however, reinforce that opposition.

Strategies for Integration: The Role of Illustration and Example

Illustration

In much recent homiletic theory and practice, the answer to the question, "What do you do after you have decided on the points of the sermon?" came rapidly and without much reflection. The answer is: "You illustrate the points." By illustration was meant a rather extended story that was intended to make memorable the conceptual material comprising the point. Typically, these story-illustrations had an overly subjective, affect-laden quality about them, presenting polar contrasts to the propositions and thematics of the points. These anecdotes were also of high market value among preachers, "like baseball cards being traded among kids."[48] Whatever else, the method of preaching advocated by David Buttrick rejects the subject-object split in modern homiletics. "We may be moving," he concludes, "into an age when sermons will no longer split between a rational denotative prose in which we

176

declare ideas, and highly emotive illustrations in which we pump up feeling."[49] Instead, illustrations will function to catalyze the single meanings of a move within the hearing of the congregation. So although an illustration's identity remains that of a story imported into the sermon from outside the immediate experience of the congregation, with Buttrick, the other criteria of successful illustrations differ widely from those of prior practice in preaching. The main criteria for effective illustrations Buttrick lists as follows:

1. There must be a clear analogy between an idea in sermon content and some aspect of the illustration.
2. There ought to be a parallel between the structure of content and the shape of an illustration.
3. The illustration should be "appropriate" to the content.[50]

We will explore these criteria now, though in reverse order.

An illustration's *appropriateness* to its content has to do with its relative strength and integrity. The former is easy to grasp—locate more powerful illustrations within moves that are themselves central to the effectiveness of the sermon. Conversely, when employing a particularly strong illustration, it is necessary to provide more conceptual content prior to its use. Buttrick adds, "We must always have a frame of meaning well established before an illustration is used."[51] A further consideration regarding the appropriateness of an illustration deals with the alignment of the positive or negative character of the move itself. A negative/negative alignment may be seen quite easily in a move, for example, dealing with Paul's well-known image of God's people as clay jars in 2 Corinthians 4:7-12. A preacher may import an illustration into this "We are clay pots, all of us" move, perhaps drawing on a story told by an ecclesiastical official about his or her humble origins and childhood in a little country church. Now moving on to the positive move about the treasure God has placed within us clay pots, our preacher attempts to employ a negative story, reversing its meaning within the move. So, after hearing about the treasure given us in Christ, the congregation is served an illustration about an old man who hides his money in the walls of his house, refusing to entrust his wealth to a bank or other savings institution. Then, the preacher tries to reverse the story by announcing, "But God is not like that old man. God does an amazing thing, entrusting even to people like us, the treasure of Jesus Christ." The problem here, for Buttrick, is that "the illustration will be saying one thing and the move statement another. . . . The result will be a confusion in consciousness, and, quite possibly, a disruption in the logical continuity of a sermon."[52] The rule, Buttrick states, is clear: relate negative illustrations to negative moves while illustrating positive-move statements with positive illustrations.[53]

An illustration, moreover, needs to parallel the content of a move with regard to structure. Since the intent is to build the single meaning of the move's statement within the consciousness of the hearers, a necessary congruence must obtain between the illustration and the shape of the move. Initially, Buttrick identifies several approaches that violate this criterion. First, if the story illustration grows beyond a certain proportion, it renders its function as analogy null and void. Moreover, the congregation may well become lodged in the expanded story-world of the illustration and become incapable of tracking the sermon's sequence of plotted moves. A second transgression here, and a controversial one as well, is that first-person illustrations will split consciousness between the move's single meaning and the point of view provided by the preacher's own experience. Buttrick's none-too-subtle caution is this: "To be blunt, there are virtually no good reasons to talk about ourselves from the pulpit."[54] We need to hear Buttrick with care at this point. He insists that a first person story told from the pulpit will rarely (never?) function as analogy with congregational experience.[55] Rather, the story will function to shape the hearers' point of view *toward* the preacher. "The illustration will fix like glue on the minister who is speaking."[56] The fix here is rather straightforward— shift the point of view so that the story is heard by the people from their own point of view, that is, as second-person plural.

The illustration's function as analogy begins with its content. The congregation will need to be able to locate the illustration quite readily within the conceptual material the preacher has been expanding. (Recall that the illustrations will be placed, for Buttrick, toward the middle of the move, following some development of the move's statement.) Once the congregation has been provided the necessary conceptual development within the move, it is time to enter rather immediately into the illustration's story world. Therefore, we will not append lengthy "introductions to introductions," once more separating a move's content from its imaging. In addition, the analogy between the move's statement and its illustration must be unequivocally clear. "Close," Buttrick notes, "is never close enough."[57] For example, in a sermon that opened with the message that while we may know Jesus, we may not know him fully enough, an illustration followed:

> A man in New York was alone at dinner in a restaurant. He soon struck up a relationship with another diner and they ranged over a number of topics of discussion, finding that they had many interests in common. After a

long, enjoyable time together, the new friend, a singer, got up to leave and bought the man's dinner. Afterward, the man learned from the manager of the restaurant that the "singer" was the famous rock star, Sting. The preacher then concluded, "Even as Gordon Sumner, the pleasant dinner companion, is also Sting, the world-renowned rock star, so Jesus our friend is also the very Word of God Incarnate."[58]

The preacher's aim toward analogy in the illustration is clear—a friendly stranger at dinner is discovered to be a person of renown. The problem is, of course, that the analogy also insists on a rather tight congruence between Jesus and Sting, a fit that may not be what the congregation is willing to accept or the preacher intends. Again the dictum regarding the employment of analogy in illustration: Close is never close enough!

Now it is precisely the dynamics of analogy that collide with a preacher's intuitive sense. The question easily emerges: "If one illustration in this move is good, wouldn't two be better?" Buttrick's answer comes immediately: "No!" This counterintuitive reasoning again relates to an illustration's analogical role. A story inevitably builds up a world within the congregational mind and by confronting the listeners with two worlds attending to the same meaning in a move, the result is a weakening of analogy rather than a strengthening of it. "If several illustrations are used in sequence," Buttrick observes, "they do not come together to illustrate a single meaning; instead, they will weaken each other and produce a confusion of meaning."[59] The rule, then, derives from the analogical power of the illustration; build one story-world only per move.

Examples

If illustrations are anecdotal material imported into the sermon, examples are drawn from the lived experience of the congregation. There is no need to import, and therefore the need to build examples into a full-blown story-world is obviated. Examples are typical to a congregation and only need to be evoked by the preacher to be brought into congregational consciousness. Such examples, Buttrick indicates, "will tend to be either 'moments in consciousness' or very simple narratives."[60] The imperative is that they be imaged concretely, and that they be received by the listeners as real slices of their lives. Initially, then, the success of an example depends on the degree to which the congregation will assent to its being true to their lived experience. Examples drawn from experiences not held in common by the hearers will not be validated as real. These idiosyncratic examples—frequent references to the preacher's hobby of collecting computer viruses—are homiletical oxymorons.

179

If the example is too unique to the preacher or a small segment of the congregation, then it is not really an example. There are two steps that lead to the discerning of homiletical examples. First, we search our own consciousness, turning to memory and our own experiences and, second, we will "assess our own experiences to see if they are common to most people."[61]

We have already heard Buttrick's insistence that each move will need to be imaged in some way and have examined the use of illustrations in such imaging. As with the illustration, one well-chosen example may serve to image the statement of a move. Returning to our sermon on the treasure in clay pots, an alternative strategy to providing illustrations to both moves would be to turn to an example as we image the clay pots first move. Instead of importing the well-worn illustration of the church official's humble upbringing, the sermon might be better served by turning to the lived experience of the congregation itself. In a rural congregation, an example of the small town itself, describing local landmarks that have not changed and reflect a clay pot identity could be easily designed. Such an example might begin: *"Here in Hatfield, we're almost Paul's original 'clay pots,' aren't we? Duffy's General Store doesn't ever seem to change, the Post Office goes back years, and our church, years before that. Of course, the co-op did build a new farm store out on the highway, but it's us plain 'clay pot' folks who meet out there to browse."* But since the preacher is drawing on some true-to-life images in this example, the congregation will be able to track a chain of two or three examples as well. A set of three examples (the most Buttrick will allow per move) related to the clay pots move may be formed as follows:

"Clay pots? Well Paul describes us right down to our southern Indiana twang and the jokes about our Kentucky kinfolks. Clay pots, that's us. Just look around our beloved Hatfield—Duffy's, the Post Office, our church itself, none of them changed much over the years. And think back. Seems like almost everybody had Mrs. Ballentine for second grade. Remember all those 'clay pot kids' in our class? Look, nobody here is going to disagree with old Paul when he says we're all clay pots. That rings true for us, has rung true for years."

Use of chained examples in an image system is possible because, on one hand, an illustration's narrative world is not being assembled in the congregation's consciousness. (More than one illustration per move unavoidably involves conflicts between these narrative worlds.) On the other hand, examples can be provided in a short series within a move. That multiple examples are chained, though, is crucial. "When we do chain examples," Buttrick notes, "they must be shaped in a similar stylized manner so they may come together to form a single sense of 'trueness' in consciousness."[62] However, preachers may well use only one example, again providing that it relates easily to the lived experience of the listeners.

The Role of Imagery

As consciousness is invited to imagine or think out an idea, it cannot do so in a vacuum. Rather, consciousness moves toward imagery, literally trying to see what comes to mind. For a sermon to form in the consciousness of the congregation, the preacher will, to be sure, need to elaborate the statement of each move, its ideas and conceptual material. However, communal consciousness both thinks toward imagery (the reason we need to image each move if it is to form) and is structured by the image (the reason *that* selecting images is a crucial issue). Images thereby function in the sermon to form ideas within each move, they also connect across moves to structure faith in the consciousness of the hearers. Recall one of Buttrick's most emphatic dictums: "Homiletical thinking is always a thinking of theology toward images."[63]

We derive the imagery for our preaching from a remarkably diverse collection of sources, including the biblical text itself, the tradition of interpretation, and the church's rituals, symbols, and praxis. Images also emerge from the examples and illustrations we employ within the sermon's moves. More broadly, we live in a wildly imagistic culture, and our social consciousness is littered with the images of our age.[64] Images from this latter source can serve in ways similar to examples and illustrations within each move and therefore become one additional element in the preacher's imagistic palette. (Buttrick frequently uses the phrase "illustrations, examples, and images" when speaking of the possible ways to image any move.) Images will find their way into a sermon, then, by virtue of the image system of the biblical text (e.g., "clay pots," "treasure"), as components of the illustrations and examples we choose, or as additional illustrative devices within each move. All of these images have one central characteristic in common: They all come equipped with a point of view.

Point of view is integral to imagery and, indeed, to all language for David Buttrick. "Consciousness is perspectival," he announces.[65] At a macrolevel, each move will embody some perspective, seeking to structure consciousness in some way. At a microlevel, every image will enter consciousness from a distinctive point of view that is an aspect of its meaning and affective significance. Whether a perspective that shapes an entire move in consciousness or the point of view of an image or image system, there are categories that are held in common, ways of speaking about point of view. Stance, orientation, and distance are attributes of all perspectives and points of view. Buttrick notes, "they shape congregational consciousness."[66] By "stance," Buttrick means the space and time given by the speaker that locates the hearers. A spatial example of stance is easily given—think of all the perspectives available to image an airplane flight. We can be a family member watching as the jet takes off or a passenger in the window seat, looking out at the rapidly receding ground. Other stances include the pilots and even the flight controller, in which case the flight is a computer-generated icon on a monitor. Another aspect of stance involves memory. We can remember our first flight or recall an early childhood experience of seeing a plane up in the sky. "Orientation," Buttrick suggests, "is what we aim toward, the direction of our intending."[67] One example of this intending in consciousness is the preacher's aim toward the hearers' inward depth, toward matters of the heart. So, a section of a move might orient the congregation inward:

> Wilderness is also a place we find down at soul-level, . . . sometimes the worst wilderness is deep down inside. Everything is dry and parched there, and we're not sure God is there, not sure God even knows we're there.

Finally, "distance" is a way of speaking of an aspect of consciousness and may be "visual or temporal, attitudinal or emotional."[68] For example, we can present an image as rendered through someone else's experience or more immediately, as our own. So:

> A pilgrim goes on a tour of the Holy Land, lands at a modern airport, makes it through customs, and is herded with the rest of the group to the bus. Then, it's up to Jerusalem. But just before entering the city, the bus pulls over and stops. The tour guide announces to the group that like all other pilgrims, the first entry into the Holy City will be by foot. Pilgrims walk into the Holy City. Maybe they even walk praying a psalm.

Now notice how the distance closes:

> Ever been on a pilgrimage to the Holy Land? You fly for hours and hours, land at a bustling airport. After standing in line for customs, the tour guide greets you and with your other pilgrims, herds you on a bus. Then it's up to Jerusalem. Just before you get to the city gate, the bus pulls over and stops by the side of the road. The tour guide picks up the mike and gives some information. "Pilgrims have always walked up to Jerusalem. Now it's your turn. We'll get off the bus and walk up through the gate." Minutes later, you are puffing up the walk, remembering a prayer from the psalms.

The issue of the distance relates strongly to emotion and feeling. How close the congregation is to what the sermon aims toward has everything to do with how the hearers feel about the experience that is intended.

David Buttrick refines the categories of point of view by adopting the image of a camera along with its terminology as a model. A hearer's perspective toward imagery is analogous to that of a camera toward its subject, and several aspects of photography are helpful in understanding, and using, point of view. The three elements Buttrick selects are focal field, lens depth, and focal depth.

Focal field

The issue of focal field relates to the relative expanse of the scene we wish to depict in our preaching. On one hand, that field may be quite broad, inviting the congregation to "look out on the fields alive and green with the new crop." On the other hand, the focal field may narrow down: "But that grove of trees out there in the field, it was the old homestead, remember? That little house the place where your mother was born." Here, we have narrowed the focal field to select one feature in a broad landscape. Notice, too, that we invoked memory in the second example. Here, field could relate broadly to an entire generation or historic era or, narrowly, to a moment in our past-lived experience.

Lens depth

Lens depth, Buttrick admits, "is somewhat more difficult to describe."[69] One way of interpreting the concept is to ask "how much of the self is engaged in a point-of-view."[70] In this respect, lens depth relates to the already-discussed aspect of "distance," especially of emotional distance. Interestingly, a somewhat close distance to the image does not necessarily provide for a more intensive lens depth. For example, we could image the experience of receiving ashes at a service of worship on Ash Wednesday:

> Kneeling there before the altar, the priest says the words and applies the ashes. Eyes closed, you kneel there. There is a gritty feeling as the pastor's thumb streaks across your forehead. As you arise and return to your seat, you smile awkwardly, aware of the smudge on your forehead.

A more intensive lens depth would image the same experience differently:

> The routine of the worship is much like Sunday, hymn, prayers, lessons. But now it's time to receive your ashes. A trip up front, and you kneel at the

altar. The priest comes down the row of kneeling worshipers. Your eyes are closed—don't know why—and you are surprised by the pastor's thumb on your forehead and the gritty feeling of the ashes. Then it hits you, those words, like you've never heard them before. "Remember you are dust," spoken directly to you. Shaken to the core, you find your way back to your seat, dazed by this new information that you will someday die.

Both examples are from a very near-distance point of view; however, the second imaging of the imposition of ashes embodies a much more intensive lens depth.

Focal depth

If lens depth relates to the relative degree of personal and communal involvement, there are similarly varying degrees of depth of perception. The congregation can be invited to look more at the surface of a situation: "There they all are, you think, as you watch the congregation sitting down to one of the church's famous potluck suppers. One big happy family." Increased focal depth might revise the observation: "There they all are, you think, as you watch the congregation sitting down to one of the church's famous potluck suppers. One big happy family. But you don't know that over in the corner two members are talking quietly over their meal. One is asking forgiveness of the other for things said that were hurtful and demeaning." Again, the distinction between lens depth and focal depth has to do with the point of view. The former deals with the degree to which the viewer enters into the experience; the latter relates to the relative depth the viewer perceives in the situation that is presented.

The Image Grid

For David Buttrick, there is a vertical and a horizontal dimension to the shaping of a sermon, dynamics we have already observed. The vertical component is the homiletical plot itself, the sequence of moves, each comprising a single meaning plotted to function in consciousness. The horizontal component is one we have been tracing through the analysis of the theological statement and its elaboration, a caution regarding the possible need for contrapuntals to defuse resistance to hearing the move, and necessity of imaging the move through illustrations, examples, or images. These horizontal and vertical elements interact to form a grid within which the content of the sermon itself takes shape.

Viewed from a vertical perspective, the statements on the left, containing the single meaning of the moves, will be designed to be easily followed by the hearers and to form naturally as thought forms in consciousness. What

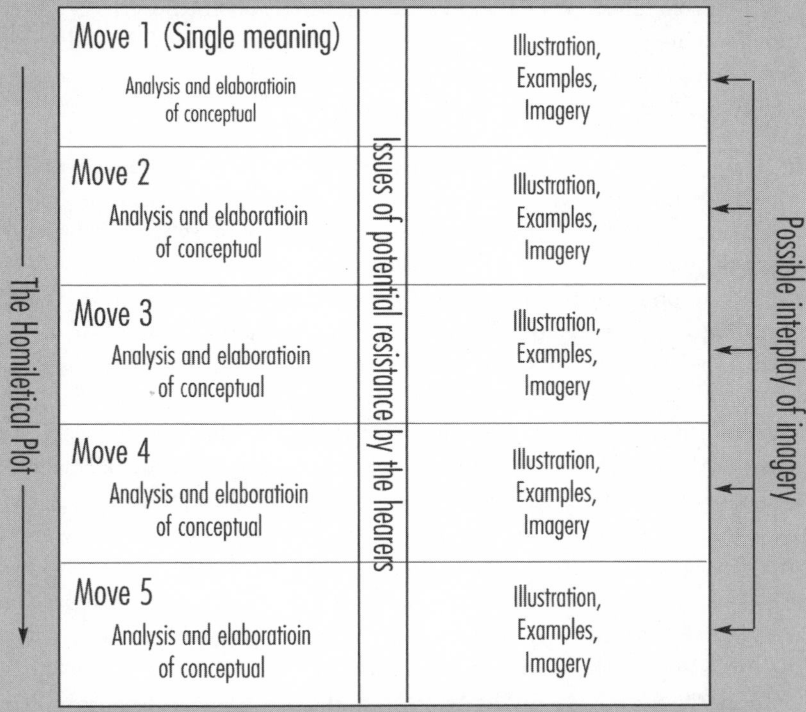

Figure 4A
The Image Grid

has not yet been scrutinized is the vertical aspect of the succession of imagery Buttrick has insisted must be present within each move. Could it be that these illustrations, examples, and images represented in the right-hand column will also function to shape a particular structure of thought? Buttrick would answer, "Absolutely! They will interact in consciousness." Our choices of illustrative materials, then, will be made with their interaction in mind. As we form the sermon, we are shaping an image grid as well.

In *Homiletic,* Buttrick sketches out the body of a sermon, without introduction or conclusion, as a way of calling attention to the variety of considerations that go into the development of an image grid. We will adopt the same pedagogy, though the sermon, based on Mark 9:38-50, will be our own. (The moves are numbered for reference only.)

The Image System

We are now aware that the image system of a sermon following the Buttrick method will both illustrate the single meaning of each move and interact among the moves to form a structure in consciousness. It follows, then, that our imagery related to each move will appropriately bring to concretion the statement of the move and its elaboration. It also follows that we will need to look across the sequence of the moves at how the images are aligned forming an image system. With respect to the four moves of our sermon on Mark 9:38-50 concerning "these little ones," an initial overview of the moves yields the following reflections. First, the interaction of the first and fourth moves is one of reversal and opposition. The point of view of the images in the two moves, then, should also reflect this reversal by shifting points of view. In the first move, we look for an image that looks down, a looking down by the disciples on the one not following them and a churchly looking down on those who do not follow us. The fourth move, with its biblically derived imagery of "little ones" and children, could be provided by a point of view that looks up. Also, as we review the moves in their plotted sequence, we are reminded of Buttrick's dictum that strong moves demand strong imaging. The third move, then, might well need an illustration rather than an example or image. We now look at the moves in succession regarding their imaging.

Move 1: If the sermon is preached in an old-line Protestant denomination's church, a persisting divide between liberal and evangelical factions might provide a rather well-recognized example. If the congregation has located itself within either of the opposing groups, the case for the example becomes even stronger. Our first attempt at an example here was as follows:

"Today we hear the cry from liberals and evangelicals looking at one another across the 'great chasm' within our churches. Each side accuses the other of splitting the church, of 'not following us.' The conclusion is inevitable—the other side is really not welcome."

Recalling that if at all possible we want to design an image here that has the point of view of looking down, a later revision involved changing the phrase "looking at each other" to "staring down at each other." This point of view with its built-in sense of disapproval and rejection will be reversed in Move 4.

Move 2: Here, we opt for a more scattershot series of examples that are intended to raise pastoral issues within the congregation. Again, recalling Buttrick on such series of examples, we will "chain" the examples together with a recurring closure system.

Just imagine who would be sitting in church here if we welcomed those not against us:

- Young adults whose tastes in music do not have much in common with our own styles of church music, but are about electric guitars and synthesizers and drums.
  "Not against us," Jesus says, "then for us!"
- Rough-living folks who drive pickups rather than Accords and BMWs, work the night shift down at the plant, and listen to country music all the time.
  "Not against us," Jesus says, "then for us."
- Persons whose sexuality is not our own, rejected in many church families as outcasts.
  "Those who are not against us," admonishes our Lord, "they are for us."

(Notice that in order for the set of three examples to form in consciousness, Buttrick would have us alter that last of the rhetorical closure systems. In this case, we altered by extending it and substituting "admonishes our Lord" for "Jesus says.")

Move 3: Here, we develop an illustration that aims at analogy with the statement of the move.

Amazing how sudden this shift can be, from a place of secure identity to becoming one of the "little ones." Health professionals slam into this when they become seriously ill. In no time at all, the badges of office—the name tag and, maybe, the stethoscope draped around the neck—these badges of honor are gone, exchanged for one of those skimpy hospital gowns like all the other patients. But that is the greatest change of all—from being in charge to becoming a patient.

Move 4: The opposition with Move 1 involved a shift in point of view and a transformation from the status of "in-group excluders" to little children dependent on the hospitality of others. We use an example from the lived experience of the congregation:

"And now, Jesus announces, we are welcomed, too. It's like when our new day care opened last month. Those little ones coming to church for the first time. Maybe they were anxious about being welcomed. But no children on God's earth received more hospitality than our new day care's children. They are part of the family now, along with the rest of us here."

We move horizontally as we shape images that serve to bring concretion to the theological and conceptual material of the move. But there is a vertical component, too, as the images within the moves-in-sequence interact with one another in the hearing of the congregation.

Framing the Sermon

Introductions

Sermon introductions do a precise kind of double work. On one hand, an introduction serves to focus the congregation toward the aim of the sermon in general and the first move in particular. On the other hand, the introduction functions to orient hermeneutical understanding toward what the congregation will be hearing. In all cases, these functions will need to be achieved within disciplined parameters regarding length and rhetoric. Regarding the question of focus, Buttrick indicates that the introduction must ready the congregation to hear the first move. We do not introduce the entire sermon, although introductions "may well be evocative of the entire sermon—its mood, intention, or general thematic concern."[71] Buttrick continues,

> But also introductions set up a congregation so that the first move may start. If an introduction is too general, it may seem oddly disconnected from the first move. If the introduction is too particular, it will, subsequently, seem irrelevant to the whole sermon.[72]

Focusing the congregation on the opening move of the sermon, the introduction also anticipates the tone of the entire sermon. These tasks will both need to be designed into the introduction—orienting the congregation to hear the first move and building a field of meaning related to the body of the sermon. Language that is too general serves neither purpose. So, for example, let us imagine an introduction to a sermon on Luke 17:11-19 (the story of the ten lepers) that begins:

"As you know, in Jesus' day, the land of the Samaritans lay between Judea to the south and Galilee to the north. Anyone traveling from Galilee to Judea would need either to travel through Samaria or go around it. The pious among the Jews would avoid that unclean area entirely. But Jesus chooses to cross through the land of the Samaritans, and as he crosses the border, he is approached by some lepers, ten in number."

We have made this example both unnecessarily ponderous and overdone on geography. Note that in its generality, the introduction really does not function to orient the attention of the listeners. The focus is as vague and scattered at the end of the unit as its beginning. Now, consider another approach:

"Border country is different. It is the place for outcasts, for cast-off folks who can't make it back 'in country.' They all gather there, a nation of exiles, of those who cannot return home as the lepers out there in border country between Galilee and Samaria. Not welcome in their homelands, unclean to their kin, they collect out there in border country.

"Of course, others must make the crossing, from one country to the other. And the lepers wait at the border, wait for the opportunities that come with the travelers. As they make the crossing, those lepers swoop in behind, like seagulls trolling behind a fishing boat.[73] *They troll for alms dropped nervously in the dust by the travelers. It's all the lepers can expect from those making the border crossing. One day, though, Jesus made his own crossing from Galilee to Samaria. And the lepers swept in behind, once more begging for mercy."*

The difference is apparent at once. A point of view is established along with a sense of place. Also built into the latter introduction is the limited expectation held by the lepers there in border country—"They troll for alms. It's all the lepers can expect." At the end, Jesus is introduced, making his crossing on his way to the cross. And once more the lepers beg for mercy. Buttrick also calls attention to the importance of the last sentence of an introduction: "(It) is difficult to write: it must *stop* action."[74] Above all, the introduction needs to collect the attention of the hearers and focus them, readying them to hear the first move of the sermon.

In order to do their work on behalf of hearing the Word, certain disciplines and parameters come into play for sermon introductions. Put simply, the specs for introductions are essential if the preacher intends them to function with regard to hermeneutic orientation and congregational focus. The obverse is also true: If the preacher intends the purpose of the sermon introduction to be that of warming up the audience or setting a mood of congregational good feelings for the preacher, then Buttrick's approach is not recommended. However, an introduction to a sermon embodying moves and structures will reflect the following characteristics:

1. The introduction usually will range in length between seven and twelve sentences.
2. The first two or three sentences will need to function much like the opening system of a move, acquainting the hearers with the speaker's voice and beginning the process of focusing the assembly toward the first move. Therefore, "the first few sentences in an introduction must be lean, simple sentences without clausal intrusions or extra adjectives."[75]
3. The last one or two sentences in the introduction, similarly, function much like the closure system of a move, they need to stop the action. Buttrick adds,

The end of the introduction and the start of the first move must be clearly separated. We do not want to fill the gap between the two with smooth-over transitional sentences. . . . The last words in an introduction, like a firm period at the end of a sentence, must establish a strong sense of "it's done."[76]

4. Because the purpose of an introduction is to focus consciousness, humor is especially suspect, defeating the orientation toward the first move and focusing instead on the preacher's wit or need to be liked.
5. As with illustrations within the moves, employment of first-person stories in the introduction subverts the focusing of congregational consciousness. Buttrick is unequivocal here:

As a preacher, you are attempting at the outset of a sermon to focus congregational consciousness on an image, or an idea, or a scriptural passage, or whatever. But, by speaking about yourself, inevitably the congregation will focus on *you*. There is no way to prevent the split. Personal narratives will always introduce a preacher and the intended subject matter will not form in congregational consciousness in any satisfactory fashion.[77]

The payoff is that within a sermon based on the method of David Buttrick, the introduction will be a carefully designed unit of language serving to focus the congregation in readiness to hear the first move and to orient the congregation with regard to hermeneutic concern. Buttrick's final word on introductions is this: "Write an introduction for the sake of a congregation and not as a form of personal expression." He adds, "Motto for introductions: Love your neighbors—in the pews."[78]

Conclusions

As is the case with introductions, sermon conclusions also serve two main purposes. The introduction is a unit of language designed to focus congregational attention and to orient congregational consciousness. Conclusions also have two functions: They must express the sermonic intention and they must conclude. Performing these two tasks, conclusions will, similarly, be disciplined language systems working under several constraints. First, as with the moves themselves, conclusions will need to be long enough that congregational consciousness is able to dial in on the content. That expectation in itself mandates a conclusion of more than three sentences. (Any shorter in length and the unit of language will not form.) At their outer limits with respect to length, most any conclusion needs itself to conclude in about eight sentences. The limits, then, are a minimum of five and a maximum of eight sentences for the conclusion. Moreover, within the body of the conclusion, there will not be introduced any new ideas; the conclusion "will work from a series of moves that have comprised the body of the sermon."[79]

The concluding function of a conclusion is addressed by taking into consideration how communal language does and does not work in consciousness. Initially, Buttrick suggests that the rhetoric designed to stop consciousness— the language of a sermon conclusion—is different from the consciousness that deals with the mobility of sermonic moves. "Thus, one of the tasks of a conclusion is to establish a stopped, reflective consciousness in a congregation."[80] It is the first two sentences of a conclusion that shift the hearers from a traveling to a stopped consciousness.[81] On the other hand, there are contraindications here as well. These "do nots" include the following: signaling that the conclusion has indeed begun by the use of "finally" or "in conclusion" will invite the congregation to drift away from attending to the conclusion. Additionally, serving up an obvious reiteration of the sermon introduction is profoundly ill advised. "The practice," Buttrick states, "totally destroys motivation" by creating a closed circle in consciousness.[82]

191

Besides the obvious need for conclusions to conclude, they also need to embody intention. There is, Buttrick notes, an "intending to do" both of scriptural texts and of sermons as well. In the case of a sermon developed in the mode of immediacy, the intention of the sermon is, presumably, the intention of the biblical text. In any mode of preaching, however, there will be an intending to do that will vary according to the moves and structures of the sermon. What this aspect of a conclusion's performance denies is any stereotyping of its role. That is, "we must be wary of suggestions that a conclusion will have *one* invariable form or purpose."[83] Whether that single purpose be one of evoking altar call decisions, moral uplift, and readiness to receive the sacrament (these examples are Buttrick's), the imposition of a predetermined function for the conclusion defeats its role as intending to do the distinctive intention of each sermon. So, for example, a sermon based on Luke's transfiguration story (Luke 9:28-36) seems to have a twofold intention: ratifying that Jesus is the chosen Son and that disciples are to listen to him, and following Jesus as he makes his departure *(exodos)*. Mark's consistently negative presentation of the disciples has as its rhetorical strategy invoking a response in the reader of a true discipleship. Therefore, the conclusion of a sermon on Mark 8:14-21 embodies the text's intention that aims toward the hearer's correct understanding of what it means to have the one loaf in the boat. The disciples fail the test by murmuring; their hearts are hardened. The conclusion of a sermon on this story will invite hearers to respond with a sense of irony and rejoice with faith that the one loaf is with them.

Buttrick sees this concluding intention becoming realized through a strategy that on one hand avoids a wooden repetition of the sermon's content and on the other avoids the necessity of beginning an entirely new idea or image system. One trick is to use a reiterative strategy, assembling fragments from throughout the sermon, which weave "images and phrases together into a patterned conclusion."[84] Another strategy is to track the natural outcome of the sequence of moves in the sermonic plot. In this case, very little, if any, material will be drawn from the body of the sermon for use in the conclusion. Rather, the aim of the sermon is quite naturally developed in the conclusion—the moves have now led the preacher and assembly to the sermon's intended outcome. In conclusion, Buttrick adds, "Conclusions are acts of obedience; we are doing what is intended. They are practical matters; we stop."[85]

Epilogue to Moves and Structures

If the homiletic method of David Buttrick seems to play out its specific implications in ways that seem overly constrained, he would probably respond by saying, "You betcha you're constrained." A sermon preached in the mode of immediacy is constrained by the scope of the text's structural logic and performative intention. The modes of reflection and praxis require other restraints specific to their own performance as well. And all preaching is constrained by the nature of human consciousness and by the need for the sermon to form within the human mind. Faith does come by hearing, Buttrick would remind us. But there is another side to the argument as well. What is offered in this method is "a whole new way of preaching which does not nail you down, but sets you free to preach the Word of the Lord, which is after all, what preaching is about."[86] What initially appears to be undue restraint, it is argued, actually provides for a liberating of the awesome power of preaching. So Buttrick concludes:

> When a new homiletic, tuned to hermeneutic sensitivity and a tough phe-nomenological analysis of language, emerges and filters down to the pastor's study, we may find a generation of preachers who find Scripture exciting and who find speaking in grace an act of radical obedience.[87]

Evaluation

With David Buttrick's *Homiletic* in print now for more than ten years and with his subsequent publication of numerous other volumes on preaching, it is generally acknowledged in homiletic circles that his method is an endur-ing aspect of the new homiletics. Not only is Buttrick's hermeneutics and methodology regarded as a highly significant groundbreaking approach to preaching, but also other colleagues exploring other avenues of faithful preaching continue a (mostly) implicit conversation with their phenomeno-logical colleague. For example, when preachers of all sorts of methodological stripes turn to consider how imagery can serve the Word, Buttrick is a pri-mary source of insight. Similarly, preachers are migrating more and more toward sermon shapes that are marked by mobility and some kind of plotted sequence. In so doing, they are borrowing from Buttrick both the notion of the sermonic plot and the very language to speak of such dynamic forms—moves, intention, and plot itself. Those of us whose place in the new homilet-ics is more fully in the narrative camp nevertheless depend on Buttrick for insights into how language works with regard to opening and closing systems, point of view, and the cautions about tense shifts and many other rhetorical concerns. (Buttrick's rhetorical insights, I have suggested to colleagues, are like "five finger exercises" for preachers.) Put succinctly, David Buttrick is a continuing conversation partner around the web of preaching. He speaks to the contemporary situation in preaching and is the subject of ongoing debate and controversy within the field.

What David Buttrick continues to contribute to the homiletical enterprise includes his constructive homiletic on one hand and his critique of modern preaching on the other. Beginning with the latter, it remains the case that the hermeneutic of distillation continues to be a largely reflexive habit of many preachers as they approach Scripture. Isolating texts without regard to context, extracting main ideas and other thematics from narrative lections, distilling entire portions of Scripture to one or more points—these homiletical echoes of the Enlightenment are still very much with us. Among all the postmodern homileticians, Buttrick continues to lead the battle against such misuses of the text. His alternative constructive approach, may continue to have a widely diverse reception from his colleagues and from new homiletic preachers. Nevertheless, most of us across the contemporary web of preaching begin our critique of preaching's recent past with David Buttrick's analysis of its hermeneutics of distillation.

A more controversial aspect of Buttrick's program is his insistence that homiletics must renew its partnership with rhetoric, with the study of how language functions in an oral, social environment. Those who oppose this insistence that the performative issue regarding pulpit speech is an essential consideration do so for a variety of reasons. For some preachers, of course, a kind of first naïveté persists in which it is assumed that most words used in the sermon will find a warm reception in the minds of the audience. Others, operating out of a Barthian perspective take umbrage at any attention to the rhetoric of preaching. If preaching is truly God's Word, they argue, then questions of rhetoric are at least beside the point and may even be symptoms of an unbelieving church! More generally, it is Buttrick's obdurate certitude regarding how the oral and communal language of preaching works along with oblique references to research that is not documented, which has exposed him to the most intense critique from colleagues. Whether seen in the initial reaction of John Melloh just after *Homiletic*'s publication ("unfortunately, the text appears arrogant"[88]) or that of others within the field of homiletics since then, the central criticism of *Homiletic* is its perceived dogmatism regarding matters of rhetoric. It is odd that those who rise to offer this critique then head off in opposite directions when it comes to proposed alternatives to Buttrick's assertorial remarks.

The persistent attack on Buttrick's (overly) confident mandates regarding language and consciousness, for some critics, leads to a conclusion that any such thoroughgoing analysis of the rhetoric of preaching is inappropriate. Apparently, the only way to avoid manipulating—or brainwashing—the congregation is for the preacher to remain naïve about language's function in oral communication within the assembly. That such preacherly innocence leads to pulpit disasters is a reality apparent not only to Buttrick, but also to many parishioners. On the other hand, the critique that Buttrick has at least overstated those rhetorical certainties does merit consideration. As it stands, the critics insist, Buttrick's approach is not in itself wrongheaded, but rather overstepping in its certainties. Do all doublet sentences delete immediately from consciousness? Eugene Lowry comments that "at least my computer asks if it's all right."[89] To this issue, Ron Allen questions whether all doublets, in fact, do delete from consciousness when preached.[90] The same critique obtains across the sweep of Buttrick's claims regarding how consciousness works. What particularly irritates many commentators is that, in the words of Thomas Long, "Buttrick, however, doesn't make suggestions; he states scientific *laws*."[91] Long then adds,

> The problem here is that critical research is never documented. Buttrick announces in the preface that, "though the technical information I offer does rest on years of research, at the risk of dogmatism I neither describe nor document the studies." This is particularly troubling not only because empirical research is so crucial to his argument, but also because some of Buttrick's findings seem to fly in the face of ordinary preaching experience and other research on the human listening process.[92]

David Buttrick may respond here with two points (deleting the other point and a poem). First, Buttrick may note that his homiletical specs, while extensive, are also quite specific in their application. For example, we hear repeatedly that doublet illustrations do not function in congregational consciousness. This is not to say, however, that other doublet systems will not, in fact, function in the congregational hearing. Buttrick would most likely label them as another sort of twofold language system than true doublets. That is, Buttrick is careful to define doublets as a binary language set in which both express the same single meaning. Second, Buttrick would likely ask his critics to subject their beliefs regarding pulpit language to a lab setting. The fact of the matter, Buttrick would argue, is that none of his critics vis à vis language and consciousness would retain true doublets when they served as the auditors. Of course, the critics would respond that it would be nice to see the research that originally led Buttrick to these assertions.

A final concern regarding David Buttrick's homiletic relates to his (profoundly positive) insistence on the communal context for hermeneutics and the various modes of preaching. That is, Buttrick invokes the notion of a "Christian consciousness" within which a text's structure and intention forms in the mode of immediacy, evokes reflectivity, and underpins the mode of praxis. Now while the modes of immediacy and reflectivity retain some degree of attachment to the biblical texts, the mode of praxis detaches itself from any specific pericope, finding its location within Christian hermeneutic consciousness. (Recall that as situations are raised within the sermon, we exegete both our worldly, human assumptions and that consciousness shaped by revelation and Christian faith.) The issue here is that for the mode of praxis to function in our preaching, two rather distinct aspects of consciousness must be available to both preacher and assembly, the human, worldly consciousness—rather easily evoked—along with a Christian, being-saved consciousness. It is the latter that is problematic in this distinctly postmodern era. That the mode of praxis depends upon a Christian consciousness within hearers implies, at minimum, a community of faith steeped in the biblical narrative, formed by a liturgical and eucharistic piety, practiced in personal and communal prayer, and tested by praxis in witness, service, and evangelism. Buttrick frequently refers to the latter elements of a Christian consciousness, those of biblical literacy and missional praxis, but does not attend much to the others. Perhaps, Robert Waznak wonders, "Buttrick's suspicions about the stirrings of Pietism prevent him from taking his readers into the intuitive world of prayer and imagination."[93] In an age when so many who are found in the churches of liberal Protestantism have an almost total amnesia regarding the narratives of Scripture, the formation of a Christian consciousness is rendered spotty at best. However, these same congregants come well formed in the worldly consciousness of their secular neighbors. (Recall that Buttrick admonished, "Worldly readings of situations will invariably lead us to wrong scriptural analogues."[94]) To the extent that the mode of praxis depends for its effectiveness on a fully formed Christian consciousness in order to function in tension with the worldly one, we may need a restrictive clause about its use. "Warning," the placard might read, "the use of the mode of praxis is restricted to certain congregations in the African American church and certain others well formed in biblical narrative, liturgical and sacramental piety, and personal and communal prayer." Those of us called to preach in less well-formed communities of faith might do well to remain with the modes of immediacy and reflectivity for a rather enduring season.

Going Home Christian

Robert Howard

Acts 2:42-47

Every Sunday, something most peculiar happens. Have you noticed it? Take a close look: We drive into the parking lot, enter the church building, and sit down in a pew. And then strange events begin to occur. Consider: we *sing praises*. Now, how often in ordinary life do you find any collection of human beings doing that? We *pray* out loud. Well, maybe you'll hear one person in some group say *one* prayer, but all together? We collect cash—to give to other people. Mighty peculiar! And we *eat and drink together* in a special ritual. Not your ordinary household event by any means. What do we think we are doing? Let's drop in on First Christian Church, in a city called Jerusalem, around 33 A.D. Maybe they can give us a clue.

Well, look at this: Luke gives us a shining ideal. See? Right there in Acts: an idyllic picture, viewed through rose-tinted glasses. A fine Christian example of church. *This* is the way to be, says Luke. Oh, great! Thanks a lot! Don't you just love an "example"? "Dear, why can't you be like Ronald?" Ronald makes straight A's, he's in the glee club, and he doesn't drink, smoke, do drugs, cuss. His shirts are always neatly pressed, he's always polite, he goes to bed at 10:00 sharp, he always turns his homework in *a day early. . . .* YECCHHH! Who in the world wants an example like that shoved down their throats? Ahh, but Luke is wise, Luke knows: Unless you have a clear idea of where you want to go, how do you know you're on the right track? A man wants to build a house. "Where are your blueprints?" "Oh, I'll just start hammering, and see how it turns out. I'll come up with something." Can you guess what's going to happen? So Luke hands us this snapshot of the infant church. (And you could even say he got double prints—check out the end of chapter 4.) *Here,* says Luke, *this* is what it means to be a Christian church. The gathered, they ate together, they rejoiced in the Lord, they heard the Word of God proclaimed, they shared *whatever* folks needed. Every day, breaking bread, praising God, sharing their stuff gladly! Here's your goal, says Luke. An *example* for us to shoot for.

So, how do we stack up? To tell the truth, not very well. We've sort of slid over the years. Just look at preaching. In the 1940s, every Monday, the *New York Times* would print an entire page of sermons from the previous day. Every Monday, the Word of God thundered, a yardstick of American conscience. And today? Not so much as a filler squib. Well, except to mention the sermon stridently warning us of that notorious threat to Christendom: Tinky Winky. But no Word of the Lord protesting American militarism smacking its lips at the prospect of another war. No pulpits denouncing the widening gap, as the stock market soars, yes, but real wages for ordinary folks plummet. No voices pointing out that it seems to be open season on gays and African Americans these days—and not just in Wyoming and Texas! No, the gospel of righteousness has been smoothed into a smiley-faced, therapeutic band-aid—a feel-good sermonette that makes giddy Christianettes. Or look at worship. A few churches today might bustle with excitement, all right, but too many of them have become mere feeding troughs. Individuals belly up to the bar, dip in, take whatever feels good, and go their merry way. No commitment, no sense that God was doing something grand and glorious long before they stepped onto stage, and will continue long after they have finished their part. No sense that we've been brought together to fulfill a mission. No, no, just: "I'm getting mine, thank you very much. Dip in, and then I'll be on my way. Enjoyed the music; the preaching sure made me feel better about myself. See you next week." And look at church life. For too many, the fire of faith has simply slumped into dull habit, week in and week out. The same folks trade church offices around, the Sunday school teachers play their annual musical-chairs shuffle. All too often Christianity in the good old U. S. of A. is simply weary, played out, with faith threadbare, numbers dropping. Joy? It took the last train to. . . . Seems we're not doing so well these days. Lost our edge, so to speak.

Okay, how do we get our act together? I'll tell you how, says Luke. I'll tell you exactly: Do what they did at First Christian Church, Jerusalem. Teach! Tell them the story of Jesus. Think, now: Every one of us here is here today because someone touched our life. That is how faith is taught: human mouth to human ear. One beggar telling another where to find the whole wheat Bread of Life. So tell them the stories—the story of how God flung great handfuls of stars into the velvet canopy of night, lit the sun with the fire of a word, knelt down and scooped up a handful of clay, tenderly shaped it into human form. Tell of Moses, doggedly herding those rebellious, griping Israelites through the dust, and of Amos planting his feet in the center of the king's crystal cathedral and bellowing out doom. Tell the stories. Tell them!

Jesus, tramping all over Galilee with twelve dum-dums who just don't get it. A supper in an upper room, lonely prayer in a midnight garden, a kangaroo-court trial, the slash of a whip, stumbling along the streets while carrying the crosspiece of his own execution, the ring of hammer on nail, the scream, "My God, my God, why have you deserted me?" The body, limp as a dishrag. The tomb. And that unbelievable Sunday morning, early, early, at dawn. Raised? Raised? *Not* dead? Tell them the stories, all of them saying one thing: This is who you are. This is what you're part of. Scott Momaday tells of a time when he was twelve or so, when his father took him to his grandmother's house. From before the sun rose until long after it set, she told him stories of his Kiowa ancestors, their victories, their defeats, the quirks, the heroes, the traitors, the grand dreams. All day long, stories of his ancestors. Sunup to sundown, all day long, the stories. He says, "That day I went home a Kiowa."[95] Tell the stories, says Luke, in Sunday school, in worship, singing, praying, preaching. Tell them! So that *we* can say, "Today I went home a Christian." Teach. Teach the Story.

But Christians also learn by doing. Head knowledge alone just won't cut it. Christianity is not a spectator sport. Oh, no. The love of God travels into the ears, to the heart, and then out through hands and feet and lips. Christianity means putting all that we have at God's disposal: "Here it is. I give it over to you, lock, stock, and barrel!" It means being willing to share our stuff at a moment's notice, whenever we see the need. So Christians will do quite ordinary actions, like buying an extra can at the grocery store and bringing it to church for the food pantry. They will dream up creative ways to minister to God's beloved children. Like the day after the ice storm hit, a few years ago, when Eastwood Christian Church in Nashville, Tennessee, was scheduled to put up a few homeless men for the night with the "Room at the Inn" ministry. But the church had no power. No power meant no heat. But, as one of the homeless guys said, "Well, at least we'll have a roof over our heads tonight. And we won't be any colder." No power meant no lights. So we brought the candelabras in from the sanctuary. No power meant no freezers. So the food committee emptied out their freezers at home, brought the goodies to church for the evening meal. The food wouldn't last anyway, and the church had a gas stove. So we had the grandest banquet by candlelight— us and a dozen homeless men. Christians will live their faith. They will pass around a beat-up plastic butter tub in Sunday school every month, collecting money for a member with cancer. Christianity means an athletic faith, not afraid to roll up its sleeves and get its hands messy. A faith that says, "We care for you." Christianity is a show-and-tell game. We act our way into being Christian. We learn by doing.

Aw, but come on now. Who can do all this—really? Let's get real. Oh, says Luke, you don't have to do it alone. Oh, no! That same Holy Spirit that brooded over the surging waters of creation will be with you all the way. The Holy Spirit, you see, is the very power of creation, busy re-creating every moment of every day. The power of God who doesn't know the meaning of the word "can't." Habitat for Humanity sprang from one man's conviction that no person made in the image of God should have to sleep in a shack. Each child of God, said he, ought to have decent housing. Habitat for Humanity now puts up dozens of houses every week, across the globe: in Uganda, Venezuela, Bangladesh—even Nashville, Tennessee. Habitat projects have attracted former presidents and withstood the furies of Hurricane Andrew in Miami. Ordinary people—just like you and me—changing lives for the love of Jesus, through the power of the Holy Spirit. Whenever they finish a Habitat house, they hold a public ceremony with the new homeowner, present a Bible, and invite them to say a few words. One woman stepped up to the microphone, hesitated, then raised her hands and shouted, "Yippee! Yippee! Yippee!" And of course, everyone in the crowd laughed, delighted. Again, she hollered, "Yippee! Yippee! Yippee!" And again, everybody chuckled. And a third time: "Yippee! Yippee! Yippee!" And this time, nobody laughed, because they were too busy crying. "Holy Spirit!" cries Luke, "hard at work." For Luke, you see, the Spirit shoves the Christian Church first out onto the streets of Jerusalem and then out into the world. The Spirit opens new doors: Peter's eyes were opened as a sheet full of all kinds of animals drops out of the sky: "Eat anything? But I didn't think we were supposed to—okay, okay, if you say so!" Always pushing, always making a way out of no way, breaking the rules, sending folks where no Christians had gone before. A small congregation starts their "Give-A-Dime" program, asking each person to give one dime a week to support Church World Service ministries. Within a year, the tinkle of dimes in their glass pickle jar with a slot in the lid has doubled their yearly giving figure. Just the Holy Spirit, doing the impossible. Over, under, around, and through, working with us, working on us, working through us. We are not alone. Unrealistic ideal? Hah! Not with the Holy Spirit at the controls! God's Holy Spirit just loves working miracles using ordinary hands and unrealistic plans. With the Holy Spirit, there's nothing we can't do! Nothing.

So let's take a look around First Christian Church, Jerusalem, 33 A.D. Now look around at another Christian church. Telling the story. Rolling up our sleeves. In the miraculous power of the Holy Spirit. Do you see a resemblance? Yeah . . . we might even go home Christians today. Amen.

CHAPTER 5

The Sermon in Four Pages: The Homiletic Method of Paul Scott Wilson

Paul Scott Wilson offers a homiletic method in which the elements of the sermon are examined and ordered according to a series of considerations. Ultimately, these aspects of the sermon will be configured into preaching's "Four Pages." However, the journey to that homiletic quartet starts at the beginning, with a glance at prior considerations, providing a count up to the Four Pages, but beginning with one. Starting at the beginning, then, involves some reflection on the ways that the unity of the sermon is achieved.

"One" Is for Unity

Wilson observes what many congregations know from firsthand and bitter experience—many sermons wander aimlessly, feel rushed and disconnected, or fail to achieve an ending. In order for preachers to avoid these pitfalls, they need to be guided by six signs along the highway of sermon composition. Observing these six signs is essential to achieving the unity of the sermon. Wilson summarizes the signs, these places to stop along the homiletic highway as follows:

> Preachers should stop six times to identify: one **text** from the Bible to preach; one **theme** sentence arising from the text; one **doctrine** arising out of that theme statement; one **need** in the congregation that the doctrine or theme sentence addresses; one **image** to be wed to the theme sentence; and one **mission**.[1]

The six signs, Wilson suggests, may be recalled using the somewhat awkward acronym, TTDNIM, more easily remembered as "The Tiny Dog Now Is Mine."[2] Each of these elements of the sermon's unity needs elaboration.

1. The One Text

Here, Paul Scott Wilson admonishes that the preacher should base his or her sermon upon one text of Scripture. Theologically, this one text is essential to preaching's task because it is through the Scriptures that God speaks to the people; proclamation involves hearing the text both read and then preached. And while some in both the pulpit and the pew turn to other sources, we have really no other authority to preach—the Scriptures are God's Word—and no other matter upon which to preach than the biblical text.[3]

In order to achieve this primary element of unity, the preacher will need to identify the one text upon which the sermon will be based. Some church traditions strongly value the independence of the preacher in choosing the text for each Sunday, based on the needs of the congregation, an interest in extending congregational exposure to unfamiliar texts, or in service of thematic series. Those who employ the three-year lectionary, whether the original Roman Catholic version or the Revised Common Lectionary, have three texts presented each Sunday over the course of a three-year cycle. Given this structure to the service of the Word, some preachers have settled on an approach to preaching that attempts to weave together all of the readings within their sermon. However, Wilson cautions against this practice for reasons relating to both the preacher and the people. The preacher rarely has time to develop more than one text appropriately, whereas the people will be able to attend to at most one text each Sunday. "In other words," Wilson concludes, "even with a lectionary, a choice of a text must be made."[4] One text is the basis for most every sermon.

2. The One Theme

Each biblical text, once its unity has been established, will yield to the careful interpreter one theme statement. This statement is an important initial point of contact between the text and the sermon—the text offers one theme as its central, concrete meaning; the theme statement also provides a clear path through the process of writing the sermon. The theme is, therefore, both a handle for the biblical text as well as an organizing principle for the ensuing sermon.[5] Once the theme statement has been identified, moreover, it has a capacity to shape the homiletic reading of the text from which it is drawn. "A good theme sentence leads the preacher to restructure and retell the biblical passage, to add nuancing, qualifications, stories, explanations, and grounding in experience and doctrinal tradition."[6]

Anticipating objections from recent authorities in biblical studies, hermeneutics, and homiletics, Wilson immediately assures his readers that such a theme statement should not be equated with old single-meaning approaches to interpretation. Wilson freely joins with recent scholarship in asserting that every text has multiple meanings, not just one main idea. In fact, Wilson notes, "every time we restate the meaning of a biblical text as a theme statement for the sermon, we may be offering a different meaning."[7] The preacher will need to assess the centrally important theme statement of the text with an awareness that what is not occurring is the naming of that text's main idea. Confronted by the multiple meanings of the text under consideration, the preacher will want to identify for this particular sermon what theme, among the variety expressed within the pericope, will serve as the text's handle and sermonic organizing principle.[8]

Since the preacher will be selecting from among several available meanings of most any text for the sermon's theme statement, two guidelines are offered to assist in the decision. First, the theme statement should be cast in a declarative mode and not as a question. When a question is made to serve as a theme, "it functions (a) to mask or blunt a more direct statement the preacher is reluctant to make, but nonetheless wants the congregation to hear, or (b) to identify a general topic and avoid saying anything specific about it."[9] Since Wilson has already insisted that this theme be as concrete as possible, a question tending toward the most general will not work. Likewise, a question may mask a concrete statement the preacher decides is risky. (Thus, we may use the question, "How do people sin?" as a cover for the declarative statement, "We are all sinners.") Second, the most appropriate question to ask about this declarative theme statement relates to the identity of God. "What is God doing in or behind this text?" Wilson asks.[10] When this question is asked of the text, the answer will be couched in a declarative mode, with the most action-oriented language possible. With Buttrick and others, Wilson points to the role of strong verbs in effective pulpit speech.[11] Moreover, the interest in God's action in the text is most urgently raised when the text in question does not mention God explicitly. Since a huge number of biblical texts make no direct mention of God, there is a likelihood that a sermon based upon such texts will also shy away from any mention of God. Given this tendency, preachers will need the discipline of seeking God "behind the text in the purpose or function of the text, or in the larger sweep of events to which the episode belongs."[12] Again, having discerned what God's action is in the text, the theme statement needs to articulate this witness in clear, declarative language. God should be the subject of the sentence, with an emphasis on grace. And again, Wilson emphasizes the need for strong action verbs.[13]

3. The One Doctrine

Just as a text yields multiple meanings and is therefore open to a number of themes, so, too, most any text offers more than one doctrine. Simply put, "a biblical passage of some length typically may suggest half a dozen doctrines."[14] The preacher's task, therefore, is to choose among the alternatives based on several considerations. However, Wilson notes that the initial problem here is that many preachers never come to the place of considering the doctrinal aspects of their text in any respect. This serious omission of the doctrinal aspect of the text may be due to a last-minute approach to sermon preparation, or to some other, more systemic factors. There is a problem regarding the other side of the coin as well: Our attempts at doctrinal clarity may result in an overly abstract and jargon-laden thesis.[15] Some guidelines are clearly needed to negotiate between doctrinal laxity on one hand and doctrinal abstraction on the other hand.

Among the doctrines available in the text, Wilson invites preachers to ask, "which doctrine most accurately 'says the text in other words.' "[16] There is a need for both clarity and conciseness in stating this "best" doctrine. This initial stage of sermon preparation is not the place for building a chapter in one's own systematic theology. First, the sermon that is about to be fashioned will not be able to explore too much doctrinal terrain. Second, since the purpose of considering the one doctrine is to shepherd and guide the sermon's development, a too complex doctrinal statement will be more of a barrier than a homiletical aid. A few sentences should suffice to express the one doctrine chosen as the central meaning of the text. And this brief summary of the text's doctrinal core should, of course, relate to the theme statement and should, in fact, arise out of that theme.

4. The One Need

To say that preaching must address some need or other is a truism in today's church. However, Wilson notes that this conventional wisdom must be approached with caution; a simplistic construal of the sermon's relevance will result in a distortion of the gospel. On one hand, the one need that will help guide the sermon is not to be reduced to what the congregation thinks their needs are this morning. On the other hand, it cannot be what the preacher thinks the congregation really needs this morning. The real need will be assessed in relation to the theme statement already identified, and the preacher will inquire of the theme, "What question does this answer in the life of a person or people in the church?"[17] The same question can be asked regarding the doctrinal statement as well. As with both the one theme and the one doctrine, the one need will be articulated in terse, concrete language. Overly vague or abstract thinking here will not help the preacher as he or she moves to the actual work of preparing the sermon.

5. The One Image

One image will emerge out of the text, aligning itself with the theme, the doctrine, and the need. As expected, Wilson observes that the sermon will contain a number of images as finally preached. The issue early in the process of working on the sermon is to identify one image that may "become dominant and unifying."[18] However, such a dominant image is not to be considered essential for every sermon—in contrast to the theme, doctrine, and need. Some sermons may never possess a central, unifying image. For the highly intuitive preacher, though, who overfunctions in the use of imagery, the discipline of selecting one dominant image will be essential.[19]

An image is to be distinguished from an abstract idea in that the former is a "word picture," bringing some specific concrete object to mind.[20] We think more in images, Wilson notes, than in abstractions, and we remember best what is presented with perceptual immediacy. And while a dominant image is not essential to the sermon's unity, when employed, it gains its power through careful repetition. "Because preaching is oral," Wilson observes, "repetition is the preacher's equivalent of the highlighting marker or colored text on a computer screen." He adds: "A recurring image can add conceptual unity to the sermon. However, it becomes of greatest force and usefulness if by the end of the sermon it adds theological unity as well."[21] Once more, we notice Wilson's caveat regarding the one image. A dominant image is not needed for every sermon or every preacher. However, when used effectively, its repetitive usage will contribute both sermonic unity and enduring perceptual experiences.

Images for preaching come from a variety of sources, and the preacher needs to be alert to these potential sources as the Four Pages of the sermon are considered. First of all, the text itself may be the best source for the sermonic imagery. Some texts abound in imagery—Wilson notes that prophetic texts are especially abundant in imagery—while other biblical texts may seem devoid of images entirely. Again, the issue when confronted by the text's multiple meanings expressed through multiple images is the same: Select from among the skein of images the one image that will remain dominant throughout the sermon and that will best express the one theme of the text. Images may also derive from our world, Wilson adds. Potential images, he notes, surround us. Two problems present themselves when contemporary images are used in the sermon, paralleling the concerns we have previously encountered. First, there is such an abundance of imagery in our world, and especially in our visual culture, that the sermon could become overdone with contrasting or conflicting images. Second, there is a care needed that images "communicate clearly what we intend."[22] David Buttrick, for example, cites a sermon illustration in which Jesus is inadvertently likened to a plate of asparagus![23]

A final source of imagery has to do with certain rhetorical systems that may be used in the course of the sermon. A refrain or repetitive system, though not employing a specific word picture, will function much like an image. Such a refrain may be taken from the culture, especially from the media, but in any case will need to be related closely to the theme statement. In fact, Wilson notes: "The theme statement is an excellent candidate for this repetition."[24] So imagery from the biblical text, the contemporary world, and from various rhetorical systems provides potential sources for the word pictures of the sermon. In any and every case, the images used will be constrained by the one theme and the one doctrine.

6. *The One Mission*

While the issue of the mission of the sermon will be addressed chiefly in Pages Two and Four of the sermon, during this early process of considering the "one thing necessary," the sermon's mission deserves some attention. "By mission," Wilson comments, "I mean primarily one act, one action of ministry that listeners may contemplate doing as a result of the sermon."[25] Some of these acts may be expressed in a general way—our mission to feed the hungry or advocate for justice throughout the world. At other times, the mission may well be articulated in a specific manner, inviting the congregation to join in an ecumenical food pantry project, for example. Related to these more specific aspects of mission, Wilson points out that one variety of concrete actions also serves in a symbolic way, indicating "the kind of action an individual or group might undertake."[26] By symbolic, Wilson means that while certain specific actions are proposed to the congregation, they are meant as both real, specific suggestions and examples of the types of missions the listeners might come to live out in their lives together or as individuals. The intent of raising the question of mission here in the opening considerations is the theological affirmation that preaching will ultimately call for specific outcomes in faith and in action.

The Two Metaphors of Preaching

Paul Scott Wilson, along with many of us, inherited a dominant metaphor of the sermon that assumes a literary, essayist quality to the work. The rules relate to writing an essay: "Do not repeat yourself; use as many big words as possible; give only the facts and no detail; avoid descriptive material; eliminate conversations."[27] Clearly, in our oral and visual culture, none of these qualities will serve proclamation very well; the decline in church membership in many denominations indicates that a change in metaphors is overdue. Wilson invites us to think of the sermon as an event of movie making instead of as the place of the literary metaphor. Immediately, the admonitions related to the essay are turned on their heads. Repetition is a time-honored quality of oral language, big words may get in the way of communication, and so on. Conceived as a kind of movie, the notions of mobility and visual immediacy are introduced. The sermon is going somewhere and will offer the listeners a vivid portrayal of that journey. Wilson concludes:

> Thus, if we imagine that we are directing a film we allow ourselves to think and compose sermons in a visual manner—which is how most of us think in any case. More than simply telling plots, or becoming one character in a narrative, we will create entire worlds that address the senses, the mind, and the heart.[28]

Conceived as an activity of moviemaking, the sermon is construed quite differently than by means of the literary model of preaching. Moviemaking is one metaphor for the sermon that can guide the process from beginning to end.

Held in tension with the metaphor of moviemaking is its companion analogy that speaks of the "Pages" of the sermon. The reader may well raise questions here regarding the literary implications of the sermon's Pages. However, Wilson insists that the metaphor of the Page is both appropriate to his method and, in fact, complementary to the other metaphor of moviemaking. Regarding the latter, Wilson indicates that while rejecting the metaphor of the book, the sermon as a book, he recognized that "even movies need scripts, and scripts have pages."[29] Moreover, we may think with some advantage of the Web page on the Internet as a model for the sermon. Here, we find information and imagery, words and pictures, and in some of the best sites, we may experience a movie along with the other information. In other words, the Web page provides for an integration of the two metaphors, moviemaking and the Page. On one Web page, all sorts of information is presented, through words and pictures, through movies and static imagery. "Conceive of the sermon as an act of movie making," Paul Scott Wilson may well suggest, "and think of it as a quartet of pages, too."

The Three Elements of the Sermon

An overview of Paul Scott Wilson's homiletic indicates that his method, though not specified directly, emerges at the intersection of three dominant elements—an interest in the biblical text, in the theological task, and in rhetorical skill. For Wilson, Scripture is the revelation of God, addressed to the human family and to the church. Authentic preaching is the act of speaking this Word to a community of believers in a way that is particular and concrete. Therefore, the sermon will be grounded in a text of Scripture both as the source of its authority and as the Word that authorizes the preacher to speak. In fact, preaching on something other than Scripture for Wilson may not really be Christian proclamation! We must, he advocates, allow the text to "speak" the sermon.[30]

Coupled with this affirmation in the biblical grounding of preaching is Wilson's interest in the theological element of the sermon. When this interest is absent from preaching, all sorts of distortions occur. Chiefly, a disinterest in theology in preaching has led to a minimalism regarding the presence and action of God, both in Scripture and in the world. Specifically, Wilson points to a pervasive graceless quality to much of the preaching of today. Wilson intentionally proposes a homiletic method that majors in grace. "With good news," Wilson affirms, "the burden of the action falls on God, not on the listener."[31] The Four Pages of the sermon are structured in such a way that God's actions are proclaimed and God's grace in Jesus Christ is named.[32]

A third element of the sermon relates to the language of preaching, oral communication within a communal context: "Revelation is not revelation until it is received."[33] Wilson teaches, and the preacher will therefore have a lively interest in the rhetoric of preaching. Most important, this interest means that sermons will become much more visual and immediate in their language, drawing on word pictures and stories and more discursive speech. If revelation needs to be received, then the preacher will remain in a dialogue with contemporary rhetoricians. The language of preaching is a vital servant of the Word.

While Paul Scott Wilson understands homiletic method to emerge at the intersection of these three elements of preaching, he explicates their meanings and interplay as each of preaching's Four Pages is interpreted. Each of those Four Pages will consider the roles of Scripture, theology, and rhetoric within the distinctive context of that particular page. It will become our interest, then, to watch for the interplay of these three elements of preaching within each of Wilson's Four Pages of preaching.

The Four Pages of Preaching

Conceiving of a sermon composed of Four Pages is for Wilson a metaphor that achieves several homiletic virtues. First, Wilson is quick to note that the metaphor is not to be taken literally—it is not as if the preacher brings four and only four pages into the pulpit at each preaching occasion! Rather, he invites the preacher to conceive of them as four distinct moments within the course of the sermon. Each component page, then, is not to be taken literally, "but as a metaphor for theological function and appropriate creative endeavor."[34] Primarily, the Four Pages provide a theological focus to the sermon and its internal structure and movement; lacking such a structure has led to a kind of preaching that is mostly joyless and innocent of the presence of God. In addition to providing for an essential theological focus to the sermon, these Four Pages also function to structure the homiletic imagination and liberate it to serve the Word. Simply put, "the pages can be a guide to greater creativity and imagination, for they provide specific focus for creative endeavor that helps prevent imagery from becoming excessive, stories from going astray, and doctrines from becoming mere turbid or turgid discourse."[35]

The normative components of the sermon include Four Pages, arranged in sequence and developed according to a series of biblical, theological, and rhetorical considerations. These Four Pages are:

1. Trouble and conflict in the Bible
2. Trouble in the world
3. Grace and good news in the Bible
4. Grace for us and for our world

Wilson emphasizes the importance of each of these pages as essential to a successful sermon. However, he also allows for a variety of arrangement as regards their sequence. (Therefore, a sermon, for example, could begin with Page Two, developing some aspect of sin in the world, move to Page One to explore the biblical expression of that trouble, then move to pages Three and Four, focusing on grace in the text and in the present world.) Wilson, however, clearly prefers the logic and sequence as originally conceived, keeping the Pages, and the sermon, ordered to consider biblical trouble, contemporary sin, biblical grace, and grace in our present age.[36] Wilson also admits to the possibility that a sermon may omit one of the pages from time to time. He is quick to observe, though, that "if one or more of these pages is consistently absent, or is not given adequate focus and development, at least from a biblical and theological perspective, there may be room for us to grow."[37] The four-page model best retains the theological functions of the sermon and pre-sents an optimal point of view on the text. While we may rearrange these pages from time to time, we begin with the basic model—preaching's Four Pages, its four biblical and theological functions.

Page One: Trouble and Conflict in the Bible

Each of the Four Pages of the sermon will need about an equal share of explication. Therefore, the First Page will comprise about one quarter of the entire length of the sermon. This first 25 percent of the sermon deals with trouble in the biblical text. And as a crucial corollary, the Third Page, grace and good news in the Bible, will comprise an additional one fourth of the sermon's expanse. The reason we begin with the First Page, for Wilson, is theological: "The sermon is God's Word, not merely a human word."[38] Most every biblical text presents a theological constant, a revelation of the world's discord and sin. In even the most positive, grace-filled texts, there is an underside that is at least implied, since it is where sin abounds that grace abounds all the more (Rom. 6:1). Wilson turns to Bryan Chappell's work to best express the quality of the biblical trouble.[39] Chappell speaks of a necessary focus on the fallen condition of humanity that is revealed in the text. This "fallen condition focus," for Chappell, is an essential aspect of biblical interpretation, pointing to the sinful and broken nature of the world. Wilson relates that this fallen condition focus for Chappell becomes clear as three questions are asked of the text: "What does the text say? What concerns did the text address in its context? What do listeners share in common with those to (or about) whom it was written or the one by whom it was written?"[40] Assumed here is that texts in Scripture are not theologically or morally neutral; a theological claim is made by the text regarding the human condition.

Moreover, that theological claim is the consistent analysis that the world is a fallen world.

It is at this point in the initial interrogation of the text that Wilson's concern for sermonic unity is first raised. Recalling that a sermon will focus on one theme, along with the other elements of its unity (The Tiny Dog Now Is Mine), it is axiomatic that the preacher will locate and expand on one idea within this First Page. This theological idea is not to be confused for the overall theme statement of the sermon, but is the concise theological focus of the First Page of the sermon. Obviously, we would err in equating Page One's theological focus with the sermonic theme—we would once again omit any reference to God's grace if we were to do so. On the other hand, the one idea of the First Page will, of necessity, serve the sermon's theme and lead the hearers finally to a consideration of grace, developed in Pages Three and Four. We may well recall Wilson's comments relating to the multiple meanings within almost any biblical text. When acknowledging this richness in ideas and images, it is essential that the preacher select from among these meanings related to the fallen human condition for one single idea. Both students and seasoned preachers are encouraged to write the focus of each Page at the top of the page.[41]

While the biblical trouble of the First Page will remain focused on one idea, there are several strategies for structuring the content of this first quarter of the sermon. Most honored in usage perhaps is the traditional approach to preaching as exposition and then as application. In this approach, the preacher begins with an exposition of the text, a beginning that assures that Scripture will form the foundation of the sermon. Then, the preacher will turn and make an application of that expository within the present situation. Notice, Wilson hastens to add, that this exposition is not guided by the canons of modern historical criticism. Rather, the expository "is commonly doctrinal discussion of theology found in the text and elsewhere in the Bible."[42] However, there are clear warrants for adopting a fourfold pattern to the sermon instead of remaining with this dual structure of traditional expository preaching. Preeminent is the need for the sermon to say something about God's merciful dealings with us, to speak of grace. Although we cannot speak of God's grace without first understanding the underlying sin and brokenness of the human condition, we cannot serve the Word while remaining only fixed on trouble. Usually, sermons that begin and end with trouble place all of the responsibility for remedial action on the hearers. But the good news is that God has acted in Jesus Christ, making possible a transformation of the human condition. "At the heart of our faith," Wilson states, "is this very important paradox: the burden God places upon humans is the burden that God has already accepted in Jesus Christ."[43]

Page One of the sermon, Wilson insists, will invite the congregation to hear trouble in the text yet will not initiate a sermon devoid of the good news. The underlying causes of sermons that remain innocent of good news are methodological, approaches to the text that wind up predetermining theology. In addition to the drawbacks of the expository method mentioned above, other approaches to preaching may result in a homily almost devoid of good news. The preacher will need to exercise care and caution when it comes to selecting a method for preaching the sermon. For the most part, such approaches as doctrinal and topical sermons can embody balance between the negative of the human condition and the grace-filled positive of God's act in Jesus Christ. Narrative preaching with its reliance on the canons of literary analysis, however, will frequently err with regard to the bad news–good news equation. Narrative preachers, Wilson insists, fail at this point first because they do not bring theological reflection to the sermonic process; literary considerations have almost entirely displaced theological concerns. These narrative preachers "have given priority to literary matters over theological ones; that is, they preach good news only if their biblical text sounds to them like good news, and frequently they fail even then."[44] The only evidence of any good news in these narrative sermons may be found just at the end of the sermon. Still, such a minimal gesture fails the theological test for Christian preaching. An all-bad news sermon fails to meet the minimum standards for Christian proclamation.

A quite different challenge for the preacher is encountered when the text at hand presents little or no evidence of biblical bad news. What, then, will become of the First Page of the sermon? Wilson has insisted that the sermonic journey will begin with trouble in the text (with a few exceptions related to the sequence of the Pages). What is a preacher to do when the text for the Lord's Day seems untroubled? Paul Scott Wilson mentions several strategies that may result in an adequately expanded (25 percent of the sermon) First Page. First, he suggests that the text under consideration might be too narrowly defined. Thus, a small portion of Scripture that seems unbounded in good news is quite likely to be a positive word in the face of some trouble present in the larger context. For example, Paul's encouragement to sing with grace in Colossians 3:16 seems at first to be a trouble-free text. However, we need to back up only several verses to bump into all kinds of trouble related to "the old self," including "anger, wrath, malice, slander, and abusive language" (Col. 3:8). Now, with a wider context in mind, the preacher has no difficulty in exploring all sorts of trouble in the Bible. The lesson to be learned here is the virtue of choosing a complete pericope for the sermon. That way, ample material will be provided for both the First and the Second Pages. A happy by-product of this approach that sees not just the verse, but the entire unit of Scripture, is this—the congregation also benefits!

Another factor detected by Wilson results in a one-sided rendition of the biblical witness, dwelling on either all-bad or all-good news. "Most preachers," he states, "have not been taught or encouraged to look for trouble and grace, thus for some it is easy to forget that the Christian message is hope."[45] Both our culture and the spirit of the age within the church works to blind us to the full witness to God's Word in the Bible. While Wilson does not spell out these cultural forces that tend to blind us to the two-edged Word, we may assume that our culture's two minds, a strangely upbeat esteem-based message, and a simultaneous fixation on violence and disaster contribute here. At any rate, Wilson concludes:

> As John Wesley once said, every law contains a hidden promise. Every door of judgment is an opening of grace; every sinful act of humans is met by God in Christ. When we exclude trouble or grace from a sermon we make a choice. We opt for a theology in preaching that is an incomplete expression of the faith, a less than full encounter with God's Word.[46]

Having begun by looking at the trouble in the text, we are encouraged, then, to look for grace, aware that both are needed for this full encounter with the Word.

Page Two: Trouble in the World

Again, we are anticipating that this page will comprise about another 25 percent of the full body of the sermon. In this quarter, the focus is shifted to the contemporary situation, in which trouble analogous to the trouble in the Bible is identified and interpreted. We can make the leap across the millennia with confidence since fallen human nature has remained much the same, although thankfully, the character of our God is unchanging. However, Wilson insists that the leap not only be made across the ages with regard to human trouble and sin, but also be made in any sermon as well. Trouble afflicts us in every age. The argument for a Page Two in every sermon is as follows: "We need to be convicted of our sin, convinced that our ways are often the ways of death, shown that we misuse our freedom to trust other than the gospel, persuaded of our broken social systems, unmasked of our pretensions, shown the world as it really is, know in the depth of our saying no to God."[47]

There is, once more, an "on the other hand" to consider. While Page Two focuses on necessity of trouble in the world, care should be given to discern those children within God's human family who bear the brunt of that trouble. In some situations, it is a devastating natural disaster that victimizes. More often, it is human sin. Whenever the question of evil in our world is raised, the preacher is called to point out the victims of the abuse of power, of discrimination, and of oppression. There is the temptation, Wilson notes, to construe each and every instance of trouble in our world as entirely individual. But sin is both personal and institutional, and guilt is societal as well as individual. Page Two will avoid the temptation to interpret our trouble as originating either solely within the individual heart or solely within institutional structures. What is needed then is a more nuanced interpretation of trouble in our world than had been employed by conservatives (the individualistic model) and liberals (the institutional model). Imagine a three-part understanding of trouble, Wilson suggests. Trouble in the human family can be conceived of in three categories: transcendent or vertical trouble, immanent trouble, and human trouble.

1. Transcendent or vertical trouble

The transcendent model of biblical trouble derives from an emphasis on the otherness of God, on divine sovereignty and divine justice. On the other hand, the human condition is evaluated as one of sin and rebellion—we are guilty as charged. Consequently, the call is for human beings to change their behavior for the present and future and to be forgiven for their errant ways in the past. Wilson notes some common elements usually encountered within this transcendent model of trouble:

> The mood is imperative; the sin tends to be personal or individual sin before God; a sentence of judgment is passed from on high; the recipient experiences guilt (or anger); repentance and forgiveness are the only way out; responsibility for change rests mainly on the individual; the only recourse is to turn to God for grace and mercy.[48]

These common elements are in some cases to be found in tension with the full dimensions of vertical trouble in Scripture. In the biblical witness, God's sovereignty as much addresses social as individual culpability, and the call to repentance is often spoken to a whole people.

As transcendent trouble is preached, a range of discourse is available, spanning from direct challenge and confrontation to a more descriptive, but less confrontational, approach. The former, Wilson notes, is stereotyped as the finger-wagging, scolding preacher. The sermon is filled with "must's," "ought's," and "should's." However, a less confrontational stance may be a more effective strategy when presenting vertical trouble. Here, an indicative mode can be at once empathetic yet not condoning. Adults do not respond well when scolded as children. Hence, an approach that is descriptive and emphatic may be the best strategy in dealing with most types of transcendent trouble. "Congregations are made up of God's children," Wilson affirms, "and children need affirmation in the process of correction."[49]

2. Immanent trouble

Of course, there is a horizontal dimension to human trouble that is a necessary correlate to the vertical and transcendent. There is a brokenness in the world, along with the suffering of the innocent. And here, there is no possibility of adequately naming immanent troubles without focusing on both the individual and the social dimensions of the fallen human condition. The center of gravity within horizontal trouble, though, lies with the social aspects of sin and guilt before God. Guilt and shame are first collective and then individual, as the needs of those who suffer are faced openly. Wilson adds:

> This kind of trouble creates a sense of urgency, because people are suffering. Some social analysis is needed for the power of evil is present in human systems. . . . Moreover, a change of individual hearts is not enough to accomplish God's will on earth. People need to commit themselves to social change, even as God is committed to overturn the powers of the world that seem to be having the final say.[50]

To speak of God's commitment to reverse and defeat the power of evil, then, necessarily focuses on the suffering and compassion of God, and especially on the suffering and crucifixion of God's servant Jesus.

Two other cautions confront us as we seek to preach about horizontal trouble. As with vertical trouble, we can adopt an indicative stance that puts our hearers off so intensely, denouncing social sin from our particular theological perspective. The outcome, as was seen within the transcendent model of trouble, is that the congregational resistance may well be hardened by the ought-must-should kind of preaching. It is certainly more divisive and alienating in its effects upon the hearers. Wilson's advice remains the same to the preacher as before—an indicative mode of discourse may best serve the Bible's message of trouble in the horizontal plane. Another caution Wilson directs to preachers who simply ignore the social dimensions of immanent trouble. Focusing solely on the individual manifestations of horizontal trouble obscures the biblical witness and shortchanges "the fullness of the gospel message and make[s] God irrelevant to the larger issues of the day."[51] There is a cumulative effect of individuals as they gather together as congregations and as collections of congregations as they oppose social evils: "And many congregations can begin to make a large impact of the kind that God both desires and empowers."[52]

3. Human trouble

In many cases, contemporary preaching is crammed with appeals to human responsibility, with our obligation to act. In that respect, we could locate these injunctions within the scope of the Fourth Page. However, there is an important sense in which these calls to act can become trouble instead of grace. Paul Scott Wilson is emphatic that sermons that focus almost exclusively on human actions lose the essential emphasis on God's initiative in Christ. Reiterating a Pauline theme, Wilson insists on the priority of divine action in the death and resurrection of Christ. Lacking the central theme regarding the initiative of God, many sermons become trouble even as they appeal to human action. Wilson states:

> Since humans cannot do what is required, however, and since these sermons point only in the human direction, as though law is all there is, these sermons preach false hope. They preach the impossible as though it is possible; they thus preach our utter destruction. The primary doctrine they imply, when examined from a distance, is the doctrine of human limitation and condemnation. Humanity needs "to get its act together" and do better. Change of the sort that is required will not take place, without God.[53]

People need to become empowered by God in Christ before any call to act simply results in further trouble. The preacher as agent of the law is not a liberating servant of the gospel. We remain in our sin.

As the preacher considers these three elements of trouble in the world, there are a number of factors that come into play, a series of guidelines for shaping this Second Page of the sermon. The initial instruction from Wilson regards length—as was the case with Page One, the Second Page will comprise approximately one fourth of the complete sermon. And since the First and Second Pages are so closely related—trouble in the Bible and trouble in the world—a smooth transition between the Pages can be accomplished if the focus of the Second Page derives clearly from the First. Thus, the sequence of the First Page of a sermon might be:

1. Hostility persists between Jews and Samaritans.
2. Each people use their tradition to set up walls.
3. There is a social barrier between men and women in both camps.
4. And a woman drawing water from a well at midday speaks of her isolation from the other women of the community.

In this case, the ordering of the Second Page might become:

1. Our world is a place of hostility between ethnic groups, tribes, and nations.
2. Each group claims its own priority, often based on religious claims.
3. Within these groups, there are all kinds of discrimination, too. Men are privileged over women.
4. And individuals can become outcasts, even among peoples suffering discrimination themselves.

Use of these focus sentences is a helpful way to organize the internal development of each Page in the sermon. Moreover, in the transition between Pages One and Two, these sentences help us retain the originating force and logic of the biblical Page One. A particularly smooth transition can be made between the two Pages, Wilson notes, if the focus sentence of the First Page is restated toward its end, whereas the focus sentence for Page Two appears at its opening.

Page Three: Grace and Good News in the Bible

This Third Page is crucial. Without its presence our sermon will become like many, if not most, preaching law, obligation, moral imperatives, yet lacking the action of God. Once we have analyzed trouble in the world, we cannot simply apply a Page Four human solution to those woes. We will first need to return to the Bible, to the text, and focus the congregation's attention on God's grace. And since God's grace-filled acts are directly toward our human condition in general and in particular, there must be a Page Three in our preaching. The first two Pages have, in fact, led us to this place where grace is proclaimed. The problem is, though, that the bulk of the sermons preached on any given Sunday are devoid of much, if any, attention to God's actions, and especially to the activities called grace. In typical preaching today, the sermon remains at the level of moral injunction, hardly making any mention of God's grace.[54] And even when grace is noted in the sermon, Wilson finds another disturbing pattern. Often, the preacher refers to God's actions of grace only when the text most explicitly witnesses to that grace. In these cases, "the sermons preach grace only when the text is readily perceived as grace."[55]

It is an impoverished hermeneutic, however, that serves up grace to the congregation only when the preacher cannot avoid its obvious presence in the text. Rather than presenting a stance of neutrality before the text, this practice may disclose a culture-conforming tendency to look away from God and from grace. A more centered hermeneutic rests on this theological foundation—"God's actions may be found in or behind nearly all biblical texts."[56] Wilson adds:

> It is as though many preachers have been taught excellent exegetical skills but not the use of theology in reading Scripture. If we have not been trained to see God in the biblical text or to name God acting in the world, we will find it hard to speak about God in ways accessible to congregations.[57]

By insisting on a Page Three, Wilson is establishing an *ordo homiletica* that will provide for the good news of God's grace and provide that good news in every sermon. Put simply, our sermon is not yet proclamation of the gospel if it ends with trouble. God's grace is a new beginning.

Before depicting the internal qualities of Page Three, Wilson pauses to consider the reasons for this strange omission of God and grace in much of the preaching in the churches. He identifies eight problems that contribute to the lack of good news in so many sermons:

1. "Preachers identify God's action in a sentence or a paragraph and then shift the focus back to human tasks, as though afraid to continue."[58] It is as if there is much more comfort in Page Two; and the preacher who ventures into the Third Page notes grace briefly, but then scurries back to a more familiar homiletical home.
2. "Preachers confuse imperatives with grace."[59] The imperatives belong on Page Two: "The church needs to open its doors to the needy." But a Page Three affirmation becomes, "God invites us into the covenant—us and all of the human family."

3. "Preachers confuse nonaction verbs with grace."[60] By this, Wilson means to say that pulpit talk about God in general, impassive ways prevents any speaking of grace.

4. "Preachers stop short of the fullest expression of grace."[61] There is a distance implied in language that speaks of God calling or inviting us, but never coming to the place of naming the new life God has bestowed upon us in Christ.

5. "Preachers fail to establish a tension between trouble and grace and emphasize one or the other, or switch rapidly back and forth."[62] A tension needs to be established between trouble and grace, and of a very specific sort of connection (between Pages One and Three and Two and Four). This tension is eroded if only one side of the relationship is developed adequately (usually the trouble side), or if the preacher toggles back and forth so rapidly that neither side has the chance to become fully developed.

6. "Preachers delay the introduction of grace in a sermon. . . . Grace commonly appears only in one, perhaps the last paragraph of the sermon."[63] If the entirety of the sermon deals with trouble, law, and obligation, a gesture toward grace at the very end will not restore balance.

7. "Preachers mistake trouble and grace for problem and solution."[64] To link God's action specifically to our felt needs is to diminish grace as well as the sovereignty of God. Wilson also notes that this problem-solution model distills out any sense of ambiguity from either our human condition or God's mysterious ways.

8. "Preachers employ sermon forms that work against grace such as: a single exposition/application; a lecture/essay format that stresses information rather than communication . . . ; and a single narrative format that has the preacher playing a role that may impede speaking God's grace directly into the lives of the congregation."[65]

Grace in the Bible: The shape of Page Three

The focus of Page Three is God's action revealed in Scripture that constitutes grace. Page Three begins, therefore, by returning to the text. (Recall that in Page Two, the focus of the sermon was trouble in our world.) Once the text's witness to God's grace is discerned, the dual challenges for the preacher are, first, to establish that particular witness to God's grace forcefully enough and, second, not to be lured into focusing once more on human action. Page Three is about God's action, and the preacher will need to demonstrate some discipline to retain the focus on God. Regarding the issue of establishing the witness to God's grace, the theme sentence needs to be stated and restated as the Third Page is introduced. Wilson suggests that a transition sentence or two may be needed to shift the focus from being on human action to God's action. In much the same way, David Buttrick urges the opening sentences of a move to contain little new material, but restate in simple language the conceptual meaning at stake in the move, Wilson advises such reiteration of the Page's theme sentence. Keeping the focus on God's action, however, is more the challenge. Preachers have been formed to talk about people's activities and not those of God.[66] One device Wilson advises as a corrective is to transform "human action" statements into "God action" ones. For example, if the issue comes to mind during our work on Page Three that we must welcome children within our church life and especially within our worship (an issue for many aging congregations), the temptation emerges to focus on our human actions: "We must include children in our service and not send them off to children's church for the hour!" However, Page Three is about God's actions and focuses on divine grace. We may translate our human focus back into a focus on God by depicting Jesus welcoming a child, taking the child in his arms, and announcing, "Whoever welcomes one such child in my name welcomes me, and whoever welcomes me welcomes not me but the one who sent me" (Mark 9:37). Wilson would want us carefully to review our material within Page Two to discover whether we have inadvertently reverted to a focus on human action. If such a backsliding is detected, a simple process of translation is the remedy.

The theme sentence for the Third Page will function not only as an opening or transitional system as the Page is introduced. Rather, the entire development and content of the page needs to be shaped by the theme sentence related to God's grace. Hence, Wilson teaches:

> Across the top of Page Three the preacher writes the theme sentence of the sermon. This is the only topic of Page Three. It is God's action in the biblical text, with reference to other biblical passages and theology as appropriate. Page Three is not mere repetition of the thought, as though a sentence parroted often enough will be accepted. Rather, we repeat the theme sentence against the backdrop of concrete language, stories, and deepening thought, perhaps dissecting the theme sentence and developing each component of its meaning as we make its case.[67]

It may surprise the reader that Paul Scott Wilson refers here to the theme sentence of the sermon as comprising the conceptual focus of the Third Page dealing with God's action in the text. However, we recall that the **theme** ("The Tiny Dog Now Is Mine") derives from the biblical text of the sermon. And if we have ascertained the underlying theme of the text, the implication here is that it points to grace. Accordingly, we will not expect to encounter the theme of the sermon during our work on Page One, since the focus there is on trouble in the text and not grace. Moreover, Pages Two and Four deal with human trouble in the text and grace in the world. We will not expect the theme sentence to dominate certainly the former, and perhaps not the latter page. No, Wilson is adamant here; the theme sentence will derive from the text of the sermon and will focus on God's action for grace. Its appropriate locus, therefore, is within Page Three.

The remaining elements that exercise control over the sermon—doctrine, need, image, and mission—are similarly qualified by the special character of Page Three. **Doctrine,** we also recall, is to be shaped by the theme sentence of the sermon; we should likewise expect that Page Three, along with Page Four, is the place for an elaboration of the sermon's doctrine. There is, Wilson states, a "plot" or "argument" that is inherent in even the most conceptually expressed doctrine of the church. Our development of this doctrine, then, will not proceed according to points and propositions. Rather, we may want to look to the narrative origins of the doctrine at hand, particularly in the text itself: "Doctrines are rooted in, and should not be separated from, scriptural narrative; they begin somewhere, something happens, and they end somewhere."[68] Thus, our development of the aspects of the doctrine related to the Third Page will have a mobility about it, a plot. We will then seek to isolate from among the rich facets of the doctrine which one to expand within the Third Page. This chosen aspect of the doctrine will also never stray too far from the witness of the text itself.

The sermon's **need** is also at stake in Page Three. And once more, the unique quality of the Third Page shapes the way in which this element is presented. The movement is from the text to theme to doctrine and now to need. The appropriate question for Wilson relates to how some aspect of the doctrine identifies with some specific need within the lives of the listeners. Once that practical need is identified, it will be developed by means of "textual action and lifelike situations."[69] The need for a lifelike and vivid presentation of doctrine and need leads to a consideration of the image within Page Three. Wilson noted previously that the dominant image of the sermon should perhaps be presented early in the sermon. Now, it will need to reappear within Page

Three and probably within Page Four. This recurrent use of the sermon's dominant image serves for Wilson as a means to bring unity to the diverse interests of the Four Pages. Also, its repetition will provide the hearers with a pedagogical device—every time the congregation hears the dominant image, the sermon's theme is thereby enhanced and reinforced.[70]

We may expect that **mission** not appear on Page Three. Mission, as Wilson has defined it, has to do with congregational action, more with human response than divine activity. There still may be some glimpses of mission in Page Three, perhaps as we reflect on "the biblical characters' response to God's action."[71] Mission, however, will find its homiletical home much more fully within the Fourth Page than the Third. In response to God's grace disclosed in the text, it is now time to make the transition to our God's actions in the world and our response.

Page Four: Grace for Us and for Our World

Page Four will point to God's action in the world. Just as God acts in grace in the text, so God's character remains the same, and we should expect to see God at work in our contemporary world. Of course, we may overfunction in making claims for how God acts in today's world. (This writer had a United Methodist district superintendent tell me that God wanted me to serve in a new appointment in his district rather than serve a church in another!) The far more serious issue, however, is in a kind of homiletic hiding, describing God's action in the world, if at all, in entirely too passive a voice. So Paul Scott Wilson remarks, "passive claims about God are safe; we risk little because they are general propositions and they require little evidence in experience—but they also do little to foster faith."[72]

Perhaps it may help to sharpen the focus of Page Four. It is not the entirety of God's action in the world that is our focus, but specifically the divine activity of grace. The focus of Page Four will connect by way of alternation with Page Two—trouble in the world. It is this trouble, as illuminated by the biblical text, that will become the counterpoint to God's grace in the world. The two will connect. Also, the theme of the Fourth Page will derive from the powerful, concrete witness to God's grace in the text that was developed in the Third Page. In order to assist in making these connections, Wilson proposes four functions of Page Four that serve to assist in the development of the last page and to help locate it with reference to the other three:

1. Page Four applies God's grace from the Bible times to now. It
   proclaims biblical truth today, however inadequate our words

may be to express such truth. Just as Pages One and Two followed exposition/application of trouble, Pages Three and Four repeat that process from the perspective of God's loving action.

2. It provides a sustained focus on God's action in the world. This allows not just for information about God's grace to be communicated, but an experience of God's grace in the present moment—listeners are encountered by the resurrected Christ in the proclamation and reception of the Word, and part of that proclamation is the ideas, images, and stories that we tell.

3. It provides a balance to Page Two and the trouble there. If Page Two presents mainly vertical trouble, listeners need vertical grace—forgiveness—on Page Four. If Page Two presents horizontal trouble and the fallenness, suffering, and brokenness of the world, Page Four will need to develop horizontal grace; it must point to God overturning the powers of this world and restoring what needs restoration.

4. Page Four puts the world into appropriate juxtaposition or tension with grace. It returns listeners to the most powerful or emotive story or issue on Page Two and identifies what the good news might be for that troubled situation, in light of God's grace.[73]

So there will need to be a Page Four, appropriately connected to the preceding Pages of the sermon.

We now have arrived at the Page in the sermon where **mission** is a dominant concern. If the theme we identified quite earlier in our work on the sermon came to its fullest expression in Page Three, the mission we named in our initial efforts now becomes the matter of Page Four. We recall that mission was also of interest in Page Two, which dealt with trouble in the text, and that in that context Wilson urged an avoidance of a works righteousness that attended solely to human actions. Now, as mission is centrally before us as the concern of Page Four, we are once more cautioned about leaving grace out of the discussion. We will speak of our actions in the world in the Fourth Page, but from the perspective of our partnership with God and in response to God's love. "God is the actor bringing forth God's purposes in which we have an important part to play." And Wilson adds, "Mission on Page Four is not a task but a privilege, honor, and opportunity."[74]

If we must speak of God's actions in the world within the scope of Page Four, there are several pitfalls we will need to avoid as we proceed. We have already mentioned the tendency to become vague by speaking of God's action only in a passive voice. Other pitfalls include identifying God with the trivial and piling up rather generic instances of how God acts. The former can be seen when a preacher shares that a sign of God's hospitality is experienced when she is welcomed by her dog at the end of the day. An instance of the piling-on problem might be a preacher's reference to God at work in every church meeting listed in his date book over the past week. Another pitfall is more serious: "Some preachers might portray God's action as though it were automatic and mechanical, part of the nature of the universe."[75] By this Wilson means the rather culture-conforming habit of celebrating principles of healing or redemption that are simply intrinsic to the way things are. So, a preacher might use the quote from *Jurassic Park* when speaking of the Christian understanding of hope—"Life finds a way." Two other pitfalls confront the preacher as she or he attends to this Fourth Page. We may locate God's action only in a future world, rather than in our own present day. Better to claim God's action in the past, Wilson notes: "Future-tense grace leaves us humans still deep in trouble and the grace is conditional."[76] Finally, we can become ensnared by interpreting nature as an unequivocal sign of the grace of God. Although creation is certainly the expression of the grace of the Creator, it, too, is fallen and groans in travail. Only an overly romanticized view of nature can fail to see the tragedies of natural disasters and the evil of disease.

So preachers will need to risk naming grace in the world, especially in this final 25 percent of the sermon. We will need to turn to good news and speak of it concretely and in a way that invites our listeners to respond. Following Wilson's disciplines regarding Page Four, for example, there would have been more celebration in preaching at the time of the fall of the Berlin Wall and the Iron Curtain as to God's liberating actions in our world. Of course, in naming grace, we will speak of Jesus not only as our example, but also as our Savior. Wilson notes the sermons that are filled with references to what Jesus does and that place an obligation on us, but insists that these comments belong back in Page Two. Especially for the preacher whose theology begins and ends with the virtue of justice, Jesus will be presented as "Model and Exemplar" with little or no acknowledgment of him as Savior. So Wilson concludes that "on Page Four we should be portraying Jesus as our Savior, the one who equips and empowers us, and whose endeavors we join."[77]

Introductions and Conclusions

Introducing the Sermon

A sermon introduction serves rhetorically to introduce the preacher to the congregation and to allow the latter to adjust to the former. Throughout the introduction, the listeners are listening to the content of the opening and also listening for clues about the preacher, his or her character in general, and physical or mental situation in particular. All of this goes on during a sermon introduction. With regard to Wilson's homiletic method, the introduction will need to provide the listeners with the theme statement and will need to suggest the ways in which that theme will be addressed. And since the introduction leads to Page One, "Trouble in the Bible," there may be occasions when the opening theme is in tension with the theme of the First Page. One strategy Wilson suggests is to tell a story that is the flip side of the theme statement of the sermon. This approach has two advantages. First, it provides an introduction that may lead naturally to a consideration of the trouble in the text, and second, we may thereby pique the interest of the congregation.[78] The alternative, of course, is to develop an introduction that is in harmony with the sermon's theme statement. One way to achieve this harmony or congruence, Wilson suggests, is to provide "a not-too-serious experience of the general theme."[79] A variation of this congruence or harmonious approach is to shape an introduction that begins in the text itself and leads quite naturally to Page One's trouble lurking there.

The contemporary contexts of the Second and Fourth Pages may also become a gateway into the sermon. Presenting a justice issue in today's world may nicely lead to a consideration of an analogous issue of justice in the text (to be developed in Page One). We may begin with a news item or even a fictional account, but with the following provisos. These contemporary lead-ins will either present the flip side of the positive theme statement or serve to undergird that dominant topic of the sermon. A fictional account, however, should never "manipulate the listeners into believing and feeling something that is just a trick."[80] One example of this manipulation occurs when the congregation has been drawn into the pathos of some opening story and the preacher then states, "And then, I woke up."[81] Other examples of problematic approaches to the sermon introduction Wilson lists as follows:

1. Beginning the introduction with a question is a frequently used device—"How many of you have ever been to the Washington Monument in our nation's capital?" The problem here, Wilson states, is that the listeners are presented with the work of imagining some event or location on their own, with little or no time provided to do that work. Employing a question in an

introduction is a "lazy route" for preachers. "The best way to involve listeners is to give them something involving."[82]

2. Telling a joke at the beginning of the sermon is, if anything, a more frequent miscue than asking a question. The problem here, Wilson agrees with David Buttrick, is that such a use of humor within the introduction disconnects that material from what follows. A second, "real" introduction is then needed in order for the hearers to track what follows in the First Page.[83]

3. "Oblique suspense" is David Buttrick's description of the tactic of withholding essential information from the congregation at the sermon's opening. This device really becomes "a false means of obtaining suspense."[84]

4. Another caution from David Buttrick that Paul Scott Wilson also endorses is against the "step-down introduction." Here, the subject is at first broadly introduced and then is narrowed through a succession of field of vision shifts. Thus, a step-down introduction might first describe the architectural glories of the Herodian Temple, proceeding then to depict the surrounding walls, and Solomon's Portico in particular. Finally, we arrive at the winter temple scene as portrayed in John 10:22. Far better, Buttrick and Wilson agree, to simply begin with the scene itself.

5. A final problem for preachers regarding introductions "is telling a story or event chronologically, rather than beginning at the place of action."[85] What results from such extended lead-ins to the action is boredom and distraction, two congregational states of mind the preacher needs to avoid at all costs, especially at the sermon's opening moments! Begin *in media res*, Wilson encourages, in "the middle of things."

Concluding the Sermon

The sermon conclusion "is very important and exceptionally difficult," Wilson cautions.[86] The conclusion may need to address any of the essential components of the sermon—the "The Tiny Dog Now Is Mine" considerations. In other words, the conclusion may need to revisit the sermon theme, its doctrine, or dominant image system, for example. Yet, as we all know, the demands for closure parameter us with regard to any conclusion's length. We cannot merely rehash the entire sermon. Still, the conclusion will attend to the theme of the sermon; after all, that theme has served as the organizing principle throughout the sermon's Four Pages. Wilson adds:

Thus, by the conclusion everyone should be clear that this sermon was about one idea and only one idea. . . . The conclusion is not a place to introduce new ideas *per se* that move the sermon in a new direction; it should draw the congregation back to the theme statement by some means.[87]

Wilson would also be quick to add here that the purpose of the theme statement is not simply to provide new information to the hearers, but to lead them to a specific mission derived from the text and its main idea.

While the goal of the conclusion may be stated in summary as restating the theme statement of the sermon, a number of strategies are available to the preacher by way of achieving this goal. They are as follows:

1. "Return to a story or use a new story."[88] This approach can involve returning to the text if it is a narrative or to a contemporary story that, we assume, would have appeared earlier in either Pages Two or Four. If the preacher returns to a prior story, then a tag line would be added "that draws listener attention back to the theme statement [that] will often secure both the preacher's point in telling the story and the thrust of the sermon."[89]

2. "Return to the doctrine."[90] The doctrine of the sermon, of course, connects to the theme statement and needs to be re-established at the conclusion. Wilson points out that since the liturgical year is organized around central doctrines of the church, by returning to the occasion or festival, we are in so doing returning to the sermon's doctrine as well.[91]

3. "Return to the dominant image."[92] Just as the dominant story of a sermon can derive either from a biblical text or a contemporary experience, similarly, the sermon's master image also may have its origins in text or contemporary world. Again, just as the doctrine of the sermon is tied to the theme, any image serving a unifying function will likewise be related to that theme statement. Wilson adds that "even if this image appeared only in the introduction, returning to it now signals completion."[93]

4. "Return to the congregational needs."[94] During the course of the development of Page Four, some particular need of the congregation has been addressed in light of the good news. If attention to the need of the congregation has not been adequately dealt within the Fourth Page, then the conclusion is the place for treating this particular need. Wilson concludes here:

Declare, proclaim, confirm that God is already at work in the listeners' lives, bringing forth transformation according to the new life they have in Christ. Name circumstances where people may expect that God has already gone ahead of them. Encourage their reliance upon God's resource. Such an ending is a close parallel to a benediction at the end of a worship service: it is literally the speaking of goodness, the bestowal of blessing upon the gathered community.[95]

5. "Return to mission."[96] Similar canons of usage apply to mission as to meeting congregational needs. We expect that both—mission and need—will appear within the scope of Page Four, and, if some completion is lacking, it will be attended to at the conclusion. Mission may be quite concretely stated by the preacher, calling the congregation to specific acts of outreach to the world or new ways of being together in Christ. If the issues of mission relate more to individual circumstances, there may need to be some provision for each hearer to determine those specifics under the guidance of the Holy Spirit. Nevertheless, a conclusion that calls for congregational action, if that call has an integrity and has grown out of the sermon's theme and sequence, remains a living option in homiletic method.

6. "Move to the cross and resurrection."[97] This strategy may appear redundant if strong attention has been provided for the Paschal mystery in either Page One or Four. However, there are sermons in which the cross and resurrection of Christ are only alluded to or implied. In these instances, the conclusion becomes the location for a strong witness to the saving work of Christ. Wilson alertly notes that in those traditions where the Eucharist follows the sermon, the warrant for this strategy is perhaps diminished.[98] Likewise, those church traditions that locate an altar call or invitation after the sermon will have this focus on the cross and Christ's resurrection built into that ritual act. Even considering these liturgical contexts, moving to the Paschal mystery "serves as a further means for the preacher to ground what has been said in the heart of the faith—after all, the cross is both the occasion and the content of Christian preaching."[99]

From Text to Sermon in Four Pages

Employing Paul Scott Wilson's method of preaching, for example, we could shape a sermon for Ascension Day/Sunday along the following contours:

TTDNIM (text, theme, doctrine, need, image, mission)

Text—The Gospel lesson for the Ascension in Year A of the Revised Common Lectionary is Luke 24:44-53. This text is also offered as an alternative reading for the Seventh Sunday of Easter in some traditions.

Theme—Although the pericope deals with a number of thematics— the authority of Scripture and its witness to Christ, the Lukan program of the church's mission emanating from Jerusalem, the promise of the gift of the Spirit, and such—the two centers of reading deal with Christ's self-disclosure as the suffering Messiah and his command to his followers to witness to all nations. Perhaps a theme statement could be devised that includes both poles of the ellipse: "The risen Christ points to his suffering and sends us out to witness to his death and resurrection."

Doctrine—The text links together the witness to Jesus as the suffering yet risen Messiah and an ecclesiology of mission. We are sent by our Lord to witness to these things.

Need—In the pastoral setting anticipated as this sermon is being formed, the congregational need also reflects the binary character of the theme. The hearers need to consider Christ's work of suffering for them more fully and to hear Christ name them not only as his followers, but also as witnesses.

Image—The dominant image in the text is presented by Luke at the end of his Gospel. Jesus, with a priestly act of blessing, ascends into heaven.

Mission—The mission here is mission. The issue is, more specifically, which mission or missions are the call to the specific community of believers gathered on the Lord's Day.

Page One: Trouble and Conflict in the Bible

Primary trouble here deals with the scandal of a suffering messiah. An opposition is thereby developed in the text between Luke's church and the Jewish community that resists such an interpretation. An implicit opposition might be found within the New Testament Christian community, between the followers of Jesus who focus solely on his glory and those, like Luke, who insist on a theology of the cross. In the text, Jesus speaks of all of "the law of

Moses, the prophets, and the psalms" (24:44) as proclaiming him as the suffering Messiah of Israel. Hence, one commentator observes:

> To search for specific references to a Davidic figure or a suffering Messiah in each of these portions is to miss the point. All of Luke's specific and allusive use of the OT illustrates what he means in this passage. From Luke's perspective, the OT prewrites what the people of God in the New Age confess concerning Jesus Christ.[100]

Trouble in this text, then, deals with a central conflict of interpretation: "Is Jesus the Messiah of Israel from God?" If so: "Do the Scriptures point to his suffering and his rising from the dead?"

A further aspect of the text's trouble is the issue that will propel the plot of the entire Acts of the Apostles. There is a shift in identity as Jesus renames his followers "witnesses." It is no longer sufficient for them to be simply "disciples." Moreover, their witness is to all of *ta ethnē,* to all "peoples" or "nations." Again, the book of Acts describes in detail the prodding of the Spirit and the resistance of Jesus' followers as they learn how seriously Jesus intended this command. So while the scene, and the Gospel, concludes with Jesus' followers in the temple in Jerusalem continually blessing God and worshiping their Lord, trouble is brewing. They cannot remain there; their stay is only until Jesus sends *(apostelō)* the Spirit. Their new vocation is to become witnesses to all peoples.

The master image of the sermon is the Paschal mystery—the suffering, death, and rising of Jesus Christ. Given the way that both hearing and seeing are featured in the text, an image that deals with both senses is appropriate. One that might function here is an illustration from a concert by a Russian cellist and composer. The work was entitled "Resurrection." At the climax of the piece, the music she wrote ascended in thrilling repetitions of joy. Yet to achieve this glory, the audience watched her left hand move downward across the strings, and her right hand repeatedly made the sign of the cross with the bow. Here, the music was of glory and joy. To create this "ascension," her body spoke of suffering and of the cross.

Page Two: Trouble in the World

Trouble in the world with regard to the text's dual theme remains much the same. The world continues to look at the cross of Christ with disinterest or even opposition. Suffering is something to be avoided; it is a sign of weakness. The irony here, among many, is that even in the church, there is resistance to Jesus' self-disclosure as the suffering Messiah. In every age, sincere church folk try to revise the biblical witness to Jesus Christ, his passion, death, resurrection, and ascension. An early attempt was in New Testament times—the Docetists, who wanted a Jesus who remained unsullied by human life with all its pain and suffering. So their answer was to deny Jesus' humanity. He only "appeared" to go through these things. The real Jesus was fully spirit, not human, not of the earth. You can see this Docetism in the paintings of Salvador Dali (a favorite in many clergy studies). There is Jesus, hanging from the cross. But the cross is suspended up in the air, not touching the ground. And the Jesus who hangs there is diaphanous, you can see right through him. Clearly this Jesus cannot be the one who told his followers that all of Scripture spoke of his suffering and of his rising! But the tendency continues in our own day. We would like to get Jesus up out of our messy world, but not in the way he chooses to ascend. Our version of the Ascension is to permanently banish Jesus to some spiritual world quite unlike our own.

Of course, the connection between this resistance to Jesus' words about himself and the later words about us goes this way: The risen and now ascending Christ can certainly speak of his suffering and call us to be witnesses *(martyres)* as well as followers (Acts 1:8). But if the church removes the scandal of Christ's suffering, including his bloody work on the cross, there is no basis for our being witnesses of these things. We have detached the resurrection and ascension of Jesus from his earthly suffering and death. So the Christ becomes a cipher for justice or a new-age notion of human potential. Jesus is left here among the dead, his body probably eaten by dogs according to one New Testament scholar. The trouble here is that there is no need to be witnesses to such things. Once more, the church is seduced into following the spirit of the age.

Page Three: Grace and Good News in the Bible

The good news in the text is that it is now "the third day." The promise of all Scripture has come to fulfillment and Jesus is risen from the dead. By virtue of this mighty act of deliverance, repentance and forgiveness are now to be preached to all peoples. Notice that the focus is not on judgment and repentance as with the Baptist (Luke 3:1-17). John's prophecy concerning the coming baptism of the Holy Spirit is about to be accomplished. But instead of the apocalyptic images of the threshing floor and unquenchable fire, Pentecost will bring the rush of a mighty wind and tongues of fire. The immediate outcome of these gifts of the Holy Spirit is the proclamation of the kerygma—"This Jesus God raised up, and of that all of us are witnesses," Peter proclaims (Acts 2:32). The good news about Jesus, then, is proclaimed by spirit-filled witnesses of these things. Forgiveness is offered, first to Jerusalem, and then to the entire world. There is no boundary that privileges one people as regards God's grace while excluding others.

The theme of the sermon, as Paul Scott Wilson insists, is to be found here in the Third Page, with its attention to God's action in the text. We will want to match the strength of this page's theme with a master image that speaks of God's grace-filled action in Jesus Christ. Since we have been developing image systems in the first Two Pages that have a visual as well as an audible component, the challenge here is to provide the congregation with a master image they can both see and hear. Several possibilities come to mind:

1. The final, jubilant scene of *Godspell* could be depicted as we watch all of those diverse followers of Jesus joining with their risen Lord in singing "Prepare the Way of the Lord." In one production, the characters exit the worship space where the performance has been occurring and dance out onto the city streets, still singing their witness to Christ.

2. An Ascension Day/Sunday scene outside a church in which the children release helium-filled balloons into the air. The balloons are brightly colored and each one has a brief message written by a child, attached by a ribbon. Some read, "Jesus is alive," while others proclaim, "Jesus loves you." As the wind carries the balloons up and away, the crowd of worshipers sings, "He's Got the Whole World in His Hands."

3. In Russian Orthodoxy liturgy for Easter, the choir and people sing, "Hos Podi Pomilui" ("Holy Is God, Holy and Strong"). As the chant is repeated, the crucifer lowers the cross to dramatize the suffering and death of the Lord. The chant becomes quiet and somber. Then, the crucifer slowly raises the cross and the singing becomes triumphant. Christ is risen and ascended into heaven! (In order to add the component of witness, the preacher could image a procession by priest and people out into the town square.)

Which illustration is selected, it must serve our twofold theme statement: Jesus is the suffering yet risen Messiah of Israel; and our joy and our task is to witness to his cross and his glory.

Page Four: God's Grace for Us and for Our World

The good news of the text is that Jesus is our risen and ascended Lord. He is worthy of our praise and devotion, and has authority to gather us and to name us as witnesses and to send us out into the world to proclaim this good news. Moreover, the Ascension is a theological claim about Jesus' relationship to the world outside the church as well. If Christ is risen and ascended, he is Lord of all creation, and his authority is not bounded or compromised by any earthly authorities or powers. Consequently, our Christian witness can stand up to any human claims of ultimacy and denounce their idolatry. One aspect of bearing witness to Jesus Christ in the world, then, is to expose the fraudulent claims made by the world regarding its own power and authority. One reference that comes to mind is the action of the Confessing Church at the Synod of Barmen in 1934. In opposition to the idolatrous claims of Adolf Hitler and nationalist socialism, the Confessing Church spoke forcefully of its allegiance to Jesus Christ who remained the only Lord of all the earth. Jesus, as the Word of God, is the One who reigns in heaven and, thereby, dethrones all earthly claims to such glory.

Since the theme statement is composed of two elements, the preacher has a responsibility to point to God's action in the world by way of the church's witness to all nations. Here is the opportunity to speak most directly to the witness of the congregation, both locally and "to all nations." One parish may sponsor a missionary overseas, and this is the opportunity to celebration God's grace made concrete through such a ministry. Another parish may be vitally engaged in local mission, including housing the homeless or participating in Habitat for Humanity. Other congregations may be involved in "naming the name" of Jesus through evangelistic outreach by way of a billboard campaign, a revival, or other public renewal emphasis. Also, public liturgical witnesses such as a Palm Sunday procession through town or an ecumenical gathering of churches for public prayer and praise might be the focus of local witness. In any case, the preacher has the opportunity here in Page Four to specifically name the ways in which the congregation is already witnessing to the lordship of Christ. Page Four in this sermon also provides the preacher with the occasion to speak of other possible ministries through which the listeners might fulfill Jesus' command that his followers also become witnesses. (Note: A word of caution should be raised here regarding the special programs and priorities that our denominational bureaucracies promote on a regular basis. Unless there is concrete and compelling warrant for the latest promotional campaign to be understood within the text's theology of witness, it should have no mention here. There is already an excess of denominational promotionalism from American pulpits. Perhaps on Ascension Day/Sunday we may look elsewhere for our instances of effective witness and grace in God's world.)

The Introduction and Conclusion

Introducing the Four Pages

We recall that Paul Scott Wilson insists that the sermon introduction be oriented in same fashion to the theme statement of the sermon. In many instances, this means that the introduction will provide the first glimpse of the sermon's theme, perhaps presented through a contemporary story. With a positive-positive relationship between the introduction and the theme statement, it will be the cases that the First Page of the sermon will function in a way similar to David Buttrick's notion of a contrapuntal. That is, if the sermon introduction embodies the theme statement of the sermon—always a positive articulation of God's action of grace—then Page One will deal with the flip side of the theme as it explores trouble in the text. On the other hand, Wilson also sees the opposite strategy as viable. Here, the introduction would probe the flip side of the theme statement, and in so doing, would lead quite naturally into the First Page's attention to trouble in the text. Employing this approach, the introduction would consequently become a contrapuntal to Page Three, the Page within which the sermon's theme is most likely to be found.

If the preacher decides on the first of these two prominent options in Wilson's understanding of the introduction, a contemporary but not too serious presentation of the theme statement may serve effectively. This preacher was surprised to note that one of the illustrations not chosen when Page Three was being formed could quite nicely fit within Wilson's specifications here. That is, if the illustration from the Russian liturgy was chosen for Page Three, the *Godspell* scene could function as the core of the sermon's introduction. Wilson may not have explicitly noted this dynamic, but it seems to follow from his methodology—candidates for the illustration of Page Three may serve as the sermon introduction if not selected for that crucial Page.

Evaluation: The Four Pages of the Sermon

For a methodology arriving so recently, there is a wide consensus among homileticians about Wilson's solid achievements that advance the ministry of preaching. Similarly, there are some points of disagreement—as would be expected—among Wilson's colleagues in the academy and among preachers themselves. In between lies a more complex field of matters raised by Wilson that remain under negotiation, issues in which the pros and cons continue to be assessed. First, we celebrate Wilson's strong contributions represented by his Four Pages homiletic.

Achievements and Contributions

Paul Scott Wilson is among those leading a recovery of preaching as a theological task. At a microlevel, Wilson insists that the preacher ground each of the quartet of Pages in doctrine that is both derived from the theme and grounded in the biblical text. That theological reflect is urged upon the preacher at each step (or Page) along the homiletic journey is to be commended without qualification. Implied in Wilson's insistence on doctrine as a necessary component within homiletic method is a mature level of theological competence by the preacher. The method requires of the preacher a familiarity with doctrinal matters that stretch far beyond a narrow, ideological solution to complex theological issues. Put simply, the preacher must be a pastoral theologian.

At a macrolevel, the method itself embodies a theology, articulates some doctrine. Woven into the Four Pages of the sermon is the law-gospel dialectic with a heritage going back through Martin Luther, to Augustine, and ultimately to Paul. Wilson shapes his *ordo homiletica* out of this theological tradition, namely, that God's Word comes to humanity as both judgment and grace (or trouble and grace). To adopt Paul Scott Wilson's method, then, is to take up the dialectical imagination and preach within its doctrinal framework. This dialectical stance enables the preacher to navigate around several pitfalls within the contemporary theological situation. Faithfully employing Wilson's Four Pages compels the preacher to take human sin and evil seriously. A feel-good pulpit message cannot be derived from this method. (Such an approach would not get beyond Page One, "Trouble and Conflict in the Bible.") On the other side of the coin, Wilson is on target when he concludes that much of contemporary preaching is almost devoid of grace. This moralizing and prophetic approach would be challenged by fully one half of the normative content of the sermon represented by Pages Three and Four ("prophetic" in its misunderstood sense of imposing "ought's" and "must's" and "should's" on the congregation). The Four Pages of the sermon embody a mature doctrinal template by means of which an almost limitless number of specific sermons can be shaped and preached.

The place of Scripture is securely grounded in Paul Scott Wilson's homiletic method. Of the constitutive elements of the sermon ("The Tiny Dog Now Is Mine"), the text is central, giving birth to the sermon's theme and evoking the doctrine that will guide the shaping of its Four Pages. The image as well derives either directly from the scriptural text along with the mission that will become the sermon's performative goal. Wilson does caution against attempting to employ more than one biblical text in any given sermon, yet the role of that one portion of Scripture is foundational. While Wilson may well agree with David Buttrick's assertion that "the Bible itself is *not* the subject of our sermons," the former may add a proviso that the gospel can become rather vague or even distorted apart from the grounding provided by the biblical text.[101] Literally 50 percent of the matter under consideration in a Four Pages sermon derives explicitly from a biblical text, its theme, imagery, and implied doctrine. Of course, the other two Pages of the sermon compel the preacher to address trouble and grace in our world. Therefore, a sermon in Four Pages cannot be preached with integrity either detached from the words and the world of Scripture or removed from the text's intersections with the contemporary world of the hearers. Wilson agrees with Buttrick that it is the gospel that we are called to preach. Wilson offers a method for preachers that will bind the gospel to particular texts of Scripture.

Paul Scott Wilson's method is pedagogically accessible. Put simply, his Four Page sermon is quickly learned by students and practicing preachers and easily taught by teachers of preaching. Though by no means simple in its scope and insight, the guiding elements of text, theme, doctrine, image, and mission can easily be learned by the student of preaching. The Four Pages themselves are nicely clear in their focus and relationship with one another. We have here a method of preaching that commends itself as an introduction to preaching.

Contentions and Disagreements

The primary criticisms of the Four Page sermon originate from the homileticians and preachers who have come to see a wisdom and effectiveness in preaching sermons in the form of Scripture. The literary critics have trained a significant minority of preachers in the skills necessary to analyze a biblical text regarding its genre, structured plot, and intention. "Why not shape the sermon to reflect rather closely the movement and structure of the biblical text?" they ask. And if the preacher invites the sermon to be shaped by the form and movement of the text, it is unlikely that the result will look much like Paul Wilson's Four Page model. Moreover, the preacher who is guided by these literary critical insights will also raise the question to Wilson as it is addressed to the remaining adherents of topical preaching about whether a text's meaning can be so radically separated from its form. Therefore, the question of preaching the parables by way of the Four Page sermon collides with the distinctive manner in which the meaning of a parable is conveyed through its distinctive sequences of scenes with their reversals, their tragic and comic surprises. Deprived of the parable's own form by Wilson's *ordo homiletica,* the resulting sermon may be hobbled in achieving the intention embodied within the parable's world. For example, the parable of the good Samaritan in Luke 10 intends a primary point of view in solidarity with the man robbed and beaten, lying in the ditch. The reversal in the parable—spotted by Robert Funk, John Dominic Crossan, Bernard Brandon Scott and others—is conveyed through its successive scenes. In a sermon that is not shaped by that parable's own plot and movement, the subject of reversal within the realm of God's reign may be discussed and even celebrated (as in Page Four). However, we would in those cases be talking about, rather than speaking of, the parable's reversal. Alyce McKenzie nicely sums up this dissenting position:

> Genre and meaning work together. The meaning of a text and its form do not exist in the same relationship as a candy bar and its wrapper, in which you can unwrap the candy bar and throw the wrapper away. . . . When preparing a sermon so that the form and function of the text can shape the form and function of the message, the pastor must name the genre of the text, its literary and rhetorical qualities, and its intentions.[102]

Related to the critique concerning the form of the sermon vis à vis that of the sermon is a more specific observation made by those who locate themselves at the narrative center of the web of preaching. We have noted with commendation Paul Scott Wilson's critique of sermons that are deficient in grace or lacking any gospel entirely. Decrying sermons that position grace only as a tag line (or paragraph), Wilson comments that "grace that is quickly dispensed is soon forgotten."[103] In a note on this issue, Wilson specifically identifies Eugene Lowry as one who advocates this tag-line approach to grace. Lowry, he adds, "gives priority to dramatic surprise instead of to the theological urgency of listeners meeting God and discerning God in the world around them."[104] In response, Lowry and others may raise two points. First, it pertains to the quality of narrative that the sense of the ending typically is one of denouement, or resolution. A sermon embodying a narrative movement and structure, then, will most likely locate grace within this final stage of the plot. It would be odd, these advocates of narrative preaching might argue, for the storyteller to give away the punch line halfway through the narration.

Second, the narrative homilecticians would agree with Wilson that an abundance of grace within the sermon is essential. They would heartily concur with Wilson that preaching today is entirely too moralistic and overburdened with law rather than gospel. That said, the issue now can be raised as to whether the measure of preaching's component of grace is primarily a quantitative or qualitative question. That is, Wilson clearly adopts a quantitative approach to the presence of grace in a sermon. (The "minimum Sunday requirement" is 50 percent—including 25 percent grace in the text and 25 percent grace in our world.) Such a sermonic recipe certainly ensures the ample presence of grace in preaching! However, the nature of grace is such that often a more qualitative approach is needed when shaping the sermonic plot. To be sure, such quality cannot be embodied within one tag line of a sermon. All would agree here. On the other hand, when the biblical narrative leads the preacher and people to a grace-filled concluding move that is vividly stated and experienced, then the intention of the text and an important theological concern has been met. Naming grace may well become the burden of one or two ending sections of the homiletical plot. The criteria for the success of such a sermon cannot be adjudged on simply a quantitative measuring of percentages of a homily's content.

Issues under negotiation

At the heart of Paul Scott Wilson's model of biblical interpretation is the insistence that a **text** under consideration have one **theme** leading to one **doctrine** and evoking one image. (The "one **mission**" aspect of the text is a related but distinct question.) We have earlier noted that when Wilson speaks of the text's one theme for its homiletical appropriation, he is not advocating a main idea "hermeneutic of distillation." Wilson notes that a text may have a number of themes, only one of which needs to be appropriated for the sermon at hand. That theme, among the others homiletically left behind, will serve both to unify the sermon—especially as that theme plays out in the two pages on grace—and to link the text to a doctrine. Wilson additionally indicates the way in which a text's one image serves to focus one or more of the sermon's Pages. The challenge presented to the preacher by Wilson's "Tiny Dog Is" approach to the text is that biblical texts vary so greatly with regard to the three aspects of interpretation. There are texts in which the "TDI" elements present themselves as a well-balanced triad.

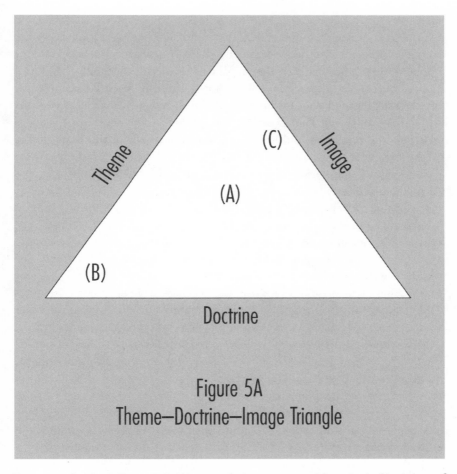

Figure 5A
Theme–Doctrine–Image Triangle

For example, in 1 Peter 2:2 (A) several themes are evident including that of the nurture offered in the Spirit to the new believer as he or she begins a growth into salvation. The doctrine attached to this theme deals with the church's whole understanding of the sacrament of Christian initiation (baptism, first Eucharist, confirmation). The text also offers a strong image connecting the theme and the doctrine: "Newborn infants" who "long for the pure, spiritual milk." First Peter 2:2 clearly embodies all three elements of Wilson's triad. A sermon in Four Pages can derive from such a text with relative ease.

The problem confronts the preacher as texts range over toward one apex of the triad of theme, doctrine, and image, leaving at least one of the three nearly unattended. Some texts—one thinks of some of Paul's strong doctrinal statements of the faith such as Romans 3:21-26 (B)—do come with thematic and doctrinal force, but seem almost devoid of imagery. Other texts are strongly imagistic, perhaps embedding the imagery in a narrative or prophetic pronouncement. In the one-liner parable in Matthew 13:33 (C) a series of odd and unclean images are aligned, evoking more a sense of mystery than doctrinal clarity. In this textual world, the one theme may be difficult to discern. Given Paul Scott Wilson's model, therefore, the preacher is challenged by texts that, unlike text A, lean toward one of the triad's poles. To the extent that the preacher needs all three elements as the basis for Wilson's Four Pages, some attention may be needed regarding adjustments to the method in cases where the biblical text does not provide theme, doctrine, and image in some balanced relationship.

Finally, the question of mission ("The Tiny Dog Now Is **Mine**") and the biblical text confronts the preacher. Once again, there is such diversity among texts that a central question of interpretation is raised. Obviously, the preacher will have no problem finding the mission in the "Great Commission" text of Matthew 28:19-20. Perhaps a great majority of texts yield a clarity of mission without much interpretive challenge. On the other hand, a collection of texts comes to mind, in which mission is not immediately discernible or even available. There are those "texts of terror" presented to us with force by Phyllis Tribble.[105] Also, preachers enjoy commenting to one another about the challenge of preaching some texts that reflect a situation in antiquity but do not seem to have much to say to our contemporary context. (Any number of texts in Leviticus confront and challenge the preacher here, such as 25:29-34 dealing with property rights in walled and nonwalled cities.) Just as David Buttrick has commented that, employing his method, some psalms perhaps cannot be rendered into a moves and structures sermon, so, too, Wilson's sermon in Four Pages may need to draw on the canon's texts that do yield some sense of mission.

The Creator's Design

Paul Scott Wilson

Genesis 2:15-17; 3:1-24

In our increasingly complex age, we may long for a simpler time. We see reruns of *Leave It to Beaver* in black and white and long for an age when drugs were unknown. We hear about the devastating effect automobiles are having on the globe and long for an age when we did not have to think about such things, hence the success of the Volkswagen New Beetle and Ford's proposed return of the classic 1950s Thunderbird. We hear dire predictions about the future from all over the world: from the Bering Sea, where the world's largest collection of nuclear reactors is gathered in rusting hulks of the former Russian fleet without even minimal maintenance; from Brazil, where the Amazon rain forest, the world's largest producer of oxygen, continues to be burned away; from our own country, where the gap between richest and poorest continues to widen. We might love to be able to turn the clock back. But this much is clear. There is no turning back to a simpler time. And God does not need us to turn back though we certainly need to turn things around. God has ordained that we move ahead. As we go into the future, we may rest assured that God's love goes on ahead of us.

Have you ever wondered what the weather was like in the Garden of Eden? Until the departure of Adam and Eve from Eden, I imagine the weather was perfect, eighty degrees, sunny skies in the day, and rain at night. After they ate the forbidden fruit, the weather no doubt took a turn for the worse, like everything else. A cold front moved in, and clouds covered the sun. They might even have had four feet of snow and had to put on their lambskin coats.

Eve has been given so much of a bad rap throughout history, when in many ways she is the more likeable of the two. When the serpent engages them in conversation, she is the one who responds. We know Adam is with her; the Bible says so. We just don't know what he is doing, for he is silent. He is doing something. Maybe he is drinking his double latte mocha java, reading the sports page, and daydreaming about going for an off-road ride in his SUV. Maybe he is channel surfing on a big screen TV. We are not told. Whatever Adam is doing, he is not stretching his mind. When the serpent asks, "Did God say, 'You shall not eat from any tree in the garden'?" Eve responds, "Of course God did not say from any tree, we just cannot eat of the fruit of the tree in the center of the garden, 'Nor shall you touch it or else you will die.'" Did you hear what she said? Did you hear that last sentence? "Nor shall you touch it or else you will die." Now God had said nothing about touching. Eve added that herself. She was interpreting what God had said. She is the first person in the Bible to interpret God's Word. She is the first preacher. She is the mother of all preachers. She added those words herself. Maybe she knew that if she or Adam started touching a tree so beautiful, they would soon touch the fruit, then pick the fruit and rub its smoothness against their cheeks, and before they knew it, they would let their tongues run over it and open their mouths to test the firmness with their teeth, and suddenly they would find that juice was running down their chins. In her conversation with the serpent, Eve is thinking ahead. In her conversation with the serpent, she is not trying to be evil. She is trying to be faithful, interpreting to the serpent not only what God said, but also what she understood God to mean.

Eve did not plan to violate God's command in a premeditated way. She did not get up out of bed and say, "This is too much of a good thing. I have to get a ticket out of here. I'm calling a travel agent. We need a last-minute club." Eve did not do that. She wants to do good. She assesses the serpent's argument about the tree. The serpent says the fruit is good to eat. Eve examines the goodness of its fruit. The serpent says she will not die. She admires the beauty of the fruit. The serpent says she will know good and evil. That is what she cannot resist. She wants to be an ethicist. She had no previous opportunity to learn that the nature of evil is to look good. She only wants to serve God, and she knows that one way to do that is to study theology. She wants to get her Ph.D. by eating from the tree. So she takes a risk. She wants knowledge. She uses the freedom God gave her to make her own choices, and so she eats of the fruit.

Now what is Adam doing during all of this? Does Adam say anything? If someone is your partner, you expect that person to give you a nudge if you are about to make a mistake. Does Adam do anything to stop Eve? She offers the fruit to him, and he bites it, no questions asked. And when God comes walking in the garden, Adam finally finds his voice and tells on his wife. The only words he can muster are, "She made me do it."

Later that day, as they were leaving Eden, we don't know what Eve said the Adam. No doubt the conversation turned a little frosty, along with the weather. She might have let him know that if he was to be her partner as God intended, he had let her down. In any case, they had messed things up. It would be great to get back to the way things were.

Have you ever made a decision only to find out that it was a defining moment of your life? Perhaps it happened in the fourth grade when you made a friend promise not to tell, cross-your-heart-and-hope-to-die, that you had a crush on your teacher, and the next day when you came to school everyone knew about your private secret. Your sweetest fantasy was now the common stuff of the school playground. Or perhaps it was as a teenager, on a Friday night, in a small town, when there was not anything to do except walk down the main street and over to the fairgrounds and back up the main street, when you and your friends, without permission and on a whim, stole your father's Chevrolet—the car he let no one drive and if you closed the door too hard, he would say, "Softly, just close it softly." The car ended up in the ditch, and you ended up in the police station awaiting the arrival of your parents by foot, after midnight, while the police captain, an elder in your church, your former Sunday school teacher, watched over you.

Of course, we make far more serious kinds of decisions, and it is not possible to go back with those either. Someone decides to drive after drinking; and in the accident that follows, someone is left paralyzed or dead. Or a manager tries to cut corners and ends up losing the company hundreds of thousands of dollars and throwing twenty employees out of work and one of them returns with a gun. How can you go on with life when you face that kind of responsibility? How can we go on with often even much lesser failings? Eve's mistake and sin, which was Adam's too, was not that she used her intelligence to make a decision, but that she used her intelligence to make a decision separate from God, in contradiction of what God had instructed. But even if we consult God continually, we can still mess things up. Being a Christian is no guarantee of success. Faithful Christians still fail exams, have bad interviews, suffer needlessly, have accidents, succumb to illness, and face untimely death. These are the times we want to turn the clock back.

I wonder how Adam and Eve could have borne leaving Eden. They could not have done it if they did not know that God's love was going ahead of them. They were leaving behind favorite animals, birds, plants, and places. They were leaving universal health care, dental plans, full employment, day care, perfect pensions, and old-age security, and for what—danger from animals, sickness and suffering, violence, failed crops, pollution, depleted natural resources, racial discrimination, unequal rights? Eve must have had a conversation with God: "O God, I know we have brought this upon ourselves. But is there no way we could stay, not for ourselves, but for the sake of our children?" We don't know exactly what she said, but we know something of how God must have answered. God said, "Eve, it breaks my heart that you have to leave. This is what I planned for you and Adam and your descendants. But Eve, when your teeth bit the fruit, your feet stood still, but you already left, because when you bit the fruit, you lost your innocence. Now you know good and evil. When you lose your innocence, Eden effectively does not exist anymore." Eve pondered God's words in her heart. "Well God," Eve said, "I can stand leaving, if I must. I can stand facing hardship, if I must. I can stand almost anything, if I only know that I am not leaving you." In spite of messing up her own life, Eve knew what she needed, and she needed God. She needed God to walk with her and Adam out into the world, not to forsake them as they had forsaken God. She needed God's love to go ahead of them into that unknown future. She needed still to be able to call on God. She needed to have God answer in the middle of the night when she was anxious about her children. She needed God to be in charge of the world, to know that God still would heed her cries.

And of course her need was exactly what God had in mind. One of the most remarkable pictures of God found anywhere in the Bible we discover immediately after God tells Adam and Eve what awaits them beyond Eden. It is a picture of extraordinary love and devotion. The verse reads, "And the LORD God made garments of skin for the man and his wife, and clothed them." What a loving picture that is: God sewing garments for beloved children as they leave home and head out for the school of hard knocks. "Eve, there is no turning back to a simpler life" God must have said in words God also addresses to you and me when we have messed up. "You are leaving Eden, but you are not leaving my love. 'Where can you go from my spirit? Or where can you flee from my presence? . . . If you take the wings of the morning and settle at the farthest limits of the sea, even there my hand shall lead you' (Ps. 139, adapted). I am not finished with you. You may have messed up, but I still have purposes for you. My forgiveness is from everlasting to everlasting. There is no wrong that you have done that I cannot work for good, for those who love me. 'I have come that you might have life and have it abundantly' " (John 10:10, adapted).

In your life and in mine, we cannot go back to a simpler time. Some of us may think that Eden is behind us: Jesus said repent ye, not return ye to a previous time. Some of us may think we are in an Eden right now: Jesus said comfort ye, not get ye comfortable. Some of us may be searching for Eden up ahead, and we may be looking in all the wrong places. The only Eden worth having is the paradise God promises. We can taste that paradise every time we taste Holy Communion, the eternal love of God that we experience even in this moment. We need to change directions; we certainly need repentance, some readjustment, some turning around, some shifts in our attitudes and actions, but we do not need to go back to Eden. God wants us to go ahead, to move into the future with justice, peace, and mercy in mind, and God will go ahead of us. The future is God's future, not just yours and mine.

In one town I grew up, there was a doctor at the local hospital who many thought was simply mean, ill tempered, and unkind. In fact, he was an alcoholic. Patients in the know would seek another doctor. He was unreliable. One fall, he simply disappeared. In the spring, he reappeared wearing the same gray cap. Everyone had assumed he had gone south for the winter without telling anyone. Eventually, as his alcoholism worsened, the hospital staff would see him coming and lock the doors to keep him out. Then, one day he received a phone call. His nineteen-year-old son had been killed. He realized that his son, in all his life, had never seen him sober. The doctor had messed up big time. But he used his experience to turn things around. He went off the booze. He started the only Alcoholics Anonymous group in that part of Saskatchewan at that time. And he went on to devote much of his practice to helping hundreds of people with the same addiction.

I do not know how you have messed up in your life. But I do know that God can use our mistakes to help others. As individuals and as a society facing change, we cannot go back to Eden. But we can go ahead with God, for God always goes ahead of us in love. And in God, we find the forgiveness that counts as innocence and the courage to act that is God's grace.

CHAPTER 6

A Homiletics of Imagery: Rhetoric and the Imagination

The history of the relationship between homiletics and imagination theory has been more than rocky or unstable. At times, the two have remained alienated or estranged, over long periods in the tradition. At other times, preaching and some notion of imagination have seemed to overcome their differences, embraced, and even fallen in love. Of course, this odd on-again, off-again relationship may be attributed in part to the changing notions of homiletics (and rhetoric) and imagination theory. In the classical age, rhetoric was dominated by a Hellenistic model of persuasion, and preachers borrowed a model that located logic *(logos)* at the heart of the speaker's persuasive arsenal.[1] Given a rhetoric of argument and persuasion, with its rationalistic bias, the imagination was held in suspicion by classical writers. Aristotle, for example, held metaphor to be simply a figure of speech and therefore as a decorative but ultimately disposable trope. And for most of the classic and medieval period, the image was construed as a copy of some object or concept in the real world. Imagining, then, was "the equivalent of imitating or copying through the construction of an object that resembled the model."[2] The reformers inherited this tradition along with its distrust of the imagination, especially as seen in the antipathy of the Calvinist movement for any images in worship and in preaching. At the Enlightenment, the estrangement between preaching and imagination continued, but with a new twist. Now, as Paul Scott Wilson observes, Peter Ramus (1515–72) reinterprets rhetoric as belonging to the imagination, while logic "became the property of reason and intellect."[3] Rhetoric becomes just rhetoric and therefore remains simply ornamental. There was a dark side to imagination for the Enlightenment scholars as well. So, with John Locke and others:

> Imagination was as likely to produce fictions, dreams, visions, and emotions as it was to assist reason, and because it was akin to an instinctive or sensory power, it tended also to be suspect as a wild, unpredictable faculty that threatens natural order, needs tight control, and that should, if necessary, be minimized.[4]

Preaching followed along, remaining shaped largely by a model of argument and persuasion.

The fortunes of imagination improved, along with its liaison with homiletics, as it first encountered Immanuel Kant and, later, the Romantics. There was a familiar cast to Kant's dealings with imagination—he equates it in religious terms with an inauthentic, "empirical" mode of knowing constituted by images. The alternative is that which appropriates the ideal or essence of religion, only achieved by way of pure reason. Given that imagination is constituted of images, with all its illusions and distortions, popular religion is therefore "indistinguishable from illusion and therefore in need of apologetic support."[5] Kant finds that apologetic support in pure reason's apprehension of the ideal, the essence, which coincidentally is the essence of Christianity. Preaching's task within a Kantian world becomes that of articulating the essence of religion while relating it to the practical reason that governs how persons conduct themselves. The preacher will carry along a hermeneutics of suspicion as regards popular religion's distortions and illusions; they are works of the imagination. Now given this Kantian world, it is striking what little alteration is needed to transform it into the new world of the Romantics. In the latter, imagination is rehabilitated to become, first, the supreme human faculty and, second, "the point of contact between divine and human creativity."[6] All that is needed, with Samuel Taylor Coleridge, is to split the work of the imagination in half, with the primary imagination becoming that universal, necessary faculty of knowing. The secondary imagination, which Coleridge labels as "Fancy," is really the faculty of poetic creativity and religious expression. Put together, there is content to the form, a unity of the secondary and primary imagination. Preaching, of course, was profoundly affected by this retrieval of imagination's work by the Romantics. Within a few decades of the early Romantics, preachers and homileticians would be extolling the "historical imagination" and regarding imagination as an ally in the quest for truth.[7]

Modern homiletic orthodoxy, however, became a marriage of Enlightenment notions of rationalism and the Romantic construal of imagination. The latter could bring near what was far away—a thesis that remains important to preachers—whereas what was brought near was most frequently assumed to be the ideational message behind the biblical text or the main idea of the parable story. Even the shape of the sermon came to embody this strange marriage of Rationalism and Romanticism. There becomes a methodological schizophrenia in modern homiletics—rationalistic points, propositions, and subthemes illustrated by emotive, pathos-laden anecdotes. Imagination's role becomes that of providing the illustrations whereby the truths of the sermon will be driven home and the sermon's themes kept interesting to the audience. Charles Rice comments on this "homiletical docetism": neither the discursive content nor the affective material embodies full human life. "The Word does not become flesh."[8] Modern homiletics, then, continued the tradition of emphasizing imagination's role in bringing near what was far away, especially by way of the "historical imagination." Beyond this function of reconstructing a past, biblical world for the listeners—a task whose product yielded in many respects a world much like the preacher's own world—the other chief role of imagination in preaching was focused on imaginative illustrations. What was almost entirely absent in these appeals for more "imaginative" sermons was any sense of the imagination's profound hermeneutical implications. The latter—the interpretative dimensions of imagination—would only come to the front in later, postmodern inquiry from such diverse locations as phenomenology, aesthetics, cognitive psychology, and narrative criticism (especially focusing on the dynamics of metaphor). Perhaps it would be accurate to reverse the previous observation: The emergence of the postmodern era is in no small part dependent on a recovery and reinterpretation of imagination theory.

Postmodern Models of the Imagination

In the way of an overview of postmodern imagination theory, Edward Murray's caution is well taken. Noting that philosophy has experienced a new awakening on the area of the imagination, he adds, "Nevertheless, to expect at this time the formulation of a full-blown theory of imagination is unrealistic."[9] In spite of this "nevertheless," several models for the postmodern imagination have emerged and have become evocative for a number of fields of inquiry and practice including homiletics. In his seminal work, *The Burning Fountain*, Phillip Wheelwright proposes a sequence of four stages to imagination especially as regards poetic creativity.[10] These four stages include the *confrontative, stylistic, compositive,* and *archetypal* imagination. The first is essential to any creative act; there needs be an initiating immediacy with the poetic object that at the same time particularizes and intensifies it. The poetic object of this engagement is not to be confused with either a conceptual object or an object in the out-there world of artifacts. Rather, the poetic object so engaged is a product of an aesthetic consciousness that "largely makes and articulates its own phenomenological object."[11] By way of imagining a sermon, then, the preacher will not begin with an objective relationship to the text as implied in the historical-critical method of interpretation. Rather, learning from the tradition, the disciplines of *lectio,* of praying the text and ruminating upon it, will begin the work that will come to fulfillment in proclamation. The stylistic phase of the poetic imagination involves a necessary distancing of the artist from his or her work. This imaginative distance is a place of rest and discernment. It is essential to the creative process and stands as a warning to preachers not to leap immediately from a reading of a biblical text to shaping the sermon. Patience is a homiletic virtue; we wait before the coming of the Lord. The third stage, the composite imagination, is the occasion for combining a variety of disparate elements that require some kind of blending or other integration. Poets might take this opportunity to juxtapose the imagery of the poem with other images either having some shared qualities or some contrapuntal elements. Here, the preacher begins to weave together the images and ideas and stories of the text with some homiletic method or other. However, preachers will want to take time to bring a number of voices into the conversation with the text—not only Karl Barth's famous newspaper, but also other sources that reflect the culture's "spirit of the age" along with the myriad voices of contemporary criticism. Unfortunately, a number of preachers begin here, with some cultural or ideological commitments that will override the text's ability to speak to the community of faith. Notice that the composite imagination is a creative possibility *only* after an immersion in the scriptural text and a season of prayer and reflection. Finally, Wheelwright proposes archetypal imagining whereby a profound sense of depth and vision is provided to the reader/listener. A poet/composer/preacher always needs to have as the *telos* of the creative endeavor this movement from the one particular object to some profound universal of the human spirit. For those called to preach, we may speak of this goal as that of revelation, whether dialectical or sacramental in nature.[12]

Another model of the imagination is provided by Richard Kearney.[13] Kearney notes that modern interpretation developed the core understanding of imagination "as presence-in-absence—the art of making what is present absent and what is absent present—while generally reversing the negative verdict it had received in the tribunal of tradition."[14] However, in a postmodern context, imagination considered from the perspective of the ethical arena embodies three functions: the utopian, the testimonial, and the empathic.[15] A related model has been developed by homiletician Thomas Troeger. In this variant of the Kearney schema, the categories within which imagination functions include the conventional or communal, the empathic, and the visionary imaginations.[16] The conventional imagination serves the essential functions of providing continuity and predictability to persons and communities. Specifically, "it is the imagination that a local congregation shares together" and is shaped by hymn books, worship traditions, church architecture, the symbol system of the congregation.[17] The obvious positive function of the conventional imagination is that a congregation "can do things together" without needing to pause and reinvent itself at each new occasion of coming together. The negative side of this imagination is that it can become hardened, excluding people and essentially reliving the past with its injustices and prejudices. Nevertheless, the preacher depends upon the conventional imagination every time she or he gets up to preach. A second way imagination functions is by providing an empathic sense of our neighbors or congregants. In fact, the possession of this empathic function is essential for ministry. Preachers must have some empathic sense, "some feeling of what our hearers are going through."[18] Once more this type of imagination has a positive and a negative side to it according to Troeger. The former, the positive, is most obvious—the ability to empathically live within the world of another person or another community. The latter, negative side to this imagination is often less noticed or even celebrated. "We can get completely swept into the person's feeling world without any objectivity whatsoever."[19] Finally, there is the visionary imagination for Troeger. Here, imagination operates in a constructive manner, putting things together in a new way. It is akin to Kearney's utopian imagination and predictably conflicts with the conventional imagination whenever the latter is challenged. Indeed, for Troeger, the very definition of a reformer is a person who challenges the conventional imagination. Regarding any negative outcomes of the visionary imagination, Troeger offers no suggestions. However, we have seen enough visionary ideologies emerge with great hope only to become hardened and authoritarian. The visionary imagination, too, can become detached from the biblical tradition to the point that an imaginative reshaping or that tradition is traded for outright repudiation.

A construal of the imagination that has similarly proved quite fruitful for homiletics has been provided by Edward Murray. Here, imagination is proposed to include three models: the perceptual, the hypothetical, and the linguistic-semantic.[20] The first open us onto the field of perception, the role of the senses that remains at the heart of imagination's work. The hypothetical imagination is in a way a refinement of Troeger's visionary model. Here, Murray observes that a person can "imagine-that" a circumstance transpires or, in a similar way, "imagine-how" a circumstance comes to be.[21] We will look at metaphor and the turn to the linguistic with regard to its implications for homiletics. However, we turn first to a much-needed study of the perceptual model, this "seeing-as," which lies at the center of imagination's roles.

Perception and Preaching

While the discussion of the imagination "is not confined to that of the image,"[22] it does begin here. Whatever else imagination achieves, its core function deals with perception, with the ways in which human beings perceive their world. With a number of commentators, we may label this central function "seeing-as." Consequently, David Bryant concludes: "The ability to create an image of something, a form that possesses a certain significance, and apply that image or form to things we experience is what makes it possible to see something as meaningful."[23] Much more than serving to ornament cognitive thinking, images perform an essential function in the human process of knowing—and feeling. Images perform an essential work of mediation between the self and the world rather than an aesthetic but optional reflection upon that world. Mary Warnock assigns to imagery, first, the ability to bring objects in the world to mind and, second, to mediate between perception and recognition. Hence, with Warnock, images "do not take the place of objects of perception, of a world transcending our subjectivity, but mediate between the world and the self in a way that opens the self to the world."[24] Seeing-as is a way of locating the work of the imagination in the entire process of knowing anything about the world, especially as that knowledge is achieved through perception. Our knowledge of the world is achieved largely through the imagination's ability to elicit and retain the image or shape of our perceived world's objects. And quite obviously, the roles of imagination and memory are closely entwined. "Both," Philip Keane notes, "work with images and both are partly sense functions."[25]

The dominant workings of the imagination, then, are crucial to the work of the preacher; we are not talking here of a decorative or ornamental glaze upon reason's higher way. Rather, our knowledge of the world and our memory of the constitutive events of knowing depend upon the imagination, and more specifically upon the role of imagery. However, this seeing-as needs to be more carefully nuanced, especially as we consider imagination's homiletic implications. At this point, David Bryant proposes three distinct though related functions of the imagination. Each provides rich suggestions for preaching. Through the imagination:

1. "We see everyday objects as every day"[26]

We recognize objects, persons, places, and other experiences of perception as familiar by associating them with images already formed within our memory. Thus, "through its capacity to form these images and subsume objects under them, the imagination enables this sort of familiarity with our world."[27] The homiletical implications of this simple yet profound insight are abundant. Initially, can we conclude that we need not as preachers restrict our illustrative sermonic content solely to stories or anecdotes? In many cases, providing the congregation with a familiar image will bring to mind an entire experience or series of experiences held in common. And since images are born within some narrative or other—about which more will be said— the latter can often be brought to mind by the shaping of an image that powerfully evokes the story. So, for example, if we decided that a reference in a sermon needs to be made to the attacks of September 11, an extended narrative of that horror-filled day may not be needed or possible. Since almost every congregation—except for those nearby in New York City—perceived the tragedy through the media, we may evoke the event by portraying that view across the river of the two buildings afire, with towering columns of smoke rising up into that beautiful blue sky. This image has become seared into the communal consciousness of almost every congregation!

A related homiletic function of imagery has to do with calling into question the image systems that the world has plastered upon the consciousness of believers—often shaping actions and attitudes more profoundly than the images and narratives of the biblical faith. There is a dialectical imagination that is in service of proclamation. Again and again, the faithful preacher finds himself or herself engaged in a struggle between the images that constitute the world's conventional imagination and those that embody the gospel. (One of the most appalling locations for this conflict of image systems is when the preacher is called upon to proclaim the gospel at the occasion of the death of a child. Here, the conventional imagination of the culture may well drape the event with romantic images of the child as a flower plucked by God and of death as an event overcome by the funeral director's art.) Repeatedly, faithful preachers will exegete the conventional imagination of the listeners in order to call into question the images purporting to accurately identify the individual and the world. This confrontative task is not only between the community of faith and the world in its unbelief, however. Rather, the preacher will be called to speak as well against the conventional imagination of the church when it becomes too conformed to the spirit of the age. One constant in faithful preaching is what Walter Brueggemann terms "a fresh liberating return to the memory."[28] Such a return is at once prophetic and sacramental.

2. Images allow us to focus on one particular aspect of what we experience

In one sense, this statement is a truism. It is never the case that our perceptive apparatus furnishes us with the entire object. Precisely by virtue of our location and point of view, the sensory object comes to us partially, never in full. This is most evident in visual imagery—we see only the near-to-us side of persons and things, yet imaginatively assume and construct the whole. Once more, the role of memory is decisive. Perceiving only one perspective of an object, our memory engages with imagination to provide other points of view. Therefore, Paul Pruyser observes that "no one can perceive a whole solid object from a static position—all we can see at any moment are the surfaces facing him (or her). Yet we know, and perhaps even perceive, the whole object, including its unseen sides."[29] Without memory's function, we could not go beyond the partially perceived object to a recognition of the whole. On the other hand, this always-partial grasp of perception's object makes for an ambiguity that at times can be misleading. We periodically mistake one thing for another because of similarities in form, texture, taste, or color. Our environment also contributes to this difficulty in truly perceiving, for example, on those dark and stormy nights when vision is clouded by mist and rain. Homiletically, then, we will want to provide enough context for the recognition of an image by our listeners while retaining an economy of speech that imagistic talk provides. Speaking of a rumbling sound without locating it in the ground (an earthquake, as in Matthew's resurrection account) or from the sky (as in a thunderstorm) may be too terse. Nevertheless, it remains the power of imagery how few cues are needed to provide the necessary recognition.

In preaching, however, we may trade on this ambiguity of images and thereby build up an interplay of meaning and effect. Sometimes, we may want the congregation temporarily to be held back from full recognition. And at other times, we may want the listeners to relate a series of events or objects or persons on the basis of some shared but partial perceptions. Withholding full recognition is an effective tool within the storyteller's workshop. A "stranger" walked along the road to Emmaus with Cleopas and his companion in Luke 24, revealed fully only at the meal and the breaking of the bread. And in Mark 8:22-26, full recognition does not come to the blind man upon Jesus' first ministrations. "I can see people, but they look like trees walking," responds the man (8:24). After a second touch, however, full recognition comes at last: "He saw everything clearly" (8:25). At times, we may want the sermon to progress in a like manner. At first, the congregation may recognize only in part on the basis of the images we have presented. Then, with further elaboration and contextualization, the full perception is provided. A further use of the inherent ambiguity of images in preaching relates to image systems and the depth of meaning provided by the interplay of images as the sermon sequences through its plot. Thus, an image provided early in the sermon—perhaps of children being excluded from sharing in an activity—can be transformed later in the sermon as another image is provided in which children are valued participants. Here, the images are in opposition to one another and the hearers are called upon to choose which image to adopt as their own. The alternative is to provide an image system in which each successive image in the sermon reinforces and deepens the meaning already provided earlier. Each of these approaches gains its effectiveness from the insight provided by Bryant. Images allow us to focus on one particular aspect of our experience.

3. Images offer us new and different perspectives on everyday reality "by focusing on their hitherto hidden or largely ignored features"[30]

The ability of the imagination to recognize objects on the basis of partial forms and other sensory data has already been explored. On the basis of this information, imagination and memory combine to identify and, equally important, signify the object for ourselves. Mary Warnock admits that this achievement is not without a certain "sloppiness," since our information about the object may be too incomplete for an accurate identification.[31] We may be misled. Nevertheless, we grow accustomed to conventional readings of the data mediated through our perception and the work of images. We learn to live within worlds shaped by both narratives and imagery. However, by focusing on those "hitherto hidden or ignored" features of the imagery, we receive surprising new insights into ourselves, and our world can be received. For Bryant, the example relates to our perception of a tree. The same perceived features are present, yet the significance shifts remarkably if a lumberjack comes to see that tree from the perspective of a birdwatcher![32] Both see the same tree, yet their emotional and even ideological vantage points differ. Once more, we are reminded of

Mary Warnock's insight regarding the inherently interpretive function of perception. And we notice, too, that with such a different way of seeing the tree also comes a shift in the imaging of the person's own identity and vocation.

Whatever else calls a preacher's attention to the power of imagery, this insight of Bryant's and Warnock's regarding the achievement of new and surprising perspectives on self and world becomes central. It is, moreover, built into the biblical witness again and again. In Scripture, it is not as much the shift in seeing-as from lumberjack to birdwatcher, but at the center from the location of faith or from disbelief. The apostle Paul begins his first letter to the Corinthians by calling to awareness the mutually exclusive perspectives on the cross as seen from the world and from those who are "being-saved" (1 Cor. 1:18-25). The former see the cross as weakness and folly, while the latter see the same cross as the wisdom of God and the power of God. Scripture also portrays the shift to new or hitherto largely ignored perspectives as resulting from circumstances that almost compel the empathic imagination into action. So, Peter, in his vision on Simon the tanner's roof, is given the images of a whole net full of unclean things and he hears a voice announce, "Get up, Peter; kill and eat" (Acts 10:13). In response to Peter's profession of ritual cleanness, the voice is heard once more: "What God has made clean, you must not call profane" (10:15). Shortly after the vision, there is a knock on the gate of the tanner's house. Three men have arrived to invite Peter to come with them to visit Cornelius, a Gentile and a centurion. Peter's world and his ideology will never be the same. His seeing-as has become irrevocably altered. Images can perform their powerful work on behalf of transformation.

Vision and the Suite of Imagery

The achievements of the imagination are based upon the perception's capacity we have denoted seeing-as. There is a dialectic at work between imagination's larger work—such as its emphatic achievements—and the workings of the human senses. "Vision," in this regard, involves all of the achievements of imagination as ably assisted by memory as well as cognition—the models of imagination we have surveyed above. Yet vision also relates to one of the senses and its visual grasp of objects in the world. The dialectic, then, involves this interplay between imagination's cosmic reach on one hand and its perceptual apparatus on the other. Hence, David Harned notes, "because the self is a creature that imagines best when it relies upon the full range of its resources, all its senses become, in greater or lesser measure, contributors to vision."[33] We do need to introduce a cautionary word at this point, however. Notice how easy it is to bias our perceptual model toward a visual modality solely. Speaking of imagination, we have found Mary Warnock's seeing-as to be a helpful shorthand; we speak also of vision in a similar manner. Then, when we turn to perception and begin to speak of imagery, the visual is once again privileged in our discourse. It is wise, then, to remind ourselves that perception's suite of imagery derives from all the senses, and not solely from those achieved through eyesight. We not only see images, but also hear them, taste them, smell them, and feel them—and in many cases in multiple modes of perceiving (seeing as well as smelling the rose). Perhaps it is time now to focus more specifically on the modes of perception and the qualities of imagery provided by each of the senses.

1. Visual imagery

The visual image is for our age the dominant mode of perception. We live in an ever-increasing visual, media-driven world culture. Visual images are everywhere. There is perhaps preeminently in the visual images an ability to focus attention involving both meaning and emotion. Visual images are capable of "training desire" (Margaret Miles) in ways that Christian tradition has known since the earliest days of the church. The spirituality of the icon is the preeminent example of this formation or training desire. Yet, as Miles notes, "advertising images act in the same way . . . [but] attempt to capture—to break off—a piece of the infinite longing of a person and dispense it in the acquisition of an immediate satisfaction."[34] The walls of our social consciousness are plastered with visual imagery provided through the media.[35] These images are crucial for proclamation since they become the lenses through which we envision a world.[36] And a person's ethics is shaped by the world they envision! On the other hand, Scripture comes laden with images of its own—images through which we are invited to see quite a different world and to live and act within its realm. More accurately, we may speak of Scripture's families of images, clusterings of images within such categories as nature and vegetation, substantive artifacts (ships, houses, Temple), and social metaphors related to God as well as God's people.[37] Preachers stand in the midst of congregations already formed and informed by the images of the culture. They also come with some awareness of the imagery of faith. The sermon is at ground zero in this contest between the worlds that shape us.

One key characteristic of visual imagery holds important implications for both theology and method. "We know only in part," the apostle Paul argues (1 Cor. 13:9). Our perspective will provide some aspect of the object, some shape, texture, color, while denying us other simultaneous perspectives with their information. This seeing-in-part recalls Bryant's insights into the functions of imagination noted above. However, the inherent perspectuality of visual imagery cautions preachers to take point of view quite serious. We will heed that caution. On the other hand, this seeing-in-part is also construed in relation to the visual images' multivalence or even ambiguity. The point of view on the image is a complex issue in itself though the image itself never yields the object in its entirety. Miles concludes:

> For the viewer, an image is interpreted according to the viewer's interest, as informed by her or his physical appearance, status within the community, education, and spirituality. The image offers a floating chain of signifieds, a wide but finite range of possible meanings.[38]

Given this floating chain of signifieds, the theological task presented most directly by visual imagery—especially the images of Scripture—is to contextualize, but not unduly limit this floating chain of meanings. Preachers may well not have a choice about whether to employ imagery in their sermons— both the faith tradition and the contemporary culture will insist on their use. Images, though, as Harned points out, are "slippery, ambiguous, and obscure until they are named."[39]

2. Oral and aural images

We hear images as well. The sounds impinging on our ears we perceive differently as a church bell, the call of a flight of geese, or, perhaps, the sweet exhaust note of a 1950s British sports car. Images we hear are also notoriously ambiguous and need imagination and memory's fuller powers to attempt to discern. Is the church bell sound from a real bell or a digital reproduction? Was that really a flight of geese or (as recently happened to me) sounds made by the church's preschool children racing around the hall on their new scooter toys? And was that really an old Triumph's exhaust note or somebody's mid-80s clunker with a hole in the muffler? Aside from this shared multivalence or ambiguity, oral/aural images do diverge at points that are significant for preaching. Visual and aural images contrast first in their modes of receptivity. The former, visual, involves the agent more directly in perception. For the sighted, the day is one constant maneuver of neck-turning, eye-focusing, head-lifting, depth- and range-adjusting actions. The latter, aural, is quite a bit more passive. We may turn an ear now and then, but most of our hearing does not involve the intentionality of visual perception. (One reason for this relative passivity of hearing is that especially at lower frequencies, the direction of the sound is less discernible.) To the contrary, this more passive stance of the oral/aural perception lends other assets not available to visual perception. Walter Ong has become the foremost advocate of these other assets of the world opened to us through hearing.

> In a visual cosmos, the self is an agent; in an aural world it is a patient. In the former, the individual is safe, at least for the moment; in the latter, the individual is always vulnerable. In one world the self is free; in the other, it is claimed, called to account, and asked to respond to the initiative of others. In one realm, the self is distinguished sharply from its environment; in the other, sounds bind it tightly to its social context and remind it of its contingency. One world contains only surfaces; in the other there are many and various clues to the interiority of selves.[40]

The genius of preaching is that it offers to the hearers all of the qualities of this aural world while also being able to picture for those hearers images for recognition of self, church, and world.

3. Tasting and smelling images

A minority of biblical images pertains to the senses of smell and taste. More centrally, it is remarkable how profound these images are to persons of faith as they are invited to "taste and see that the LORD is good" (Ps. 34:8); or to rejoice that "we are the aroma of Christ to God among those who are being saved and among those who are perishing" (2 Cor. 2:15). Certainly when preaching from such texts, these images of taste or smell will become the master images of the sermon, orienting the listeners to analogous images out of their lived experience. And although relatively infrequent in Scripture, images of taste and smell abound within the experience of the congregation. Especially rich are the images of taste and smell provided through sacramental praxis. In one church, the Sunday Eucharist was anticipated by the smell of freshly baked bread drifting up from the church kitchen. Homiletic usage of this proleptic smell, then, became a natural and easy image when needed in preaching. Also, churches that use incense in the liturgy thereby provide another strong image of smell related to prayer and to sacrifice. While the preacher would not want to wear out these references, when appropriate, they provide a rich source of powerful images for the sermon.

What is held in common within the entire suite of perception's ways of imaging are several core characteristics. Imagery by its very nature provides essential contributions to knowledge and our experience of self and world. Its distinctiveness also involves limits, boundaries to our knowing and our feeling. In the first instance, we have noted that across the range of perceptual imagining, a persistent multivalence and residual ambiguity obtain. The former, multivalence, is a way of speaking of the images' "finite range of possible meanings."[41] Part of this multiple meaning of imagery stems from the variations in point of view, not just with regard to location vis à vis the object, but related to the varieties offered by age, gender, class, and social and religious perspectives. However, the multivalence of the image is never reduced to the question of the perceiver's social location. Rather, there is an inherent resistance within the perception of an image to being reduced to one single discursive definition. Simply put, an image will yield more than one finally settled meaning for a community—always. In fact, the play of imagery within Scripture uses this quality of multivalence as the covenant people re-imagine themselves and their God. For example, the biblical image of the lamb would, at first glance, seem rather stable and focused on a limited range of meanings derived from Israel's nomadic origins. The Lord, then, is imaged as Israel's Shepherd, the covenant being God's flock. However, a related skein of meanings derives from the association of lamb with the sacrificial cult. Now lamb is not simply an image of the covenant faithful, but reconceived as their offering, their vehicle for atonement and cleansing. Within the New Testament, both of these image systems persist—those baptized in Christ are like the lost sheep that are found, restored to the one flock with the one shepherd. At the same time, Jesus is identified by the Baptist as "Lamb of God" and is envisioned at the *parousia*—the fierce lamb upon the throne. The two image systems—covenant people as flock, God/Christ as shepherd and Jesus as Lamb of God—both weave their way through Scripture. The multiple meanings of the image of sheep and flock derive not simply from the two complementary systems. Rather, there abide rich multiple meanings within each. Preachers will draw on these meanings while exerting some care and precision to avoid mixing the two image systems into a confusing pastiche.

Precisely by virtue of the multivalence and ambiguity of imagery, the question arises regarding the context or location of the image. It is not that we can ever nail down an image to one discursive point—images resist such ideational redaction as much, say, as metaphors. Rather, the challenge is that lacking some sort of location of rootage, images can be made to mean almost anything, or nothing. For example, most assemblies of the faithful have listened to homilies in which images tumbled over one another in what became "buzzing, blooming confusion." Then, too, the church has struggled with recent attempts to re-imagine God, which were for many a profound distortion of Christian faith. Moreover, the never-ending barrage of images generated by the media present subtle ideological messages about personal and communal identity. But this is precisely a central issue for preaching—Christian life and work will be shaped for better or for worse by the images held by the believer. Craig Dykstra puts it directly: "The configuration of images that constitute the shape of each person's imagination determine what we can do and see, think, feel, and how we act."[42] Images constitute the vision by which we recognize ourselves, the community of faith, and the world. They determine in large part "how we act." The question is critical for those called to preach:

> The work of the preacher must begin with knowledge of that cache of images that already reside in the individual and corporate psyches of our parishioners. Do we have any idea which images buttress or destructively engage their views of life?[43]

What is needed is, then, is a hermeneutic of imagery for preaching that retains their wonderful multivalence yet enables the preacher to speak imagistically with theological integrity. Images need a certain discipline if they are to become faithful servants of the Word. For all its importance, a celebration of imagery's multivalence is not yet an adequate model of interpretation. We now turn to several theses that are offered to flesh out a hermeneutics of imagery for preaching.

4. Images come laden with a language

There is a "grammar" of the image that will need to be decoded. We encounter this most forcefully in the icon. An icon, Ella Bozarth-Campbell teaches, cannot be encountered other than through "a growing process of self-transformation . . . and through growing with the word within the literary text: listening to it, learning it, becoming it."[44] As a meeting place with the divine, the icon's power resides not in its ability to imitate any thing, but in its capacity to disclose the Word *(logos)* itself. Put simply, "The presence of logos in the image constitutes the seat of its energy."[45] However, there is a sense in which, to put it negatively, all images are inevitably "contaminated by language."[46] More positively stated, one of the tasks of the preacher is to exegete the "language" the image is speaking—images already held by the community and those considered for use in the sermon. We have already noted with Troeger that the images of mass media reveal an "implicit gospel."[47] Here, the language is one of personal identity by ownership and consumption and of communal identity as a market. Other language games images play are equally in need of careful exegesis for preaching. A preacher may reach for a sports image in professional football by way of illustrating team spirit or character, yet all the while the image will be shouting its language of competition, violence, and the triumph of technology. Another preacher may attempt to image a biblical notion of sacrifice through the ordeal of American prisoners of war during the Vietnam War. Yet the language of the image may speak both of noble sacrifice as well as of a contaminated language offered in post–Vietnam War films starring Silvester Stallone and Arnold Schwarzenegger. Even within the explicit imagery of Christian faith, the same image may speak differently depending on the context. So, Martin Marty observes: "The cross on the Crusaders' shields is 'other' than the one on whom the cancer patient fixes in desperate and consoling prayer."[48] (We might also add with Marty that the cross worn by a young adult with the pierced body parts and tattoos may be "other" than the cross worn by a girl at her Confirmation.) Homiletically, this deciphering of the language or languages of an image can provide for some of the richest irony within a sermon. On one hand, the media frequently couch their marketing pitch with an implicit language of religion and spirituality. So, the enduring quality of love used to be imaged through a South African diamond. Now, it is imaged by a digital camera. On the other hand, a good many of the ostensibly secular images offered by the world will reveal a quite religious content when interrogated by the person of faith. It is ironic to watch such television spectacles as the opening ceremonies of the Olympics with an eye of faith. Here, postmodern humanity struggles to image a world of harmony yet without the particularity of any national tradition or faith tradition. The resulting pageant is oddly religious, stretching for transcendence yet predictably falling back into a Hollywood theme-park version of the meaning of life.

5. Images are best located within a narrative

In the beginning is the story and the images that are born within them. In fact, every image has a hereditary home within some story or other. Devoid of some narrative context, David Harned notes, "images grow ambiguous and opaque. . . . Images can be named in a variety of ways, but until they are named in some fashion or another they will not divulge their precise significance."[49] One of the preacher's perennial tasks, then, is to name the images of church and world by locating them within some story. It is the story of the crusades and the story of the cancer patient that names the image of the cross differently in those respective contexts. And it is the narrative location of a face radiant with joy that discloses whether we are seeing a mother after giving birth to her first child, a believer freshly come from the waters of baptism, or a model putting on a good face to sell a car. Therefore, the crisis of imagining God within the churches is at its core not as much a question of proper or improper imagery, but of the narrative that is either privileged or suppressed in the image's presentation.[50]

An alternate perspective is crucial as well. By virtue of its location within stories, imagery provides ports of entry into the world of the narrative itself. That is, once an image suggests its narrative home, an interpretive point of view is thereby provided with regard to that story. So, for example, to evoke the image of manna in sermon or song is to evoke as well the wilderness narrative with its drama of hunger, murmuring, and divine provision. Also notice that images are persistently itinerant. For those of the new Israel in Christ, manna also evokes the bread of heaven discourse in John 6, again with its themes of hunger, murmuring, and divine provision. "Images afford a critical perspective upon particular renditions of a story," David Harned concludes, adding, "the story provides critical perspective upon different interpretations of the imagery."[51]

6. Images convey an epistemology along with their message

More accurately, we may say that images convey an epistemology that becomes their message. Therefore, Thomas Troeger comments that watching television "conditions us to a way of knowing reality."[52] Exegeting that epistemology in its best light discloses a world shaped by narratives and images that profoundly illuminate human life. Such an analysis also uncovers the chronic passivity of the audience—the proverbial couch potato—who substitutes vicarious experiences for a real-lived experience of his or her own. It is also inherent in the epistemology of the visual media, whether television, film, or the Internet, that the experience is primarily individualistic even in the company of others. The images of the media are consumed passively and privately, and with a pace that allows for little personal or communal reflection. We will be aware of the ways in which this epistemology shapes us as we then shape our sermons to speak to these images or speak with these images. By shaping preaching to be a dialogue, the African American homiletical tradition is a strong counterculture experience in the midst of a media-driven world. Television's images do not invite us to talk back! In another church context, too, we will need to move with considerable caution in the use of visual media projected on a screen during our preaching. The problem here is twofold: First, the epistemologies are different regarding communal consciousness. The hearers of the sermon must shift to a different consciousness to be viewers of the images on the screen. This is more than a challenge; it may be impossible to shift back and forth rapidly between these two types of consciousness. Second, the epistemologies differ in that proclamation is inherently communal and dialogical, whether the hearers talk back or feel back. Once a visual media presentation takes center stage, the event becomes a monologue and the experience largely individual. Community and dialogue become sublimated or even lost. And in the contest between the two epistemologies, most of the time the media event will win over that which is spoken and heard.

7. *The liturgy as essential arbiter*

If preaching is divorced from the other aspects of worship, then its images will be received by the worshipers as having little or nothing to do with the images embodied in the rest of the service. Perhaps some image from the sermon will be picked up in a hymn that follows, but otherwise, there will be minimal connection. However, if preaching is viewed as a liturgical act, then the images of the sermon will become interwoven with the images of the other acts of worship. Moreover, the images of the sermon are offered by the preacher within a liturgical event whose theology and practice stand as arbitrators of the church's preaching and its doctrine. Margaret Mary Kelleher, therefore, speaks of the liturgy as "the censor of the Christian imagination."[53] Just as the church's doctrine is finally measured by its worship and sacramental practice *(lex orandi, lex credendi),* so the sermon and its images are finally arbitrated by the liturgical context of proclamation. We may then speak of a related norm applicable to the imagery of preaching: *Lex orandi, lex imagi.* Therefore, returning to an earlier example, to image a child's death in a funeral sermon by a poem in which God gathers beautiful little flowers for his garden is not only a maudlin example of pietism, but also heresy. The funeral liturgy itself speaks of the God of Jesus Christ as good shepherd and compassionate friend. This dreadful image of God as child taker needs to be censored by the liturgy and the preacher!

There is in these considerations a hermeneutics of suspicion regarding imagery and the task of preaching. The careful preacher will be in a stance of interrogating the imagery formed by the world and brought to the community's worship. Preachers will inquire concerning the language of the images, their particular ideological content and message. She or he will also look for the narrative location of the image in its specific presentation, recalling that images are not only slippery but itinerant. They migrate quite easily from one narrative context to another. The preacher will furthermore assess the epistemology of imagery with regard to the oral art of proclamation. And finally, the images will be held up to the light of the gospel embodied within the church's liturgy and sacraments. There, as the community gathers to praise the triune God, the image finds its best narrative home—water, bread, wine, oil for anointing, and the images of the saints and martyrs. All are located within the narrative of our salvation in Jesus Christ.

Imagery and Point of View

Being objects within the human act of perception, images come to awareness with some point of view or other. We look up, watching a flock of geese in their V formation, while hearing their honking encouragements fade away as the flight disappears beyond the tree line. To be sure, the aural point of view is less focused than the visual—we could turn away from the geese and still hear their honking—nevertheless, point of view is essential to the image. In fact, we should begin our consideration of point of view with an axiom: images, being objects of human perception, are always experienced with some point of view. Moreover, that particular point of view in many cases provides significant affective content as well as cognitive significance with regard to the perceived object. The emotional dimension of imagery is achieved in no small part through several qualities related to point of view. *Distance* is a rather obvious quality within point of view. Typically, increasing the distance from the perceived object tends to diminish its affective power. Therefore, images of potentially harmful objects—snakes, spiders, velocoraptors (those nasty meatasaureses in *Jurassic Park*)—may evoke heightened fear if perceived as nearby. Perceived from some safe distance, those emotions may then diminish. *Duration* is another quality of point of view that affects the emotive significance of an object. While it may seem intuitive to conclude that longer exposure to some negatively experienced object will bring with duration an increased emotive power, there are circumstances in which an extended experience of that negative object actually diminishes its capacity for emotive power. Hence, the strategy of desensitization by which an extended exposure to an object reduces its prior negative emotional power. Point of view also has a potential *dynamic* quality. That is, whether the object is moving closer or farther away may well serve to intensify or diminish its affective power. (Remember the characteristic "click" of the velocoraptor's stalking approach in *Jurassic Park*, produced by the scythelike middle claw of its feet?) The dynamic quality of an object's point of view relates to the issue of duration as well as distance. It certainly helps when your dentist announces, "Just another minute and we're done," as you endure the sound and feeling of a seemingly endless drilling out of a tooth cavity. Now, it can be endured just a little longer!

It will be noticed by now that we have selected a series of negative examples to illustrate the qualities of distance, duration, and dynamic change in point of view. However, a series of positive examples may also be provided. A photographer uses distance as she or he zooms in to get a close-up of a child's face or a single flower in bloom. A worship service may be other than the stereotyped endless boredom—it may involve instead an ecstasy that seems timeless as images of faith are contemplated and experienced. And the dynamic quality of point of view is exploited by filmmakers in those classic shots of someone running toward their lover, finally to meet in a joyous embrace. The positive quality of an object's dynamic point of view may also be experienced by way of its duration. In soaring flight, a glider pilot experiences both relief and exhilaration when a thermal is encountered, lifting the glider upward and prolonging its time aloft. (Here, the object that is experienced is both visual—the rising pointer on an instrument gauge—and through the bodily sense of that lift that is produced.) In every case, the qualities produced by point of view function to shape experience in both negative and positive directions. Preachers alert to these qualities now can turn toward the more methodological considerations deriving from these capacities of point of view.

Models of Point of View

The camera model

David Buttrick in his *Homiletic* first explored point of view from the perspective of a model related to preaching. Buttrick borrowed the image of a camera to image the model of imagery (see pp. 183-84 for an analysis of Buttrick's camera model). Just as a camera incorporates the elements of focal field, lens depth, and focal depth, preachers may (and should) exploit these elements as they image moves within their sermons. Given our analysis of the qualities of point of view, the camera model offers itself particularly as a means of shaping images that are relatively static in distance and duration. That is, the camera model excels at guiding the preacher to image for the congregation an object that remains fixed in proximity. Thus, we can invite the listeners to view a thunderstorm cloud off on the horizon or have them squint to thread a needle. The emotive capacity of an image is shaped here mainly through lens depth, the degree of self-engagement in the image. As Buttrick comments, differing degrees of self-involvement are capable of reaching "different depths in consciousness."[54] Observe differing lens depths at work in the following three examples:

Have you ever observed someone sitting on a bank, maybe in a little boat, whiling away time just fishing? Maybe a child with a bamboo pole? The red cork float is watched, waiting for a nibble. Who knows how long they have waited, doing nothing, really. Just watching the red bobber out there beyond their pole.

Fishing has a quieting tranquillity about it. Most of us have participated in this contest of wills with a fish lurking there under the water's surface. We get into a hypnotic trance almost, staring at the fishing line and the float we have flung out to a likely spot for a big one. And even if nothing happens, well, that, too, is good enough.

Your therapist invites you to close your eyes and relax. "Think back to a time with pleasant memories," the familiar litany begins. And soon your tension fades and a scene comes into view. You are back once more, sitting on the hard boards of the wharf, warmed by the summer sun. You bait the little hook, send it arcing out into the water. Then you watch the red float. Watch and watch. The feelings grow huge and warm like the boards. It is your father's float out there, now a brilliant red in color. You peer at it and even hope it doesn't disappear under the water. Dad let you use his tackle box when you were a kid. Fish or no fish, that was good.

Now each of these examples is designed with a different lens depth. All of them involve a middle-range focus on that red fishing bobber. But a somewhat distant third-person observer perspective shapes the first. There is some reflectivity—about how long the individual remained there fishing—but the level of emotional engagement was minimal. In the second example, there seems to be a more intimate lens depth. The scene is shaped through a second-person point of view, although it is diminished somewhat by an annoying rhetorical excess. In the third scene, the reader or hearer is invited to imagine a hypnotic trance in which the image of the red float has vivid and poignant significance. Here, lens depth is magnified to an immediate proximity within consciousness. In each case, the emotive quality is intensified as the lens depth is compressed. Point of view contributes significantly to the emotional power of images in general and in preaching in particular.

Beyond the question of emotive range, point of view provides for other aspects of meaning and significance as well. Images mean differently in some cases as their point of view is shifted. One striking example in biblical interpretation relates to the field of meaning discovered within the world of the parable of the mustard seed (Mark 4:30-32 and parallels). Here in Mark, the smallest of all seeds is planted in the ground "and becomes the greatest of all shrubs" (Mark 4:32). The point of view even for a great shrub, however, remains a downward glance. On the other hand, the image system implied by the coordinates of kingdom of God-seed planted-great tree for Jesus' hearers is provided in Ezekiel 17:23. Here, Israel's fortunes will be reversed and the covenant people will become like a cedar sprig planted by God upon "a high and lofty mountain," which will grow, produce fruit, and "become a noble cedar" (Ezek. 17:22-23). Moreover, the birds of the air will find rest and nesting in its branches—an allusion to the nations including those that have afflicted God's people. Since cedars grow only on the heights of Lebanon (while mustard grows abundantly and is controlled in its planting by Jewish law),[55] the parable takes on a strong quality of reversal as well as advent and surprise. From a homiletical perspective, the reversal is embodied within the relative points of view of "cedar upon the lofty mountains" and "common mustard shrub of Israel." The meaning of the lofty tree is literally embodied—you have to look off to the north and look up to those heights for that majestic tree. Conversely, the point of view on mustard shrubs remains downward. A sermon whose image system is shaped by the parable and its mytheme in the Hebrew Scripture will likewise embody this reversal in point of view. After an opening section expanding upon the Ezekiel pericope and its image of the triumphal great tree, the preacher could then explore contemporary images of power and glory. The latter, contemporary imagery, will need to retain the point of view established in the Ezekiel text. We will need to provide images whose points of view invite the congregation to look up in pride and glory. The alternate image system will then be explored beginning with the mustard seed and its performance in the parable. The preacher then invites the hearers to look down as signs of God's humble reign in Jesus Christ are envisioned. Here, the entire sermonic plot is shaped by a reversal in point of view. Certainly, there is an affective component to these respective points of view. But notice, however, that the two points of view are integral to the thematic structure and movement of the sermon. Point of view on images conveys both emotive power and participates in the conceptual meaning of the object as well. Both meaning/theme and emotion are shaped by the image's point of view.

The videocam model

David Buttrick's camera model of imagery's point of view may be supplemented helpfully with two additional models. The videocam model retains the strong orientation toward the visual mode of perception but now allows mobility of the image. Visual images may be perceived as stationary, in which case the camera model is fully adequate to interpret the dynamics of their points of view. However, images also move in relation to the perceiver and for those experiences another model is needed. Here, the qualities of the camera—focal field, lens depth, and focal depth—all continue to obtain for the viewer, but each is now capable of dynamic change experienced over time. We may invite the congregation to imagine themselves *reading a psalm praising God for creation and then looking up, smiling as they take in a glorious sunset with a flock of birds flying off in the distance.* Here, focal field has been shifted. Or the preacher may use a videocam approach to alter lens depth as the congregation is asked to imagine themselves *at the airport arrival curbside, watching the cars and vans trundle by. Finally, one vehicle is spotted as it approaches in the stream of traffic. Everything is different; this is your sister whom you haven't seen in years.* Or, focal depth can be shaped into a dynamic experience by providing a growing depth of insight. So, we might image *a young husband and wife watching the ultrasound screen as it images their newly created life of only a few weeks, but they can see the heart beating within that little form there on the screen. It is their child.* In every case, the three qualities of the camera model obtain with the videocam. However, the mobility offered through the latter model provides for possibilities of emotion and conceptual meaning unavailable in the former. Both have their place in preaching.

Of course, the added benefit of the videocam model is that the perceptual range is expanded to include sound as well. Video cameras come equipped with microphones so that objects may be both seen and heard. Imaging by way of the videocam model, for example, allows the congregation to "see" *a busload of the church's children driving off to camp, their happy clamor and good-bye's diminishing as the bus heads down the road.* Quite frequently, the objects of our perception convey much of their dynamic quality to us through sound and not through sight alone. Before they even come into view, the next band in the parade can be heard approaching our place among the spectators. A confirmand kneeling before the altar can hear the words said as the bishop lays hands on others, kneeling there as she awaits her moment of confirmation. Recalling the discussion on perception and the ambiguity of images, the videocam allows us to present an image whose identity is not fully revealed by one mode of perception until another is added. We employ our vision and hearing to resolve these ambiguities without much conscious thought. We hear footsteps approaching from behind us and turn to see, and confirm, the identity of the person drawing near. Or, we may strain to identify an unrecognizable automobile until we hear the familiar sound of the air-cooled Volkswagen engine as it drives by. This car is a classic replica shell hiding an old VW! (Of course, we also turn to other senses to resolve ambiguity—tasting some pale yellow stuff stored in the refrigerator to see if it is vanilla pudding or mayonnaise!)

The addition of the aural quality of perception provided by the videocam model also grants the preacher the capability to envision some object—static or mobile—and invite the congregation to listen to some reflective, internal comments or questions. With this imaging strategy, the sound that is heard is an internal one of consciousness acting in reflection to what it sees. We can invite the congregation to watch the scene of the disciples in the boat making the crossing in Mark 8:14-21, to hear them complain about having only one loaf in the boat. (Here, the voices we hear are external.) As that scene is established, certainly Mark invites a reader-viewer-hearer response: *"And we wonder what kinds of boneheads Jesus has for disciples. I mean, didn't they just assist Jesus as he fed a hungry crowd out in the wilderness?"* (In this case, the voice we hear is internal, a response to the irony of the Markan scene.) Once again, this reflective voice may serve to resolve ambiguity or to let it remain. In the former mode, we might invite the congregation to watch Jesus approach a Samaritan well at midday, meeting a woman who had come there to draw water. *"Well, you wonder what the disciples think of this?"* you question, adding, *"Oh, that's right. They aren't here to see it. They're off in town shopping for provisions."* Here, our internal reflection has clarified the response of the disciples—there is none—allowing their response to come later in the story. At other times, the reflective voice in response to the perceived scene simply retains or even deepens the ambiguity. Thus, at the end of a sermon dealing with the prodigal son, we may have focused on the older son standing out there in the field, arms crossed in front of him, speaking words of bitterness to a servant. Then, we might let our reflective voice intrude over the scene— *"I guess the question is, does he uncross those arms, go down to the house, and open them in welcome to his brother, or does he remain out there in his anger? But Jesus doesn't tell us, leaves him standing there. We just don't know about that older brother's outcome, do we?"* (The sermon could conclude by shifting the focus to ourselves. At least we will know if we come to the Father's house and open our arms and welcome a repentant sinner.) This reflective voice in response to our external perceptions is a powerful resource for the preacher. Like other such tools, it should not be frivolously or frequently used. Only when the issues at hand in the sermon invite, or demand it.

The flight simulator model

A flight simulator brings along the perceptual complement of the camera model as well as the videocam model of imaging. That is, first, a strong visual orientation remains. Under visual flight rules (VFR), the pilot at the simulator is constantly shifting from glances inside the cockpit to scans through the canopy. The former, inside visual references are to various instruments indicating airspeed, altitude, aircraft attitude, and location. The outside scanning corroborates all this information in the real world of flight. The camera model obtains as an image is spotted in close focal range on the aircraft's radar screen. As the contact approaches, the pilot looks out to locate in far range the other aircraft alerted by the radar. Of course, all of this is moving in real time, so the videocam model is more appropriate to speak of the various points of view and the perceptual experience in general. The videocam model is also more inclusive of the pilot's experience because of the varieties of sounds that accompany any kind of flight. The pilot increases the throttle and hears the jet engines spool up. The pilot extends the air brakes and hears a bit of the increased turbulence of the airflow over the wings. Some instruments give audible warnings or translate flight information through a variety of sounds—beeps, clicks, and, if needed, hornlike warning whoops. But the entire experience in the simulator is also one of bodily sensation. Get the signal to take off, push the throttle forward, and you can feel the tires on the runway. Upon liftoff, the sound and feel changes as the wheels leave the ground. Hit the gear-up control, and you hear the motors retracting the wheels. When they bed home, you hear and feel a satisfying thunk. Soon, you are vectored into a turn, and the world outside tilts. A bit more power is needed, so once more the throttles are pushed forward. The sound of the engines deepens, and you feel the vibration change through the seat of your pants. A flight simulator model includes bodily, kinesthetic sensations while retaining the visual and aural perceptions of the camera and videocam models.[56]

Preachers need this latter model of point of view and perception from time to time. Different circumstances call for its richer suite of sensations. The first reason to invoke the flight simulator model is when the biblical text speaks of deeply felt bodily sensations. The most compelling example in the New Testament may be found in John 11 as Jesus confronts the mourners of Lazarus's death (John 11:1-44). Once Jesus arrives at the home of Lazarus, Mary, and Martha, he becomes "greatly disturbed in spirit and deeply moved" by the weeping of Mary and the Judeans (11:33). The Koine Greek translated "greatly disturbed" and "deeply moved" are terms that invite a flight-simulator model of imaging. The former, *embrimaomai,* can equally be translated as "groaned" or even "snorted." Wes Howard-Brook comments: "It has its root in the sound of a horse snorting and clearly expresses deep anger."[57] The latter term, *tarassō,* can mean deep fear, but in this context is more complex. Again, Howard-Brook notes that these meanings "show a side of Jesus we have not seen in this Gospel, a deeply emotional stirring that is enraged and perhaps fearful about some aspect of what is presented before him."[58] Clearly, these two descriptions of Jesus' response to the mourning and the unbelief of the crowd involve strong bodily sensations, experiences not fully conveyed by the usual translation choices of "greatly disturbed" and "deeply moved." Therefore, it is the responsibility of the preacher to convey these bodily and emotional responses of Jesus through analogous images out of the lived experience of the congregation. Perhaps the experience can be imaged by an example: *"It's like Jesus had simultaneously caught a bad case of the stomach flu while being enraged at the sexual misconduct of some ordained clergy in his church."* Here, we try to entwine the cognitive and bodily dimensions of the meaning of the Johannine text. Only a flight-simulator model is up to the task of this kind of imaging.

In addition to the task of interpreting biblical terms with strong bodily sensations, the flight simulator model relates as well to the project of depiction as we provide contemporary examples and illustrations. Psychologists speak of "bodily memories" and these imprints of childhood experiences may provide an entry into the adult client's early traumas. However, bodily memories are not by any means limited to a negative set of experiences. So by way of providing an example of Jesus' admonition to "become like a child" (Matt. 18:2-4), we might shape an image designed for a largely older adult congregation:

Becoming like a child is many things; we need to recover much that has gotten lost over the years. Take our worship, for example. Becoming childlike in worship means worshiping our God with our entire being, bodies and all. Remember as a child, when you played hopscotch on the grid that somebody had drawn on the pavement with chalk? Then throwing, what, the old shoe heel, trying to get it to land up there at that arch-shaped place near the top. Then you hopped in and headed toward the heel—alternating two-foot and one-foot jumps, hair bobbing up and down, your whole body leaping and landing, never stepping on a line. Such energy and enjoyment. Maybe one of the psalms should sing, "Let us hopscotch before the Lord our God!"

And while older persons of faith may well need to recover more of this sense of bodily sensation for their worship, it is becoming clear that for younger generations, references in worship and preaching that omit references to bodily sensation will be experienced as odd or irrelevant.[59]

Imagery and the Homiletical Plot

The three models of imagery and point of view relate most naturally to the task of illustrating a move or unit of the sermon. That is, once a conceptual focus and single meaning is established for some component, with Buttrick, the preacher will turn to the challenge of imaging that meaning out of the lived experience of the listeners. And along with the deployment of an image or image system comes the related and essential task of providing a point of view—hence the three models of camera, videocam, and flight simulator. However, it is also possible in certain circumstances to elevate the role of an image to a macrolevel of determining the movement and structure of the sermon's entire plot. The sequence of episodes aligned to form the plot of the sermon, as we have seen in preaching around the web and at its center, may be shaped by the scenes of a biblical narrative, a narrative but nonstoried plot, the expansion of a biblical theme, or the logic, for example, of a Pauline convictional system. At least one other approach to shaping the movement and intention of the sermon is available to the preacher—a sermonic sequence guided by an image or image system derived from Scripture or contemporary experience. While this latter approach remains part of the preacher's suite of methods, with regard to certain biblical texts, a homiletics of imagery is almost mandated. The particular texts doing this mandating are those whose meaning and intention are grounded in a dominant image that remains indispensable to the purposes of the text. We may speak of these pericopes as having a master image at the heart of their meaning

The master image of the text and the homiletical plot

Certain passages of Scripture are aligned with reference to a dominant or master image such that the text could not convey its conceptual and affective meaning if the image was either deleted or drastically altered. The metaphors of Jesus' parables certainly fall into this category—mustard seed, shepherd and lost sheep, pearl of great price. Most of these parables, however, extend into an explicit or implicit narrative such that their narrative plot can orient the direction of the sermon. In other lections the master image dominates and will insist on becoming the grounding motif of the sermon. Among this genre of Scripture, a most instructive example is Paul's evocative image of God's treasure that is Christ being in clay pots (in 2 Cor. 4:7-12). The context for the clay pots reference is a prior alignment by Paul of Christ as the image of God (4:4) with the vision of believers and the lack of sight of unbelievers (vv. 1-3). The concluding line of the argument is foundational: "For it is the [same] God who said, 'Let light shine out of darkness,' who has shone in our hearts to give the light of the knowledge of the glory of God in the face of Jesus Christ" (4:6). Perhaps noting that believers could be led into pride and arrogance by this witness to the glory of Christ revealed to them, the apostle then shapes the image system of believers as clay jars that are graced to hold the treasure that is Christ.

The challenge homiletically, then, is twofold in preaching on biblical passage embodying dominant or master images. First, we are invited to shape a sermon plot whose movement and intention are guided by the text's master image and, second, we are challenged to image each unit of the sermon in ways that are congruent with the image system of the text. Using the 2 Corinthians text as a test case, we may shape the sermon plot as a series of Buttrick-like moves:

1. Christ is the image of God, Paul shouts. Look at Christ, and you see the light and glory of God.
2. Problem is, we human types go for the glory, imagine ourselves to be its source and its goal. Then, "we proclaim ourselves."
3. "But we are only clay jars," Paul says. Humble but useful vessels, that's who we are. We are God's earthenware.
4. The good news is that God entrusts such a treasure to our clay pots. Christ is given to God's clay jar people.
5. So we may be afflicted or struck down, but we are not overcome. Given up to death, Christ is our life.

Looking at the logic and movement of the sermon's plot, we may want to shorten its number of moves for the sake of the liturgical context. If so, the first move could become the introduction, while the last move could become a spirited conclusion/celebration. However, the basic sequence would need to be retained: Christ as image of God—proclaiming ourselves—ourselves as clay jars—Christ as God's treasure—admonition to persevere.

The related challenge is to image each of these units of the sermonic plot in ways that allow the text's master image to remain central while at the same time keeping faith with the conceptual elements of each respective move. Of course, point of view will emerge as a concern and opportunity whenever a move is imaged.

Image "overlays" as homiletical plot

In the preceding discussion, imagery has functioned with reference to the sequence of the sermon's units or moves and has been utilized to illustrate the meanings of various respective moves. However, there is another option when dealing with a biblical text embodying a master or dominant image. In this approach, the aim is not a coordinated sequence of moves that shape a progressive logic, as we explored with the clay jars example.

Here, the objective is to establish the dominant or master image through some rhetorical device or other—we shall explore several—and then choose a series of storied fragments that are congruent with the master image. In other words, the sequence in the sermon is experienced more as a series of overlays on an overhead projector screen. Each of the segments of the sermon is its own narrative world, yet each draws its direction from the master image system of the text. But notice that Buttrick's sense of overall intention is violated here. The segments are given in some order, yet that order lacks a plottable logic. The intent is to provide the congregation with a scattershot of imaged scenes, all connected to the organizing image of the text yet not necessarily connected to one another. (More accurately, we could say that the segments are connected to one another only as they participate in the symbolic world of the biblical image.) As the scenes or segments build, a quite powerful sense of reinforcing conviction or insight can build, with the listeners given freedom to align and arrange, select or delete the segments themselves. Perhaps it is best once again to chose a biblical text embodying a master image and shape a sermon whose segments aim at this overlay effect. In Ezekiel 34, the prophet establishes the master image of the shepherd and the flock. The pericope looks at the image first and, in an extended exploration, at the tragic consequences for Israel—God's flock—when the shepherds of Israel are only out for themselves (vv. 1-10). Then, the image is transformed; the God of Israel will be shepherd to the people. Clearly, the overlay strategy will depict these two options in course: first, the unrighteous shepherds and consequences for the flock; and second, the transformation wrought upon Israel as their God takes up the role of shepherd. A series of scenes suggest themselves for each performance of the flock and shepherd image:

Introduction: The Historical Context of Ezekiel's Prophecy Is Depicted

Sequence I: Unrighteous shepherds and their consequences

A. A television evangelist preacher pleads for seed money to keep the ministry going. Week after week, the appeal goes out, the 800 number scrolling across the screen. Week after week, the money comes in, largely from the elderly on fixed incomes. When the preacher is finally indicted, it is revealed that the funds have gone to him and his family for a lavish lifestyle.

Even the evangelist's doghouse is air-conditioned. "Thus says the Lord GOD, I am against the shepherds; and I will demand my sheep at their hand."

B. Two bishops of the church battle each other. Each has a holy cause—one, justice; the other, redemption. Supporters line up with their leader and against the enemy. The church is divided, and anger displaces forgiveness. Later, it is discovered that each of these bishops is living a double life. There is a public stance of fervor and commitment to a cause. But under the cover of darkness, each has broken covenant, it is revealed, again and again. "Thus says the Lord GOD, I am against the shepherds; and I will demand my sheep at their hand."

C. There is yet another meeting for the church bureaucrats, this time to facilitate new guidelines for implementation of proactive initiatives for the marginalized A facilitator has come to lead the process. When one of the group mutters, "You already know what it is we're supposed to come up with," the facilitator smiles knowingly. "Yeah, I guess it's really all a bunch of boiler-plate." She turns, writes the guidelines on the newsprint, and walks out of the meeting. "Thus says the Lord GOD, I am against the shepherds; and I will demand my sheep at their hand."

D. A priest is discovered to be a pedophile. The bishop is alerted along with his staff. The priest is quickly and quietly removed from his parish and sent immediately to a new assignment where the pattern repeats itself. "Thus says the Lord GOD, I am against the shepherds; and I will demand my sheep at their hand."

E. The preacher has the congregation in his hand. He has just fin-ished telling them a gripping illustration about the time he sat next to a man on a plane who spoke of his desperation and depression. The preacher shared how he listened carefully to his seatmate and then told him about the love of Jesus that can heal any illness, forgive any sin. There, up over the clouds, that man came to Christ and received salvation. Just about then, they landed and the man parted with a radiant joy, thanking the preacher for offering him new life. The story is true. Only it did not happen to this preacher. He heard it told by a speaker at an evangelism conference the previous summer. "Thus says the Lord

GOD, I am against the shepherds; and I will demand my sheep at their hand."

Sequence II: Righteous shepherds sent by God

A. A student walks into the preaching class, weary after a full day's work at a tough city school. She is still a teacher but has received the call to preach, and this evening is her first sermon. After raising three children to young adulthood, she is now completing her seminary education and looks forward to ordination. Her text is from John's Gospel where Jesus announces, "I am the good shepherd." It is a sermon from the heart. "For thus says the Lord GOD: I myself will search for my sheep, and will seek them out."

B. It was an assignment nobody wanted in the diocese—an inner-city parish with a huge old church building, a wheezing boiler in the basement, and a declining, aging group of faithful parishioners. A young priest is sent by the bishop, and his energy is infectious. It seems that in no time at all, the old church is filled to overflowing by joyful worshipers, and a gospel choir now adds their praise and celebration. The assembly is now a glorious rainbow of the faithful—black, white, and Asian, too—and the church has once again turned to mission in its community. "For thus says the Lord GOD: I myself will search for my sheep, and will seek them out."

C. He could have made it big in the industry. Excellent guitarist, outstanding voice, and he writes lyrics that have a punch and power. But instead of making MTV appearances, he and his band are the music ministers for a new church's young adults ministry. They meet every week in a V.F.W. hall, and his salary is below minimum wage when counted up. Still, young adults are being reached, and the new church is growing. "I wouldn't change my life for all the world," he commented after one celebration. "No, not for all the world." "For thus says the Lord GOD: I myself will search for my sheep, and will seek them out."

Notice two qualities about this overlay method of aligning images with a master image. First, it is important to cast your homiletical net widely and with a scattershot kind of diversity. One common problem in sermons in these days is that both positive and negative examples are drawn from only a narrow, ideologically constrained in-group. This image-based approach invites—or better, insists on—a wide range of examples selected intentionally not to conform to some prescribed and political list. Second, it will be the case that while the preacher intentionally builds in a wide diversity of image fragments and scenes, the hearers will probably align the set of examples they retain in consciousness with order and intention. In other words, the congregation will not hold onto the images in a scattershot fashion, but select and deselect the examples according to personal or communal concerns. These arrangements will vary among the listeners, but the likelihood is that some intention will shape the alignment of images retained by the hearers.

Contemporary image systems and the homiletical plot

We have explored several methods for shaping the sermon based on a biblical master image system. In each of these approaches an image derived from Scripture becomes the foundation and organizing principle for the sermon. With care, a preacher may turn to a contemporary image and exploit it using one of these same approaches. The homiletical care is that the contemporary image is theologically appropriate and relates well to the biblical text and liturgical occasion. The issue is similar to that encountered when a preacher considers an extended story illustration, especially when it is proposed as an introduction. Often, the story will be a good one with some theme or image shared in common with the lesson. However, the story's scope and interest may extend beyond those of the pericope and, in some cases, may be in conflict with it. With reference to this concern for theological congruence in contemporary master images, let us look at two examples, one that serves its purpose effectively and one that presents real problems:

1. For a sermon on a Sunday in which the Gospel lesson is from John 12, a preacher focused on the Dominical saying, "Very truly, I tell you, unless a grain of wheat falls into the earth and dies, it remains just a single grain; but if it dies, it bears much fruit" (12:24). The contemporary image that became the sermon's orga-nizing system involved an old Midwest farmer who knew that it was time to begin plowing his fields and planting. But winter had kept its grip on the land that year and snow still covered the fields. Finally, the farmer hitched up his team and began plowing, a square of dark earth growing in the midst of the white cold field. Once this image system was developed, other contemporary-lived experiences were related to it, always

in touch with the Gospel text about the grain of wheat that must fall into the earth and die in order to bear much fruit.[60]

2. In another sermon, the preacher chooses a scene from *Star Wars,* in which Darth Vader and son Luke Skywalker have been battling with their light sabers. Luke now knows that he fights his father. He is struck and wounded by one of Vader's blows and hangs now by one hand over a precipice, the central core within the death star. The moment freezes, and Vader extends his hand to Luke. His father can save him. The preacher uses this scene as the contemporary image related to the biblical story of Jesus' walking on the water and reaching out for a sinking, fearful Peter. Emotionally, the choice may have worked; the hearers were deeply moved. However, upon later reflection, the choice was a disaster theologically. Yes, the two scenes shared the image of an outstretched hand reaching down to save a person in quite dire straits. But the *Star Wars* scene brings with it all of Steven Speilberg's pop-Buddhism notions that are certainly in tension with biblical faith. Far worse, our preacher has linked through analogy Jesus Christ and Darth Vader!

With appropriate theological care and homiletical caution, a contemporary master image may serve as effectively as a biblical one. The two examples—both from actual preached sermons—indicate the opportunities as well as the pitfalls accompanying such a strategy.

The interplay of biblical and contemporary imagery

In the sermon that follows these discussions of the homiletics of imagery, Susan Briehl has shaped a brilliant sermon by juxtaposing a biblical and a contemporary image of water. At their intersection is her master image—the estuary, a place where two waters meet. This brief introduction serves two purposes. First, it establishes the image for the congregation. Second, it links the two waters organically—you cannot have an estuary without such an intersection—and points to that place as the source of life. Method and content are both evoked in only four sentences. Each of the moves in the sermon are developed as estuary scenes. We may track the succession of moves as Briehl continues to explore this estuary master image:

Move 1. First, Israel's long wait for the Messiah will at last be rewarded as two waters come together: "the salty tears of the people will be met by the fresh water pouring from the fountain of God's deep mercy." The coming together of these two waters is then imaged for the hearers. We are the exiles, those "brokenhearted and rejected." Even the earth itself mourns: "the salt and silt and sun will grieve all that is trampled, broken, and lost."

Move 2. Now Jesus is introduced, and the two waters meet in him. In Christ, "the life-giving river of God's presence meets and becomes one with the persistent tide of human suffering and death, frailty and failure." It is by this suffering and death of the Messiah—a reality lost on Peter—that Jesus "will gather the sorrow and grief, the suffering and wounds of every people in every time and place." Then the preacher invites the listeners to look around at how we have failed to love one another, a rhetorical system that ends, "We have walled ourselves off from sand and silt and water and sun, denying our dependence upon the earth and neglecting our responsibility to it." Once more, the master image of the estuary is evoked to conclude the move.

Move 3. Now comes the concluding baptism scene. Things that must drown in our baptismal waters are intimated—our attempts at safety and security at the expense of others. But in our "estuarial waters of baptism," Briehl continues, "the walls we have built are washed away like sand castles in a rising tide." The related and newly introduced image of a sand castle melting away by the rising tide is now applied to the walls we have so fervently held on to, including our economic and even religious systems. None of these walls can stand "in the community born in the estuary of Christ's death and resurrection."

Conclusion. The conclusion invites the hearers to come again into the waters of their baptism. The preacher builds up the typology—a form of the overhead projector approach to imaging—to include the waters of creation, the Red Sea, the Jordan, Rachel's tears, "the birth waters breaking, and the fountain of abundant life leaping." The conclusion is remarkably and intentionally like the "Flood Prayer" of thanksgiving over the water at the sacrament of Holy Baptism. The listener is invited to a very kinesthetic experience of these waters while adding the sign of the cross to the estuarial imagery in powerful, image-laden words:

> Feel the cool waters fall upon your face, your body, your life. Let your own tears flow, if they will. They will be met by a river of grace. As the water touches you, make a water crossing on your body, a reminder of who you are and to whom you belong, a sign of the shape of our new life together.

The conclusion ends with an invitation: "Let us become what we receive, the very Body of Christ: an estuary for the sake of the world where life can stir, awaken, and arise again and again."

Perhaps the power of the Briehl sermon derives from this preacher's insight and spirituality, certainly shaped by a sacramental imagination. But the sermon is also shaped by its careful use of imagery as images of tears, birth, walls, sand castles, baptism, and the cross all orbit around the one organizing master image of the estuary. In and through that image, Scripture's stories and signs of grace in our world mix together again and again.

Evaluation

Given the ever-accelerating focus on images in a culture driven by the visual media, it is no surprise that homiletics would be seeking ways in which to proclaim the gospel by way of imagery. In fact, we may come to the conclusion that a pulpit rhetoric mostly devoid of imagistic language will be perceived as increasingly odd, if not foreign to contemporary listeners. If the perennial challenge of preaching is to employ the vernacular of the age to speak of the power of the gospel, then we will learn how to image ourselves, the world, and our God. To preach in nonimagistic ways is in this postmodern context to lose the vernacular of our people. However, there is an even greater cost than the loss of vernacular in our preaching. Those who come together to worship in Christ bring with them personal and communal consciousness strongly shaped by the imagery of the world. These images are never ornamental—they convey an epistemology weighted toward consumption, individual autonomy, and self-gratification. These images not only think, but also provide the lens through which contemporary persons imagine their world. And we can act—for better or for worse—only within the worlds we envision. On one hand, therefore, our sermons will engage with the imagery inhabiting the personal and communal world of our listeners in a kind of hermeneutics of suspicion. We will hold up for scrutiny the images of the culture for critical evaluation and prophetic challenge. On the other hand, we will speak of the biblical faith in ways that privileges its narratives and imagery. And we will raid the culture's continually shifting storehouse of images for those that can do service on behalf of the gospel. Images think, they shape our sense of world, and they dominate our social discourse. We will use imagery, then, as we preach.

At a deeper level, a homiletics of imagery is emerging by virtue of the rich fruitfulness of imagination theory over the last century. We have been instructed in imagination's perceptual functioning, in the pragmatics of "imagining-that" and "imagining-how" and in imagination's turn toward the linguistic in metaphor and irony. With Hans Gadamer, we have been tutored in the notion of imagination as play and have extended his model into a construal of preaching as performance.[61] Contemporary hermeneutics is rarely much distant from some aspect or other of the play of imagination. Whether in the fields of aesthetics, literary criticism, ethics, or hermeneutics, the work of imagery is an essential aspect of the discipline's continuing conversation. Moreover, an interest in the hermeneutics of the image within biblical interpretation has drawn on these diverse movements, especially as literary critics and structuralists have been turned toward Scripture. Whether related to narrative or structuralist criticism,[62] the role of the image in biblical texts has come under careful and fruitful scrutiny. At one level, this is to say that the contemporary preacher has at her or his fingertips a wealth of interpretive resources that take image-laden texts quite seriously. But at a deeper level, those called to preach now have access to a wide range of interpretive approaches spanning across a number of disciplines, all of which offer rich insight into imagination theory in general and the work of the image in particular.

Postmodern homiletics certainly reflects this deepening interest in the play of the imagination and the work of the image in preaching. At a rhetorical level, there is a wide consensus that pulpit language will need to employ imagery simply in order to function and be heard by today's congregations. At a hermeneutic level, recent homiletics also acknowledges that imagery has a profound capability in conveying affective significance as well as personal and social meaning. To be sure, the first homiletician to integrate the rhetorical and hermeneutic dimensions of imagery into a full postmodern homiletic is David Buttrick. Buttrick has also been the pioneer in point of view studies with regard to the use of imagery, and I have sought to expand upon his camera model of perspective. Notice, however, that every position on the web of preaching surveyed with these chapters now takes imagery quite seriously and cautions preachers to employ imagistic language from the pulpit. One profitable exercise might be to compare and contrast the dynamics of imagery within the approaches of David Buttrick and Paul Scott Wilson. We may readily assemble the points at which they concur and differ regarding the use of imagery in preaching.

Points of Convergence Between Buttrick and Wilson

1. Both homileticians agree that each unit of the sermon dealing with a single meaning will need to be imaged. For Buttrick, each move in the homiletical plot will need to be imaged in some way out of the lived experience of the listeners. This imaging can be achieved through several ways—by use of an illustration or through one or more examples or images. Wilson also insists that that each of the Four Pages of the sermon contain

one image in addition to the other necessary components—text, theme, doctrine, and mission. A Page of a Wilson sermon devoid of one working image would be as deficient for him as would a Buttrick move lacking imagery. Both agree on the essential character of the image within each unit of the sermon having a single meaning.

2. Both Buttrick and Wilson concur that imagery has a potential for connecting in the hearing of the congregation a sequence of units of single meaning across the span of the sermon. For Buttrick, this interplay of imagery can be achieved by retaining a common point of view while changing the imagistic content, or by employing a recurring image but changing point of view. In the former alternative, for example, you could image a move on sadness and depression *by "looking out the window at the gray day, the clouds weeping a cold drizzle that matches your own deep mood."* Later in the sermon, a time of healing might be imaged as you invite the listeners to *"open the door after the sun comes out, warming the fields. A hawk now soars overhead in celebration. Thank God for the healing warmth of the Spirit!"* (Both images retain a look-outside point of view.) The latter approach can also be demonstrated as point of view is shifted with regard to a similar or the same image. Here, we might image looking down at "an infant lying in a high-tech little bassinet in pediatric intensive care. This little child came into the world three months too soon." In a subsequent move, we might image this child later during the service of Holy Baptism, as *"we look down at her lovely face as she delights in the water streaming over her little head."* For Wilson, a dominant image—one powerfully evoked by a biblical text—may be repeated within more than one sermonic page. Given the presence of such a dominant image, Wilson suggests that it may be seen in the introduction, and within perhaps one or two of the other Pages.[63] Most probably the reason Wilson limits such repetition to two of the sermon's Pages is that this sort of dominant image will either deal with trouble—thereby appearing in Pages One and Two—or grace—appearing in Pages Three and Four. Wilson adds that such multiple use of a dominant image can add both conceptual and theological unity to the sermon. It "forms a chain through the sermon and adds to its unity."[64]

3. Buttrick and Wilson both issue strong cautions with respect to the analogical power of contemporary imagery. It is easy to select an image out of contemporary experience that may seem nicely analogous to the biblical context, but upon reflection will not communicate what we intend. So, Buttrick mentions a sermon where a student analogically turned Jesus into a plate of asparagus and Wilson refers to a homily where Jesus was likened to a red Porsche! Images come crammed with multivalent meanings. The preacher will employ imagery with analogical precision. Upon this, both Wilson and Buttrick fully agree.

Points of Opposition Between Buttrick and Wilson Regarding the Homiletic Image

1. There is more than a shading of difference between Buttrick's notion of a move's conceptual and Wilson's insistence on a theme of a sermon's Page. The selection of appropriate imagery within a move is constrained for Buttrick by the clear meaning of the move's conceptual content. A theme statement for Wilson, however, may need to exert more discursive force since each of the sermon's Four Pages relates to one theme shaped around trouble (in the text and in our world) and grace (in the text and in the world). Once again, both colleagues would take up the project of imaging within a conceptual environment—the move or the Page. Of the two, however, Wilson may need a more forceful linkage between the theme statement and the image than Buttrick needs between the move's conceptual and the image. However, we should hasten to note at this point that we are speaking of shading rather than radical differences in their approach to the relationship between conceptual and imagistic aspects of the sermon.
2. Perhaps a more explicit distinction in the homiletics of imagery for Buttrick and Wilson deals with the image's role in contemporary rhetoric. Imagery is needed in order for a move to form within the consciousness of the hearers for Buttrick. Here, Buttrick is not as much making an assertion in constructive homiletics as he is judging the contemporary rhetorical context for preaching. As the world continues to be about the sloppy process of "changing its mind," the importance of imagery only continues to heighten with regard to the

formation and retention of pulpit speech in the listener's mind.[65] Wilson certainly agrees that besides adding to the unity of a sermon, images can help make it more memorable. Moreover, Wilson notes that "much of human thinking is in mental pictures, and most people remember best what they can visualize."[66] On the other hand, Wilson may not emphasize the rhetorical necessity of imagery as much as does Buttrick. Here, a more significant distinction between the two exists beyond mere shading.

3. It is with reference to point of view that Wilson and Buttrick diverge most fully. The latter insists on point of view considerations as organically related to the issues of the meaning and affective capacity of the image. The former insists on the presence of an image within each Page of the sermon, but does not consider point of view with Buttrick's level of seriousness. With even further refinements in the qualities provided by point of view, it would seem that Buttrick's hunch regarding the essential role of perspectuality is a crucial aspect of postmodern homiletic theory and practice (see pp. 169-71).

Beyond Buttrick and Wilson

What has developed over the recent past is that some courageous preachers have stepped out into a homiletics of imagery beyond the scope of both David Buttrick's and Paul Scott Wilson's systems. This preaching—largely pioneered by women in the pulpit—has seen the power of imagery not only to concretize some conceptual meaning within the sermon, but also to organize and propel the homiletical plot. It is the preaching of these risk-taking servants of the Word that has lured us to consider the implied methods, often unarticulated. We have noticed how sermons can be composed of a series of imagistic overlays, based upon some biblical dominant image. We have also experienced the power of images thrown into a homiletical nexus, with an outcome emerging with grace and surprise. Susan Briehl's sermon, "Two Rivers Meet," is an excellent example of this homiletic strategy of allowing images to intersect and evoke surprises of the Spirit for the listener/viewer. It remains to be seen where a homiletics of imagery will lead God's people. However, we can quite happily reintroduce David Buttrick and Paul Scott Wilson to the conversation once more. A biblical homiletics of imagery, with Buttrick, will involve some sequence of episodes comprising the sermon that head toward some intention or other. And with Paul Scott Wilson, any homiletics of imagery will need to keep up a steady conversation with Christian theology along the way. That way, the way of the image, beckons preachers to take the risk along a modestly slippery homiletic slope. Then too, most of our locations within the web offer great potential for proclaiming the gospel, while all involve some certain risk.

Two Rivers Meet

Susan R. Briehl

Zechariah 12:7-10; Galatians 3:23-29; Luke 9:18-24

Two waters meet. A river runs into the sea. Fresh water flows to the salty deep. The river current dances with the ocean tides. Salt and silt and sun and water mingle to make muck so fecund that some people believe life first stirred, awakened, and arose in such a place: an estuary.

When the Messiah comes, the prophet Zechariah tells the children of Israel, two waters will come together—the salty tears of the people will be met by the fresh water pouring from the fountain of God's deep mercy. The day is coming, the prophet says, when God "will pour out a spirit of compassion and supplication on the house of David and the inhabitants of Jerusalem" (12:10). And on that day you will weep. You will weep tears of grief over all the little ones gone: the orphan and the widow, the weak and defenseless, the unwelcome stranger within your gates. You will weep as Rachel weeps for her children who are no more, as the households of the Egyptians wept at the slaughter of their firstborns, as David wept for his fallen son, Absalom. You will lament your own lost children and childhood.

Tears of sorrow will flow for all the dreams dashed, the dancing turned to mourning, the songs turned to dust in your mouth. As the exiles wept, so you will weep. As those conquered and oppressed in every generation weep, so you will weep. As the brokenhearted and rejected weep, so you will weep, the prophet declares. On the coming great day even the wounded earth will mourn; the salt and silt and sun will grieve all that is trampled, broken, and lost.

Tears of repentance will flow as you remember how far you wandered from the source of your life when you turned from God's steadfast love and entered the embrace of others. You will weep to see the prophet whom you pierced, the prophet sent to you from God to awaken you from your death sleep and call you home again. And yet, even while you weep, God will turn you toward the dawn of a new day, and you will see mercy flowing like a river into the sea of your sorrow, "a fountain will open for the House of David" whose waters will cleanse and heal you, your families, and your land. The current of God's compassion will dance with the tide of your tears and create among you an estuary where you will stir from your sleep, awaken, and arise to life again.

Two waters meet. In Jesus, the life-giving river of God's presence meets and becomes one with the persistent tide of human suffering and death, frailty and failure. Jesus tells the disciples that he "must suffer many things and be rejected . . . and . . . be killed and on the third day be raised to life" (Luke 9:21 NIV). This isn't the response Peter expected to his declaration that Jesus was God's promised Christ. He, like we, had rather hoped for a messiah who would pull the people out of the mire and place their feet on solid ground, saving them from the whole messy business of being human, not a messiah who would willingly enter it.

Jesus is clear; by his own suffering, rejection, and piercing, he will gather the sorrow and grief, the suffering and wounds of every people in every time and place. He will receive the tears of every Rachel weeping for her children who are no more, the sighs of all the exiles with dust in their mouths, the groans of the captive and the conquered, the pleas of the battered and the defenseless. He receives our sorrow, too, our wounds deeply personal and widely universal.

In his presence we dare to tell the truth. We have failed to love one another. We have built a bulwark to protect ourselves, to safeguard our way of life, and to secure our own future. We have divided the human family into those whom we will receive and those whom we refuse or ignore. We have walled ourselves off from sand and silt and water and sun, denying our dependence upon the earth and neglecting our responsibility to it.

We bring our broken promises and the whole broken world to Jesus who receives the muck and mess of our lives, and takes it to himself and descends with it to the deep. And on the third day a fountain of fresh water springs forth, a river of healing flows to the seas of sorrows, resurrection life meets suffering and death. An estuary is born where life stirs, awakens, and arises anew.

Jesus says, "If any want to become my followers, let them deny themselves and take up their cross and follow me" (Matt. 16:24). We follow him into the sea of human suffering, and we taste the tears of those near and far. We let drown in that sea our own attempts to create a safe life for ourselves, dying to the ways we take life from others, releasing what we hoard and clutch. And we are raised by God to a life not of our own making nor in our own control, but life given as a gift in Jesus.

We follow Jesus, day after day into the estuarial waters of baptism where we first put on Christ, his suffering and death, his resurrection life. In these waters, the walls we have built are washed away like sandcastles in a rising tide. The powers of political and social systems that make of some masters and others slaves are eroded. Economic systems that widen rather than bridge the chasm between the rich and the poor begin to crumble. And all religious systems that declare some people worthy and others unworthy are revealed to be nothing more than futile human attempts to play God. For in the community born in the estuary of Christ's death and resurrection, there is neither Jew nor Greek, slave nor free, male nor female, says Paul. There is neither rich nor poor, gay nor straight, black nor white, for all are one in Christ Jesus.

Come to the baptismal estuary again. Here are the waters of creation by which God nourishes and sustains all living things: rivers and rain and waterfalls, lakes and oceans and tide pools. Here is the deep salt sea of human suffering and the suffering of all creation. Here is the Red Sea parting, the water gushing from the rock in the wilderness, the Jordan washing, the tears of Rachel flowing, the birth waters breaking, and the fountain of abundant life leaping. Feel the cool water fall upon your face, your body, your life. Let your own tears flow, if they will. They will be met by a river of grace. As the water touches you, make a water crossing on your body, a reminder of who you are and to whom you belong, a sign of the shape of our new life together.

Then let us arise to live as Christ calls us to live, not with walls that divide, but washed and united in these estuarial waters and gathered around the table of grace where all are welcome and fed. Let us become what we receive, the very Body of Christ: an estuary for the sake of the world where life can stir, awaken, and arise again and again. Amen.

Notes

Introduction

1. Kenneth L. Woodward, "Heard Any Good Sermons Lately?" *Newsweek,* March 4, 1996, 50-52.

2. The "new homiletics" is my phrase used in the introduction to *A New Hearing: Living Options in Homiletic Methods* (Nashville: Abingdon Press, 1987). It was not intended to be used in the singular implying one privileged position, but always in the plural. There continues, thankfully, a rich diversity of methods by which faithful preachers may speak forth the Word.

3. F. Wellford Hobbie, "The Play Is the Thing: New Forms for the Sermon," *Journal for Preachers* 5 (1982): 17-23.

Chapter 1: Inductive and Narrative Homiletic Plots: Fred Craddock and Eugene Lowry

1. Eugene L. Lowry, *Doing Time in the Pulpit: The Relationship Between Narrative and Preaching* (Nashville: Abingdon Press, 1985), 12.

2. Ibid.

3. Eugene L. Lowry, "The Revolution in Sermonic Shape," in *Listening to the Word: Studies in Honor of Fred Craddock,* ed. Gail R. O'Day and Thomas G. Long (Nashville: Abingdon Press, 1993), 93.

4. Fred B. Craddock, *As One Without Authority* (Nashville: Abingdon Press, 1979), 54.

5. Fred B. Craddock, *Preaching* (Nashville: Abingdon Press, 1985), 100.

6. Fred B. Craddock, "Recent New Testament Interpretation and Preaching," *The Princeton Seminary Bulletin* 66, no. 1 (October 1973): 77.

7. Craddock, *As One Without Authority,* 54.

8. Ibid., 55.

9. Ibid., 56.

10. Ibid.

11. Ibid., 5.

12. Ibid., 6-7.

13. Craddock, *Preaching,* 31.

14. Craddock, *As One Without Authority,* 7.

15. Ibid., 37.

16. Craddock, *Preaching,* 52.

17. Craddock, *As One Without Authority,* 12-13.

18. Ibid., 29.

19. Ibid.

20. Ibid., 9.

21. Ibid., 10.

22. Craddock, "Recent New Testament Interpretation," 77.

23. Craddock's "new angle of vision" implies approaches to the text that can traverse the distance between the contemporary church and the biblical world, though not annihilate that distance. It is neither desirable nor possible, he believes, "to collapse their difference in contrived harmony" ("The Sermon and the Uses of Scripture," *Theology Today* 42, no. 1 [April 1985]: 8).

24. Craddock, "Sermon and the Uses of Scripture," 8. Craddock insists that what authorizes any sermon—whether evoked by an occasion or given through the lectionary—is grounded in the Scriptures. Therefore, a sermon can feel quite biblical to the listeners if it is "sprinkled with words and phrases from Scripture. . . . However, there is here the illusion rather than the reality of listening to the text" (*Preaching,* 100).

25. Craddock, *As One Without Authority,* 45.

26. Ibid.

27. Craddock, "Sermon and the Uses of Scripture," 8.

28. Craddock, *Preaching,* 27.

29. Craddock, "Recent New Testament Interpretation," 78.

30. Ibid.

31. Craddock, *Preaching,* 115.

32. Craddock, *As One Without Authority,* 134.

33. Fred B. Craddock, "Occasion-Text-Sermon," *Interpretation* 35, no. 1 (January 1981): 60.

34. Ibid., 63.

35. Craddock, *Preaching,* 106.

36. Ibid.

37. Fred B. Craddock, "The Commentary in the Service of the Sermon," *Interpretation* 36, no. 4 (October 1982): 386.

38. Ibid., 387. In this article, Fred Craddock more precisely defines the sequence by which various resources are to be consulted. Following the first reading on Monday; then follows lexicons, Bibles, dictionaries, and theological wordbooks of the Bible on Tuesday. Wednesday is commentary day, while Thursday's work turns the preacher to commentaries dealing more immediately with the text's implications for the present situation. Friday's resources will be of various types and all will focus on the contemporary context for preaching (pp. 386-87).

39. Fred B. Craddock, "Preaching and the Nod of Recognition" (paper delivered at The Hickman Lectures I, Duke University Divinity School Convocation, Durham, N.C., October 29, 1984).

40. Craddock, "Occasion-Text-Sermon," 65.

41. Craddock, *Preaching,* 117.

42. Ibid., 118.

43. Craddock, *As One Without Authority,* 139.

44. Craddock, *Preaching,* 122.

45. Ibid.

46. Ibid., 123.

47. Ibid.

48. This approach of Craddock's, distinctly separating the interpretive and sermonic functions differs considerably from that of David Buttrick. The latter insists on the mediating function of personal and communal consciousness. See pp. 151-52.

49. Ibid., 85.

50. Ibid., 87.

51. Ibid., 88.

52. Ibid., 88-89.

53. Ibid., 90.

54. Ibid., 91.

55. Ibid., 97.

56. Craddock, "Preaching and the Nod of Recognition."

57. Craddock, *Preaching,* 161.

58. Ibid., 162.

59. Fred B. Craddock, "Preaching and the Shock of Recognition" (paper delivered at The Hickman Lectures, II, Duke University Divinity School Convocation, Durham, N.C., October 30, 1984).

60. Ibid.

61. Craddock, *Preaching,* 160.

62. Ibid., 85.

63. Craddock, *As One Without Authority,* 132.

64. Craddock, *Preaching,* 153.

65. Craddock, *As One Without Authority,* 57.

66. Ibid., 57.

67. Craddock, *Preaching,* 170.

68. Craddock, *As One Without Authority,* 146.

69. Craddock, *Preaching,* 166.

70. Craddock, *As One Without Authority,* 151.

71. Ibid., 156.

72. Ibid.

73. Ibid.

74. Ibid., 100.

75. Ibid., 101.

76. Ibid., 80.

77. Ibid., 78.

78. Ibid., 92.

79. Ibid.

80. Ibid., 95.

81. Ibid., 96.

82. Craddock, *Preaching,* 172.

83. Ibid., 174.

84. Ibid., 176.

85. Fred B. Craddock. "Preaching as Storytelling" (paper delivered at Lecture III, Furman University Pastor's School, Greenville, S.C., June 3, 1980).

86. Craddock, *Preaching,* 178.

87. Ibid., 177.

88. Ibid.

89. Eugene L. Lowry, *The Sermon: Dancing the Edge of Mystery* (Nashville: Abingdon Press, 1997), 58.

90. Ibid., 23.

91. Eugene L. Lowry, *The Homiletical Plot: The Sermon as Narrative Art Form* (Atlanta: John Knox Press, 1980).

92. Eugene L. Lowry, *Doing Time in the Pulpit: The Relationship Between Narrative and Preaching* (Nashville: Abingdon Press, 1985).

93. Eugene L. Lowry, *How to Preach a Parable: Designs for Narrative Sermons* (Nashville: Abingdon Press, 1989).

94. Lowry, *Homiletical Plot,* 20.

95. Lowry, *Doing Time,* 66.

96. Ibid., 67.

97. Lowry, *Homiletical Plot,* 21.

98. Ibid., 23.

99. Ibid., 25.

100. Ibid.

101. Ibid., 30-31.

102. Ibid., 33.

103. Ibid., 35.

104. Ibid., 38.

105. Ibid., 37.

106. Ibid., 40.

107. Ibid., 48.

108. Ibid., 60.

109. Ibid., 62-63.

110. Ibid., 65.

111. Ibid., 67.

112. Ibid.

113. Ibid., 69.

114. Ibid., 70.

115. Ibid., 72.

116. Ibid., 78.

117. Ibid., 76.

118. Ibid., 77.

119. Lowry, *Sermon,* 57.

120. Ibid., 59.

121. Ibid., 64.

122. Lowry discusses a sequence of these strategies in *The Sermon* (pp. 70-72).

123. Lowry, *Sermon,* 71.

124. Ibid., 72.

125. Here I was observing David Buttrick's caution against repetitive illustration strategies in successive locations within the sermonic plot. See my *Pitfalls in Preaching* (Grand Rapids, Mich.: W. B. Eerdmans Publishing, 1996), 89-93.

126. Lowry continues to insist on the necessity of a stage of complication separating the initial stage of conflict and a successive stage of resolution. See *The Sermon,* 66-74.

127. Lowry, *Sermon,* 81.

128. Ibid., 85.

129. Ibid., 86.

130. Ibid., 85.

131. Ibid., 87.

132. Fred Craddock's contributions to preaching through excellent commentaries is stunning in both quality and quantity. He has authored commentaries on the Gospel of John and many of the Epistles and texts in seasons and ordinary time of the church year and lectionary.

133. Ronald J. Allen, ed. *Patterns of Preaching: A Sermon Sampler* (St. Louis: Chalice Press, 1998), 64-65.

134. Lowry, *Sermon,* 54-55.

135. Ibid., 75.

136. Ibid., 76-77

137. Ibid., 77.

138. Ibid., 78.

139. Allen, *Patterns of Preaching,* 94.

140. Ibid.

141. Lowry, *Homiletical Plot,* 78.

Chapter 2: The Narrative Center

1. See Hans W. Frei, *The Eclipse of Biblical Narrative: A Study in Eighteenth and Nineteenth Century Hermeneutics* (New Haven: Yale University Press, 1974).

2. David Buttrick, *Homiletic: Moves and Structures* (Philadelphia: Fortress Press, 1987), 264-76.

3. For an excellent survey of some recent contributors to hermeneutics, see Richard Kearney, *Poetics of Imagining: From Husserl to Lyotard* (New York: HarperCollins, 1991).

4. Stephen Crites, "The Narrative Quality of Human Experience," *Journal of the American Academy of Religion* 39 (September 1971): 291-311.

5. John S. McClure, "Narrative and Preaching: Sorting It All Out," *Journal for Preachers* 15, no. 1 (Advent 1991): 24-25.

6. Eugene L. Lowry, "The Revolution of Sermon Shape," in *Listening to the Word: Studies in Honor of Fred B. Craddock,* ed. Gail R. O'Day and Thomas G. Long (Nashville: Abingdon Press, 1993), 96.

7. Ibid., 96-97.

8. Ibid., 97.

9. E. M. Forester, *Aspects of the Novel* (New York: Harcourt, Brace & Company, 1927). Quoted in Mark Allan Powell, *What Is Narrative Criticism?* (Minneapolis: Fortress Press, 1990), 40.

10. This notion of causality, of course, is intimately linked to the distinctive biblical depictions of character along with a sense of God's providence working through these actions and characters. That there appears a providence at work in and through these literary techniques of biblical narrative comes as no surprise "since they are associated with the conception of human nature implicit in biblical monotheism: Every person is created by an all-seeing God but abandoned to his own unfathomable freedom" (Robert Alter, *The Art of Biblical Narrative* [New York: Basic Books, 1981], 89). Consequently, we might conclude that the particular literary devices and their usage in Scripture are in some sense dictated by the Bible's theology of God and of humanity.

11. See Bernard Brandon Scott, *Hear Then the Parable: A Commentary on the Parables*

of Jesus (Minneapolis: Fortress Press, 1989), 7-62. Also see David Buttrick, *Speaking Parables: A Homiletic Guide* (Louisville: Westminster John Knox Press, 2000), 3-21.

12. R. Alan Culpepper, *Anatomy of the Fourth Gospel: A Study in Literary Design* (Philadelphia: Fortress Press, 1983), 54. See also pp. 53-57 for an excellent treatment of narrative time as related to the Gospel of John. Culpepper acknowledges his dependence on "the pioneering, yet highly acclaimed work of Gérard Gennette, *Narrative Discourse: An Essay in Method,* trans. Jane E. Lewis (Ithaca, N.Y.: Cornell University Press, 1980)," 53. Also see Eugene L. Lowry, *Doing Time in the Pulpit: The Relationship Between Narrative and Preaching* (Nashville: Abingdon Press, 1985).

13. Gennette, *Narrative Discourse,* 40, quoted in Culpepper, *Anatomy of the Fourth Gospel,* 56.

14. Ibid., 114-16.

15. For an extensive study of the techniques of repetition within biblical narrative, see Alter, *Art of Biblical Narrative,* 88-113. Insightful commentaries on John 4 include Gail R. O'Day, *Revelation in the Fourth Gospel* (Philadelphia: Fortress Press, 1986) and Wes Howard-Brook, *Becoming Children of God: John's Gospel and Radical Discipleship* (Maryknoll, N.Y.: Orbis Books, 1994).

16. Mark Allan Powell, *What Is Narrative Criticism?* (Minneapolis: Fortress Press, 1990), 42.

17. Robert Fowler notes that Mark's literary strategy of questioning by the characters in his gospel is a masterful achievement. In particular, the employment of double questions in 1:24 "serves to train the reader to follow the lead of the narrator as he takes incremental steps in his discourse." Robert M. Fowler, *Let the Reader Understand: Reader-Response Criticism and the Gospel of Mark* (Minneapolis: Fortress Press, 1991), 133.

18. Daniel Patte, *Structural Exegesis for New Testament Critics* (Minneapolis: Fortress Press, 1990), 24.

19. Ibid.

20. Ibid., 25.

21. Daniel Beaumont, "The Modality of Narrative: A Critique of Some Recent Views of Narrative in Theology," *Journal of the American Academy of Religion* 65 (Spring 1997): 132.

22. Ibid., 133.

23. See Culpepper, *Anatomy of the Fourth Gospel,* 79-84, for an analysis of this dynamic of cause and effect along with other elements of characterization. Also see the treatment of characterization in Meir Sternberg, *The Poetics of Biblical Narrative: Ideological Literature and the Drama of Reading* (Bloomington, Ind.: Indiana University Press, 1985), 322-64.

24. Alter, *Art of Biblical Narrative,* 116-17.

25. Culpepper, *Anatomy of the Fourth Gospel,* 166, points out that such ironic statements in the Fourth Gospel serve to invite the reader to share the narrator's point of view.

26. See Meir Sternberg, *The Poetics of Biblical Narrative: Ideological Literature and the Drama of Reading* (Bloomington, Ind.: Indiana University Press, 1985), 354-64, for an analysis of outward appearance and character depiction in the Hebrew Scripture.

27. For an analysis of the parable of the rich fool, see Bernard Brandon Scott, *Hear Then the Parable,* 127-40.

28. Wayne C. Booth, *The Rhetoric of Fiction,* 2nd ed. (Chicago: University of Chicago Press, 1983), 3-4. Quoted in Powell, *What Is Narrative Criticism?* 25.

29. Powell, *What Is Narrative Criticism?* 25.

30. Meir Sternberg, *Expositional Modes and Temporal Ordering in Fiction* (Baltimore: Johns Hopkins University Press, 1978), 88-89.

31. The variety of information a narrator can provide through footnotes is remarkable. In the Fourth Gospel, as M. C. Tenney discovered, at least ten types of narratorial comments abound, rang-

ing from notes on the time and place of an event to theological discussion and an omniscient knowledge of Jesus. See his "The Footnotes of John's Gospel," *Bibliotheca Sacra* 117 (1960): 350-64.

32. Powell, *What Is Narrative Criticism?* 26.

33. Sternberg, *Politics of Biblical Narrative,* 84.

34. Ronald F. Thiemann, "Radiance and Obscurity in Biblical Narrative," in *Scriptural Authority and Narrative Interpretation,* ed. Garrett Green (Philadelphia: Fortress Press, 1987), 30.

35. Ibid., 30-31.

36. Culpepper, *Anatomy of the Fourth Gospel,* 165-66. See also pp. 43-49 for an analysis of the distinction between an "implied author" and the narrator.

37. See Culpepper's treatment of misunderstanding in *Anatomy of the Fourth Gospel,* 152-65.

38. See Sternberg's penetrating analysis of the ironies lurking in the narration of the David and Bathsheba account (*Poetics of Biblical Narrative,* 190-219).

39. Booth continues, that ironies "are deliberately created by human beings to be heard or read and understood with some precision by other human beings" (*Rhetoric of Irony,* 5).

40. Robert M. Fowler, *Let the Reader Understand: Reader-Response Criticism and the Gospel of Mark* (Minneapolis: Fortress Press, 1991), 13-14.

41. Ibid., 14.

42. See D. C. Muecke, *The Compass of Irony* (London: Methuen, 1969), 19-20.

43. Fowler, *Let the Reader Understand,* 12. See my *Narrative and Imagination: Preaching the Worlds That Shape Us* (Minneapolis: Fortress Press, 1995), 117-27.

44. See, for example, Edmund A. Steimle, Morris J. Niedenthal, and Charles L. Rice, *Preaching the Story* (Philadelphia: Fortress Press, 1980); Thomas E. Boomershine, *Story Journey: An Invitation to the Gospel as Storytelling* (Nashville: Abingdon Press, 1988); Terrence W. Tilley, *Story Theology* (Wilmington, Del.: Michael Glazier, 1985). Also see my *A New Hearing: Living Options in Homiletic Methods* (Nashville: Abingdon Press, 1987), chapter 1, for an analysis of the early work of Charles Rice in preaching as storytelling.

45. John C. Holbert, *Preaching Old Testament: Proclamation & Narrative in the Hebrew Bible* (Nashville: Abingdon Press, 1991), 21.

46. Mark Ellingsen, *The Integrity of Biblical Narrative: Story in Theology and Proclamation* (Minneapolis: Fortress Press, 1990), 22.

47. Thomas G. Long, *Preaching and the Literary Forms of the Bible* (Philadelphia: Fortress Press, 1989), 58.

48. See, for example, Leo Purdue, *Wisdom and Creation: The Theology of Wisdom Literature* (Nashville: Abingdon Press, 1994); and Alyce MacKenzie, *Preaching Proverbs: Wisdom for the Pulpit* (Louisville: Westminster John Knox Press, 1996).

49. Richard L. Eslinger, *Narrative and Imagination,* 22. Marc Saperstein reports that in early medieval Jewish preaching, the sermon generally began with a verse from the Writings, the book of Proverbs being the most frequently used. This citation, mainly from Wisdom literature, then served as a hermeneutic lens with regard to a narrative text from Torah. See Marc Saperstein, *Jewish Preaching 1200–1800: An Anthology* (New Haven: Yale University Press, 1989), 63-75.

50. William Beardslee, "Uses of the Proverbs in the Synoptic Gospels," *Interpretation* 24 (January 1970): 65.

51. See Elisabeth Schüssler-Fiorenza, *The Book of Revelation: Justice and Judgment* (Philadelphia: Fortress Press, 1985). Also see Thomas G. Long, "The Preacher and the Beast: From Apocalyptic Text to Sermon," in *Intersections: Post-Critical Studies in Preaching,* ed. Richard Eslinger (Grand Rapids, Mich.: W. B. Eerdmans Publishing, 1994), 1-22. A fine resource by David Schnasa Jacobsen for preaching apocalyptic texts is *Preaching in the New*

Creation: The Promise of New Testament Apocalyptic Texts (Louisville: Westminster John Knox Press, 1999).

52. Paul Ricoeur, "Biblical Hermeneutics," *Semeia* 4 (1975): 110.

53. David Buttrick, *Preaching the New and the Now* (Louisville: Westminster John Knox Press, 1998), 62.

54. Ronald F. Thiemann, *Revelation and Theology: The Gospel as Narrated Promise* (Notre Dame, Ind.: University of Notre Dame Press, 1985), 83.

55. See George A. Lindbeck, *The Nature of Doctrine: Religion and Theology in a Postliberal Age* (Philadelphia: Westminster Press, 1984), 17-25.

56. Hans Frei, "Literal Reading of Biblical Narrative in Christian Tradition," in *The Bible and the Narrative Tradition*, ed. Frank McConnell (New York: Oxford University Press, 1986), 61.

57. Charles L. Campbell, *Preaching Jesus: New Directions for Homiletics in Hans Frei's Postliberal Theology* (Grand Rapids, Mich.: W. B. Eerdmans Publishing, 1997), 196.

58. See my *Narrative and Imagination* for an analysis of the varieties of this experiential/expressive model of interpretation (pp. 14-18).

59. Mark Ellingsen comments: "To say that Jesus has not risen is to manufacture a Jesus different from the one depicted in the biblical text," *Integrity of Biblical Narrative,* 37.

60. Walter Brueggemann coined the phrase concerning Scripture's "vested interest" in a community of interpretation endowed with certain distinctive virtues. See his "The Social Nature of the Biblical Text for Preaching," in *Preaching as a Social Act: Theology and Practice,* ed. Arthur Van Seters (Nashville: Abingdon Press, 1988), 130.

61. Stanley Hauerwas, "The Church as God's New Language," in *Scriptural Authority and Narrative Interpretation,* ed. Garrett Green (Philadelphia: Fortress Press, 1987), 193.

62. See Paul S. Minear, *John: The Martyr's Gospel* (New York: Pilgrim Press, 1984), chapter 9.

63. See Edward Foley, *Preaching Basics: A Model and a Method* (Chicago: Liturgy Training Publications, 1998). Foley introduces the helpful concept of a "liturgical Bible," by which he means the resources for and content of preaching within the worship of the church. This liturgical Bible includes the texts of the liturgy themselves and "ritual actions and objects and spaces, and even the feasts and seasons that we celebrate throughout the year" (p. 13). The homiletical capacity for thanksgiving, of course, is centered on the Eucharist, its narrative text, ritual actions, communal song, and sacramental imagery.

64. See my *Pitfalls in Preaching* (Grand Rapids, Mich.: W. B. Eerdmans Publishing, 1996), 28-31.

65. The reader is referred to David Buttrick's insightful analysis of the history of parable interpretation in his *Speaking Parables: A Homiletic Guide* (Louisville: Westminster John Knox Press, 2000), 1-21.

66. Amos Wilder, *The Language of the Gospels: Early Christian Rhetoric* (London: SCM Press, 1964).

67. Robert Funk, "The Parable as Metaphor," in *Language, Hermeneutic, and Word of God: The Problem of Language in the New Testament and Contemporary Theology* (New York: Harper & Row, 1966).

68. Eta Linnemann, *Jesus of the Parables,* trans. John Sturdy (New York: Harper & Row, 1966).

69. John Dominic Crossan, *In Parables: The Challenge of the Historical Jesus* (New York: Harper & Row, 1973).

70. See Eugene Lowry, *How to Preach a Parable: Designs for Narrative Sermons* (Nashville: Abingdon Press, 1989) and David Buttrick, *Speaking Parables: A Homiletic Guide* (Louisville: Westminster John Knox Press, 2000).

71. See, for example, the diversity of approaches to the narrative project in *Theology Without Foundations: Religious Practice and the Future of Theological Truth,* ed. Stanley Hauerwas, Nancy Murphy, and Mark Nation (Nashville: Abingdon Press, 1994).

72. Several approaches to homiletic method reflecting a narrative strategy are surveyed by Ronald Allen in his edited work, *Patterns of Preaching: A Sermon Sampler* (St. Louis: Chalice Press, 1998), including Alyce McKenzie, "The Form of the Text Shapes the Form of the Sermon"; Jana Childers, "Sermon Developed as an Author Develops a Novel"; and Serene Jones, "Preaching from the Perspective of Postliberal Theology."

73. Intending "a serious and thorough approach to preaching from a clearly articulated theological position" (i.e., process theology), the contributors to *Biblical Preaching on the Death of Jesus* ([Nashville: Abingdon Press, 1989], 11), offer commentaries and sermons. Contributors include William A. Beardslee, John B. Cobb Jr., David J. Lull, Russell Pregeant, Theodore J. Weeden Sr., and Barry A. Woodbridge.

74. See, for example, Justo L. González and Catherine G. González, *The Liberating Pulpit* (Nashville: Abingdon Press, 1994).

75. Therefore, "the homily is not so much *on* the Scriptures as *from* and *through* them, *Fulfilled in Your Hearing: The Homily in the Sunday Assembly, The Liturgy Documents: A Parish Resource* (Chicago: Liturgy Training Publications, 1991), 359.

76. Hauerwas, "Church as God's New Language," 192.

77. Ibid., 193.

78. Holbert, *Preaching the Old Testament,* 22.

79. Don Wardlaw, ed., *Preaching Biblically* (Philadelphia: Westminster Press, 1983), 1-15. Also see Allen, *Patterns of Preaching,* 73-79.

80. Many preachers retain John H. Hayes and Carl R. Holladay's *Biblical Exegesis: A Beginner's Handbook* (Atlanta: John Knox Press, 1982) on a bookshelf in their study. The chapter "Textual Criticism" is a starting point for most any work of scriptural interpretation. See pp. 30-41.

81. Bernard Brandon Scott points out that "the passage of three years indicates that the fig tree is hopelessly barren." The possibility of future fruitfulness can only be a miracle (*Hear Then the Parable,* 337).

82. See David Buttrick's interpretation of Luke 7:1-10 in his "Interpretation and Preaching," *Interpretation* 35 (January 1981): 46-58. In this early exposition of his approach to scriptural interpretation, Buttrick finds what appears to be a miracle story—the centurion's slave in Luke 7:1-10—to reveal a structure embodying law and grace.

83. See Howard-Brook, *Becoming Children of God,* 76-85, for an insightful analysis of the events clustered at the first Passover in the Gospel.

84. Robert Beck (*Nonviolent Story: Narrative Conflict Resolution in the Gospel of Mark* [Maryknoll, N.Y.: Orbis Books, 1996], 78), identifies several "textual links" between the two stories and adds that most noticeably, "there is a convergence of the two themes: birth threatened, death threatening" (p. 85).

85. See my *Pitfalls in Preaching,* 60-62.

86. See, for example, Culpepper's excellent study of point of view in the Gospel of John in his *Anatomy of the Fourth Gospel,* 20-49.

87. See particularly Robert Funk, *Parables and Presence: Forms of the New Testament Tradition* (Philadelphia: Fortress Press, 1982).

88. Lowry, *How to Preach a Parable,* 121.

89. Buttrick, *Homiletic,* 50-53.

90. See my discussion of the preacher as hero and victim in *Pitfalls in Preaching,* 96-97.

91. See my "Fwd.; Fwd.; Fwd.: Mega-story in the Untaught Homiletic," *Journal of Theology* 106 (Summer 2002): 3-22.

92. Holbert, *Preaching the Old Testament,* 43.

93. Lowry, *How to Preach a Parable,* 79.

94. William F. Turner, "Divine Appearances and Erecting Altars," in my *Narrative and Interpretation,* 176-86.

95. Lowry, *How to Preach a Parable,* 115. Also see Lowry's sermon, "Who Could Ask for Anything More?" 115-20.

96. Holbert, *Preaching the Old Testament,* 43.

97. Ibid., 43-44.

98. Campbell, *Preaching Jesus,* 171.

99. Ibid., 178.

100. See Charles Campbell's footnote critiquing the hermeneutics proposed in my *Narrative and Imagination.* Campbell notes: "Not surprisingly, in the practical section of the book, Eslinger focuses on 'preaching narrative and imagery' (p. 141), rather than on 'preaching Jesus.' " Ibid., 181.

Chapter 3: Narrative Preaching in the African American Tradition

1. James Weldon Johnson, *God's Trombones: Seven Negro Sermons in Verse* (New York: Viking Press, 1965), 20.

2. James H. Love, *God of the Oppressed* (New York: Seabury Press, 1975), 90.

3. David G. Buttrick, "Laughing with the Gospel," in *Sharing Heaven's Music: The Heart of Christian Preaching. Essays in Honor of James Earl Massey,* ed. Barry L. Callan (Nashville: Abingdon Press, 1995), 133.

4. Warren H. Stewart Jr., *Interpreting God's Word in Black Preaching* (Valley Forge, Pa.: Judson Press, 1984), 42-43.

5. Ibid., 43.

6. Henry H. Mitchell, *Black Preaching: The Recovery of a Powerful Art* (Nashville: Abingdon Press, 1990), 23-38.

7. Ibid., 30.

8. Ibid.

9. Ibid., 33.

10. Ibid., 34.

11. W. E. B. DuBois, in Evans E. Crawford, *The Hum: Call and Response in African American Preaching* (Nashville: Abingdon Press, 1995), 19.

12. Ibid.

13. Ibid., 13-17.

14. Olin P. Moyd, *The Sacred Art: Preaching and Theology in the African American Tradition* (Valley Forge, Pa.: Judson Press, 1995), 89.

15. William E. Pannell, "Preaching: Pew Rights and Prophecy," in *Sharing Heaven's Music,* 17.

16. Moyd, *Sacred Art,* 91.

17. Jon Michael Spencer, *Sacred Symphony: The Chanted Sermon of the Black Preacher* (New York: Greenwood Press, 1987), 5.

18. Ibid.

19. "The Drum Major Instinct," see Richard Lischer, *The Preacher King: Martin Luther King Jr. and the Word that Moved America* (New York: Oxford University Press, 1995), 99-100.

20. Spencer, *Sacred Symphony,* 5. Cheryl J. Sanders underscores this connection when she notes that "in the twentieth century, gospel music has emerged as a significant vehicle for women to perform sermons." See "God's Trombones: Voices in African American Folk Preaching," in *Sharing Heaven's Music,* 161.

21. Moyd, *Sacred Art,* 91.

22. Crawford, *Hum.*

23. Spencer, *Sacred Symphony,* 2.

24. Ibid.

25. Ibid., 2-3.

26. Ibid., 55.

27. Stewart, *Interpreting God's Word,* 61.

28. Crawford, *Hum,* 55.

29. Stewart, *Interpreting God's Word,* 62.

30. Henry H. Mitchell, *The Recovery of Preaching* (New York: Harper & Row, 1970), 83.

31. Crawford, *Hum,* 59.

32. Ibid., 60. Crawford's term, "bold particularity," is derived from Don M. Wardlaw, "Preaching as the Interface of Two Social Worlds: The Congregation as Corporate Agent in the Act of Preaching," in *Preaching as a Social Act: Theology and Practice,* ed. Arthur Van Seters (Nashville: Abingdon Press, 1988), 62-68.

33. Ronald J. Allen, ed., *Patterns of Preaching: A Sermon Sampler* (St. Louis: Chalice Press, 1998), 15. Allen makes this observation by way of prefacing Henry H. Mitchell's sermon, "Living Epistles," 16-21.

34. Henry H. Mitchell, *Celebration and Experience in Preaching* (Nashville: Abingdon Press, 1990), 64.

35. Ibid., 34.

36. Ibid., 41.

37. Ibid., 67.

38. Ibid., 69.

39. James Earl Massey, *The Responsible Pulpit* (Anderson, Ind.: Warner Press, 1974), 102-8. See Sanders, "God's Trombones," 169-70, for a discussion of Massey's insights.

40. Crawford, *Hum,* 68.

41. Ibid., 67.

42. Moyd, *Sacred Art,* 109.

43. Johnson, "God's Trombones," 17-20.

44. See Frank A. Thomas, *They Like to Never Quit Praisin' God: The Role of Celebration in Preaching* (Cleveland: United Church Press, 1997), 1-2.

45. Eugene L. Lowry, "Preaching the Great Themes," in *Preaching on the Brink: The Future of Homiletics,* ed. Martha J. Simmons (Nashville: Abingdon Press, 1996), 62.

46. Stewart, *Interpreting God's Word,* 15.

47. Ibid. See pp. 15-21 for Stewart's elaboration of these qualities of God.

48. Edward Farley, "Toward a New Paradigm for Preaching," in *Preaching as a Theological Task: World, Gospel, Scripture,* ed. Thomas G. Long and Edward Farley (Louisville: Westminster John Knox Press, 1996), 165. Also see a considered response by Ronald J. Allen, "Why Preach Passages in the Bible?" in *Preaching as a Theological Task,* 176-85.

49. Moyd, *Sacred Art*, 53.

50. Jerry L. Cannon, *Church Growth Through Afrocentric Preaching in the Presbyterian Church* (D.Min. Thesis, United Theological Seminary, Dayton, Ohio, 1998), 53.

51. Stewart, *Interpreting God's Word*, 42.

52. Ibid.

53. Mitchell, *Recovery of Preaching*, 34.

54. Massey, *Responsible Pulpit*, 101-4.

55. Thomas, *They Like to Never Quit Praisin' God*, 43-44.

56. Ibid., 45.

57. Mitchell, *Celebration and Experience*, 22.

58. Ibid., 25.

59. Melva Wilson Costen, *African American Christian Worship* (Nashville: Abingdon Press, 1993), 104-5.

60. Mitchell, *Celebration and Experience*, 30.

61. Ibid., 31.

62. Costen, *African American Christian Worship*, 55.

63. William B. McClain, "The Importance of Holy Communion: The African American Church and the 'Circament,' " in *Worship Arts, the Feast of Many Meanings: Preaching at the Holy Meal* (March-April 1997): 10.

64. Eugene L. Lowry, *Doing Time in the Pulpit: The Relationship Between Narrative and Preaching* (Nashville: Abingdon Press, 1985), 95-98.

65. Gerald L. Davis, *I Got the Word in Me and I Can Sing It, You Know: A Study of the Performed African American Sermon* (Philadelphia: University of Pennsylvania Press, 1985), 76-77.

66. Mitchell, *Celebration and Experience*, 57.

67. Davis, *I Got the Word in Me*, 90.

68. Ibid.

69. The Reverend Lymon Gaines is pastor of First Missionary Baptist Church in Addyston, Ohio.

70. Davis, *I Got the Word in Me*, 77.

71. Ibid., 78.

72. Ibid. See pp. 128-29 of this book for an analysis of these and other phrasing structures.

73. Mitchell, *Celebration and Experience*, 57.

74. Davis, *I Got the Word in Me*, 83.

75. Ibid., 86.

76. Ibid., 87.

77. Mitchell, *Celebration and Experience*, 57.

78. Moyd, *Sacred Art*, 93.

79. Davis, *I Got the Word in Me*, 88.

80. Hortense Spillers, quoted in Dolan Hubbard, *The Sermon and the African American Literary Tradition* (Columbia, Mo.: University of Missouri Press, 1994), 7.

81. Stewart, *Interpreting God's Word*, 43.

82. See Henry Mitchell, *Celebration and Experience* for an analysis of the sermon as character sketch (pp. 42-43).

83. See my *Narrative and Imagination: Preaching the Worlds that Shape Us* (Minneapolis: Fortress Press, 1995).

84. See David Buttrick, *Homiletic: Moves and Structures* (Philadelphia: Fortress Press, 1987), 57-68. Also see chapter 6.

85. Stewart, *Interpreting God's Word*, 44.

86. Davis, *I Got the Word in Me,* 29.

87. William B. McClain, *Come Sunday: The Liturgy of Zion* (Nashville: Abingdon Press, 1990), 69.

88. Eugene L. Lowry, *The Sermon: Dancing the Edge of Mystery* (Nashville: Abingdon Press, 1997), 61.

89. Ibid.

90. Massey, *Responsible Pulpit,* 108.

91. Moyd, *Sacred Art,* 108.

92. Thomas, *They Like to Never Quit Praisin' God,* 46.

93. Mitchell, *Celebration and Experience,* 64.

94. Martin Luther King Jr., "I've Been to the Mountaintop," April 3, 1968 speech in Memphis, Tennessee, in James W. Washington's, *A Testament of Hope: The Essential Writings of Martin Luther King, Jr.* (San Francisco: Harper & Row, 1986), 286.

95. Thomas, *They Like to Never Quit Praisin' God,* 48.

96. Ibid., 90.

97. Ibid.

98. Ibid.

99. Ibid., 93.

100. Ibid., 95.

101. Ibid.

102. Ibid., 96.

103. Ibid.

104. Ibid., 97.

105. Ibid., 98.

106. Ibid.

107. Davis, *I Got the Word in Me,* 73.

108. Regina C. Anderson, "Faithful Mothers: Stewards of the Spirit," in *Those Preaching Women: African American Preachers Tackle Tough Questions,* vol. 3, ed. Ella Pearson Mitchell (Valley Forge, Pa.: Judson Press, 1996), 1.

109. United Methodist Bishop Leontine Kelly has preached sermons with this introduction on many occasions.

110. See Eugene L. Lowry, "Preaching the Great Themes," in *Preaching on the Brink: The Future of Homiletics,* ed. Martha J. Simmons (Nashville: Abingdon Press, 1996), 62-63.

111. Henry H. Mitchell, "The Providence of God," in Richard L. Eslinger, *A New Hearing: Living Options in Homiletic Method* (Nashville: Abingdon Press, 1987), 57. For an elaboration of the core themes of African American preaching, see Henry H. Mitchell and Nicholas C. Cooper, *Soul Theology: The Heart of American Black Culture* (Nashville: Abingdon Press, 1991).

112. Ella Pearson Mitchell, "Human Reclamation," in *Those Preaching Women,* 72.

113. Davis, *I Got the Word in Me,* 76.

114. Mitchell, *Celebration and Experience,* 12.

115. Moyd, *Sacred Art,* 109.

116. Ibid., 108-9.

117. Massey, *Responsible Pulpit,* 108.

118. Davis, *I Got the Word in Me,* 80.

119. Ibid., 33.

120. United States Catholic Conference, *Fulfilled in Your Hearing: The Homily in the Sunday*

Assembly, in *The Liturgy Documents: A Parish Resource* (Chicago: Liturgy Training Publications, 1991), 347-74.

121. William B. McClain, *Come Sunday: The Liturgy of Zion* (Nashville: Abingdon Press, 1990), 68.

122. Mitchell, *Celebration and Experience,* 64.

Chapter 4: Moves and Structures: The Homiletics of David Buttrick

1. David Buttrick, *Homiletic: Moves and Structures* (Philadelphia: Fortress Press, 1987), 265.

2. Ibid.

3. There is an interesting parallel between Buttrick's analysis of the rationalist and Romantic elements in modern hermeneutics and George Lindbeck's cognitive and "experiential-expressive" models of doctrine. See his *The Nature of Doctrine: Religion and Theology in a Postliberal Age* (Philadelphia: Westminster Press, 1984).

4. Adolf Jülicher, *Die Gleichnisreden Jesu,* 2 vols. (Darmstadt: Wisenschaftliche Buchgesellschaft, 1899).

5. See my *Pitfalls in Preaching* (Grand Rapids, Mich.: W. B. Eerdmans Publishing, 1996), 28-36.

6. David Buttrick, *A Captive Voice: The Liberation of Preaching* (Louisville: Westminster John Knox Press, 1994), 92.

7. Bernard Brandon Scott, *Hear Then the Parable: A Commentary on the Parables of Jesus* (Minneapolis: Fortress Press, 1989), 224.

8. David Buttrick, "On Doing Homiletics Today," in *Intersections: Postcritical Studies in Preaching,* ed. Richard Eslinger (Grand Rapids, Mich.: W. B. Eerdmans Publishing, 1994), 90.

9. Ibid.

10. Buttrick, *Homiletic,* 302.

11. Buttrick asks, "Is it possible that all scripture is a plotted language intending to *do,* a performative language?" (*Homiletic,* 301). The parables are therefore representative of any biblical text's plot and intention. However, many homileticians have turned to the parables by virtue of the prominence of their plotted language.

12. Buttrick, *Homiletic,* 276.

13. Ibid., 277.

14. Ibid.

15. Ibid.

16. Ibid., 277-78.

17. Ibid., 278.

18. David Buttrick, *Captive Voice,* 79.

19. Buttrick frequently turns to give attention to this profound shift in communal language and therefore communal consciousness. See, for example, "On Doing Homiletics Today," 92-94; also see *Captive Voice,* 64-67.

20. David Buttrick, *Captive Voice,* 79.

21. Buttrick, *Homiletic,* 320.

22. Buttrick notes that the congregation hears Scripture read in a present-tense mode of consciousness. Hence, for the preacher to begin his or her sermon by referring to that text in the past tense already involves a rather extensive shift in point of view; see *Homiletic,* 55-68.

23. Ibid., 322.

24. Ibid., 323.

25. Ibid., 322.

26. Buttrick insists that the sequence of moves in a sermon be capable of being easily followed by the hearers. If the sequence of single statements related to the moves do not connect in sequence with a rather straightforward logic, the congregation will not follow the sermon's now garbled plot.

27. Buttrick, *Homiletic,* 323.

28. Ibid.

29. Ibid., 325.

30. Ibid.

31. Ibid., 328.

32. Ibid.

33. Ibid., 326.

34. Ibid., 327.

35. An abysmal example: At a recent "retreat" for new clergy about to enter their first pastorates, a United Methodist district superintendent announced, "You need to know how it is. *We* are the company and *you* are our franchise operators. We expect you to deliver!"

36. Buttrick, *Homiletic,* 327.

37. Ibid., 28.

38. Ibid., 26.

39. Buttrick will tolerate no excuses from preachers with regard to mental meandering during the sermon. "When congregations drift off into wanderings of mind, it is *always* the fault of the speaker" (*Homiletic,* 39).

40. Ibid., 51.

41. Ibid.

42. See *Homiletic,* 30-32, for a discussion of these oppositions.

43. Ibid., 29.

44. Ibid., 32.

45. Ibid., 34.

46. Ibid.

47. Ibid., 47.

48. Eslinger, *Pitfalls in Preaching,* 89.

49. Buttrick, *Homiletic,* 151.

50. Ibid., 133.

51. Ibid., 148.

52. Ibid., 139.

53. See my discussion of the difficulties that emerge when these positive/positive and negative/negative relationships are inverted; *Pitfalls in Preaching,* 101-5.

54. Buttrick, *Homiletic,* 142.

55. Eslinger, *Pitfalls in Preaching,* 95-101.

56. Buttrick, *Homiletic,* 142.

57. Ibid., 136.

58. Mark D. Roberts, "Jesus the Word," in *The Library of Distinctive Sermons,* vol. 3, ed. Gary W. Klingsporn (Sisters, Ore.: Questar, 1996), 169.

59. Buttrick, *Homiletic,* 135.

60. Ibid., 131.

61. Ibid., 133.

62. Ibid., 132.

63. Ibid., 29.

64. See *Captive Voice* (pp. 64-75) for a discussion of contemporary culture and its implications for preaching.

65. Buttrick, *Homiletic,* 55.

66. Ibid., 58.

67. Ibid.

68. Ibid., 59.

69. Ibid.

70. Ibid.

71. Ibid., 84.

72. Ibid.

73. I am indebted to Thomas Long for this fine imaging of the lepers at the border crossing.

74. Buttrick, *Homiletic,* 87.

75. Ibid.

76. Ibid.

77. Ibid., 94.

78. Ibid., 96.

79. Ibid., 98.

80. Ibid., 101.

81. See Buttrick, *Homiletic* (p. 101) for examples of the elements within a sermon's conclusion.

82. Ibid., 105.

83. Ibid., 98.

84. Ibid., 102.

85. Ibid., 109.

86. David Buttrick, "First Steps for a New Homiletic," videotape produced by the General Board of Discipleship of The United Methodist Church, for use as the national preaching event for "Proclamation," Nashville, Tenn., July, 1983.

87. Ibid.

88. John A. Melloh, "Response to David Buttrick," in *Worship* 62 (May 1988): 266-69.

89. Eugene L. Lowry, *The Sermon: Dancing the Edge of Mystery* (Nashville: Abingdon Press, 1997), 33.

90. Ron Allen, review of Richard Eslinger's *Pitfalls in Preaching,* in *Homiletic* 23 (Summer 1997): 26.

91. Thomas G. Long, review of David Buttrick's *Homiletic: Moves and Structures,* in *Theology Today* 45 (April 1988): 111.

92. Ibid.

93. Robert P. Waznak, "A Second Response," review of David Buttrick's *Homiletic: Moves and Structures,* in *Worship* 62 (May 1988): 278.

94. Buttrick, *Homiletic,* 328.

95. I am unable to locate precisely this citation. It is from a sermon in a series preached by Fred Craddock for the NBC Radio Pulpit in late 1978 or early 1979.

Chapter 5: The Sermon in Four Pages: The Homiletic Method of Paul Scott Wilson

1. Paul Scott Wilson, *The Four Pages of the Sermon: A Guide to Biblical Preaching* (Nashville: Abingdon Press, 1999), 38. Wilson has published a number of other works including *A Concise History of Preaching* (Nashville: Abingdon Press, 1992); *Imagination of the Heart: New Understandings in Preaching* (Nashville: Abingdon Press, 1988); and *The Practice of Preaching* (Nashville: Abingdon Press, 1995). We will draw his methodology, however, primarily from his most recent work, *The Four Pages of the Sermon*.

2. Wilson, *Four Pages,* 36.

3. Wilson responds to one central question also posed by Ronald J. Allen, "Why Preach from Passages in the Bible?" in *Preaching as a Theological Task: World, Gospel, Scripture*, ed. Thomas G. Long and Edward Farley (Louisville: Westminster John Knox Press, 1996), 176-88.

4. Wilson, *Four Pages,* 37.

5. Ibid., 39.

6. Ibid., 42.

7. Ibid., 41.

8. The preacher may need to be reminded often that the theme selected for service in the sermon at hand is not the one enduring single meaning of the biblical text. Assuming the latter would reintroduce a main-idea hermeneutic that Wilson desires to avoid.

9. Wilson, *Four Pages,* 39.

10. Ibid.

11. See David Buttrick, *Homiletic: Moves and Structures* (Philadelphia: Fortress Press, 1987), 217-21. Also, see my *Pitfalls in Preaching* (Grand Rapids, Mich.: W. B. Eerdmans Publishing, 1996), 10-12.

12. Wilson, *Four Pages,* 40.

13. See Wilson, *Four Pages,* 42-44, for a discussion of these attributes of the theme sentence.

14. Wilson, *Four Pages,* 45.

15. Ibid.

16. Ibid.

17. Ibid., 48.

18. Ibid., 50.

19. See my *Pitfalls in Preaching* (Grand Rapids, Mich.: W. B. Eerdmans Publishing, 1996), 7-10.

20. Wilson, *Four Pages,* 50.

21. Ibid., 51.

22. Ibid., 55.

23. Buttrick, *Homiletic,* 133-34.

24. Wilson, *Four Pages,* 55.

25. Ibid., 56.

26. Ibid.

27. Ibid., 10.

28. Ibid., 11.

29. Ibid.

30. Ibid., 36.

31. Ibid., 43.

32. See Mary Katheryn Hilkert, *Naming Grace: Preaching and the Sacramental Imagination* (New York: Continuum, 1997).

33. Wilson, *Four Pages,* 28.

34. Ibid., 15.

35. Ibid., 16.

36. See pp. 243-56 for Wilson's analysis of variations in the Four Page sermonic form.

37. Ibid., 17.

38. Ibid., 73.

39. See Bryan Chappell, *Christ-Centered Preaching: Redeeming the Expository Sermon* (Grand Rapids, Mich.: Baker Books, 1994).

40. Ibid., 43.

41. Wilson, *Four Pages,* 81.

42. Ibid., 76.

43. Ibid., 78.

44. Ibid., 79.

45. Ibid.

46. Ibid., 79-80.

47. Ibid., 108.

48. Ibid., 110-11.

49. Ibid., 111.

50. Ibid., 113.

51. Ibid., 114.

52. Ibid., 114-15.

53. Ibid., 115.

54. Note on Wilson's analysis of LDS sermons, pp. 198-99.

55. Wilson, *Four Pages,* 160.

56. Ibid., 161.

57. Ibid.

58. Ibid., 162.

59. Ibid.

60. Ibid.

61. Ibid., 163.

62. Ibid.

63. Ibid.

64. Ibid.

65. Ibid., 164.

66. "Most students will state the theme sentence [of grace] and quickly shift back to discuss human action" (Ibid., 168).

67. Ibid., 170.

68. Ibid., 171.

69. Ibid., 172. This sequence is almost an exact reversal of the approach advocated by Eugene Lowry based on his advocacy of a narrative homiletical plot (see pp. 33-47).

70. David Buttrick growls that linking the moves of a sermon with a common image or even images that are similar in content or point of view "is full of dangers" (*Homiletic,* 164). Contrary to the approach advocated by Paul Scott Wilson, Buttrick insists that "We may never reuse images in connected moves" (Ibid.).

71. Wilson, *Four Pages,* 173.

72. Ibid., 199.

73. Ibid., 202-3.

74. Ibid., 206.

75. Ibid., 204.

76. Ibid.

77. Ibid., 209.

78. Ibid., 59-61.

79. Ibid., 61.

80. Ibid., 67.

81. Ibid.

82. Ibid., 68.

83. For an insightful reassessment of humor in preaching, see Joseph M. Webb, *Comedy and Preaching* (St. Louis: Chalice Press, 1998).

84. Wilson, *Four Pages,* 68.

85. Ibid.

86. Ibid., 209.

87. Ibid., 209-10.

88. Ibid., 210.

89. Ibid.

90. Ibid.

91. Ibid.

92. Ibid.

93. Ibid.

94. Ibid., 211.

95. Ibid.

96. Ibid.

97. Ibid.

98. See Charles Rice, *The Embodied Word: Preaching as Art and Liturgy* (Minneapolis: Fortress Press, 1991).

99. Wilson, *Four Pages,* 211-12.

100. Frederick W. Danker, *Jesus and the New Age: A Commentary on St. Luke's Gospel,* rev. ed. (Philadelphia: Fortress Press, 1988), 397.

101. Buttrick, *Homiletic,* 374.

102. Alyce McKenzie, "The Form of the Text Shapes the Form of the Sermon," in *Patterns of Preaching: A Sermon Sampler,* ed. Ronald J. Allen (St. Louis: Chalice Press, 1998), 73.

103. Wilson, *Four Pages,* 163.

104. Ibid., 5, 269.

105. Phyllis Tribble, *Texts of Terror: Literary-Feminist Readings of Biblical Narratives* (Philadelphia: Fortress Press, 1984).

Chapter 6: A Homiletics of Imagery: Rhetoric and the Imagination

1. Various commentators have analyzed the three core elements of classical rhetoric as *logos, ethos,* and *pathos.* See, for example, Paul Scott Wilson, "Beyond Narrative: Imagination in the Sermon," in *Listening to the Word: Studies in Honor of Fred B. Craddock,* ed. Gail R. O'Day and Thomas G. Long (Nashville: Abingdon Press, 1993);

and David Buttrick, *Homiletic: Moves and Structures* (Philadelphia: Fortress Press, 1987), 319.

2. Edward L. Murray, "Imagination Theory and Phenomenological Thought," in *Phenomenological Psychology,* ed. Edward L. Murray (Pittsburgh: Duquesne University Press, 1987), 178.

3. Wilson, "Beyond Narrative," 133.

4. Ibid.

5. Garrett Green, *Imagining God: Theology and the Religious Imagination* (San Francisco: Harper & Row, 1989), 15.

6. Ibid., 18.

7. See my "From Beecher to Buttrick: Imagination in Modern and Postmodern Homiletics," in *Narrative and Imagination: Preaching the Worlds That Shape Us* (Minneapolis: Fortress Press, 1995), 213-23.

8. Charles Rice, "Just Church Bells: One Man's View of Preaching Today," *The Drew Gateway* 49, no. 3 (Spring 1979): 22.

9. Murray, "Imagination Theory and Phenomenological Thought," 176-77.

10. Phillip Wheelwright, *The Burning Fountain: A Study in the Language of Symbolism* (Bloomington, Ind.: Indiana University Press, 1968).

11. Ibid., 38.

12. See Mary Catherine Hilkert, *Naming Grace: Preaching and the Sacramental Imagination* (New York: Continuum, 1997); also see my *Narrative and Imagination,* 95-102, for an analysis of the homiletical imagination after Wheelwright.

13. Richard Kearney, *Poetics of Imagining: From Husserl to Lyotard* (London: HarperCollins Academic, 1991).

14. Ibid., 4.

15. Ibid.

16. Thomas Troeger, "Imagination and Metaphor in Preaching," *Staying Alive in the Pulpit* videotape (Nashville: Discipleship Resources, 1966).

17. Ibid.

18. Ibid.

19. Ibid.

20. Murray, "Imagination Theory and Phenomenological Thought," 181.

21. I have analyzed Murray's model of the hypothetical imagination in some detail in *Narrative and Imagination,* 60-66, 90-109.

22. Murray, "Imagination Theory and Phenomenological Thought," 179.

23. David J. Bryant, *Faith and the Play of Imagination: On the Role of Imagination in Religion* (Macon, Ga.: Mercer University Press, 1989), 88-89.

24. Mary Warnock, *Imagination* (Berkeley: University of California Press, 1976), 194.

25. Philip S. Keane, *Christian Ethics and Imagination* (New York: Paulist Press, 1984), 127.

26. Bryant, *Faith and the Play of Imagination,* 90.

27. Ibid.

28. Walter Bruggemann, *Hopeful Imagination: Prophetic Voices in Exile* (Philadelphia: Fortress Press, 1986), 102; also see his *The Prophetic Imagination* (Philadelphia: Fortress Press, 1978); and *Finally Comes the Poet: Daring Speech for Proclamation* (Minneapolis: Fortress Press, 1989).

29. Paul W. Pruyser, *The Play of Imagination: Toward a Psychoanalysis of Culture* (New York: International Universities Press, 1983), 10.

30. Bryant, *Faith and the Play of Imagination,* 91.

31. Warnock, Imagination, 194. Because perception never provides complete and exhaustive

data of the object (we always perceive one aspect at a time), imagination's achievement is the largely unnoticed way in which our perception yields a knowable world. Warnock adds, "We cannot separate the interpretive function of the imagination from its image-forming function. . . . The images themselves are not separate from our interpretations of the objects in the world" (Ibid.).

32. Bryant, *Faith and the Play of Imagination*, 90-91.

33. David Bailey Harned, *Images for Self-Recognition: The Christian as Player, Sufferer, and Vandal* (New York: Seabury Press, 1977), 14.

34. Margaret Miles, *Image as Insight: Visual Understanding in Western Christianity and Secular Culture* (Boston: Beacon Press, 1985), 129.

35. David Buttrick, *Homiletic: Moves and Structures* (Philadelphia: Fortress Press, 1987), 115-19.

36. Harned, *Images for Self-Recognition*, 155.

37. See Gerd Theissen, *The Sign Language of Faith: Opportunities for Preaching Today* (London: SCM Press, 1995), 24, for an analysis of these biblical fields of imagery.

38. Miles, *Image as Insight*, 34.

39. Harned, *Images for Self-Recognition*, 130.

40. Walter Ong, *The Presence of the Word* (New Haven: Yale University Press, 1967), 6. See my *Narrative & Imagination*, 78-85, for a further exploration of the relationship between visual and oral/aural imagery.

41. Miles, *Image as Insight*, 32.

42. Craig Dykstra, *Vision and Character: A Christian Educator's Alternative to Kohlberg* (New York: Paulist Press, 1981), 77.

43. Gijsbert D. J. Dingemans, "A Hearer in the Pew: Homiletical Reflections and Suggestions," in *Preaching as a Theological Task: World, Gospel, Scripture*, ed. Thomas G. Long and Edward Farley (Louisville: Westminster John Knox Press, 1996), 87.

44. Ella Bozarth-Campbell, *The Word's Body: An Incarnational Aesthetic of Interpretation* (University, Ala.: University of Alabama Press, 1979), 104.

45. Ibid.

46. W. J. T. Mitchell, ed., *The Language of Images* (Chicago: University of Chicago Press, 1980), 7.

47. Thomas G. Troeger, "Imaginative Theology: The Shape of Postmodern Homiletics," in *Homiletic* 13, no. 1 (1988): 31.

48. Martin Marty, "The Long Road to Reconciliation," *Newsweek*, 27 March 2000, 61.

49. Harned, *Images for Self-Recognition*, xix-xx.

50. Hence, the problem with the rituals at the "Re-Imagining Conference" in Minneapolis, in the early 1990s was not specifically with the images of milk and honey (Hippolytus reports their use along with bread and wine at the Easter Vigil Eucharist). Rather, it was the suppression of the narrative of the Paschal mystery that left the milk and honey with only an implied "other" story.

51. Harned, *Images for Self-Recognition*, 155.

52. Troeger, "Imaginative Theology," 31.

53. Margarete Mary Kelleher, "Liturgy and the Christian Imagination," *Liturgy* 66, no. 2 (March 1992): 133.

54. David Buttrick, *Homiletic: Moves and Structures* (Philadelphia: Fortress Press, 1987), 60.

55. For a brilliant study of the parable of the mustard seed, see Bernard Brandon Scott, *Hear Then the Parable: A Commentary on the Parables of Jesus* (Minneapolis: Fortress Press, 1989), 373-87.

56. See my *Narrative and Imagination*, 148-51.

57. Wes Howard Brook, *Becoming Children of God: John's Gospel and Radical Discipleship* (Maryknoll, N.Y.: Orbis Books, 1994), 261.

58. Ibid.

59. See my *Pitfalls in Preaching* (Grand Rapids, Mich.: W. B. Eerdmans Publishing, 1996), 108-10.

60. A seminary preaching lab sermon by former student and friend, Denise Dieter-Rankin.

61. Hans Gadamer's notion of imagination as play is most fully developed in his *Truth and Method,* 2nd rev. ed. (New York: Crossroad, 1989), 101-34. For an excellent exploration of preaching as performance, see Jana Childers, *Performing the Word: Preaching as Theatre* (Nashville: Abingdon Press, 1998).

62. For a fine survey of structuralism's interest in signs, see Jonathan Culler, *The Pursuit of Signs: Semiotics, Literature, Deconstruction* (Ithaca, N.Y.: Cornell University Press, 1981), 18-43.

63. Paul Scott Wilson, *The Four Pages of the Sermon: A Guide to Biblical Preaching* (Nashville: Abingdon Press, 1999), 51.

64. Ibid., 53.

65. Buttrick concludes that "when language changes in every major tongue on earth, then a whole world is in process of changing its mind." *A Captive Voice: The Liberation of Preaching* (Louisville: Westminster John Knox Press, 1994), 72.

66. Wilson, *Four Pages,* 51.

Contributors

Susan R. Briehl is a pastor in the Evangelical Lutheran Church in America, Spokane, Washington.

Lymon Gaines Jr. is Pastor of First Missionary Baptist Church, Addyston, Ohio.

Robert Howard is Visiting Professor of Preaching, Lexington Theological Seminary, Lexington, Kentucky.

Eugene L. Lowry is Professor Emeritus of Preaching, St. Paul School of Theology, Kansas City, Missouri.

Maurice J. Nutt, C.Ss.R. is Pastor of St. Alphonsus Rock Catholic Church, St. Louis, Missouri.

Marjorie J. Thompson is Director of the Pathways Center, The Upper Room, Nashville, Tennessee.

Paul Scott Wilson is Professor of Preaching, Emmanuel College, Toronto School of Theology.